D15887524

02.

Lo
Thi
sta
by
at
Re
m

Patricians, power and politics
in nineteenth-century towns

Themes
in Urban
History

General editor: Derek Fraser

Patricians, power and politics in nineteenth-century towns

edited by DAVID CANNADINE

Leicester University Press/St. Martin's Press, New York 1982

CANNADINE,
David

First published in 1982 by Leicester University Press
First published in the U.S.A. by St. Martin's Press Inc., New York
For information write: St. Martin's Press Inc., 175 Fifth Ave, New York, N.Y. 10010
Copyright © Leicester University Press 1982

Designed by Arthur Lockwood
Phototypeset in Linotron Times, printed and bound
in Great Britain by The Pitman Press, Bath

British Library Cataloguing in Publication Data

Patricians, power and politics in nineteenth-
century towns.—(Themes in urban history)
1. Municipal government—Great Britain—History
I. Cannadine, David   II. Series
352'.008'0941   JS3118

ISBN 0-7185-1193-X

Library of Congress Card Catalog Number 82–42544
ISBN 0-312-59803-3 (St. Martin's Press)

FOREWORD

Urban History is an expanding field of study, sustained by a considerable volume of research. The purpose of this series, originally conceived by the late Jim Dyos, is to open a new channel for the dissemination of the findings of a careful selection from that research, providing a conspectus of new knowledge on specific themes.

For each volume in the series, each of the contributors is invited to present the core of his work: the essays, originating in theses but now specially written for this volume, are combined under the control of the editor, who writes an introduction setting out the significance of the material being presented in the lights of developments in that or a cognate field.

It is hoped in this way the fruits of recent work may be made widely available, both to assist further exploration and to contribute to the teaching of urban history.

In this, the fifth volume of the series, David Cannadine brings together case studies in an area of historical enquiry which he personally has done much to pioneer. Though Cobden proclaimed 'The battle of our day is still against aristocracy', these studies show that the relationship between cities and the nobility was as much concerned with partnership as with conflict. These essays demonstrate in varying geographical and political contexts how important an influence aristocratic proprietors had on urban development.

Derek Fraser
University of Bradford

v

EDITOR'S PREFACE

The four essays in this book were written in the United Kingdom, while the subsequent editorial work has been undertaken in the United States of America. In the course of this protracted publishing process, a wide variety of obligations have been incurred.

John Davies would like to thank: the staff of the Departments of Manuscripts and Maps and Prints of the National Library of Wales, Cardiff Central Library, Glamorgan Record Office, Cardiff, Coal House, Llanishen, Register House, Edinburgh, and the British Transport Historical Record Office, London. He is also grateful to the library staff at University College, Swansea, and at the University College of Wales, Aberystwyth, and wishes to thank both colleges for grants to assist his researches.

John Liddle wishes to thank: the staffs of the Southport Public Library, the Library of the University of Lancaster, and the Wigan Record Office, for their efficient and courteous service. He is especially indebted to Colonel Roger Hesketh for his kind and generous help in allowing free access to his private collection of family papers, and for the liberal use of his home as a place of study for many weeks. He would also like to thank all his former colleagues at the Lancashire Record Office for their help and assistance, in particular the former Deputy County Archivist, David Smith. Finally, he would like to express his gratitude to Dr John Marshall, whose enthusiasm first prompted his interest in the subject, and Dr J.K. Walton for his continued help and encouragement.

Richard Roberts wishes to thank: Sir George Meyrick; A.T. Goadsby, agent to the Cooper Dean Estate; Dick Shepherd, Public Relations Officer, Bournemouth Corporation; Pauline Baker, Town Clerk's Department, Bournemouth Town Hall; and Mike Edgington, Reference Librarian, Bournemouth Library.

Richard Trainor wishes to acknowledge the assistance of: Mrs M.H. Atkins and the staff of the Archives and Local History Department, Dudley Library; Miss J. Coburn and the staff at the Greater London Record Office; Mr H.J. Heaney and the staff at Glasgow University Library; Miss M. Henderson and the staff of the Hereford and Worcester Record Office; Dr F. Hull of the Kent Archives Office; Mr E.H. Harcourt Williams of the Salisbury Archives, Hatfield; Mr F. B. Stitt and the staff at the Staffordshire Record Office and William Salt Library; and Mrs M. Reed and the staff of West Bromwich Reference Library. He also wishes to thank the following for access to records, hospitality, information and suggestions: Dr J.S. Bourne, the Earl of Dartmouth, the Earl of Dudley, Dr M.W. Dupree, Dr and Mrs J.M. Fletcher, Mr M.W. Greenslade, Mr A.W. Kwitatkowski and Lady Barbara Kwiatkowska, Miss Dorothy Meynell, Dr T.J. Raybould, Dr J.S. Rowett, Mrs E.H. Sargeant, Mrs M. Shakespeare, Mr. F.H.W. Sheppard, Dr R.W. Sturgess, Mr and Mrs P.J. Waller, Prof. J.T. Ward, Mr R.J.H. Whitworth, and Mr and Mrs J.K. Winter. In addition, he is grateful for grants from the Committee on Conference and Research Support of the University of Glasgow.

The Editor would like to thank the School of Historical Studies at the Institute for Advanced Study, Princeton, for providing such congenial surroundings in which to work, and the staff of Leicester University Press for their unfailing patience, kindness and expertise.

D.N.C.
16 February 1981

CONTENTS

LIST OF ILLUSTRATIONS

LIST OF TABLES

LIST OF ABBREVIATIONS

Note Places of publication are given only for works published outside the United Kingdom. In abbreviating less frequently cited periodical titles, commonly accepted abbreviations such as *J.* for *Journal*, *Rev.* for *Review* have been used; other abbreviations are listed below.

DNB	*Dictionary of National Biography*
PP	Parliamentary Papers
PRO	Public Record Office
RO	Record Office
VCH	*Victoria County History*

NOTES ON THE CONTRIBUTORS

DAVID CANNADINE completed his D.Phil. thesis in Oxford in 1975 and is at present a Fellow of Christ's College, Cambridge, and a University Lecturer in History. He is the author of *Lords and Landlords: the Aristocracy and the Towns, 1774–1967* (1980), and has published numerous articles and contributions to books on the social, economic and political history of modern Britain.

JOHN DAVIES is a Lecturer in the Department of Welsh History at the University College of Wales, Aberystwyth. He is the author of *Cardiff and the Marquesses of Bute* (1981), and of several articles on Welsh history. He is currently writing the *Pelican History of Wales*.

JOHN LIDDLE was a post-graduate research student at Lancaster and is researching for his Ph.D. there. He now works in industry.

RICHARD ROBERTS undertook his research for his Ph.D. at Cambridge. He is currently a Lecturer in Economic History at the University of Sussex.

RICHARD TRAINOR was a post-graduate student at Princeton and at Oxford, and obtained his D.Phil. from there in 1981. He is now a Lecturer in Economic History at the University of Glasgow.

Introduction

DAVID CANNADINE

Introduction

DAVID CANNADINE

'One of the greatest changes in England that people of my age have seen is the complete shifting of influence from the country to the town.' Thus, writing in 1914, F. Foakes-Jackson noted how the old world dominated by the landowners was superseded by the new society of great cities in nineteenth-century Britain.[1] In recent years, it has become increasingly fashionable to stress how slowly this transition occurred, and to emphasize the degree to which the *landed* élite also survived as the *governing* élite well into the last quarter of the nineteenth century, and even on into the twentieth.[2] Particularly important in such explanations is the landed élite's continued wealth, largely the result of widespread participation in non-agricultural ventures such as mining, markets, docks, harbours and urban estate development.[3] As a result, many patrician families remained the richest in Britain until the 1880s, weathered the storm of the agricultural depression, and survived, prosperous and intact, into the inter-war years of the twentieth century and beyond. As Professor Burn rightly notes, 'consciously or unconsciously, the landed aristocracy of England had come to terms, and profitable terms, with the Industrial Revolution.'[4]

Assuredly, this retention of riches was agreeable enough in itself, but it also helped to keep open the gateways to patrician political power. For it was often this sustained and augmented wealth which made possible continued political involvement and social dominance. There were, of course, exceptions. Not all latter-day patrician politicians were rich in their own right: Curzon and the later Churchills had to find (or make) their money elsewhere. Nor did all those who were wealthy make a significant impact on high politics or high society: the sixth duke of Portland, for example, was hardly a household name among Westminster politicians or Whitehall mandarins, and the third marquess of Bute was something of a recluse. But in many cases, as the pre-eminence of the Salisburys, Devonshires and Derbys suggests, the sustained financial gain from the Industrial Revolution made it easier for the great patrician families to continue to play an important part in national politics and high society at the end of the nineteenth century and on into the twentieth.[5]

Although this has been stressed at the level of *national* life, this important link has received far less study as regards *local* affairs. Sinking a mine, building a market, constructing a harbour or developing a building estate all created new spheres of patrician influence, in the form of economic leverage, political power and social initiative, in the towns of industrializing Britain. The *revenue* thus derived may have helped in the maintenance of a *national* rôle; but the *assets* thus located obliged even the most retiring landowner to assume some responsibility at the *local* level as well. Not all patricians were equally energetic in seizing these opportunities; but none, however timid, lethargic or uninterested, could completely ignore the political and social implications of their localized economic activities. There was urban development to plan and mould, urban labour to employ and manage, urban livings to finance and fill, urban society to adorn and lead, and urban government and representation to dominate and control. Accordingly, the shifting influence from the country to the town did not just mean that in the long run the city overwhelmed the land; it also meant that in the short term, there was *increased* scope for rural, patrician influence on most aspects of urban, industrial life.

This short-run influence, and long-term decline, forms the subject matter of this book, as four historians take particular landed families in the nineteenth and twentieth centuries, and describe and investigate their changing relationship with the three industrial and two seaside towns with which they had important economic links. John Davies studies the social and political activities of the Bute family in Cardiff, the town which they created by their decision, in the late 1820s, to build the docks to service the Glamorgan coalfield. Richard Trainor looks at the Dudleys' involvement in the public life of their titular town, and fruitfully compares it with the activities of another great Black Country dynasty, the Earls of Dartmouth, in nearby West Bromwich. John Liddle investigates the part played by two Lancashire gentry families, the Heskeths and the Scarisbricks, in the affairs of Southport, where they were joint and preponderant landowners. And Richard Roberts examines the more complex mosaic of property patterns in Bournemouth, and discusses the relatively lower profile which the local landowners maintained there.

Each of these studies begins by sketching in the economic links between the particular patrician family and the town with which they were connected, and then examines in specific detail the way in which that engaging and protracted encounter between the landed élite on its way down and the urban mass on its way up was played out. Assuredly, the growth of all these towns – which initially came into being largely in response to landed initiative and enterprise – may in the long run have hastened that shift of influence from the rural to the urban world on which Foakes-Jackson remarked. But, as will become clear as each of these accounts unfolds, they initially provided great opportunities for patrician intervention in urban life; so that even at the end of the nineteenth century, the influence which landowners might wield, in local as in national affairs, remained considerable. As these essays well demonstrate, it was not only in the realms of revenue that the British landed establishment came to 'profitable terms' with the Industrial Revolution.

1

Taken together, these essays greatly increase our knowledge of the fluctuating relationship between the landed élite and the towns of modern Britain. To begin with, it is gratifying to report that their findings largely conform to the six phases of that encounter which were suggested in an earlier, speculative survey: 'power then conflict, influence then confrontation, ornamental impotence then territorial abdication.'[6] As Davies shows, the power base built up by the second marquess of Bute in early nineteenth-century Cardiff was so secure that neither parliamentary nor municipal reform could shake it: until the mid-1840s, he dominated the town, in terms of its philanthropy, its local government and its parliamentary representation. In the Black Country, too, as Trainor demonstrates, the power wielded by the Dudleys over their titular town, and by the Dartmouths in West Bromwich, was scarcely less. In all three towns, there were weak, divided middle-class élites, with limited social, philanthropic and political resources and opportunities: the landowners, accordingly, still held the power and the initiative.

Gradually, however, the balance began to shift, exemplified by some bitter and painful conflicts. Between the late 1830s and the early 1850s, the Dartmouths suffered defeat over Church Rate, were unable to take the initiative in the Black-Country strike of 1842, lost the support of the West Bromwich Board of Guardians, and were largely thwarted in their attempts to dominate South Staffordshire constituency politics. Under these circumstances, their residential withdrawal, from Sandwell to Patshull, is hardly surprising. The Dudleys fared little better. From the 1840s, radical hostility towards the family grew among Dudley residents, culminating in clashes with the local Board of Health in the early 1850s and the defeat of the family's parliamentary candidate in 1857. Again, the territorial withdrawal from grimy Himley Hall to rural Witley Court is suggestive and significant. But the most spectacular, if belated, shift in the balance of power took place in Cardiff, where the death of the second marquess of Bute in 1848, who left a son only six months old, and family affairs in the hands of absentee trustees, meant that by the early 1850s, the family lost its hitherto unchallengable control of both the corporation and the constituency.

But these middle-class, urban victories were not consolidated, as weak and divided local government bodies remained, psychologically and sometimes financially, dependent on the local landowners, their largesse and their leadership. This was especially noteworthy in the many seaside towns that were coming into being at this time. In Southport, as Liddle shows, Charles Scarisbrick owned the water works company, Charles Hesketh was keeper of the town's moral conscience and dominant in philanthropy and public life, and the Board of Improvement, on which the two families were strongly represented, had neither sufficient radicals nor sufficient funds effectively to challenge them. And in Bournemouth, despite the landowners' more limited rôle in public utilities and public life, their strong – if often indirect – representation on the local board meant they remained, corporately, the most important figures in the town. In Cardiff, where the Butes' economic leverage was still large, the picture was similar. In 1868 and again in 1872, Bute family celebrations were made into parties for the whole town, and – ironically enough – between 1857 and 1880, the local anti-Bute MP was a member of the Bute family. In Dudley, after incorporation, the first mayor was the earl's local agent, and the family remained important in philanthropy and public life, as did the

Dartmouths in West Bromwich, where the town, still unincorporated, benefited greatly by their charitable endeavour and personal participation.

This phase of *rapprochement* did not last indefinitely, however, as there followed another period of confrontation, this time between local authorities increasingly conscious of their financial strength and acquisitive powers, and patricians anxious to defend their property rights and industrial assets. In Cardiff, for example, the council became increasingly hostile to the Butes in the late 1870s, and threatened to take over the docks in 1881. And the building of the Barry Dock and railway between 1884–9 by the coal masters effectively ended the Bute monopoly in the provision of port facilities for the South Wales coalfield. In Dudley, the earl tried unsuccessfully in 1874 to remove the incumbent of the parliamentary seat, and in the 1880s ran foul of the town over such matters as sewerage and the collapse of mine workings, while at the same time, the Dartmouths in West Bromwich incurred criticism because of their partial immunity from rates. At Southport, animosity between the landowners and the corporation exploded into the much-publicized confrontation over the foreshore in 1883, and in the more general campaign for leasehold enfranchisement; and in Bournemouth, there were similar disputes between the corporation and the patricians in the 1890s and early 1900s over land for parks, the municipal pavilion project, and the cliff drive schemes.

Thus did the balance of power shift again. However, having successfully asserted their political and financial dominance, in both corporation and constituency affairs, the middle-class urban leaders were anxious to re-establish cordial relations with the landowners who still, economically, held their respective towns in the hollow of their hand. And, in an age when property rights and landed assets seemed increasingly vulnerable, the patricians, too, were anxious to present a favourable local public image. So there took place that picturesque *rapprochement*, characterized by patrician mayoralties in Cardiff, Dudley and Southport, and in all the towns by grand ceremonials, at which mayors, councillors and landowners outdid each other in fulsome praise and mutual admiration. In constituency affairs, too, the patricians were happy to co-operate with the local élites they had once dominated, although it was increasingly on the local élite's terms rather than on their own. As the examples of Cardiff, West Bromwich, Dudley and Southport show, the provision of patrician candidates for parliamentary honours at this time should be explained more in terms of personal ambition and stopgap service for local parties rather than as an atavistic reassertion of a 'landed interest'.

Between the wars, the balance of power tilted ever more markedly in favour of the local councils, and away from the landowners. And as the estates themselves were broken up and sold off, the economic link which had been the basis of this last, largely ornamental phase of public, patrician involvement, gradually vanished. In Bournemouth, territorial abdication came early and quickly, as most of the central estates were sold in the early 1920s, and in Southport the same process began shortly after. Only the repurchase of part of the Hesketh estate in 1929 meant the reassertion of a vestigial patrician rôle as late as the 1950s. In Cardiff and the Black Country, the Butes and Dudleys began to dispose of their mineral assets soon after the First World War, and by 1947 they had both severed their residential, economic, social, political and philanthropic links almost completely. And, although the Dartmouths continued to play a reduced role in West Bromwich throughout the inter-war years, it hardly survived into the second half of the twentieth century, as their economic and residential links were also gradually but inexorably broken. Today, Sandwell Hall is demolished, Witley Court is a ruin, Himley Hall is owned by the National Coal Board, Cardiff Castle belongs to the Corporation, and Scarisbrick Hall is a private school. In the end, the towns' triumph over patrician power has been complete.

2

This summary of patrician involvement in the social, public and political life of Cardiff, Dudley, West Bromwich, Southport and Bournemouth largely reinforces the general picture of the encounter between the landowners and the towns which is already known in outline. But at the same time, the material presented here makes it possible to extend our knowledge of the subject, and to appreciate more vividly its complexities and diversities. To begin with, taken in conjunction with the detailed investigations of the Calthorpes and Birmingham and the Devonshires and Eastbourne which are already available, they enable us to identify more precisely some of the points on that spectrum of landed involvement with the towns of modern Britain which runs from patrician power to noble impotence.[7]

In the case of the great industrial towns, we can now see more vividly how the Calthorpes lie towards one end of that continuum, playing a very limited part in the economy of Birmingham, and keeping a relatively low profile in the town's public life. At the opposite extreme come the Butes, whose massive importance on the economy of Cardiff was reflected in their much greater and more enduring political power and social influence. Somewhere between these two, but much nearer to Cardiff than to Birmingham, are the Dudleys in the Black Country – again wielding great economic power and considerable early political influence, but never, perhaps, having quite the complete hold over their titular town that the Butes achieved in Cardiff. And, again, more powerful than the Calthorpes, but perhaps less influential than the Dudleys, were the Dartmouths in West Bromwich, whose early dominance was more stridently challenged, and who did not provide an aristocratic mayor at the end of the century.

The same spread may be seen in the seaside towns. At one extreme, the Devonshires at Eastbourne stand out even more markedly, with their immense outlay on the resort's creation and amenities, and with their correspondingly large and abiding influence over local companies and the local authority. At the other end of the spectrum are the poorer, less broad-acred landowners of Bournemouth who, with one exception, limited their activities almost completely to the development of their estates, rarely invested in the town's public utilities, and played a negligible part in its public life. While the Devonshires dominated Eastbourne, the Tapps-Gervis-Meyricks played only a vestigial rôle in Bournemouth. In Southport, the landowners were slightly more assertive, especially in the 1890s and 1900s, when they took up residence in the town again, and played some real, personal part in its affairs. But they were never as influential as were the Devonshires in Eastbourne. In Southport, as in Bournemouth, most local amenities were created, financed and managed by individual businessmen quite independent of the landowners, or by the more assertive local authority, so that the resorts were monuments to civic rather than to landed enterprise.

Brought together thus, these case studies are collectively more illuminating of the overall pattern of land involvement in modern British towns than any single study, conceived and developed in isolation, could possibly be: the whole is, indeed, greater than the sum of its parts. And these generalizations may be further extended by directly comparing patrician involvement in the resorts and in the great industrial towns. For example, it clearly emerges that the Butes in Cardiff and the Devonshires in Eastbourne played a similar part: their enterprise and initiative laid the foundations of the town and its economy, and the political and economic power they wielded was correspondingly large and relatively long-lived. But at the other extreme, the Calthorpes in Birmingham and the Tapps-Gervis-Meyricks in Bournemouth were far less significant economically, and the part they played in local affairs was also markedly less. Significantly, whereas in Eastbourne and Cardiff the great phase of ceremonial government at the end of the nineteenth century was firmly centred on the local landed representative, in Birmingham and in Bournemouth it revolved around Chamberlain and Russell Cotes, local business-men who were themselves effectively surrogate patricians.

But while these generalizations are fruitful in relating different case studies to each other, and in building up an increasingly well-evidenced and coherent overall picture, the essays in this book also serve as a warning against trying to force the varied local evidence into too rigid a framework. For generalizing about Victorian landowners is almost as hazardous as generalizing about Victorian cities: there is a constant need to do full justice to the local, the particular, the individual and the idiosyncratic. Among the patricians, such matters as the financial circumstances of the family, the location and spread of their acres, and the antiquity of their lineage and title (if any), were all of importance in influencing the money they spent and the part they played in their respective towns. Moreover, individual traits, such as party-political preference, personal quirks and characteristics, and the accidents of birth, inheritance and death, constantly cut across any attempts to offer smooth, all-embracing generalizations, or to devise neat, consistent chronological devisions. Likewise, towns which can plausibly be grouped together under such blanket headings as 'industrial' or 'seaside' frequently had divergent social structures, were of varied size and political complexion, and grew at different rates. So, when landed variety is juxtaposed with urban diversity, the *particular* picture which emerges of that general encounter between the patricians and the towns necessarily shows strong local variation.

The idiosyncracies and peculiarities of family circumstances and members, for example, are well illustrated in the essays which follow. Had the Meyricks been more assertive and adventurous and, after 1876, less devoted to Anglesea, they might have played a greater part in the public life of Bournemouth. As the career of Sir Henry Drummond Wolff shows, there was ample scope for landed leadership in the town: but the Meyricks were not interested. Likewise, if the circumstances under which both Charles Hesketh and Charles Scarisbrick acquired their respec-tive Southport estates had been less bizarre, the development policies which they pursued might have been less tight-fisted, and the clash with the Corporation over the foreshore might have taken a less strident form. In the same way, if the third Marquess of Bute had been more worldly and less of a recluse, Cardiff might never have had its incomparably splendid castle. And in the Black Country, the Earls of Dartmouth, with their estates more scattered and their income less Olympian, never wielded quite the power in West Bromwich that the Dudleys – whose acres were more concentrated and more valuable – did in their titular town.

The diversity of the towns must also be borne in mind. Holiday resorts, with their large population of servants and leisured, middle-class rentiers, were more likely to be of a 'conservative' inclination than were 'essentially radical' towns with heavy industry and strong working-class representation.[8] They were also much smaller: in 1911, for instance, Cardiff's population was 182,000 while that of Bournemouth was only 78,000. The differing rates at which towns grew is also significant. The lower profile kept by the Dartmouths in West Bromwich compared with the Dudleys in Dudley at the end of the nineteenth century, for example, may in part be explained by the fact that West Bromwich was growing much more rapidly at that time. And the relatively small size of both these towns, compared with Birmingham and Cardiff, which meant that their municipal and financial resources were limited, explains why the 'civic gospel' of the 1870s and 1880s was not articulated with the anti-aristocratic stridency which characterized these larger, wealthier, more self-confident towns.

Party politics also make generalizations difficult. Among middle- and working-class town-dwellers, civic pride, or delight in patrician glamour, might dissolve otherwise strongly-held Liberal or Tory preferences. Or, on other occasions, they might not. As for the patricians, their position was especially ambiguous: at one level, they were grand, avuncular, established authority figures, above the sordid intrigues and petty squabbling of party politics; but at another, many of them were committed political operators, tempering and modifying their avuncular benevolence in the interests of party-political calculation. In Cardiff, for instance, in 1832 and again in 1868, the opponent of the official Bute candidate was actually related to the family, but held completely opposed political views. In Dudley, in the 1840s and 1850s, the party-political position of Lord Dudley was compromised as he changed allegiance in his attempts to revive the family earldom. And in Southport, the espousal of Liberalism by one of the Scarisbrick beneficiaries in the 1890s – which goes against the general trend of patricians towards Conservatism at this time – must be seen in the context of the strong campaign in the town in favour of leasehold enfranchisement.

3

The picture is, then, a complex one, in which it is important to strike the correct balance between significant generalization and the need to do appropriate justice to the particular circumstances of urban growth and family characteristics. Indeed, in Bournemouth, landed lethargy was so pronounced that Roberts has abandoned chronological treatment, and preferred a thematic approach to the problem. Quite rightly, the other contributors have chosen chronological units which make most sense of their evidence, and all have written to a length which seemed best suited to the materials available. At the same time, it is, perhaps, appropriate to offer a further set of tentative general remarks. Having looked at the interaction between families and towns at the level of the particular and with reference to the six-stage model, it may be worth trying to relate this material to the broader themes of urban growth and landed development in modern Britain.

Very generally, it seems possible to suggest that the first three quarters of nineteenth-century Britain were characterized by leadership more powerful among the rural landowners than among the urban middle classes. The owners of broad acres remained prosperous: indeed, thanks to the Industrial Revolution they were still the richest men in the land. Rural Britain remained, if diminishingly, dominant, and its local government and parliamentary representation continued almost exclusively in the hands of the landowning classes. Parliament, too, was patrician at all levels: cabinets were still preponderantly landed, the House of Lords was as yet unsullied by industrialists, and in the Commons both Liberal and Conversative parties had large landed wings.[9] *Perhaps* the English working class was 'made'; the middle-class 'ideal' *may* have triumphed: but it was the landed élite which remained in control of a landed polity, boasting a power and a coherent sense of its own self-identity which neither middle nor working classes could rival.

Urban Britain was, by comparison, localized, fragmented and divided. This may have been the 'age of great cities': but there were not many of them; they were still, physically, small; and even as late as 1851, York was more typical of urban Britain than Leeds or Liverpool or Manchester.[10] The relatively slow rate of industrialization initially served to differentiate communities rather than make them more alike, and so created a working class more varied and diverse than coherent and self-conscious.[11] In the same way, the provincial, middle-class, entrepreneurial urban élite remained relatively small in numbers, limited in wealth, and conspicuously lacking in self-conscious, self-confident coherent identity.[12] The richest local businessmen often would not serve on local government bodies, which thus became the arena of petty, myopic, penny-pinching squabbles. And as the number of such bodies proliferated – including vestries, poor law boards, school boards, health boards, burial boards, and a whole host of voluntary societies, all in addition to corporations, where they existed – power in the industrial towns and cities became *more* diffusely located, not less.[13]

What picture of Britain from the 1800s to the 1870s emerges if these two aspects of it are coupled together, as they so rarely are? In terms of *national* government, the consequences have long been known: in Professor Vincent's words, there prevailed – as much by necessity as by design – an 'episcopal' concept of landownership, in which the rural part of Britain administered the nation's affairs on behalf of the urban part as well.[14] But the implications for *local* government and urban life have never been spelt out so clearly. In towns with divided élites, lacking any real sense of corporate civic pride, there was still ample opportunity for members of the landed élite, especially if there was some close territorial link, to wield real power if they chose – initiating schemes of economic development, taking the lead in the provision of amenities, dominating local social life, and actively interfering in local government and parliamentary representation.

Of course, as the following case studies show, that power was gradually being eroded, as the towns grew in size, and as the middle-class élites became more confident, wealthy and united. Moreover, in some towns, the local landowners exerted less power than they might have chosen to do. But it is important to remember that incorporation in the 1830s and 1840s was often presented, not as a triumph *for* some middle-class concept of civic autonomy, but as a thrust *against* patrician, landed dominance or interference.[15] In this period, the town hall was not so much the focus *for* coherent, united middle-class civic endeavour, authority and initiative: rather, it was a new, weak and insecure bastion *against* patrician interference which was still possible, easy and (in certain urban quarters) expected. Even after the struggles of the 1830s and 1840s, many landowners like the Butes and the Dudleys retained enormous economic leverage, boasted greater revenue and resources than the new, infant local government bodies, and so could still interfere – formidably if not always successfully – in local affairs. Timid local authorities, lacking funds and self-confidence, meant that landed families with greater resources could dominate almost by default, as did the Scarisbricks and Heskeths in Southport, where they never really set out to do so.

All this illustrates the danger of writing the history of urban and landed Britain, for the first three quarters of the nineteenth century, with the distorting image of hindsight. Only in the last quarter of the century did agricultural depression, the reform of county government, the extension of the franchise, the introduction of industrialists into the peerage, and the impact of Home Rule and the Liberal split, bring about a qualitative weakening and fragmentation of the old landed order. Assuredly, its tenacity was remarkable: but cabinets gradually became more middle class; the power of the Lords was clipped; and country gentlemen ceased to form the back bone even of the Tory party. Sales of landed estates, both rural and urban, began – slowly in the 1880s, but swelling into a flood, especially after both world wars.[16] The speed with which this demise took place should not be overstressed: dominance was followed, not by disappearance, but by fragmentation, adaption and survival in varied mixture. Nevertheless, it seems fair to suggest that, between the 1880s and 1930s, the circumstances of the landed élite changed fundamentally compared with what they had been during the first three quarters of the nineteenth century.

The same was true, if in a different way, for the urban middle classes and their town councils. For it was in *this* period, rather than the earlier decades of the nineteenth century, that Britain really became an urban nation, increasingly in the hands of more self-conscious, united, self-confident middle-class leadership. In parliament, the representation of towns and cities was often undertaken by local big businessmen, and in the towns, the councils increasingly became the focus of civic power, as they gradually took over the other local government bodies which had hitherto competed with them.[17] At the same time, the example of Chamberlain's Birmingham made local government ever more attractive to important local businessmen, who brought to civic affairs a corporate sense of mission and financial flair which vanquished the earlier myopic, penny-pinching bickering.[18] In terms of personnel and methods, it was the years from the late 1870s to the 1930s, the golden age of municipal collectivism, which saw the triumph of the middle-class 'ideal', rather than the generation before.

In the short run, these broader developments help to explain the battles between towns and landowners over various aspects of patrician property in the last quarter of the nineteenth century. Thereafter, a new relationship emerged between weakened (if still tenacious) landowners, and stronger (if occasionally obsequious) urban élites, in which the previously dominant patricians were replaced by the increasingly confident urban middle classes as the majority partner. Initiative and power had largely passed to the local councils, often embarking on grand, collectivist schemes of municipal enterprise, and to the constituency associations, now dominant in party politics. The patricians might support middle-class initiatives, respond to their requests and suggestions, and collaborate in civic and philanthropic schemes promoting the unity and well-being of the town. But they no longer dictated policy or held the initiative in the way they once had. The balance of civic power had shifted from the country house to the town hall. So, when the patricians participated in civic and ceremonial affairs, it was more on the council's terms than on their own.

In towns where the economic link was weak, or the personal patrician element was lacking, this might mean an ornamentally impotent phase, or even no ornamentation at all. But in other towns, where the economic link was still strong, influence necessarily remained, even if direct political power and initiative had gone. Until the inter-war years, the Butes, the Dudleys, the Dartmouths, the Heskeths and the Scarisbricks all held their respective towns, economically 'in the hollow of their hand.'[19] In particular, their local agents, like Claughton in Dudley and W.T. Lewis in Cardiff, remained men of weight and influence in the community. The formal evidence of their relationship with corporations and constituency associations, as revealed in minute books, correspondence and local newspapers, says little of the influence which such men might still wield, on behalf of the estates they served, by telephone calls, informal meetings and off-the-record conversations. Although the scope of patrician power had been much eroded by this time, the landowners still exerted influence until, and even beyond, the time when territorial abdication began. And, ironically enough, the Second World War, which brought an end to most of these lingering landed links, also spelt the end of the era of municipal, middle-class collectivism, as the power and financial independence of the councils was rapidly eroded, and the old middle-class 'social leaders' were replaced, along with their patrician colleagues, by 'public persons.'[20] By the time middle-class municipal government had completely emancipated itself from patrician thraldom, its own demise was almost nigh.

4

These reflections suggest that it may be valuable, in future, to bear in mind the changing balance between the rural, landed, patrician élite, and urban, middle-class leadership, and also the relative coherence or fragmentation of each of these groups, when writing about the towns of modern Britain no less than about the countryside. More precisely, it suggests that in the towns, the years from the 1800s to the 1870s might usefully be seen as a time of landed power and (albeit lessening) middle-class subordination, while the period from the 1880s to the 1930s saw this relationship increasingly reversed. In some other realms of British life, indeed, the patricians still remained in control – such as governing the empire and conducting diplomacy. But in the towns, they had largely traded political power and initiative for economic influence and ceremonial involvement, which usually persisted as long as their territorial links remained.

But speculation such as this should not be carried too far: for as these essays well demonstrate, the particular circumstances of any family or town are a constant reminder not to let generalizations get out of hand. Indeed, there is still much more to do before a fully satisfactory evidential framework can be pieced together. Take, for example, the town of Liverpool, where the Derbys, Seftons and Salisburys were all important landowners. We know very little about the development of their local urban estates; and their rôle in Liverpool's public life, which persisted in ceremonial guise until the Second World War and beyond, has not been studied at all. In the case of the Derbys, for instance, the recently-edited diaries of the fifteenth earl, covering the years 1849–69, do not even mention Liverpool in the index; and the local activities of his nephew, the seventeenth earl and uncrowned 'king' of Lancashire, both as a patrician figure and as Tory party boss, need a more scholarly investigation than they received at the hands of Randolph Churchill.[21]

In other cities, too, similar gaps in our knowledge abound. In Sheffield, for instance, we know something of the political involvement of the earls Fitzwilliam during the first half of the century.[22] But thereafter, the social, political and philanthropic activities of the eighth and ninth earls are completely unstudied. And, although the development of the Norfolk building estate is now beginning to receive belated attention, the public activities of the Dukes of Norfolk in Sheffield have not been investigated either.[23] Occasional hints are thrown out in local histories whose major preoccupations lie elsewhere; but no historian has yet directly addressed the question of patrician power and influence in the town.[24] Likewise, in Huddersfield, we know far less than we ought about the doings of the Ramsden family. There is some work now being done on the development of their urban holdings, and town histories and a brief survey of the Ramsden estate offer tantalizing glimpses of what may be in store for an intrepid researcher.[25] But, as with Sheffield, we still await a study which deliberately and self-consciously investigates the position of the Ramsdens in the public life of the town.

Three other big cities are equally in need of attention. Various secondary works offer material about the significance of the marquesses of Donegall and the earls of Shaftesbury in the public life of Belfast.[26] But aside from some important exploratory work on the Donegalls' finances, no systematic research has been done: we badly need a study of this second Celtic capital of the calibre of Davies's work on the Butes and Cardiff.[27] For the Potteries, we know a great deal about the economic, social and political involvement of the Sutherlands during the early decades of the nineteenth century, but nothing has been published for the later period.[28] Again, there are hints in local histories and in the novels of Arnold Bennett: but a full-scale, full-length study of the Sutherlands in North Stafford-shire, to parallel Trainor's investigation of patrician activities in the southern part of the county, is urgently needed.[29] Finally, and oddest of all, are the activities of the Astor family in Plymouth from before the First World War until after the Second: as philanthropists, MPs, benefactors and freemen, they played a major rôle in the town's affairs, and their archives must now be ripe for serious scholarly study.[30]

Among seaside resorts, a similar agenda of research may be drawn up. The part played by the Palks in the creation of Torquay, the de la Warrs and Brasseys in the making of Bexhill, the Radnors in the development of Folkestone, and the Scarbroughs in the rise of Skegness all merit attention: as much from the economic as from the social and political viewpoint. In each case, old-fashioned resort histories tell us a little: but until estate and corporation archives are systematically investigated, it will not be possible to know whether they come more at the Eastbourne or the Bournemouth end of the spectrum of patrician involvement.[31] There are other resorts which were smaller, or with a less direct landed link, which might repay some investigation, such as the Northumberlands at Tynemouth, the Norfolks at Littlehampton, the Cromers at their titular town, the Mostyns at Llandudno, the Cornwallises at Hastings and the Sitwells at Scarborough.[32]

Of equal significance are those small country and county towns which, until the middle of the nineteenth century, housed a majority of Britain's urban population, and remained thereafter an important (if neglected) appendage of landed England. Many of them, such as Arundel, Peterborough, Stamford, Wenlock and Whitehaven, were pocket boroughs both before and after the Great Reform Act. And, from the late nineteenth century until the 1950s, they boasted more patrician mayors than any other type of town.[33] Three such towns – Exeter, Lincoln and Colchester – have received outstanding, if traditional, recent histories.[34] But the majority, including all those with more marked patrician links, have hardly been studied. There is some work on Stamford, Whitehaven, Arundel, Peterborough and Buxton, of varied merit and interest: but towns such as Worcester, Warwick, Woodstock and Northampton have received no scholarly attention from this standpoint.[35]

Finally, there is the 'great wen' itself. Of course, the pattern and importance of patrician landownership in London is well known, and there have been some quite outstanding studies of estate management.[36] But the political and social consequences of this landed presence in the great metropolis remain completely unknown, at least for the nineteenth century. We know, for instance, that the first Duke of Westminster is reputed to have 'exercised a great deal of influence in the city of Westminster'; that the ninth duke of Bedford was first mayor of Holborn in 1900; that the fifteenth duke of Norfolk was mayor of Westminster in the same year; and that the earls Cadogan provided mayors of Chelsea in 1900 and again 64 years later.[37] But we know nothing of the real power – if any – which lay behind this decorative, ornamental, ceremonial façade. And the fact that Lord Rosebery was first Chairman of the London County Council, and that a variety of other grandees were Councillors and Aldermen, is something more often commented on than investigated.[38]

5

This is a long catalogue of work which remains to be done. There are some extraordinarily large gaps in our knowledge of specific families and particular towns, which must be closed before generalization can be pushed beyond the present stage of tentative speculation, and be tested and refined with reference to a fuller evidential base. Indeed, if treated in the detail which they merit, the projects outlined above should spawn several books, a dozen dissertations, and a score of articles. Thanks to the essays which have been written for this volume, we now know a great deal more about patrician involvement in the social, public and political life of urban Britain than we did before. But perhaps the most significant gain in our knowledge is the greater precision of our ignorance. The field is wide open; the archives are voluminous; the results cannot fail to be individually interesting and collectively important. From whatever angle it is viewed, the study of the power and influence wielded by the patrician élite in the towns of modern Britain – new and old, large and small – remains a subject of great interest, opportunity and potential.

NOTES

1 F. Foakes-Jackson, *Social Life in England and Wales, 1750–1850* (New York, 1916), 334.
2 See, for example: F.M.L. Thompson, *English Landed Society in the Nineteenth Century* (1963); *idem*, 'England', in *European Landed Elites in the Nineteenth Century*, ed. D. Spring (1977); W.L. Arnstein, 'The survival of the Victorian aristocracy', in *The Rich*,

the Well-Born and the Powerful: Elites and Upper Classes in History, ed. F.C. Jaher (1973); D. Cannadine, *Lords and Landlords: The Aristocracy and the Towns, 1774–1967* (1980), ch. 1.

3 The fullest account of this is: D. Spring, 'English landowners and nineteenth-century industrialism', in *Land and Industry: The Landed Estate and the Industrial Revolution*, ed. J.T. Ward and R.G. Wilson (1971).

4 D. Cannadine, 'The landowner as millionaire: the finances of the Dukes of Devonshire, c. 1800–1926', *Agricultural History Rev.* xxv (1977), 87–93; *idem*, 'Aristocratic indebtedness in the nineteenth century: the case re-opened', *Economic History Rev.*, xxx (1977), 647–8; W.D. Rubinstein, 'Wealth, elites and the class structure of modern Britain', *Past and Present*, LXXVI (1977), 103–4; W.L. Burn, *The Age of Equipoise: A Study of the Mid-Victorian Generation* (1964), 308.

5 W.L. Guttsman, *The British Political Elite* (1963), 222–4.

6 Cannadine, *Lords and Landlords*, 59.

7 *Ibid.*, pts. 2 and 3.

8 A. Briggs, *Victorian Cities* (1968), 38.

9 R.E. Pumphrey, 'The introduction of industrialists into the British peerage: a study in adaption of a social institution', *American Historical Rev.*, LXV (1959), 8; H.J. Laski, 'The personnel of the English cabinet, 1801–1924', *American Political Science Rev.*, XX (1928), 16–22; M. Ransome, 'Some recent studies in the composition of the House of Commons', *University of Birmingham Historical J.*, VI (1958), 142–7.

10 A. Armstrong, *Stability and Change in an English County Town: A Social Study of York, 1801–51* (1974), 10, 28–30.

11 Briggs, *op. cit.*, 33; A. Reid, 'Politics and economics in the formation of the British working class: a response to H.F. Moorhouse', *Social History*, III (1978), esp. 359.

12 Rubinstein, *op. cit.*, 104–5, 121; W.L. Arnstein, 'The myth of the triumphant Victorian middle class', *The Historian*, XXXVII (1975), *passim*.

13 E.P. Hennock, 'Finance and politics in urban local government in England, 1835–1900', *Historical J.*, VI (1963); *idem, Fit and Proper Persons: Ideal and Reality in Nineteenth Century Government* (1973), 31, 313; D. Fraser, *Urban Politics in Victorian England: The Structure of Politics in Victorian Cities* (1976), 92; *idem, Power and Authority in the Victorian City* (1979), 148–55.

14 J.R. Vincent, *The Formation of the Liberal Party, 1857–1868* (1966), 213–14.

15 Fraser, *Urban Politics*, 21–2.

16 Thompson, *English Landed Society*, 329–33; Cannadine, *Lords and Landlords*, 420–1, 426.

17 Fraser, *Power and Authority*, 154–73.

18 Hennock, *Fit and Proper Persons*, 35, 56; H.E. Meller, *Leisure and the Changing City, 1870–1914* (1976), 99–104.

19 See below, 110.

20 J.M. Lee, *Social Leaders and Public Persons: A Study of County Government in Cheshire since 1888* (1963), 5; Hennock, *Fit and Proper Persons*, 323–34; R.V. Clements, *Local Notables and the City Council* (1969), esp. chs 2 and 3.

21 J.R. Vincent (ed.), *Disraeli, Derby and the Conservative Party: The Political Journals of Lord Stanley, 1849–69* (1978); R.S. Churchill, *Lord Derby: 'King' of Lancashire* (1959). For the most recent work which gives some leads, see P.J. Waller, *Democracy and Sectarianism: a Political and Social History of Liverpool, 1868–1939* (1981), 288, 293–4, 310–16, 318–23, 328–9, 341–2.

22 E.A. Smith, *Whig Principles and Party Politics: Earl Fitzwilliam and the Whig Party, 1748–1833* (1975); D. Spring, 'Earl Fitzwilliam and the Corn Laws', *American Historical Rev.*, LIX (1954); F.M.L. Thompson, 'Whigs and Liberals in the West Riding, 1830–1860', *English Historical Rev.*, LXXIV (1959).

23 G. Rowley, 'Landownership and the spatial development of towns: a Sheffield example', *East Midland Geographer*, VI (1975); G. Rowley and R. Homan, 'The location of

institutions during the process of urban growth: a case-study of churches and chapels in nineteenth-century Sheffield', *ibid.*, VII (1979); D.J. Olsen, 'House upon house', in *The Victorian City: Images and Realities*, ed. H.J. Dyos and M. Wolff (2 vols., 1973).

24 H.K. Hawson, *Sheffield: The Growth of a City* (1968), 45, 135, 204, 216; S. Pollard, *A History of Labour in Sheffield* (1959), 101–2, 111, 183.

25 D. Wholmsley, 'A landed estate and the railway: Huddersfield, 1844–54', *J. Transport History*, n.s. ii (1974); R. Brook, *The Story of Huddersfield* (1968), 187; C. Stephenson, *The Ramsdens and their Estate in Huddersfield* (1972).

26 D.J. Owen, *History of Belfast* (1921), 187–92, 255–7; R.W.M. Strain, *Belfast and Its Charitable Society* (1961), 212–37.

27 W.A. Maguire, 'The 1822 settlement of the Donegall estates', *Irish Economic and Social History*, III (1976); *idem*, 'Lord Donegall and the sale of Belfast: a case-history from the Encumbered Estates Court', *Economic History Rev.*, 2nd ser., XXIV (1976).

28 E. Richards, 'The industrial face of a great estate: Trentham and Lilleshall, 1780–1860', *Economic History Rev.* 2nd ser., XXVII (1974); *idem*, 'The social and electoral influence of the Trentham interest', 1800–1860', *Midland History*, III (1975); F. Bealey, 'Municipal politics in Newcastle-Under-Lyme, 1835–1872', *North Staffordshire J. Field Studies*, III (1963).

29 E.J.D. Warrillow, *A Sociological History of Stoke-On-Trent* (1960), 157, 216, 351; A. Bennett, *The Card* (1956 edn), 9, 97, 101–5, 113–18, 130.

30 C. Sykes, *Nancy: The Life of Lady Astor* (1972), 107–9, 187–200, 226, 307, 473; M. Collis, *Nancy Astor: an Informal Biography* (1960), 57, 127, 229–31.

31 A.C. Ellis, *A Historical Survey of Torquay* (1930); L.J. Bartley, *The Story of Bexhill* (1971); C.H. Bishop, *Folkestone: The Story of a Town* (1973); W. Kime, *Skeggy: The Story of an East Coast Town* (1969).

32 For some suggestive hints concerning the Sitwells and Scarborough, see: O. Sitwell, *Left Hand, Right Hand!*, vol. I, *The Cruel Month* (1945), 59, 79–81, 131, 139, 144, 148, 157, 184, 208–9, 211, 238.

33 Cannadine, *Lords and Landlords*, 33–6.

34 Sir Francis Hill, *Victorian Lincoln* (1974); R. Newton, *Victorian Exeter, 1830–1910* (1968); A.F.J. Brown, *Colchester, 1815–1914* (1980).

35 J.M. Lee, 'Modern Stamford', in *The Making of Stamford*, ed. A. Rogers (1965); J.E. Williams, 'The growth and decline of the port of Whitehaven, 1650–1900' (M.A. thesis, University of Leeds, 1951); M. Zimmeck, 'Chartered rights and vested interests: reform era politics in three Sussex boroughs: Rye, Arundel and Lewes' (M.A. thesis, University of Sussex, 1972); T. C. Cunningham, 'The growth of Peterborough' (Ph.D. thesis, University of Cambridge, 1972); T. Marchington, 'The development of Buxton and Matlock since 1800' (M.A. thesis, University of London, 1961); R.G. Heape, *Buxton Under the Dukes of Devonshire* (1948).

36 J. Summerson, *Georgian London* (1970), chs 3, 7, 12; D.J. Olsen, *Town Planning in London in the Eighteenth and Nineteenth Centuries* (1965); *idem, The Growth of Victorian London* (1976), ch. 4; F.H.W. Sheppard (ed.), *The Survey of London*, vol. XXXVI, *The Parish of St Paul, Covent Garden* (1970); *idem* (ed.), *The Survey of London*, vol. XXXIX, *The Grosvenor Estate in Mayfair*, Pt I, *General History* (1977); H. Hobhouse, *Thomas Cubitt: Master Builder* (1971).

37 H.J. Hanham, *Elections and Party Management: Politics in the Time of Gladstone and Disraeli* (1959), 80. For some suggestive comments on patrician political power in eighteenth-century London, see: N. Rogers, 'Aristocratic clientage, trade and independency: popular politics in pre-radical Westminster', *Past and Present*, LXI (1971).

38 See, for example: The Marquess of Crewe, *Lord Rosebery* (2 vols, 1931), i, 330–8; 88, 383–5; R.R. James, *Rosebery: A Biography of Archibald Philip, Fifth Earl of Rosebery* (1963), 197–9.

Aristocratic town-makers and the coal metropolis: the marquesses of Bute and the growth of Cardiff, 1776 to 1947

JOHN DAVIES

Aristocratic town-makers and the coal metropolis: the marquesses of Bute and the growth of Cardiff, 1776 to 1947

JOHN DAVIES

1 Introduction

'No town in Great Britain', stated the *Cardiff and Merthyr Guardian* on the death of the second marquess of Bute in 1848, 'so clearly and indisputably owes its prosperity to one creative hand as does Cardiff to the late Lord Bute.' '[We] acknowledge', declared the corporation of Cardiff to his son, the third marquess, on his coming-of-age in 1868, 'how largely this Town is indebted for its high commercial position, for its many charitable and public institutions, for all that tends to the prosperity and happiness of the people, to the forethought, enterprise, benevolence and sympathy of the lamented nobleman whose name you bear.' 'There is probably no similar estate in the country', wrote the *Daily Chronicle* on the death of the third marquess in 1900, 'where an immense commercial centre has been fostered on one man's property, and the rights of the landlord preserved, as one might say, absolutely intact.'[1]

The family thus described was undoubtedly one of the richest in the United Kingdom, and the importance of the Butes in the creation of Cardiff was perhaps only equalled by the contribution of Cardiff to the revenue of the Butes. By the 1880s, as the necessarily approximate figures in table 1 suggest, the Glamorgan estate, which constituted less than one fifth of the family's landholdings, was providing at least two thirds of the total income. Indeed, the £100,000 *per annum* recorded in 1883 is undoubtedly a gross underestimate; by the last decades of the ninteenth century, the third marquess of Bute was receiving from Glamorgan, in ground rents, dock dues, mineral royalties and other payments, a gross annual income in the region of a quarter of a million pounds.

The growth of the town with which the family was connected was as rapid as the contribution which it made to their fortune was large. In 1801, Cardiff was a mere village; but the building of the docks from the 1830s onwards meant that the town became the centre for the export trade in Welsh coal. Thereafter, its population expanded prodigiously, so that, by the beginning of the twentieth century, it was being aptly described as the 'Chicago of Wales', the 'Metropolis of Wales' or, more grandly but no less realistically, as the 'coal metropolis of the world'.[2]

Table 1   The marquesses of Bute: acreage and income, c. 1883

county	acres	%	gross annual value (£)	%
Glamorgan	21,402	18.34	100,000	66.2
Durham	1,953	1.7	5,424	3.6
Bedford	72	0.0	256	0.2
Brecon	59	0.0	170	0.1
Monmouth	12	0.0	19	0.0
Ayr	43,734	37.58	22,756	15.0
Bute	29,279	25.1	19,574	12.9
Wigtown	20,157	17.37	2,936	1.9
Total	116,668	99.9	151,135	99.9

Source: J. Bateman, *The Great Landowners of Great Britain and Ireland* (1883 edn, ed. D. Spring, 1971), 69

Table 2   The growth of Cardiff, 1801–1911

	pre-1875 boundary	post-1875 boundary
1801	1,870	
1811	2,457	
1821	3,521	
1831	6,187	
1841	10,077	11,442
1851	18,351	20,258
1861	32,954	41,422
1871	39,356	56,911
1881		82,761
1891		128,915
1901		164,333
1911		182,259

Source: *Census of England and Wales*, 1801 to 1911

The rôle of the Bute family in the history of Cardiff and Glamorgan is examined in detail in *Cardiff and the Marquesses of Bute*.[3] The book focuses upon the lives of the first three marquesses, owners of the estate from 1766 to 1900; it analyses their system of estate administration, examines their relationship with the community in Glamorgan, assesses the impact of urbanization, industrialization and agricultural development upon the estate, and describes the family's involvement in docks and railways. In the essay which follows, the early history of the family and the activities of the first marquess (1744–1814) are described in part 2, and the economic background is outlined in part 3. Whereas the main emphasis of *Cardiff and the Marquesses of Bute* is upon the estate's contribution to the economic development

19

of south-east Wales, the prime purpose of this essay is to evaluate the part played by the Bute family in the public life of Cardiff and, as such, it contains material not used in the book. The core of the essay is part 4, in which the influence of the second marquess (1793–1848) upon Cardiff is examined. Part 5 is concerned with the consequences, for the family and for the town, of the long minority (1848–68) of the third marquess, and in part 6 his activities in Cardiff after his coming of age are investigated. The essay is concluded by outlining the family's territorial withdrawal from the region and its declining rôle in Cardiff public life during the first half of the twentieth century.

2 The family and political background

The family which was to become so intimately associated with the making of a nineteenth-century industrial city accumulated an astonishing array of antique, exotic and feudal sounding titles: marquess of Bute, earl of Bute, Dumfries and Windsor, Viscount Mountjoy, Ayr and Kingarth and Baron Cardiff, Crichton, Cumnock, Mountstuart and Inchmarnock, as well as a baronetcy in the baronetage of Nova Scotia. This agglomeration of titles represented an agglomeration of landed possessions, the result of shrewd marriage alliances, for the Butes, like the Habsburgs, had married their way to territorial power (see Appendix). It must be confessed, however, that they owed their origin to anything but a marriage, for the first of the Stuarts of Bute was the illegitimate son of King Robert II of Scotland, who died in 1390. The first earl of Bute (created in 1703) married the daughter of Sir George Mackenzie, Lord Advocate of Scotland and the third earl, George III's prime minister, the daughter of Edward Wortley Montagu, marriages which brought the extensive Rosehaugh estates and the vast Wortley lands into the family. The third earl's son, the first marquess (created in 1796), took as his second wife Frances Coutts, thereby giving the Stuarts of Bute a claim upon the great fortune of Thomas Coutts, the banker. The first marquess's eldest son, John Stuart (who died in 1794) married Penelope Crichton, sole heiress to the possessions and titles of the earls of Dumfries and his son, the second marquess, took as his first wife Maria North, co-heiress to the estates of the earls of Guilford.[4]

It was the first marriage of the first marquess, that to Charlotte Windsor, daughter and co-heiress of Lord Windsor, which linked the house of Stuart with Cardiff and Glamorgan. 'Your friend [Lord Mountstuart, later the first marquess of Bute]', wrote Sir John Pringle to James Boswell in 1767, 'is a married man and, I am persuaded, happy in that state although the match was made upon prudential consideration only.'[5] The 'prudential consideration' was the Cardiff Castle estate in Glamorgan which the Windsors in turn had acquired by marriage when in 1704 Thomas Windsor had married Charlotte Herbert and had thereby obtained possession of the Welsh estates of the Herbert earls of Pembroke, estates which had been granted to the Herberts by Henry VIII and Edward VI. Charlotte Windsor had little apart from her expectations to commend her. When her younger sister became engaged to Lord Beauchamp, Horace Walpole wrote: 'Lord Beauchamp is to marry the second Miss Windsor. It is odd that those two ugly girls . . . should get the two best figures in England, him and Lord Mountstuart.'[6]

The Cardiff Castle estate, held by the Stuarts of Bute from 1776 to 1947, extended by the mid-nineteenth century over 22,000 acres of Glamorgan. The

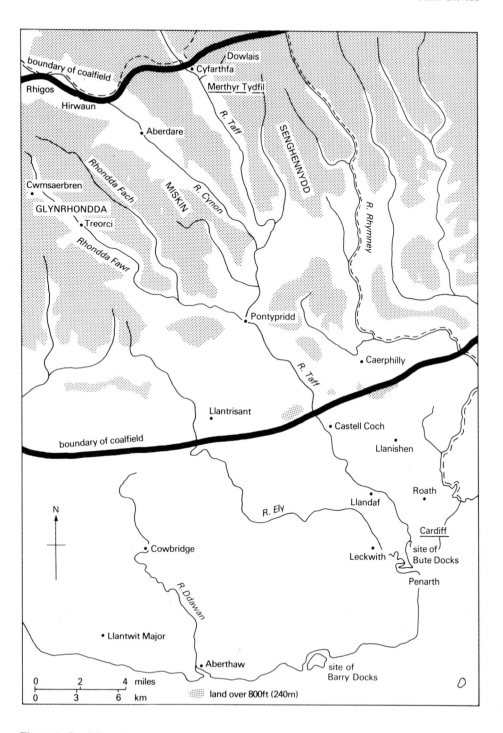

Figure 1. Cardiff and its vicinity in the nineteenth century.

estate was by then overwhelmingly preponderant at Cardiff, embracing three quarters of the ancient borough and much of the neighbouring parishes of Roath, Llandaf and Llanishen. In addition, it included a wide variety of the terrain of the county: rich agricultural land in the vale of Glamorgan, farms and mineral land at Caerphilly and Llantrisant, forests at Castell Coch and Leckwith and enormous tracts within the valleys of the Rhondda, Cynon, Neath and Rhymney. Together with the land, there were rights of lordship over the boroughs of Cardiff, Llantrisant and Cowbridge and over the great manors of Senghennydd, Miskin and Glynrhondda, bringing the Butes manorial dues, market tolls, rights of wrech, control over the Cardiff foreshore and the water of the river Taff and above all ownership of the minerals beneath the tens of thousands of acres of the commons of north Glamorgan.[7]

The Cardiff Castle estate was to become one of the richest estates of its size in the United Kingdom, and its owners were to win pre-eminence among aristocratic town-makers. None of this, however, can have been apparent when Charlotte Windsor married Lord Mountstuart in 1766. The history of the estate under the Pembrokes and the Windsors had not been auspicious. From the late sixteenth century, the earls of Pembroke had concentrated their attention increasingly upon their estates in Wiltshire. A fortune was spent on their great mansion at Wilton while the castle at Cardiff, left uninhabited, fell into ruin. The fifth earl, who died in 1669, began to dispose of his Welsh estates; the Windsors continued the process, the bankruptcy of the second viscount, who died in 1758, forcing him to sell all that remained of the great possessions of the Herberts in the county of Monmouth. Inattention by owners and agents had led to extensive encroachments by neighbouring landowners and to widespread usurpations of the rights of the estate. Industrial development, which by the early nineteenth century was to make northern Glamorgan a leading iron-making centre, brought infinitesimal returns to the Cardiff Castle estate. Valuable rights were leased for a pittance, in particular at Dowlais where 'the greatest ironworks in the world' was established under a lease granted by Viscount Windsor in 1749 for 99 years at £23 *per annum*.[8]

By 1766, therefore, the Cardiff Castle estate represented a truncated and neglected remnant of the vast tracts of Wales granted to the Herberts by the Tudor kings. When surveyed in 1774, its enclosed land consisted of 11,211 acres 'scattered within a space twenty-four miles by fourteen' and its total receipts amounted to £2,797.[9] The first marquess of Bute proved assiduous in enlarging the estate, acquiring land of immense strategic importance in the coalfield and at Cardiff, some of the latter obtained through purchase from and exchange with the corporation in a manner which subsequently gave rise to rumours of under-hand deals. The marquess proved equally assiduous in increasing the rental and, on his death in 1814, the receipts of the estate had risen to £6,168.[10] His desire to enlarge his property and increase his income was not accompanied by a will to reform the administration of the estate and to undertake its improvement. Such concerns would have been inconsistent with his character and style of life. He was described by Boswell in a letter to Rousseau as a 'handsome [man] with elegant manners and a tempestuously noble soul who has never applied himself earnestly to anything' and his brother Frederick doubted whether the marquess would 'ever be a man of business for that he would not persist.'[11] His endemic extravagance, his life in the 1760s and 1770s as a man-about-town flirting with politics, his diplomatic career in the 1780s and 1790s and the ceaseless wanderings of his last years would

Figure 2. The first marquess of Bute (by courtesy of the National Portrait Gallery of Scotland).

have been difficult to reconcile with a dedicated application to meticulous and constructive estate management. Thus, when the second marquess, his grandson, inherited the estate in 1814, he was informed by his surveyor, David Stewart: 'I never saw an estate in a more neglected condition . . . You should not allow an estate of the extent and consequence of your lordship's property to continue under its present miserable management.'[12]

The political influence of the estate acquired by the Bute family through the marriage of 1766 was as flawed as was the estate itself. In the sixteenth and early seventeenth centuries, the Herbert family had all but nominated the members of parliament for the county and the boroughs of Glamorgan, but later in the seventeenth century their political power was challenged, on the one hand by the earls of Worcester (later the dukes of Beaufort) and on the other by the county's resident gentry; it became 'virtually dormant' following the death of the seventh earl in 1683. It was revived by the first Viscount Windsor who in the election of 1734 secured the borough seat for his son Herbert and collaborated with the duke of Beaufort in strengthening the Tory cause in the county. Herbert, who inherited the estate in 1738, was also active in Glamorgan politics, committing himself in the election of 1745 to a substantial financial contribution to the Tory campaign.[13] The erosion of the acreage of the Cardiff Castle estate, its replacement as the largest landed property in the county by the Margam estate of the Mansel family, and the hostility felt by the resident gentry towards domination by absentee aristocrats, however, made it impossible for the Windsors to restore the hegemony enjoyed by the earls of Pembroke in Glamorgan politics. After the second viscount's death in 1758, it was alleged that as collector of crown rents in the Lancastrian lordship of Ogmore he had embezzled the money and that the tenants, following his insolvency, had been obliged to pay them again. 'The honest feelings of the injured', noted a Glamorgan Whig in 1789, 'glow with indignant detestation at the very name of Windsor.'[14]

While the influence of the Cardiff Castle estate over the parliamentary representation of Glamorgan and its boroughs had declined since the sixteenth century, its influence over the borough of Cardiff and its corporation had proved more enduring. In the late sixteenth century the earls of Pembroke, at the height of their power in Glamorgan, had been faced with frequent unrest among the burgesses of Cardiff but by the mid-eighteenth century the town had lost much of its vigour. Cardiff in the thirteenth century was undoubtedly the largest borough in Wales but it declined sharply in the later middle ages; a period of growth occurred under Elizabeth and the early Stuarts but the town stagnated from the mid-seventeenth to the late eighteenth centuries.[15] It has been estimated that its population in 1670 was 1,771; by 1801, when the town was described as having 'little contrivance to boast of in the arrangement of its streets, little accommodation or symmetry in the construction of its buildings', its population amounted to 1,870.[16]

To the extent that Cardiff in the mid-eighteenth century had economic functions beyond those of a large rural village, they lay in its rôles as market town for the fertile vale of Glamorgan and as port for the shipment of the vale's agricultural produce to Bristol, although in the former rôle it was challenged by Cowbridge and in the latter by Aberthaw. Although the county town of Glamorgan, Cardiff was no match for Swansea which had four times its population and the Cardiff region could not compare in vigour with west Glamorgan where the growth of metallurgical industries and of the coal trade had produced a lively economy and a vigorous social and cultural life.[17]

24

In the late eighteenth century, with the dramatic development of the iron industry of northern Glamorgan, Cardiff assumed a new rôle as the port for Merthyr Tydfil and, by the end of the century, was exporting over 10,000 tons of iron a year. Access by canal from Merthyr to the sea at Cardiff, completed in 1798, gave 'a most notable impulse to the commerce of the town' and in the 1790s Cardiff was provided for the first time with a bank, a printing press and a daily mail-coach to London; the town church of St John was repaired, street paving was improved, the sea defences were completed and a number of philanthropic and pietistic societies were established.[18]

In these new initiatives, the first marquess of Bute took little part. He had in 1776 repaired the castle and had erected along the western curtain wall a mansion which 'bore a strange resemblance to the gaol at Rothesay.'[19] The work was left unfinished when his eldest son died in 1794 and no member of the Bute family took up residence there. 'The castle', it was stated in 1818, 'has been and is still without an occupant, its chambers untrod, its portals desolate.' As the castle provided employment only for a house-keeper, a porter and occasional day-labourers, there did not exist at Cardiff a great establishment the purchasing power, employment opportunities and hospitality of which could radiate Bute influence throughout the town and the surrounding countryside.[20] The first marquess, with his 'satrap manners', did little, on his rare visits to Glamorgan, to cultivate the loyalty of the inhabitants of Cardiff.[21] Yet, such was the ingrained deference of the small town that its corporation remained loyal to the lord of the castle. Although in theory Cardiff was a free town, its corporation vested with wide powers, in fact, the constable of the castle, nominated by the lord, had a virtual veto over the choice of corporation officials and over the admission of burgesses. The corporation's land holdings within the borough were one-twentieth of those of the marquess, its loans from him had made it financially dependent upon him and its chief officials were almost invariably drawn from among the agents of his estate.[22]

His position at Cardiff also provided the first marquess with a base to capture the parliamentary representation of the boroughs of Glamorgan. The constituency consisted of eight boroughs, in all of which the vote was vested in the burgesses at large.[23] Cardiff, Llantrisant and Cowbridge were under Bute domination and pacts with the patrons of the western boroughs, along with a considerable expansion in the number of Cardiff burgesses, led to the unopposed return of the marquess's eldest son as member for the Glamorgan boroughs in 1790 at a total cost of £289. He was followed on his death in 1794 by his brother Evelyn; Evelyn retired in 1802 and was succeeded by his brother William; William died in 1814 and Evelyn took up the seat again. Both Evelyn and William were on active service in the war and between them they obtained less than ten mentions in the parliamentary records in 24 years.[24] During their period as members of parliament Glamorgan experienced rapid industrial growth and the lack of legislative initiatives by its representatives on issues such as the coal trade caused bitterness among the new industrialists. 'Is it not notorious', wrote a Bute opponent in 1818, 'that for ought that concerns our welfare, the chief of the Court of Pekin might as well profess to represent us.'[25]

Under the first marquess, it appeared that control over the town of Cardiff was an appurtenance of the castle estate and that the family's hold upon the parliamentary representation of the boroughs could be maintained with the minimum of effort and expense. By the second decade of the nineteenth century, however, there were those at Cardiff concerned to 'rescue their town from the state of political degradation in which it has been so long held by the noble Marquess and his underlings.'[26] The first marquess's successor was to learn that landed possessions and aristocratic lineage no longer, in the Cardiff of the nineteenth century, brought unquestioned influence and deference. Influence would have to be nurtured and sustained, deference earned and rewarded.

3 Economic and urban development in east Glamorgan

The second marquess of Bute, who held the Cardiff Castle estate from 1814 to 1848, was in character and personality markedly different from his grandfather. A friend of Shaftesbury and Wellington, his evangelical sense of duty was combined with an inordinate capacity for hard work and a ruthlessness worthy of a self-made industrial baron. Although half-blind, he pursued estate improvement with zealous enthusiasm, perambulating his far-flung estates in Buteshire, Ayrshire, Galloway, County Durham, Bedfordshire and Glamorgan like a medieval monarch, conducting a vast correspondence with his agents and initiating a wide range of activities aimed at developing his property and enhancing its influence. The contrast between the first and second marquesses, between the profligate nobleman of the eighteenth century and his conscientious descendant in the early nineteenth, appears to be not untypical of aristocratic families, suggesting a significant shift in that period in the values and outlook of the British ruling class.[27]

The second marquess inherited his titles and property at the age of 21 and thus held the Cardiff Castle estate throughout his adult life. It was a period of decisive change in Cardiff and Glamorgan. The industrialization of the coalfield, initiated in the late eighteenth century, gathered momentum in the early nineteenth and with the coming of the railways the iron-making districts of south Wales became one of the pivots of British and indeed of world industry. The development of the coal industry, in particular the exploitation of the matchless steam coal of the valleys of east Glamorgan, led to industrial growth outside the confines of the iron-making districts and to a substantial influx of population into the hinterland of Cardiff, the population of east Glamorgan increasing threefold between 1811 and 1848. When the second marquess inherited his estates, Cardiff was still a very small town, twenty-fifth in size among the towns of Wales and, to its inhabitants, those omens of the future, the iron-laden wharfs of the Glamorganshire Canal, seemed no more than an obstacle to herdsmen driving cattle from the back-street byres to the salt pastures.[28] By his death in 1848, 'the most sanguine imagination [could] hardly picture the greatness and importance of her future destiny'; by then, the way had been prepared for Cardiff to become the largest urban centre in Wales and the greatest coal port in the world.[29]

The industrialization and urbanization of Glamorgan, along with the development of the county's communications by land and sea, inevitably transformed the Bute estate. The second marquess was not content, however, passively to benefit from the royalty payments, ground rents, dues and capital gains which came to landowners in the wake of economic expansion. He did not wait for transport entrepreneurs to realize the strategic value of his land in terms of docks and railways, for industrialists to make offers for his coal, for surveyors to discover exploitable seams and for speculative builders to suggest housing schemes. He initiated such developments, thus ensuring that the relentless tide of industrializa-

Figure 3. The second marquess of Bute (by courtesy of the National Portrait Gallery of Scotland).

tion sweeping across Glamorgan should find a focus in his estate. In consequence, during his marquessate, the income of his Glamorgan properties rose from £6,168 in 1814 to £27,403 in 1848, the proportion coming from agricultural sources falling from nine-tenths to one-sixth.[30]

It is in his dock-building activities that the marquess showed most clearly his determination actively to participate in the development of his estates. Nevertheless, in other spheres his participation, although not so spectacular, was equally determined. A series of mineral surveys, initiated by him in 1817, provided proof of the vast mineral reserves lying beneath his property in northern Glamorgan and of the enormous wealth that could accrue to him through their exploitation. 'The whole of the country', enthused David Stewart, 'is formed as if on purpose to enable man to procure with the least possible difficulty, all the minerals necessary to convert the district into one great emporium for the manufacture of iron . . . and there is no reason that I can discover to doubt that an all-wise providence designed it for that purpose.'[31] The strengthening of his hold over this potential wealth, the recognition of his right, as lord of the manor, to the minerals beneath the common lands of his lordships and the securing of convenient access to them became to the second marquess major priorities. He was equally concerned, as were his successors, to enlarge Bute freehold properties within the coalfield and in 1919 the fourth marquess estimated that since 1814 the family had spent £220,000 on purchases of mineral land in Glamorgan.[32]

A substantial coal owner in County Durham, the second marquess was reluctant, because of the rudimentary marketing system then obtaining at Cardiff, to exploit his own coal in Glamorgan.[33] He did, however, finance considerable boring operations on his estate and at Rhigos established a small coal mine, aimed at providing employment in a poverty-stricken district. In the 1840s he purchased the farm of Cwmsaerbren in the upper Rhondda valley and there set in train operations to prove the accessibility of Rhondda steam coal. The success of the venture, carried out by his son's trustees, ushered in the dramatic development of the valley and the trustees became, in the Rhondda and elsewhere, owners of collieries which were, by the late nineteenth century, producing up to 200,000 tons of coal a year.[34]

Nevertheless, the second marquess's primary role within the coalfield was that of landlord. As the owner of the largest estate within the coalfield, his stipulations over leases and royalties and his surveillance of the activities of his lessees went far to determine the pace and pattern of the exploitation of the mineral wealth of Glamorgan. Smaller landowners turned to him for guidance, a number of them leasing their minerals to him, he in turn leasing them to ironmasters and coalowners. He was prepared to assist industrialists with loans, his mineral agent, Robert Beaumont, for example, borrowing £1,200 from him in 1839 to pay the first two years rent upon his newly acquired colliery.[35] The Bute-Rhymney Ironworks, intended to be 'the first works in Wales and consequently in the world', found in the marquess a munificent patron, his lordship negotiating and guaranteeing for its proprietor a loan of £147,000.[36] The marquess's concern to establish a successful ironworks in the upper Rhymney valley was largely motivated by his desire to contain the expansion of the great Dowlais Iron Company, whose 99-year lease of a large proportion of his mineral land at a derisory rent caused him intense mortification. Attempts to upset the Dowlais lease and to obtain compensation from the company led in the 1820s to complex litigation, the duel between the marquess and Sir John Guest of Dowlais spilling out of the industrial field into the politics of Glamorgan. The renewal of the lease, due to expire in 1848, became an issue of obsessive concern to the marquess in the 1840s, the marchioness believing that Guest's intransigence had driven her husband to a premature death.[37]

The example of the Dowlais lease before him, the marquess scrutinized mineral leases with great care. 'It is curious', he wrote in 1840, 'to compare the leases of 1748, 1763, 1803, 1823 and 1840 and to observe how landlords have been taught by experience.'[38] In this scrutiny, he was assisted by his advisers on Tyneside, in particular by his friend and confidant, the remarkable John Clayton, town clerk of Newcastle.[39] Under Clayton's guidance, the marquess brought a number of Newcastle mineral experts to Glamorgan, thus causing the Bute estate to be one of the chief channels of communication between the well-established coalfield of north-eastern England and its youthful rival in south Wales. The dead rents, wayleaves and royalty payments stipulated in the Bute leases, together with the covenants they contained regarding the pace and method of working, provided a model for other mineral landlords, particularly in the steam coal districts of the coalfield. Innovations such as sliding-scale royalties, pioneered by the Bute estate, were later adopted by other lessors. Among the recipients of income from mineral rents and royalties, the Bute family won an increasingly prominent position. In the year 1847–8, the second marquess's mineral income amounted to £10,756; in the following year, with the renewal of the Dowlais lease, his son's trustees received £24,619. In the third quarter of the nineteenth century, the expansion of coalmining in the Rhondda where the family owned 8,000 acres, led to a rapid increase in Bute mineral receipts; rents and royalties in 1872, for example, produced £55,207. By the early twentieth century, the Bute estate was the richest mineral estate in Britain, the fourth marquess receiving £117,477 in rents and royalties in the peak year of 1919.[40]

The industrial development of east Glamorgan was accompanied by urban growth at Cardiff and within the coalfield and this also brought an accretion of wealth to the Bute family. Ground rents at Cardiff which had produced an income of £214 for the second marquess in 1830, yielded £28,348 to his son in 1894. The family's receipts from urban development continued to increase in the early twentieth century as suburbs spread over Bute farms in the neighbourhood of Cardiff; when the Bute family company, Mountjoy Ltd, sold its urban estate to the Western Ground Rents Company in 1938, the sale involved over half the city of Cardiff with the leases of 20,000 houses, 1,000 shops and 250 public houses. In addition, Bute urban property included a large portion of the town of Aberdare and much of the townships of the upper Rhondda as well as more scattered settlements in the valleys of the Rhymney, the Taff and the Ely.[41]

Estate policy with regard to urban development was laid down by the second marquess and, as was the case with mineral development, the system he evolved became the pattern for neighbouring estates. Although both he and his son's trustees were on occasion obliged to become house-builders in order to accommodate essential workers, they did so with reluctance. The second marquess and his successors were even more reluctant to sell building land or to subject it to the quasi-perpetual leases of the 999-year variety. Indeed, he considered the 99-year lease which by the mid-nineteenth century was becoming the norm in south Wales to be deplorably long and leases generally contained clauses allowing the Bute estate to repossess the land before the expiration of the lease if it were needed by the estate and if adequate compensation were paid. The Bute building lease, patterned upon those of London and owing something also to the system prevailing in the watering-places of southern England, had evolved by the 1840s and hardly changed in its essentials for the rest of the century. Under it the landlord leased a building plot for 99 years on the understanding that the tenant would erect a building upon the site and enjoy the use of the property for the duration of the lease.[42]

Initially, nothing beyond the plot itself was provided but, as new building sites were mapped out, the Bute authorities increasingly committed themselves to expenditure upon drainage, sewerage and the making of roads and pavements, expenditure which increased substantially in the 1850s following horrific disclosures of the sanitary condition of Cardiff.[43] Initially also, the second marquess made little attempt to dictate the form the proposed buildings should take, his surveyor in 1824 doubting 'the propriety of . . . compelling . . . lessees . . . to build upon a uniform plan.'[44] By the late 1830s, however, the marquess was concerning himself with the details of elevations and, as the century advanced, Bute control over the activities of lessees at Cardiff, if not always in the valleys of the coalfield, became progressively more rigid. In the early twentieth century it was reported that on the Bute estate houses were built 'according to the plans supplied by the estate architect . . . The building regulations of the estate are . . . well-inforced, so that weak or insanitary construction is hardly to be found.'[45] Indeed, by then informed commentators considered that the estate officials were doing their work too well, for, as a consequence of the expansiveness of their plans and their demand for high quality materials and workmanship, most of the houses built under Bute leases were, it was alleged, beyond the means of working class tenants.[46]

As a result of Bute policies and of the readiness of some lesser landowners, in particular Lords Plymouth and Tredegar, to follow the Bute example, Cardiff was provided with some fine examples of Victorian architecture and town planning. This is especially the case in the middle-class quarters developed in the late nineteenth century, although the commercial district adjoining the dock, the area which the second marquess 'so highly approved of . . . being called Butetown,' also provides, in the midst of much dereliction, evidence of the dignity which the marquess had hoped would characterize his new town.[47] In the valleys of east Glamorgan, where evidence of enlightened town planning is rare, much of that which has distinction at Caerphilly, Llantrisant, Aberdare, Treorci and elsewhere, may be attributed to the Bute estate. In the centre of the old borough of Cardiff, however, the second marquess made no attempt at planning and rebuilding on more spacious and dignified lines, a task which was undertaken by his friend John Clayton at Newcastle.[48] Yet, adjoining the town centre, Bute activity and inactivity gave to Cardiff its chief glories. The castle, refurbished by Burges under the direction of the third marquess, is an extraordinary achievement, 'massive, learned and glittering'. Cathays Park, saved from speculative development by the Butes, became the site of a civic centre of great dignity, while Sophia Gardens and the Castle Park, also preserved from building by the marquesses, provide a vast tract of open land in the heart of Cardiff, an amenity any city would envy.[49]

Nevertheless, however considerable the Bute role in the urbanization and industrialization of Glamorgan, it was in the field of transport that the marquesses made their crucial contribution. By the mid-1820s it was obvious that the sea-lock pond of the Glamorganshire Canal, separated from the open sea by a tortuous two-mile channel and unable to accommodate ships of over 200 tons, was inadequate for the trade of Cardiff, which had grown tenfold since the sea-lock pond had been opened in 1798.[50] The second marquess owned all the land between the town of Cardiff and the sea and also enjoyed manorial rights over the river Taff and the foreshore. In 1828 he commissioned James Green, the canal engineer, to report on the possibility of constructing a dock at Cardiff. Green considered that a ship canal could be built at Cardiff for £66,000 and the marquess, satisfied that he could afford the investment, obtained in 1830 an act of parliament authorizing him to construct the canal at his sole expense. Green calculated that the expenditure would bring a return on existing trade, largely in iron, of 7 per cent; the marquess, however, looked forward to a substantial growth in the coal trade and also hoped that improvements at the port of Cardiff would lead to a more rapid exploitation of his mineral land.[51]

In the event, the enterprise, changed from a ship canal to a masonry dock by an act in 1833 and completed in 1839, cost £350,000.[52] Raising so large a sum proved a severe embarrassment to the marquess and in the early 1840s he was tottering on the brink of disastrous indebtedness. The leading ironmasters, William Crawshay of Cyfarthfa, the chief shareholder in the Glamorganshire Canal Company, and Sir John Guest of Dowlais, were suspicious of the marquess and loth to bring their trade to his dock. Most of Cardiff's growing coal exports could still in the 1840s be shipped from the sea-lock pond and from jetties in the Taff. The Taff Vale Railway Company, which linked Cardiff to the coalfield by rail in 1841, was dominated by Sir John Guest and was reluctant to make the Bute dock the sole outlet for its traffic.[53] The early years of the dock's existence were, therefore, a period of acute disquiet for the marquess. 'I hope that some vessels have entered during the month', he wrote to his dockmaster in November 1839. 'Send me a weekly return for the present. You will not be surprised at my anxiety.'[54] Concern over the success of his investment caused him great volatility of temper and in 1842 his personal physician urged him to 'get that immense and complicated [business] out of [your] hands' in order to 'secure [your] Health, Comfort and Fortune, all those now scarcely as safe as they ought to be.'[55]

Matters improved in the late 1840s. Ships' masters showed a marked preference for the new dock, the increase in the size of ships made the sea-lock pond increasingly redundant and the Taff Vale Railway Company proved unable to construct alternative docks. Furthermore, the marquess made use of his power as lord of the Taff, landlord of the canal wharfs and grantor of mineral leases in order to coerce the freighters of Cardiff to use his dock. Its trade, which hardly amounted to 40,000 tons in 1839–40, rose to 827,000 in 1849 and to 1.8 million tons in 1859. In the 1850s the third marquess's trustees were obliged to construct a new dock which, when its final section was opened in 1859, added 9,360 feet of quays to the 8,800 of the old dock. The West and East Bute Docks rapidly proved inadequate as trade rose to 2.5 million tons in the mid-1860s, to 3.5 million tons in the mid-1870s and to 8 million tons in the mid-1880s. The Roath Basin was opened in 1874 and the Roath Dock in 1887 but the provision of new accommodation lagged behind demand, causing severe congestion and delay. In the early 1880s a group of coalowners prepared plans to construct docks at Barry, ten miles from Cardiff and to build a railway linking them with the coalfield. Despite the vigorous opposition of the Bute authorities and of the Taff Vale Railway Company, the project received parliamentary sanction in 1884. The Barry Docks were opened in 1889 and they eventually captured half the tonnage of the ports of east Glamorgan. Yet such was the coalfield's capacity to expand that, despite the competition from Barry, the trade of the Bute Docks rose from the 8 million tons of the mid-1880s to 11.7 million tons in 1907 and to a peak of 13.7 million tons in 1913.[56]

The continuing increase in trade placed further pressure upon accommodation at Cardiff, particularly as the size of ships made the older docks, with their comparatively narrow entrance locks and shallow basins, virtually obsolete. In 1894 parliamentary authority was obtained for further expansion and the new dock, known as the Queen Alexandra, was, when it was opened in 1907, the largest masonry dock in the world.[57] Control of the docks had since 1886 been vested in the Bute Docks Company and its directors viewed their new project with scant enthusiasm. 'Its formation,' wrote the company auditor, 'has been forced upon the company by the exigencies of trade; it is a measure of defence and precaution, intended to preserve rather than extend the company's business.'[58] Poor returns on investment had been characteristic of the Bute Docks from the beginning. The second marquess hardly received a quarter of the annual net earnings of 7 per cent predicted by James Green and in 1874, during the great coal boom, the rate on the investment was 2.7 per cent while interest rates between 4 and 4.5 per cent were being paid on the money raised to finance dock investment.[59]

The heavy emphasis upon coal exports, never less than three-quarters of the total trade, meant that ships generally entered the port in ballast and thus the docks were denied the additional income which would have arisen through double freights. Valiant attempts were made to diversify the trade of the docks; some success was achieved but because of a combination of factors, among them the inability of the Bute authorities to provide the additional facilities needed for a wider range of trade, Cardiff failed to emancipate itself from its dependence upon coal. After 1889, fear of competition from the Barry Docks, which were not burdened with obsolete investments, caused the Bute authorities to be unwilling to raise their charges; those for shipping coal remained at $2\frac{1}{4}$d. a ton and were insufficient to cover the cost of the service. The dividend on the company's ordinary shares rarely exceeded 3 per cent and payments at that level were only achieved because of the willingness of the chief shareholder, the marquess of Bute, to forego many of his receipts. In the immediate pre-war years, when the trade of the docks had reached unprecedented levels, the dividend was 1 per cent in 1913 and nil in 1914. The degree of overcapitalization became apparent in 1922 when the entire Bute undertaking, by then called the Cardiff Railway Company, was merged in the Great Western Railway Company. The Cardiff Railway Company's capital in stocks, shares and loans amounted to £7,325,166; substituted for it were stocks and shares in the Great Western Railway Company worth £3,502,875.[60]

In financial terms, therefore, the Bute family's investment in dock-making proved disappointing. In other terms, too, the enterprise proved a heavy burden. Worry over the success of his investment undoubtedly contributed to the heart disease which killed the second marquess in his fifty-fourth year and his son's trustees found dock administration a severe encumbrance. To the third and fourth marquesses, the docks were an embarassment of which they sought every opportunity to rid themselves. William Crawshay of Cyfarthfa showed remarkable foresight when he informed the marquess in 1833: 'Your lordship would do better to let others take the Port-making, yourself keeping every ulterior and collateral advantage'.[61] Furthermore, there were drawbacks for Cardiff in the fact that its docks were the enterprise of a single family and that they were controlled by that family for nearly a century. Personal and political antagonism between the second marquess and the freighters of Cardiff added to the problems of the docks in their early days; expansion was held up in the 1860s because parliament would not sanction vast expenditure on the estate of a minor; a new dock was not constructed in the 1870s because the third marquess did not wish to commit too large a proportion of his assets to a single project; the fact that the capital invested in the docks was owned, wholly until 1886 and largely thereafter, by one man made it difficult for the mercantile community in South Wales to obtain a sense of identification with the enterprise. Indeed, the leading coalowner D.A. Thomas claimed in 1906: 'So far from the late Lord Bute being the creator of modern Cardiff, the docks, in the hands of a private individual, have greatly retarded the progress of the port.'[62]

Nevertheless there can be no doubt that the second marquess's initiative in the 1830s was of crucial importance to the development of Cardiff and the South Wales coal trade. In the 1830s, when intimations of the potential of the coal trade first became apparent, it was only at Cardiff that any decisive action was taken to provide that trade with a dock adequate to its needs. Cardiff's chief rivals, Newport and Swansea, took no steps during that decade. When the West Bute Dock was opened in 1839, Newport's coal trade was three times that of Cardiff but, by 1848, Cardiff, largely because of its superior dock facilities, had outstripped Newport and it never lost the lead it had won. A dock was built at Newport in 1842 and the town was talked of as an 'infant Liverpool' but its dock was only four acres compared with Cardiff's nineteen. Throughout the 1840s, coal ships at Swansea lay in the mud at low tide where they were loaded from small boats; at Cardiff, from 1839 onwards, they were loaded afloat in the security of the dock.[63]

As significant as that early initiative was the success of the Bute authorities in the years between the 1840s and the 1880s in retaining for their docks almost the entire trade of the basin of the Taff and, through judicious sponsorship of railways, in capturing for Cardiff the trade of the Rhymney valley to the east and much of the trade of the valleys of mid Glamorgan to the west. This enlargement of the hinterland of Cardiff was the consequence not only of the enterprise and the hard bargaining of the second marquess and his son's trustees, but also of the fact that the Bute family, as well as owning docks, was in addition the leading owner of mineral land within the coalfield. The Bute Docks' virtual monopoly of the trade of east Glamorgan was massively breached following the opening of the Barry Docks in 1889. By then, however, Cardiff had securely established itself as the leading regional capital in South Wales and as the acknowledged administrative centre of the coal trade, rôles which were strengthened rather than weakened by the growth of Barry. Cardiff's rise to the headship of the local urban hierarchy occurred between the 1840s and the 1880s and was the direct result of its superior transport facilities. The decline in the importance of those facilities after the First World War caused its administrative and commercial functions to become its primary rôle, a rôle enhanced by its recognition as the capital of Wales in 1955.[64]

4 Power and control: the second marquess, 1814–48

The involvement of the marquess of Bute in the industrialization and urbanization of east Glamorgan and in the provision of transport facilities for the trade of the coalfield is of central importance in assessing the rôle of the Bute estate and its owners in the social and political life of Cardiff and Glamorgan. Active participation by the marquesses in the economic development of south Wales on the one hand strengthened Bute power, and on the other contributed to social processes which were gravely to threaten the influence of landed possessions and of aristocratic families.

When the second marquess of Bute inherited his estates in November 1814, the town of Cardiff appeared content to be an appanage of the Bute estate, the rarely held meetings of its corporation being 'occupied with little more than the formal installation of the Bailiff and Aldermen, who were nominees of the Lord and devoted to his service.'[65] For a generation, scions of the Stuarts had succeeded each other as members for the Glamorgan boroughs and there was general rejoicing when in June 1815 the young marquess made 'his first appearance in this Borough as Lord thereof.'[66] Beneath the surface, however, the possibility of tension existed. The growing commercial interests of Glamorgan were increasingly hostile to the representation of the boroughs by absentee members of the Stuart family and their hostility mounted when the marquess, in the election of 1818, showed his determination to continue the tradition by bringing forward his 24-year-old brother, Lord James Stuart, as candidate in place of his uncle, Lord Evelyn.

Meanwhile at Cardiff, Bute agents and officials, who had been left largely unsupervised by the first marquess, quickly came to resent the greater surveillance imposed by his grandson. In particular, the Wood family, solicitors and bankers to the Bute estate, developed a deep enmity towards Peter Taylor Walker, a clerk of the Exchequer, whom the marquess appointed as supervisor of his affairs in 1815 and as Constable of Cardiff Castle in 1816. Walker demanded that the burgesses should 'show proper and respectful behaviour towards Lord Bute and those in whom his lordship had been pleased to place confidence' and instituted enquiries into the Woods' management of corporation finances in a manner 'calculated to excite a strong prejudice against [the family] in the town.'[67] The Woods responded by creating an anti-Bute party within the Cardiff corporation and by the summer of 1817 that party, although not a majority, had succeeded in outmanoeuvring the marquess's supporters, one of whom commented: 'Had gentlemen been for the last twenty years admitted to the corporation instead of tradesmen, the temporary difficulties we now experience would never have arisen.'[68] Walker sought to dismiss Nichol Wood from the office of town clerk and refused to swear in burgesses who were partisans of the opposition.

Litigation and riot followed and the Woods, in their publications, the *Cardiff Reporter* and the *Cardiff Recorder*, endeavoured to present themselves as champions of freedom against aristocratic control. Contact was made with disaffected elements in the other boroughs of Glamorgan and Lewis Weston Dillwyn, the respected Swansea industrialist, estimated that had he stood against Lord James in the election of 1818, he would have won a majority of votes in all the boroughs except Cowbridge. Glamorgan's Whigs, however, were reluctant to coalesce with the rabble-rousing Woods and in the event the anti-Bute candidate was Nichol Wood's brother, Frederick, a man of little standing. The patrons of the western boroughs refused him their support and, after one day's voting, Frederick Wood retired having gained 17 dubious votes to Lord James's 45.[69]

Although the opposition proved feeble, the election cost the marquess £5,132, David Stewart commenting: 'Real political influence must follow real wealth.

Large sums spent on elections are spent in the worst possible way.'[70] In 1820, Lord James was elected for the county of Bute, a constituency represented at alternate parliaments, and the marquess, in conjunction with the patrons of the western boroughs, successfully sponsored Wyndham Lewis, Disraeli's wife's first husband and a partner in the Dowlais Iron Company, as candidate for the Glamorgan boroughs. In 1823, however, the marquess, by then involved in protracted litigation with the Dowlais Company, determined to jettison Lewis and bring his brother forward again at the next election. Lewis resisted the substitution and preparations to ensure his defeat in the election of 1826 absorbed much of the energies of the marquess and his advisers in the mid 1820s.[71]

During the fight against Lewis, the marquess perfected the web of influence and patronage in Cardiff and Glamorgan which caused the Bute estate to be so formidable a factor in the society and politics of the town and the county in the ensuing decades. The despotism he created was a benevolent one for central to his beliefs was the assumption that leadership involved obligations to those led, assumptions apparent in his enthusiastic support for charitable institutions, in his endeavours to protect the interests of the working classes and in his determination to succour and support the church.

Between 1821 and 1848, his philanthropy in Glamorgan cost the marquess some £25,000, representing 7 to 8 per cent of the gross rental of his estate. The bulk of his donations were subscriptions to charitable societies, ranging from the Cardiff Dorcas Society to the Glamorgan Prisoners' Charity Fund. His patronage was essential to the well-being of such societies for 'other donations will be governed by your lordship's.'[72] At Cardiff and Llantrisant he organized his own system of aid, regularly distributing coal, blankets and shoes to the poor and giving special consideration to 'the class most to be pitied . . . infirm people just above applying for poor relief.'[73] In addition he was responsive to the plight of individuals and instructions such as 'pay Mr Thackeray's funeral expenses' or 'pay John Thomas £3 towards the apprentice fee for his son' were frequent in his correspondence.

Apart from assisting the poor through donations and subscriptions, the marquess considered himself their shield against the power of the new industrialists, particularly that of the great ironmasters, upon whose rapacity, pretensions and hostility towards himself he frequently dwelt. As Lord-Lieutenant of Glamorgan he resisted the notion that they were the natural guardians of law and order in the communities under their control and, rather than recommend them as magistrates, succeeded after much effort and some financial loss, in obtaining a stipendiary magistrate for Merthyr Tydfil.[47] The epitome of the capitalists' abuse of power he saw as the practice of truck which he described as 'that artificial, atrocious and cruel system.' He conducted an enquiry into its prevalence, denounced it as a major cause of unrest in Glamorgan and exerted pressure upon his lessees, the Bute-Rhymney Iron Company, to abandon it. Equally obnoxious to him was the laxity with which employers enforced safety regulations in mines, while the knowledge that some ironmasters kept private lock-ups strengthened his determination to secure a county police force for Glamorgan.[75]

He himself was anxious to be considered a model employer. When advocating the building of a hospital at Cardiff, he pointed out that his proposed construction of a dock would inevitably lead to accidents among his workmen and 'this consideration pressed strongly upon me in urging the establishment of the infirmary effectual for the relief of people hurt at our work. Insist that all cases of hurt be made known to you and you will supply them with my orders of admission to the infirmary.'[76] He joined the duke of Wellington in approving of the Poor Law Amendment Act, arguing that 'it was calculated to benefit the honest and industrious classes and brought the gentry into an acquaintance with the wants of their fellow countrymen.' He objected to large Poor Law unions, urging that 'what ought to be considered is the distance that a poor person would have to walk in order to make his appeal to the Board of Guardians'; the size of the proposed Cardiff union, he asserted, 'involves a denial of the right of appeal.'[77] More surprisingly perhaps, he was a firm opponent of the Game Laws, informing the House of Lords in 1827 that 'the existing laws against poaching were most unjust and oppressive.'[78]

There was nothing romantic about the marquess's view of the poor and his attitude to the working class was untouched by egalitarianism. Central to his Tory paternalism was his belief that the Established Church, whether English or Scottish, was the chief bulwark of the social order and his political opinions were largely determined by his conviction that it should be maintained at all costs. The patron of eight livings of Glamorgan, he chose the incumbents with great care, paying particular attention to their knowledge of the Welsh language for, as he noted, 'The Welsh language is . . . called for in almost every piece of patronage I possess.'[79] In the late 1830s, when the commissioners for the commutation of the tithe were at work, the marquess, fearing that the change would lead to a fall in the income of the church, conducted a voluminous correspondence with them and threatened to challenge their valuations in court. His agent's argument that such action 'may lead the dissenters and other discontented parties . . . to further objection to church rate' made him refrain from legal proceedings but the pressure he exerted did cause the tithe of most of the parishes with which he was connected to rise as a result of commutation.[80] Schools the marquess considered a crucial weapon in the fight against Nonconformity and in the 1840s donations to church schools accounted for a fifth of his philanthropic disbursements. Equally crucial was the provision of adequate accommodation in the growing urban areas of Glamorgan and in all the parishes of which he was patron or in which he was a major landowner, the marquess took the lead in encouraging church building and restoration, placing his emphasis on maintaining the hold of the church upon the working classes. It was to him rather than to the ironmasters that the Anglicans of the industrial areas looked for succour and churchmen considered his death a calamity to the Establishment.[81]

Wielding such a benevolent despotism presented problems for a largely non-resident landowner. The marquess rarely spent more than a month a year in Glamorgan, generally a fortnight at the time of the Spring Assizes and a fortnight in the autumn for the annual meetings of the charitable societies. He was therefore obliged to brief himself on events there by correspondence with the county's leading figures and by a minute scrutiny of the local press. He sought to extract the maximum effect from his brief visits, holding dinner parties at the castle, reviewing the militia and making a great show of his weekly progress to St John's church, where he owned the whole of the south east end of the aisle. To Cardiffians he was 'quite come-atable and would listen to the longest tale of woe with exemplary patience', one of them describing him as 'a kindly and far-seeing nobleman, father of the town and beloved by the townspeople.'[82]

In the task of maintaining and enhancing Bute influence and prestige, the marquess was ably assisted by Edward Priest Richards, a member of a Cardiff gentry family and agent of the estate from 1824 to 1867. Richards gave to the administration of the estate a new coherence and was the chief executant of the enterprises initiated by the second marquess, the *Merthyr Guardian* commenting on his death: 'If any proof of his admirable stewardship of [the Bute estate] during a period of more than forty years were wanting, a comparison between their present flourishing condition and their state when they were first entrusted to his care would give ample and substantial testimony to the energy and wisdom of his administration.'[83] Over the years he came to appear as a proxy for the marquess himself and as the embodiment of the Bute system. 'Coming to Cardiff as an absolute stranger [in 1859]', wrote the Radical, George Robinson, 'the personage who, more than any other, impressed himself upon my mental retina was Mr Edward Priest Richards – no undignified shortening of his name could be dreamt of. Tall, reserved, silent and singularly difficult of access, he was the central pivot around whom revolved the whole Bute planetary system.'[84]

By the mid-1820s the marquess and Richards, in seeking to reimpose Bute control over the corporation and the parliamentary representation of Cardiff, developed a growing awareness of the diverse forms of political influence and a determination to wield that influence with energy and circumspection. Its primary source was, of course, the estate itself. Landowners had the power to manufacture county voters by letting property on life leases, thereby creating what were in law, if not in reality, 40s. freeholders. On many estates life leases had largely been discontinued in the late eighteenth century but they survived into the nineteenth on the Bute estate, much to the disquiet of David Stewart who considered them a deplorable example of the subordination of agriculture to politics.[85] Urban property within the boroughs could also produce county voters and Richards enfranchised the tenants of Bute building ground 'by the insertion [in the lease] of a life or lives before the form of ninety-nine years.'[86] The marquess could not hope to control the representation of the county of Glamorgan, where his influence was outstripped by that of the Margam estate, but the county votes at his command were a necessary bargaining counter in his negotiations with Margam over the deployment of its interest in the western boroughs.

In the boroughs, Bute rights of lordship over Cardiff, Llantrisant and Cowbridge were fully exploited. Despite Wyndham Lewis's threat to contest in the courts 'many of our customs at Cardiff, particularly the right of the bailiffs to make honorary burgesses', the marquess, in preparation for the election of 1826, created 200 new burgesses at Cardiff and fifty at Llantrisant, paying the fees of those 'to whom £4 or £5 may be an object.'[87] Keeping the loyalty of burgesses could present problems, particularly at Llantrisant where the population was in a 'dreadful state of ignorance, depravity and barbarism' and in 1824 the marquess's adviser O.T. Bruce lamented that 'elections dress many a burgess in a little brief authority which is frequently sold at a price far beyond its worth.'[88] In seeking to retain their loyalty, the marquess turned the influence and prestige he won as a conscientious public figure to political ends. As Colonel-in-Chief of the Glamorganshire Militia, he assumed that all militiamen would vote as he wished and, when some of them defied him in 1832, their action was described as mutiny.[89] As Lord-Lieutenant of Glamorgan his was the deciding voice in the appointment of deputy lieutenants and justices of the peace while in the election of the chairman of the quarter sessions, the selection of High Sheriffs and the appointment of stipendiary magistrates, his wishes usually prevailed. Although obliged to recommend to the bench who were opposed to him politically, those who aspired to public offices but whose claims upon them were not incontrovertible found it to their advantage to support his interest. Traditions of deference continued and, even industrialized boroughs, there was diffidence over challenging the prestige attached to the office of Lord-Lieutenant. When L.W. Dillwyn considered standing for the Glamorgan boroughs in 1818, he recorded in his diary: 'Mr Bruce addressed the Neath corporation . . . and expressed his astonishment that a man who had been in business should presume to oppose the Brother of the Lord-Lieutenant.'[90]

The second marquess's philanthropic activities could also be explicitly aimed at strengthening his electoral influence. Electioneering could lead to competitive charity. 'Mrs Wyndham Lewis', wrote the marquess to Richards in 1825, 'has been ordering a great many blankets for distribution to the poor and particularly to poor freemen's wives . . . I therefore beg you will give blankets and coals in the inclement season whenever such relief appears to be most called for.'[91] The marquess enthusiastically supported the Cardiff Reading Room, established as 'a rallying point for the many respectable men devoted to the interests of Lord Bute and his brother' and barred to adherents of the opposition.[92] Despite his staunch support for the Establishment, the marquess did contribute in his own and his brother's name to the building of Nonconformist chapels and recognized in 1832 that 'Baptist ministers . . . [had] made themselves very useful in the suppression of Union Clubs.'[93] Assistance to individuals, although not lacking in altruism, could have political implications. In 1825, for example, Lady Bute was urged to make a crippled girl her protegée so that 'all her family would be secured'. Donations to individuals ceased if the recipients proved politically disloyal and Richards was active in seeking proof of such treachery.[10] The marquess's concern for those 'who struggle honestly against applying for poor relief' was not wholly disinterested, for recipients of relief were denied the vote and part at least of his philanthropy was aimed at keeping his dependents on the voting list.

To the marquess the permanent nature of his philanthropy was a telling argument against the largesse of a carpet-bag opponent. 'It is most desirable', he wrote in 1825, 'that my acts show . . . a character of permanence corresponding to my property . . . to let the permanent character of my measures . . . be held out in contrast to the temporary measures of my opponents.' The establishment of schools with estate endowments emphasized that permanence, voters being 'more thankful for what is done for their children than for themselves.' 'Much political good', wrote Richards, 'will arise from a uniform clothing of twelve or twenty-four children. They would be considered the objects of your lordship's bounty and the parents of other children in the school would be looking forward to vacancies.'[95] To the marquess, elementary education instituted and controlled by landowners and the church was a crucial contribution to social stability, Richards echoing his views when warning that 'unless education . . . is attended to by the exertion of clergymen and Conservatives . . . the time will come when Wales will be the seat of dissent and radicalism.'[96] His support for the Welsh language, shown in his patronage of eisteddfodau, in his anxiety to provide adequate accommodation for Welsh-speaking Anglican worshippers and in his advocacy of the use of Welsh as a medium of instruction in schools, reflected his hope that the language would provide a barrier to the importation of subversive ideas into Glamorgan; his wrath knew no bounds when, on discovering that the Welsh sections of the Merthyr radical paper, *Y Gweithiwr (The Workman)* were more extreme than the English, he realized that his hopes were foiled.[97]

Estate policy could also be dictated by political considerations. The marquess was anxious that it should be known that his rents were lower than those of neighbouring landowners, while his refusal to preserve game and his opposition to squatters were motivated, at least in part, by his desire to win the support of the county voters. His allotment policy, for which he was widely praised, had political overtones; in 1825 a farm at Llantrisant was divided into plots to offer to the burgesses there, after they had united in protest against 'Lord Bute's agents letting Pontypark to an occupier that hath no vote.'[98] Improvements to buildings were sometimes undertaken for political ends. 'Richard Morgan wants his house repaired', Richards was informed in 1825. 'There are a great number of votes in the family and if you accommodate him, he will be active amongst them.'[99] The political convictions of applicants for tenancies were not always taken into consideration; in 1836 the marquess let Llandaf Mill Farm to a capable farmer although 'he is a radical who might do mischief if the great body of my tenants were not too sound to be corrupted.'[100] Applicants who were open opponents of the Bute interest, however, found little favour; in 1837, John Winstone was rejected as lessee for the Blue Anchor Inn because 'he has no claim upon your lordship – he is the most dangerous and offensive character we have in the town.' Particular care was taken over the letting of the castle lodges where loyalty to Bute interests was the overriding consideration, Richards in 1837 recommending the claims of Thomas David who 'is . . . of the Old School [and] has always been a warm and honest supporter of your lordship's family.'[101]

The employment provided by an estate was an important political weapon. In 1824, when constructing a colliery pond at Llantrisant, the marquess, despite Richards's warning that 'employing burgesses will increase the expense tenfold [for] they . . . will only work at extravagant prices', ordered him 'to take care to have workmen selected who will vote for my brother.'[102] The dock-building project was partly inspired by political motives, the marquess hoping that 'the increased good feeling towards me' that it would engender would promote 'Conservative feeling'. 'The commencement of the work', wrote Richards on the eve of the election of 1832, '. . . would act as a charm upon our poorer burgesses who may thus derive employment throughout the winter.'[103] Anxious to employ Cardiff people at his dock, the marquess gave priority to those whose families had been loyal to his. 'The post of assistant tide-waiter is vacant', he wrote in 1845. 'Who has claims on me for that sort of job?' In answering Richards commented upon one of the applicants: 'Mr Riches has [no claims]. He and his family have done all in their power to promote discontent in the town.'[104] Rapid urban and industrial growth are generally considered to have hastened the decline of aristocratic influence. At Cardiff, however, the creation of docks wholly under Bute control strengthened rather than weakened castle influence, at least in the short term.

By the late 1820s, the success of the marquess's tactics was evident. Bute control over the corporation of Cardiff was restored in its entirety. The marquess's brother became constable of the castle, his friend O.T. Bruce corporation steward and his agent Richards an alderman of the borough and corporation solicitor. Richards, who was also town clerk of Llantrisant and treasurer of the county lieutenancy as well as frequently acting as deputy high sheriff, led the castle party with 'consummate skill'. He compiled lists of possible aldermen and capital burgesses from which the marquess chose those to be elected, corporation officials considered hostile to castle interests resigned and the annual election of bailiffs was carried out in accordance with Bute wishes.[105]

The restoration of the marquess's control over the borough of Cardiff and his readiness to bludgeon the patrons of the other boroughs led the way to the restoration of Bute ascendancy over the borough constituency. Wyndham Lewis retired from the contest ten days before the election of 1826 and on that occasion and again in 1830 and 1831 Lord James Stuart was elected unopposed. By 1831, however, economic distress, the reverberations of the great upheaval of the Merthyr Rising and the agitation over parliamentary reform were presenting new threats to Bute ascendancy. The second marquess, like his mentor, the duke of Wellington, was an ardent, although not a die-hard opponent of parliamentary reform. At Cardiff, the commercial and professional middle class, among them the officials of the Canal Company and the agents of the great iron companies – contemptuously labelled 'wharf gentry' by the arch-conservative Richards – together with the Nonconformists and what Richards described as 'the mob' were all enthusiastic reformers.[106] To the marquess's consternation, his brother and client member of parliament made common cause with the advocates of reform, stating in the Commons in 1832 that Cardiff supported the Bill and voting in favour of all its stages. Richards remonstrated with Lord James, arguing that 'Lord Bute's interest and your own must be the same . . . the family interest has secured your seat hitherto without reference to politicks'.[107] Lord James proved obdurate and the marquess, having failed to extract a promise from his brother that he would never again oppose him publicly, replaced him as Bute-sponsored candidate in the election of 1832 with John Nicholl, an able Tory lawyer and a member of a long-established gentry family of the vale of Glamorgan. His action was given wide publicity through an article in *The Times* which declared: 'The Marquess of Bute prefers the substitution of a Tory member for his own brother . . . The Tories themselves speak of it with deep regret and condemnation.' Although Lord James had already been brought forward as Whig candidate for Perth, his supporters insisted upon nominating him also for Cardiff, Richards lamenting that 'those always opposed to [the Bute] Interest are now the loudest in upholding Lord James against your lordship'.[108]

The election of 1832 was of course fought under the new dispositions laid down by the Reform Act. The Act divided the Glamorgan boroughs constituency into two, one based on Cardiff and the other on Swansea; it also created a new borough constituency at Merthyr and raised the number of Glamorgan's county members from one to two. Although the marquess of Bute had opposed the legislation, it did in fact strengthen his interest, for it freed him from the obligation of seeking votes in the western boroughs and of the need to pledge the county votes at his command to the Whig family of Margam. The Act enfranchised men occupying property of an annual value of £10 and above while it preserved the existing rights of resident freemen. Virtually no new freemen were created after 1832 but in that year freemen outnumbered £10 householders at Cardiff by 209 to 169 and at Llantrisant by 202 to nine while at Cowbridge where, because the burgesses 'so pique themselves on their . . . independence . . . that it is a rather delicate matter to have any communication with them', politically motivated expansion of the numbers of freemen had hardly occurred, the ratio was 50 to 55.[109]

Freemen voters had an ingrained loyalty to the lord of the borough; the same deference could not be expected from the new voters, some of whom had been denied the burgess-ship before 1832 because of doubts about their allegiance to the castle party. Yet, with the cloak of politically motivated philanthropy and patronage thrown over them, with the marquess, through his dock-building activities, becoming Cardiff's major employer of labour, along with the fact that he was ground landlord of most of the town's £10 householders, there were compelling motives for the newly enfranchised voters not to break with the tradition of the past. Furthermore, the onus of establishing one's right to the franchise lay upon the voter and, in ensuring the continuation of Bute political influence, Richards's dedication in compiling electoral lists, a task described by the marquess as 'the groundwork of political management', was of central importance, Richards claiming, 'I do not believe ten of your lordship's tenants would have registered unless I had taken good care to do it for them.'[110]

To secure the allegiance of the new voters and to retain that of the old, the marquess, three weeks before the election of 1832, launched east Glamorgan's first weekly newspaper. During the Reform crisis he had felt handicapped by the county's lack of a Conservative newspaper and the numerous press attacks he then suffered made him determined to start his own. 'A good county newspaper', wrote Richards, 'would be the means of promoting your lordship's influence and interest throughout the county . . . the proprietors should be of the old Tory, Church and King, Conservative or any more fleeting name-of-the-day Party . . . and the paper would . . . clearly pay its way in a very few years.'[111] The marquess's correspondents were told to burn all the letters which referred to his connection with the venture, but enough disobeyed to provide ample evidence that the *Glamorgan, Monmouth and Brecon Gazette and Merthyr Guardian*, launched on 17 November 1832, was a Bute creation and that the marquess was the 'generous and munficient patron of our only Conservative medium of public utterance'. Richards's optimism about the paper's financial viability was not realized and the *Guardian* remained a burden upon the estate for many years. Yet the marquess was proud of his venture. Although he often found its Toryism too virulent, leading articles on such matters as the church and the ballot, copied from more responsible newspapers, had 'an effect in the Pot-Houses'.[112] The *Guardian* spoke respectfully of the marquess, gave prominence to his personal and charitable activities, championed him in all his disputes and, when he died, devoted black-edged editions to his memory.

The Cardiff election of 1832 proved that despite the strength of reformist sentiment, the marquess's influence was more than a match for his brother's popularity. After a two-day poll, the Bute nominee, John Nicholl, defeated Lord James Stuart by 342 votes to 191, causing Cardiff to be in that election one of the rare constituencies where a sitting reformer was defeated by an anti-reformer. Although the marquess was successful in marshalling his followers against his brother, there were those among them who wondered whether it might not be to their advantage to warm to Lord James as heir presumptive and father of a large family, rather than to the childless marquess. Aware of such feelings, the marquess, during the election of 1835, warned Richards: 'If you hear the mischievous argument . . . that "I have no children and therefore people will do better to please my brother as the rising sun", you may make known as broadly as possible that every inch of my estates . . . is in my own absolute power. To cut off my brother is certainly one of the last acts I should like to carry through but I should have very little hesitation in [doing so] in order to prop the Conservative cause.'[113] In the event, Nicholl was elected unopposed in 1835 as he was at each election until the death of the marquess in 1848. He had a moderately distinguished political career, holding office as a Lord of the Treasury in 1835 and as Judge Advocate General from 1841 to 1846. The marquess warmly approved of his political conduct and pledged support to him at successive elections.

There were fears in 1842 that Nicholl's state of health would oblige him to resign from parliament and, in considering a replacement, Richards urged the claims of the marquess's friend O.T. Bruce or 'anyone connected with the government who might be supposed to have places at his command or disposal for the benefit of the £10 householders.'[114] In 1846 such fears were again current and *The Times* reported that Gladstone, whose support for free trade had lost him his seat at Newark, would be brought forward by the marquess as Nicholl's successor.[115] Although nothing came of the suggestion, the views and values of Gladstone in the earlier phase of his political career would have fitted him to be a client member of parliament of the second marquess of Bute. Like Gladstone, the marquess followed Peel and Wellington over the Corn Laws, informing the House of Lords: 'When he began public life, he approved of protection but having been . . . engaged in matters . . . connected with the commerce of the country, his views had undergone considerable change. He now thought that protection, as far as commerce was concerned, so far from being a benefit, was a positive injury.'[116] His attitude on the Corn Laws caused him, as a Peelite, to move closer to the Whigs while the fears aroused by the Chartist agitation caused middle-class leaders to look with greater favour upon the aristocratic landowner as the traditional guardian of stability and property. Nicholl was prevailed upon to stand again in 1847 and, when the marquess died in the following year, Bute influence over the parliamentary representation of Cardiff seemed, outwardly at least, to be as secure an inheritance for his son as the estate itself.

The Reform Act of 1832 was soon followed by the Municipal Corporations Act of 1835. The commissioners appointed to enquire into the state of the municipalities visited Glamorgan in 1833 and Richards was questioned for seven hours at Cardiff and for two at Llantrisant. Their report portrayed Llantrisant as corrupt and the Act did not grant it full borough status. The corporation of Cardiff was described as having no identity of interest with the inhabitants and to be among those where everything was subordinated to electoral and political ends. The marquess resented these attacks and talked in the Lords of corporations which felt aggrieved by the allegations of the commissioners and which were anxious to refute them. He followed the passage of the act with close attention, cooperating with Wellington and others in preserving life interests and the office of alderman.[117]

The act of 1835 gave Cardiff a corporation consisting of six aldermen and 18 councillors, elected by all occupiers of property rated to the relief of the poor. Before 1835, castle control of the corporation was assured as long as the burgesses admitted were loyal supporters of the marquess; as a result of the act, his power as lord of Cardiff Castle disappeared. This constituted a significant break with the past and J. H. Matthews, in the 1890s, sought to invest the change with the character of a revolution, writing of the abolition of 'the last remnants of feudalism' and of Cardiff becoming 'suddenly . . . a muncipality in the modern sense.'[118] The reality was somewhat different. For months before the first municipal elections in December 1835 the marquess had been preparing his plans. He wrote to Richards in August:

You must endeavour to keep good watch so that we are not surprised by the Radicals getting promises . . . It is advisable that we should put into our lists some of the most substantial among those persons whom we might generally be disposed to call *the other side* . . . You may depend upon it these substantial men are not sorry in the bottom of their hearts to find themselves separated from their pauper tail . . . I adopted this course in the election of the Guardians of Luton . . . I put the wealthiest Baptist in the Town, the most moderate of the Quakers and a friendly Methodist on my list. The Radicals had a meeting for the express purpose of getting up a contest but the list was so respectable that they were obliged to give up their intended agitation.

The same policy of making 'a virtue of necessity' was pursued at Cardiff and the list prepared by the marquess and Richards was, with few exceptions, the list of those elected.[119]

The first act of the new corporation was to appoint E. P. Richards as town clerk, hardly the act of a body of men yearning to throw off Bute domination. There were members of the corporation who wished to widen the range of its activities and in the mid-1830s plans were drawn up for an improvement act and for an investigation into borough lands and funds. The marquess commented sardonically: 'I am not surprised by the activity of your new town council but if they begin to make rates in proportion, they will soon become unpopular.'[120] Within a few years the vigour of the corporation had been dissipated; many meetings in the late 1830s lacked a quorum and in 1842 Richards claimed that 'our Corporation is nearly in a state of insolvency.'[121] There were elements in the town which resented the castle's power. In 1837, Sir John Guest, when canvassing the country seat as a Liberal, received a warm welcome from a section of the citizens, his wife expressing in her diary her surprise 'at such a demonstration of feeling in Lord Bute's own borough where he dominates everything.' The marquess saw such demonstrations as the consequence of a Guest plot and was loud in his denunciations of the Quaker journalist Elijah Waring 'the notorious Demon of Radicialism [who] for the last two or three years has been the secret minister employed by Sir John Guest at Cardiff.'[122]

By the late 1830s, of the 24 members of the corporation, about five were considered to be consistently hostile to the castle interest; most of them were newcomers to the town and the marquess hoped that their 'conduct would have a good effect by causing the Cardiffians of all colours, by which I mean whether they consider themselves Tories or Liberals, to join together against the insolence of strangers.'[123] Although Richards made much of the opposition, Bute control of the corporation showed little sign of weakening. 'Our six town councillors', the marquess was informed in 1836, 'have been elected as your lordship determined' and in 1839 Richards wrote: 'Mr Davies the surgeon offered himself as a councillor and I have stated that your lordship would have no possible objection to his election and I therefore expect he will be elected without opposition.'[124] While self-interest and a continuing tradition of deference kept the corporation loyal to the castle, also involved was at least a hint of coercion. When, in 1840, elements among the councillors proved recalcitrant, Richards urged the marquess to make explicit his power as landlord. 'It is not a matter of Whig, Tory, Conservative or Radical politicks', he wrote, 'but whether your lordship should have the legitimate interest [your]property ought to command . . . It is wholly impossible for any agent of your lordship's here to keep up your interest if on every occasion he is not upheld by your lordship's tenants . . . There is still time, by notices to quit, to remind the parties your lordship expects your property to have the weight it ought to possess.'[125] Yet, despite occasional unrest, the second marquess of Bute's influence over the corporation of Cardiff survived largely intact until his death and the resolution adopted by the corporation on 3 May 1848 gives the impression of a genuine awareness of loss. 'This council', it stated, 'deeply regrets the death of the Most Honourable, the Marquess of Bute – an event that has deprived this town of its most powerful and munificent friend, whose purse was always open to every call for its improvement and for the promotion of every charity.'[126]

5 New challenges and changed circumstances, 1848–68

In March 1848 the second marquess of Bute had come to Cardiff for his usual spring visit. He had 'brought his long-wished-for little heir to Cardiff for the first time' and was 'at the height of his glory . . . visiting day by day his docks and the institutions of the second Liverpool'.[127] On 17 March, after entertaining the leading citizens to dinner at the castle, he collapsed and died, leaving his titles, his property and his debts in their entirety to John Crichton Stuart, third marquess of Bute, an infant of six months. The second marquess's untimely death and the lack of an adult heir were devastating blows to the Bute system of estate management and to the maintenance of the prestige and influence of the house of Stuart in Glamorgan. 'My feeling', wrote the widowed marchioness, 'is that the entire fabric of our affairs has been shivered to its foundations by Lord Bute's death! and that the hope of knitting all together again depends mainly on the fewest possible changes of what *He* established being made.'[128]

The maintenance in its entirety of 'what *He* established' was a vain hope and even the creation of alternative working arrangements proved difficult, for the second marquess, despite his punctiliousness, had failed to make adequate arrangements for a minority. In his will he had vested the Glamorgan estate in his friend O.T. Bruce and his wife's relation James McNabb, to hold in trust for his heir but the will contained a number of anomalies and the granting of adequate powers to the trustees involved months of bitter wrangling and the passage of two acts of parliament.[129] The trustees were overwhelmed at the immensity of the task with which they were confronted. 'You and I', wrote McNabb to Bruce in May 1848, 'have already seen enough of our new office to satisfy to us that it is to be no sinecure, nor its duties a pleasure . . . The anxiety of mind which the duties of the Trust involve shake my hopes of being enabled to persevere in their performance.'[130] Ill-health forced McNabb to resign in 1852 when he was replaced by John Boyle of Calder Hall near Glasgow; Bruce died in 1853 and Boyle became the final authority on estate matters, a responsibility which he undertook until his retirement in 1880, adding to his duties as executive trustee the offices of dock manager and chairman of the Bute-sponsored Rhymney Railway Company.

Under Boyle's direction, the administrative system built up by the second marquess continued to function, although in a rather more hesitant way. Richards, who in 1853 had taken his great-nephew W.C. Luard as partner, died in 1867, when the legal aspects of Bute business became the responsibility of the firm of Luard and Shirley; the agricultural land of the estate continued to be administered by John Stuart Corbett, a Bute kinsman whom the second marquess had appointed in

1841; the mineral department was run by W.S. Clark until his death in 1864 when he was succeeded by William Thomas Lewis who was to be in the late nineteenth and early twentieth centuries the chief arbiter of the fortunes of the estate and a key figure in the South Wales coal industry.[131]

Financially Boyle and his associates had reason to be proud of their stewardship of the Bute estate. The second marquess left a confused mass of debts amounting to £493,886, almost £300,000 of which was a charge upon the Glamorgan estate. Despite heavy expenditure on the docks, the trustees made debt reduction and rationalization their prime concern and when the third marquess came of age in 1868, annual interest payments had been reduced from £16,625 to £9,343 while investments of £150,000 in Consols together with shares worth over £100,000 in railway and other companies in Glamorgan were producing a return of almost £7,000 a year. The net income from dock operations rose during the minority from £12,285 to £38,346 and net earnings from mineral rents and royalties increased from £10,756 to £44,700; in addition, while net receipts from agriculture hardly amounted to a few thousand pounds, annual income from collieries, ground rents and other sources were, by 1868, in the region of £20,000. The 'income in the distance' which the financially embarrassed second marquess had hoped for in the early 1840s had materialized and, from the Glamorgan estate alone, the third marquess could look forward to an annual overall income in excess of £100,000.[132]

The trustees had less reason to be proud of their stewardship of the political influence of the Bute estate. During the minority, the parliamentary representation of Cardiff was captured by interests hostile to the castle, Bute domination of the town's corporation was eroded beyond recall and even the burgesses of Llantrisant threw off their old allegiance.[133] At first glance it might appear that Bute political influence declined because the estate during the minority lacked a dynamic adult owner. Yet, even had the second marquess lived, it is doubtful that the Cardiff of the 1850s and 1860s would have bowed to his wishes as had the Cardiff of the 1830s and 1840s. It was not solely the loss of his guiding hand that caused the web of influence he had woven with such care to be unravelled in the years following his death. His own activities helped to undermine the political power of Cardiff Castle. Aristocratic control of small boroughs survived at least until the late nineteenth century but, largely because of the second marquess's initiative in providing Cardiff with dock facilities superior to those of its neighbours, the town was, by mid-century, ceasing to be a small borough. Between 1811 and 1851, the population of Cardiff rose from 2,457 to 20,258; by 1861, it had increased to 41,422 and by 1871 to 56,911; by the end of the nineteenth century it exceeded 160,000 and, on the eve of the First World War, Cardiff, by then a city, had a population ten times that of the mid-nineteenth century. As the town developed, its income increased, its rateable value rising a hundredfold between the 1830s and the 1880s and, as the sphere of the corporation's activities widened, it was inevitable that disputes would arise between it and the Bute estate.[134] When Cardiff expanded beyond its ancient boundaries and building took place on the land of other landowners, the shadow of the castle began to pale. As the town attracted inhabitants, not only from the immediate vicinity, but also from more distant parts of Wales, from England, from Ireland, from the empire and from continental Europe – a process which made Cardiff one of the most cosmopolitan of British towns – traditional loyalties faded. The castle came to appear to many as it did to

George Santayana who viewed it in 1974, as an incongruous anachronism, as 'the living survival of mediaeval features, material and moral in the midst of [modernity]'.[135]

Nevertheless, the replacement of an energetic and popular aristocrat by rather anonymous and alien trustees undoubtedly hastened the decline of Bute political influence. Although the second marquess was sincerely mourned at Cardiff, his death marks the beginning of the end of town's tutelage. The trustees had neither the prestige necessary to become leaders of Glamorgan society nor were they in a position to nurture the loyalty of a growing industrial community. Fearful that they would be open to prosecution if they exceeded their powers, they terminated all philanthropic subscriptions and annuities not secured by deed, an action which brought them many despondent letters from members of the clergy and from previous recipients of Bute charity.[136] It was a matter upon which they felt vulnerable. 'The most successful issue of our Exertions', wrote McNabb, 'will be to accumulate wealth for parties whose wealth will at any rate be enormous while we are denied the compensatory comfort . . . of promoting the spiritual and intellectual improvement of the people residing on the Estates under our charge.'[137]

In 1849 Lady Bute, abetted by the trustees, prised the castle from the grasp of her hated brother-in-law, Lord James Stuart, and, until her death in 1859, spent lengthy periods at Cardiff where she sought to assume the rôle her husband had played in the life of Glamorgan. Assiduous in fulfilling her duties as aristocratic patroness of Cardiff, she was unable from her own resources to perpetuate her husband's structure of philanthropy. In the 1860s, the trustees, in view of the accumulation of wealth and of their conviction that 'the heir would not tax them' for acts of generosity, felt able to make some contribution to its perpetuation. They gave substantial donations to church building and were generous in their assistance to church schools while at the docks they assumed full financial responsibility for the erection and maintenance of a sailors' home. Nevertheless, during the minority, benefactions to individuals ceased, subscriptions to local societies were drastically reduced and the trustees declined all invitations to preside at local festivities. By the 1860s the personally administered philanthropy of the second marquess had ebbed away and symptomatic of the contrast between his relationship with the local community and that of the trustees is a note written by General Stuart, Boyle's co-trustee, to Richards in 1863: 'Here is another beg. Pray advise me on it.'[138]

The difficulties facing an estate robbed of its master in retaining its hold over a community growing in size and complexity became apparent in the years immediately following the death of the second marquess. Bute control of the corporation of Cardiff survived the constitutional changes brought about by the reform of the municipalities. What it did not survive was the greater self-assertion of the corporation which was the consequence of the widening of its activities and responsibilities. It was the issue of sanitary reform in particular which led to a breach between the estate and the town authorities for, at Cardiff as elsewhere, 'economic individualism in the hour of its triumph over the Corn Laws, found itself challenged by a sanitary doctrine that involved innumerable interferences with private property, often in fields in which it was strongly and profitably entrenched'.[139]

The split began in the summer following the second marquess's death when over 300 people died of cholera at Cardiff, the disease battening upon the squalor caused by the absence of an adequate sanitary system. Richards, as town clerk, was hostile to demands for reform and proved obstructive when an enquiry into Cardiff's sanitary condition was instituted. The petition for the enquiry and the agitation in favour of the establishment of a local Board of Health at Cardiff were organized by the town's Radicals and Bute opposition, manifested by Richard's recalcitrance, gave them the opportunity to portray the estate as the enemy of the well-being of the citizens. The Board was established in 1850 and immediately pressure was placed upon the trustees. They were ordered, often in peremptory tones, to cover drains, mend sewers, fence the dock feeder, cease depositing dock dredgings within the borough and expedite the drainage of new streets. Furthermore, although the corporation was anxious above all to be economical, its increasing commitments obliged it to raise its rates and, as the Bute estate and docks were the largest concerns in the town, this proved a fruitful source of dispute.[140]

The strength of anti-Bute feeling in the corporation became apparent when, in 1853, the mayoral election was won by John Batchelor, whose lifelong hostility to the castle interest caused his friends after his death to erect a statute to him as 'Friend of Freedom'. Those agitating against Bute influence obtained a powerful ally in 1857 with the establishment of the *Cardiff Times*, its proprietors declaring that the aim of the paper was 'to deliver the borough from the degrading position of being a mere appanage of the Bute estate'. In that year, Richards came to the conclusion that his duties as Bute agent could no longer be combined with the office of town clerk of Cardiff. In resigning the clerkship, he gave as his reason that 'circumstances have . . . arisen where the Council and the trustees are antagonistic to each other'.[141]

In the 1860s the trustees stood aloof from the corporation's affairs, the *Cardiff Times* in 1864 congratulating them for not making 'use of their "interest" in this town to advance one side or another in a municipal contest'.[142] Among the members of the corporation there continued to be men prepared to argue that the interest of the Bute family 'in the welfare of the town of Cardiff and the extension of its commercial progress is one and indivisible with the general weal',[143] but they were effectively opposed by those who had rejected the notion, so assiduously cultivated by the second marquess, that the interests of the town and the estate were identical and, long before the minority was over, Bute control over the corporation of Cardiff had become a thing of the past.

The erosion of the influence of the castle estate over the corporation was paralleled by the ending of its hold over the parliamentary representation of Cardiff. In 1849, John Nicholl, his health worsening, informed the trustees that he wished to withdraw from parliament. Bruce and McNabb were deeply perturbed. 'There are no grounds for reopening the seat', wrote Bruce. 'Gratitude to Lord Bute and consideration for those left in charge of the family property ought to decide him not put put the family interest to hazard by opening the seat unnecessarily.'[144] Under pressure from Lady Bute and the trustees, Nicholl was prevailed upon to change his mind and, in 1851, when it was obvious that the Bute interest would be challenged in the forthcoming election, he agreed to stand again. His opponent was Walter Coffin, coalowner, Unitarian and chairman of the Taff Vale Railway Company, who had been petitioned by 400 of Cardiff's electors to stand for parliament in the 'commercial interest'. Coffin's supporters in the election of 1852 declared that their main concern was 'to destroy the Bute interest in the Borough' and, in seeking to do so, they could rely upon the backing of Coffin's fellow 'wharf-gentry' and upon Cardiff's increasingly influential Nonconformists.

Sir John Guest, although close to death, roused himself to instruct the Dowlais agents at Cardiff to support Coffin and similar action was taken by William Crawshay with regard to the Cyfarthfa agents and the employees of the Glamorganshire Canal Company. Coffin won by 498 votes to 461. Cowbridge gave Nicholl the overwhelming majority of 87 to six and Llantrisant the ample one of 115 to 62, but Cardiff, 'Lord Bute's own town', repudiated the castle nominee by 410 to 259, causing Lady Bute to lament 'the ascendancy of revolutionary principles and the abasement of the family'.[145] The new member proved inactive and resigned the seat in 1857. In the Commons, 'he declined to risk his reputation as a speaker' and 'in opening the borough he felt he had fulfilled his mission.'[146]

With the loss of the seat in 1852, the trustees made no further attempt to sponsor a candidate at Cardiff until the minority was over. Boyle felt less committed to the maintenance of the political influence of the estate than had Bruce and McNabb, both of whom had been close associates of the second marquess. Indeed, it was by no means certain that the recapture of the Cardiff seat by a Conservative would win the approval of the eventual owner of the Bute estate. The political creed that the boy marquess would embrace in adulthood was, of course, unknown; furthermore, he was a sickly child and, despite the threats of the second marquess in 1835, the heir presumptive to the estate was Lord James Stuart, who had sacrificed much for Liberal principles. In 1857, the Liberals of Cardiff brought forward his son, Colonel J.F.D. Crichton Stuart, as their candidate. Bute officials made no move to bring forward their own candidate and Stuart was elected unopposed and re-elected, again unopposed, in 1859 and 1865.

6 Grandeur and impotence: the third marquess, 1868–1900

In September 1868, the minority came to an end. The trustees saw the third marquess's coming-of-age as an opportunity to reassert before the people of Cardiff and Glamorgan the prestige, power and benevolence of the Bute estates and staged celebrations on an enormous scale. The *Merthyr Guardian* saw the event as a symbol: the young lord and the greatness of Cardiff had been fathered by the second marquess and had come of age together. Celebrations lasted for a week and included balloon ascents, school fêtes, two concerts, two balls, two regattas, three public dinners and a firework display, the cost to the estate exceeding £14,000. Special trains brought tenants and well-wishers from the Rhondda, Aberdare, Merthyr, Rhymney and the vale of Glamorgan and ministers of all denominations assisted in a lavish display of philanthropy. The corporation of Cardiff spent £1,500 on the rejoicings, providing illuminations, decorations and triumphal arches.[147]

The man whose coming-of-age led to such public manifestations was one of the most remarkable figures of the nineteenth-century British aristocracy. His immense wealth, his eccentricities, his conversion to Roman Catholicism, his extravagant building operations and his fame as the hero of *Lothair*, the most successful of Disraeli's novels, made him the object of much gossip and speculation. He had spent his infancy in the care of his mother at Cardiff, Mountstuart and elsewhere; following her death in 1859, it was arranged, after much quarrelling among his relations, that he should live in the household of the earl of Galloway and it was at Galloway House, near Whithorn Abbey, the mother church of Scottish Christianity, that he became entranced by medieval Scottish history and by legends of saints and monasteries. At Oxford he was befriended by C.S. Murray, a Catholic Scot for whom Pugin had designed a chapel and was much influenced by Murray's chaplain, Monsignor T.W. Capel. The marquess was received into the Roman Catholic Church on 8 December 1868, the timing dictated by his advisers who were anxious that his conversion, which they did all in their power to prevent, should not weaken Bute influence in the election of November 1868 or poison the demonstrations of loyalty at the coming-of-age celebrations.[148]

With his conversion, the marquess's life became dominated by Catholicism. 'It was like reading *Lothair* in the original', wrote Augustus Hare after meeting him in 1874, 'and most interesting at first, but became somewhat monotonous as he talks incessantly . . . of altars, ritual and liturgical differences; he often loses himself and certainly lost me in sentences about "the unity of the Kosmos".'[149] His liturgical interests led the marquess to make a serious study of the Orthodox and Armenian churches and to prepare a massive translation of the Roman breviary. He travelled widely in Italy, Greece and Palestine and left instructions that his heart be buried on the Mount of Olives. He was fascinated by the occult, publishing studies of hauntings and collecting books on sorcery and witchcraft. He played a significant part in the development of the Scottish Catholic hierarchy, gave extensive support to Scottish historical studies and advocated the re-establishment of the Scottish parliament, the symbol to him of the 'national, Catholic and feudal' era of Scottish history. His delight in building bordered upon mania. In the building and restoration he undertook at Cardiff and Mountstuart and at the numerous Scottish historic houses he purchased, he employed some of the most remarkable architects of the nineteenth century. The work he commissioned reflects his fascination with medievalism, ecclesiasticism, occultism and orientalism and makes him 'perhaps the greatest private patron of architecture in British history'.[150]

To a man of the temperament and tastes of the third marquess of Bute, the growing town of Cardiff, with its expanding docks, its aggressive coal freighters and its booming industrial hinterland, made little appeal. 'Athens and Assisi', he wrote, 'have spoiled me for everything else.'[151] Estate administration, in which his father had delighted, was to him a burden. 'At last', he stated in 1877, 'I am relieved from a more than usually tedious spell of business with lawyers and factors.'[152] 'He did not have to turn his thoughts to the accumulation of wealth', wrote the *Western Mail* on his death in 1900; 'this flowed into his coffers unsought and unbidden'. Like Lothair, he 'came into everything readymade'.[153]

The coming-of-age of the marquess made little difference to the system of estate administration. The trust established by his father continued in existence and Boyle, as executive trustee, supervised the workings of the various departments as he had done during the minority. Boyle retired in 1880, when the trust was enlarged and reconstituted and W.T. Lewis, previously mineral agent, was appointed general manager of the estate and, as such, was the only channel of communication between the marquess and his employees in Glamorgan. In 1887, with the incorporation of the Bute Docks, the marquess became chairman of the Bute Docks Company but he rarely attended meetings. The company was dominated by the masterful Lewis, although he was obliged on occasion to travel to Athens or Rome to obtain his employer's formal consent to decisions already made. The declining rôle of the owner in the management of the estate was the consequence, not only of the third marquess's distaste for administration but also of the increased complexity of estate business, reflected in the rapidly increasing returns from Bute properties in Glamorgan; overall receipts in 1879 amounted to £185,932 of which £84,000 was transmitted to the marquess's personal account at Coutts.[154]

It was rare for the third marquess during his adult life to spend any length of time at Cardiff and his long absences from the town which was the source of the bulk of his wealth were frequently criticized. He did play some part in the public life of Glamorgan, becoming the president of the Cardiff Provident Dispensary, Savings Club and Cricket Club and the chairman of the Benefit and Annuitants Society; in addition he was a trustee of the Monmouthshire and South Wales Miners Permanent Benefit Society and Honorary Colonel of the Glamorgan Artillery Volunteers. An execrable public speaker, he disliked formal occasions. He did overcome his reluctance to undertake public rôles sufficiently to play a leading part in the National Eisteddfod held at Cardiff in 1883, to undertake, for the year 1886, the chairmanship of Cardiff's Chamber of Commerce and to serve for five years as president of the town's newly-established University College. The climax of his public life came in 1890 when he was elected mayor of Cardiff, 'the first to restore the ancient association of peers with civic office'.[155]

More to the third marquess's taste were his philanthropic activities. During his lifetime he gave away many hundreds of thousands of pounds, most of the money going to Scottish causes. Nevertheless, his benefactions in Glamorgan were numerous and impressive, although it is doubtful whether, in proportion to his gross income from the county, they approached the 7 to 8 per cent which his father had given to philanthropic causes. Among his major donations were £13,000 to rebuild the Hamadryad Hospital, £10,000 to Cardiff University College, £10,000 towards building a drill hall, £5,000 to alleviate the distress which followed the failure of the Cardiff Savings Bank and almost £5,000 to the Monmouthshire and South Wales Miners Permanent Provident Society. He was generous to Roman Catholic causes at Cardiff, defraying most of the expenses of the Convent of the Good Shepherd and Nazareth House and making large donations to churches and schools. Jews in Cardiff and in Scotland benefited from his philanthropy and he was also prepared to assist the 'schismatics' of the Anglican church on the understanding that his contributions to the restoration of historic churches were not used to provide 'the auxiliaries of Anglican worship'. His gifts of land at Cardiff included Cardiff Arms Park, much of Roath Park, many squares and open spaces and the site of the University College. Among his more unusual charities were his pensions to Welsh enthusiasts of druidism and the £1,000-fund, instituted by him on the occasion of his silver wedding, to provide dowries for poor girls at Cardiff.[156]

The third marquess, on coming of age, declared himself to be a Conservative, his association with Disraeli confirming him in his romantic Toryism. Nevertheless he took virtually no part in London political life, largely confining himself in his rare speeches in the House of Lords to the affairs of the University of St Andrews, of which he was rector. He did contribute substantial sums to Conservative party funds and, although he shrank from being personally involved in political campaigning, supported the attempts of his employees at Cardiff to use the estate's interest on behalf of Conservatism.[157] The knowledge that the young marquess was a Conservative and the success of the coming-of-age celebrations made the general election of 1868 appear a propitious occasion to reactivate the political influence of the Bute estate at Cardiff. With the marquess's approval, the Bute trustees and agents brought forward H.S. Giffard, the future Lord Chancellor Lord Halsbury, as Conservative candidate against Colonel Crichton Stuart. The election, which cost the Conservatives £10,000, was fought with much bitterness and the Liberals were loud in their denunciations of intimidation by Bute agents. Crichton Stuart won by 2,501 votes to 2,055.[158]

A by-product of the election was the foundation of the *Western Mail*. Crichton Stuart had been championed by the *Cardiff Times* and, convinced by Giffard's arguments that the Conservative campaign had been 'hampered by the fact that we had no powerful press support' the Bute trustees and officials launched on 1 May 1869 the first daily paper in Wales. Ostensibly the proprietor was L.V. Shirley, the estate's zealously Tory solicitor, but the expenses of the venture were met by the marquess. The estate accounts show that £19,800 was spent on the paper between 1868 and 1871 and the marquess later claimed that it had cost him a total of £50,000. It continued in Bute hands until 1877 when Shirley arranged for it to be sold to its editor, Lascelles Carr. Under its new owner it continued to advocate the causes which had been championed by the Bute estate since the time of the second marquess, combining as it did staunch Conservatism and support for the Anglican Establishment with an informed interest in Welsh national and cultural affairs.[159]

Figure 4. Cardiff Castle (by courtesy of the Cambridge University Library).

Figure 5. The third marquess of Bute in his robes as mayor of Cardiff.

Their initiative in establishing the *Western Mail* is proof that the Bute officials were by no means reconciled to their defeat in the election of 1868. Shirley in particular was anxious to return to the fray and organized a vigorous Constitutional Association at Cardiff. Although there were those among the town's Conservatives who doubted whether a close entanglement with the castle was helpful to their cause, Shirley's activities in the election of 1874 were sufficient to ensure that Giffard, rather than the Cardiff alderman preferred by many local Conservatives, should again be candidate. By then, the Ballot Act protected voters from open coercion but the *Western Mail*, a powerful addition to the Conservative arsenal, believed that Cardiffians would support the Bute-sponsored candidate uncoerced in order to demonstrate their approval of the estate as 'the principal promoter of the prosperity of the town'.[160] Giffard succeeded in 1874 in reducing Stuart's majority to nine votes, but this was as much a tribute to the revived fortunes of the Conservative party as it was to the influence of the Bute estate. By 1880, the Conservative party at Cardiff had emancipated itself from Bute domination and its nomination of Sir John Guest's son Arthur as candidate in that year found little favour with the marquess's advisers. Indeed, in 1880, the estate officials devoted more energy to the support of W.T. Lewis's unsuccessful candidature as an Independent at Merthyr than they did to Guest's campaign at Cardiff.[161] Nevertheless, their unenthusiastic support of Guest was considered sufficient to make the result of the election doubtful. In the event, the Liberal, E.J. Reed, a naval architect, defeated Guest by 3,881 votes to 3,483.

After 1880, the Bute estate was only one of many concerns at Cardiff supporting the Conservative cause and, although Reed made much of sinister Bute influence, it had ceased to be a major factor in determining the town's parliamentary representation. Cardiff was, by the end of the nineteenth century, one of the largest single member borough seats in the kingdom. It was a highly marginal constituency, and its Conservative party was far more powerful and better organized than were those of the other major boroughs of Wales. While Bute patronage had undoubtedly assisted the establishment of the party in the town, the relative strength of Conservativism at Cardiff by the early twentieth century may be attributed to factors such as the comparative weakness of Noncomformity, the greater anglicization of the population and the existence of a large middle class – the consequence of the fact that the town was a commercial and administrative centre not an industrial one – rather than to the influence of a single estate. Reed was re-elected in 1885, 1886 and 1892 but in 1895 he was defeated by the Conservative, J. Mackenzie Maclean, who although of Scottish origin and a co-proprietor of the *Western Mail*, had no obvious connection with the Bute family.[162]

The attempts to restore the Bute hold over the parliamentary representation of Cardiff which were made in the years following the coming-of-age of the third marquess were accompanied by attempts to reactivate the castle's influence over the corporation of Cardiff. The chief protagonist, in this as in the parliamentary field, was L.V. Shirley. His Constitutional Association, according to the *Cardiff Times* 'kept alive in the town a bitter political feeling and, by its interference with elections . . . its fêtes, mountebank performances and open debauchery . . . has become obnoxious to all members of the community. Its object is to reduce Cardiff to a mere appanage of the house of Bute'.[163] The association brought party organization into the town's municipal elections, an example quickly followed by the local Liberals, causing the corporation by 1870 to be divided for the first time along party lines. The open coalition between the castle and the Conservative party, revived in 1868 and sustained by Shirley's activities, galvanized the opposition and the consequent controversy aroused the corporation from the torpor which had characterized it in the 1860s.[164]

The Liberals, advocates of municipal reform, argued that 'there are other matters to be considered and nobler purposes to be subserved than the development of [the marquess's] property and the extension of his influence.'[165] By the mid-1870s, they had won control of the corporation and in their campaign harsh and bitter things were said of the Bute agents and of the marquess himself. The *Western Mail* and Shirley more than reciprocated and the marquess allowed his hostility to the Liberal councillors to find expression even when acknowledging the corporation's congratulations on the birth of a daughter to the marchioness. 'Lord Bute', wrote his secretary in 1876, 'requests me to thank the Council as an official body; and to those members of it who have in the past, as well as in the present, acted towards him with fairness and uprightness, he desires to return his own and Lady Bute's sincere acknowledgments for the present manifestation of their kindness.'[166]

In the early 1880s, the threat that the coal-freighters would build docks to which they would divert their trade away from Cardiff raised in a critical form the relationship between the Bute estate and the corporation of Cardiff. The *Weekly Mail* exulted at the damage to Bute interests which would be caused if the proposed plans were implemented. 'Thus the high handed policy of the Bute Trustees would be effectively avenged', it wrote, 'and the craven-spirited town council which had meekly bowed its head before the iron heel of tyranny would learn that their miserable sycophancy was unprofitable as well as unmanly.' There were others, however, who heeded the warning of Councillor Carr that 'all property values depend upon the amount of shipping done in the docks and the corporation would be utterly insolvent if anything happened to them'.[167]

The corporation was dominated, not by the commercial élite of shipowners and coal-freighters, but by men drawn from the small business and professional classes. The former had no major investments within the town and their trade could, if necessary, be accommodated elsewhere, while the latter had an abiding concern for the prosperity of the docks and therefore a common interest with the Bute estate. This common interest was stressed by the Bute authorities when seeking support for their Docks Bill of 1882 and allies for their fight against the Barry Dock scheme. The Chamber of Commerce, dominated by the freighters, was opposed to the bill of 1882, which sought to increase the dock charges paid by coal shippers, but to the corporation, which saw it as proof of Bute commitment to the expansion of dock accommodation at Cardiff, the bill gave 'the liveliest satisfaction'. In the fight against rival docks at Barry the Liberals were lukewarm, their newspaper, the *South Wales Daily News*, established in 1872 as a counterweight to the *Western Mail*, commenting: 'It is not to be supposed that the coal trade of south Wales would be fatally injured . . . if Cardiff should come to a full stop.'[168] With the estate sponsoring 'dock candidates' in the municipal elections of 1882, the 1880s saw the effective revival of the Bute-Conservative coalition which led, in the mid 1880s, to the capture of the corporation by the Conservatives. Their period of control was brief and when in 1904 the party again won power at Cardiff, that power had no significant Bute dimension.

Nevertheless, attempts to ensure that there should be at least one spokesman for Bute interests on the corporation continued into the twentieth century. The grounds upon which such influence was claimed had changed markedly since the time of the second marquess; it was as a major ratepayer rather than as the lord of Cardiff Castle that the fourth marquess in 1919 sought to justify his efforts to obtain a voice in the affairs of Cardiff.[169] Yet long before the third marquess's death, Bute influence over the affairs of Cardiff was a lingering remnant rather than a dynamic force. When the corporation in 1890 invited him to become mayor, the unanimity of the decision suggests that even the Radicals considered that there was no political danger in placing the leadership of the corporation in the hands of the marquess of Bute. It was only when aristocratic influence was a spent force that the prestige of the peerage could be exploited to further civic dignity. The marquess understood his position: 'They only elected me', he wrote, 'as a kind of figure-head.'[170]

Although it was accepted before the end of the nineteenth century that the Bute family's sway over the corporation and the parliamentary representation of Cardiff had come to an end, the vast sums of money which the family drew from Cardiff and the interlocking nature of its various enterprises could still, in the early twentieth century, arouse hostility and suspicion. 'It is almost certain', wrote the economist H.S. Jevons in 1912, 'that there is no builder in Cardiff who would dare bring an action against the Bute; he never knows when he may want some concession down the Docks, from the Cardiff Railway, or from colliery or industrial enterprises out of the many [with] which Lord Bute or the trustees of the Bute estate or Lord Merthyr [formerly W.T. Lewis] or the surveyors, architects or solicitors of the Bute estate are connected.'[171]

Attacks on the estate took an antiquarian turn and much energy was spent on researching into the original grants by Edward VI to William Herbert, earl of Pembroke; at the height of the agitation against the House of Lords, the *South Wales Daily News*, which had 'a seated antipathy to titles in general and to marquesses in particular',[172] published headlines such as 'The Herbert Grant – How His Guardians Fleeced The King' and insinuated that the Cardiff Castle estate owed its origins to fraud.[173] When the fourth marquess appeared before the Royal Commission on Coal in 1919, he was questioned closely about these allegations and was treated with calculated rudeness by the miners' representatives. 'Your family is of Scottish origins?', asked Robert Smillie. 'Yes', answered the marquess. 'But they have not', noted Smillie, 'confined their attentions to Scotland.' 'No', agreed the marquess. 'Unfortunately for the Welsh people', snapped Smillie.[174]

7 Epilogue: economic and social withdrawal in the twentieth century

The fourth marquess, who succeeded in 1900, was less involved in the life of the Welsh people than were his immediate ancestors. Although he had some command of Welsh, took an intelligent interest in Welsh cultural affairs and accepted a commission in the Welsh Guards, he did not seek a leading rôle in the life of Cardiff and Glamorgan. In Scotland he was active for decades on the Buteshire County Council; a recognized authority on Scottish antiquities, he was president of the Scottish History Society and chairman of the Scottish Historical Buildings Society. When he died in 1947, the authors of his obituaries could find little to say about his public rôle in Wales beyond noting his hospitality towards the prince of Wales at the castle when the Royal Show visited Cardiff in 1919. In the first decade of the twentieth century, the marquess was overshadowed at Cardiff by his chief agent, W.T. Lewis, who was elevated to the peerage as Baron Merthyr in 1911. It was Lord Merthyr, rather than the fourth marquess, who served a term as president of University College, Cardiff and the coverage given to him and his activities by the newspapers of South Wales far exceeded that given to his employer.[175]

It was rumoured that the fourth marquess did not care for Cardiff, but he did spend considerable periods at the castle, completing his father's sensitive work on the Roman fortifications and undertaking a magnificent restoration of Caerphilly Castle. A passionate accumulator of houses, he acquired Cottesmore Hall in Rutlandshire, a house in Edinburgh, a place in Chile and an estate in Spain. The notion of the Butes as a local dynasty to which homage was due did to some extent endure. In 1928, when the earl of Dumfries, the fourth marquess's eldest son, came of age, a garden party for 7,000 guests was held at Cardiff Castle. The band of the Welsh Guards played, the Pendyrus Male Voice Choir sang, the Lord Mayor of Cardiff made himself affable and the Archbishop of Cardiff prayed. The fourth marquess, in introducing his son to Bute employees and well-wishers, declared his intention of involving the young earl in the administration of the estate and then went on to voice his worries about the future of landed property. The *Western Mail*, although hoping that the celebrations would 'give new life to the bonds of amity between the castle and the city', reported them in its women's page, which was generally devoted to fashion shows. In a later issue in the same year the paper gave more prominence to a smaller garden party at Buckingham Palace, a fact that suggests that, to the *Western Mail*, loyalty to a local dynasty had been subsumed by loyalty to a royal one.[176]

By the 1920s, the Butes' political presence in Cardiff had vanished. In 1900, E.J. Reed re-captured the Cardiff seat in the Liberal interest, and he was followed as a Liberal member in 1906 by Ivor Guest, grandson of Sir John Guest, who in turn was succeeded in January 1910 by D.A. Thomas, the powerful coalowner. Thomas's opponent was Lord Ninian Crichton Stuart, son of the third marquess of Bute and brother of the fourth. Lord Ninian stood again in December 1910, defeating his Liberal opponent, Sir Clarendon Hyde, by 299 votes. Bute officials were active in Lord Ninian's support and it was rumoured that the estate's refusal to sell land for building had been relaxed in the months leading up to the election. The election campaign revolved around general issues such as tariff reform, defence and the activities of Lloyd George. The Liberal *South Wales Daily News* made no mention of the Conservative candidate's links with the castle but the *Western Mail* stressed that, unlike the Liberal candidate, Lord Ninian was a local man with a strong personal stake in the prosperity of Cardiff. His victory cannot be seen as constituting a revival of Bute influence over the politics of Cardiff; it was the victory of orthodox Conservatism. Yet his links with the castle, stressed by his friends and ignored by his opponents, were evidently seen by both as giving an added lustre to his candidature.[177]

Lord Ninian, commander of the sixth Welsh Battalion, was killed on active service in 1915. In the election of 1918, the constituency of Cardiff having been divided into three, Lord Ninian's brother, Lord Colum, contested Cardiff East. Again the *South Wales Daily News* barely mentioned the Conservative candidate's relationship to the marquess of Bute while the *Western Mail* stressed that the marchioness and the dowager marchioness both spoke in his favour. The constituency included the Cardiff Dowlais Ironworks, the lease of which was shortly to expire. Rumours that the marquess had demanded a new annual rent of £50,000 were denied by Lord Colum who claimed that the sum charged was £1,500, 'the low rent . . . [having] the one object of benefiting Cardiff commercially'. Paradoxically, he made much of his support for the enfranchisement of leaseholders and advocated the abolition, after compensation, of mineral royalties, while the strain of paternalistic Toryism which had been present in the Bute family since the time of the second marquess showed itself in his statement that 'past administrators of noble blood had laboured to give labour some of the freedom it now enjoyed'. He lost the election to the Liberal shipowner Sir W.H. Seager and, 128 years after his great-grandfather had been elected for Cardiff, Lord Colum's unsuccessful candiature brought the direct links between the constituency and the Bute family to a close.[178]

The decline in the rôle played by the Bute family at Cardiff in the early twentieth century was accompanied by a contraction in the Bute property in Glamorgan. The third marquess had not bequeathed all his wealth and lands to his eldest son; most of his purchased estates and part of the agricultural land of the Glamorgan estate went to his daughter and his younger sons; and thus, with death duties and other charges and bequests, the fourth marquess was less rich and powerful than the third.[179] The professionalization of administration, which had begun under his father, continued under the fourth marquess and, in the first decade of the twentieth century, W.T. Lewis retained full authority over estate matters. In 1909 Lewis, at the age of 72, resigned from most of his duties. By then, the complexities of administration, the low yield of the dock investment, the virtual extinction of the political influence of landed property and the fourth marquess's desire to realize capital assets and to diversify his investments, were all inducements to him to dispose of his Glamorgan possessions. He continued the efforts which his father had been making since 1880 to divest himself of his dock responsibilities, offering the docks to the corporation of Cardiff in 1906 and supporting their take-over by the Taff Vale Railway Company in 1908.[180] During the war, a degree of common management of the transport concerns serving Cardiff did come about when in 1917 the manager of the Rhymney Railway Company also became manager of the Taff Vale and the Cardiff Railway Companies. This unified management continued after the war until all the south Wales railway companies were amalgamated with the Great Western Railway Company. On vesting day, 1 January 1922, the independent existence of the Bute Docks and the Cardiff Railway Company, along with that of all their old rivals, came to an end. Thereafter the marquess, although a substantial shareholder in the Great Western Railway Company, no longer bore final responsibility for Cardiff's docks and the problems they experienced as a result of the contraction of the coal trade in the 1920s and 1930s were not of central concern to him.[181]

In 1909, following Lewis's retirement, Bute urban land in the industrial valleys was placed on the market, a process which culminated in a series of auctions of land in the Rhondda and Cynon valleys in 1919 and 1920, a four day sale at Aberdare in December 1919 yielding receipts of £120,000.[182] Between 1915 and 1919, the Bute collieries were sold, the giant Ocean and Powell Duffryn Companies acquiring them at boom prices. In July 1923 the Bute estate at Hirwaun and Rhigos, consisting of 723 lots, was placed on the market and in July 1924 90 lots in the neighbourhood of Pontypridd were auctioned.[183] In 1926 surviving Bute property, largely urban land at Cardiff and minerals under lease, were incorporated in the private family company of Mountjoy Ltd. In 1938 Mountjoy sold its urban estate to the Western Ground Rents Company, a syndicate established by the Equity and Law and the General Life Assurance Companies. The property, which included the site of the Cardiff Dowlais Ironworks and the Mountstuart Dry Dock as well as half the city of Cardiff and those leaseholds in the coalfield which had not been sold at auction, changed hands at £5 million.[184] The year 1938 also saw the compulsory acquisition by the state of unworked minerals. In compensation, Mountjoy received £1,222,425 for coal and other minerals under a total of 36,456 acres of the south Wales coalfield.[185]

When the fourth marquess died in 1947, his son's inheritance in Glamorgan consisted of little beyond Cardiff Castle and its park. Four months after his father's death the fifth marquess presented the castle and the 434-acre park to the city of Cardiff. On 10 September 1947 the standard of the Butes was lowered from the castle keep for the last time and, as aeroplanes flew overhead in salute, the fifth marquess expressed his satisfaction in presenting to the city the castle from which it had sprung.[186]

APPENDIX

Genealogical table of the Bute family (simplified)

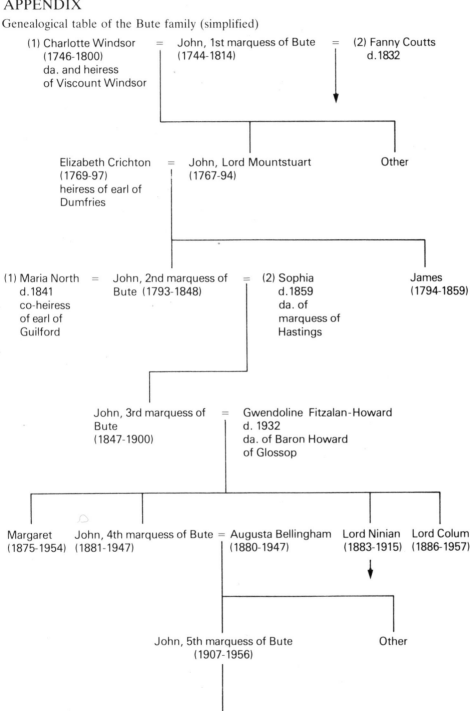

BIBLIOGRAPHY

1 Primary sources

British Transport Historical Record Office: Minute Books of Directors' Meetings: Bute Docks Company, 1886–98; Cardiff Railway Company, 1898–1922.
Cardiff Central Library: Bute Collection; Miscellaneous Bute Papers; Diary of John Bird; Letterbooks of E.P. Richards.
Coal House, Llanishen, Cardiff: Claim Files relating to the nationalization of mineral reserves.
Companies House, Cardiff: Material relating to Mountjoy Company, Ltd.
Glamorgan Record Office, Cardiff: Bute Estate Papers.
National Library of Wales, Aberystwyth: Bute Collection; Cyfarthfa Papers; Collection of Sale Catalogues; Glamorgan tithe commutation: maps and apportionments; Diary of Lewis Weston Dillwyn; Jevons Papers.
Public Record Office, London: Home Office: Letters concerning unrest in Glamorgan.
Register House, Edinburgh: Hamilton Bruce Papers.

2 Newspapers and periodicals

Archaeologia Aeliana; Barn; The Buteman; Cambrian; Cambrian Journal; Cardiff Recorder; Cardiff Reporter; Cardiff Times; Daily Chronicle; Economist; Estates Gazette; Illustrated London News; The Leader; Merthyr Express; Merthyr Guardian; The Scottish Review; South Wales Coal Annual; South Wales Daily News; Star of Gwent; The Times; Weekly Mail; The Welsh Housing and Development Yearbook; Western Mail.

3 Official publications: general

Hansard's Parliamentary Debates, second and third series; *Parliamentary Debates*, fourth and fifth series; *Census of Great Britain*, 1801 *et seq.*

4 Official publications: parliamentary papers

1835, vols. XXIII to XXIV, *R.C. on Municipal Corporations in England and Wales.*
1871, vol. XXXVI, *R.C. on Truck System.*
1874, vol. LXXII, *Return of Owners of land, England and Wales.*
1880, vol. XXXI, *R.C. on Municipal Corporations not subject to the Municipal Corporations Act.*

1886, vol. XII
1887, vol. XIII   } *S.C. on Town Holdings*
1888, vol. XII
1889, vol. XV

1890, vol. XXXVI
1890–1, vol. XLI   } *R.C. on Mining Royalties*
1893–4, vol. XLI

1894, vol. XVI
1896, vol. XVI–XVII   } *R.C. on Agricultural Depression*
1897, vol. XV

1894, vol. XXXVI–XXXVII ⎤
1895, vol. XL–XLI ⎬ R.C. on Land in Wales and Monmouthshire
1896, vol. XXIII–XXXV ⎦
1919, vol. XI–XIII, R.C. on the Coal Industry.
1926, vol. XIV, R.C. on the Coal Industry.
1938, Cmd. 5904, Central Valuation Board, Valuation Regions.

5 Published contemporary sources (local)

Anon., A Sketch of the Life of John, Second Marquess of Bute, Reprinted Principally from the Cardiff and Merthyr Guardian (1848).
Bessborough, Earl of (ed.), Lady Charlotte Guest: Extracts from her Journal, 1833–52 (1950).
Bird, J., The Directory of Cardiff (1794).
Brady, F., and Pottle, F.A. (eds.), Boswell on the Grand Tour: Italy, Corsica and France (1955).
—, Boswell in Search of a Wife (1957).
Cartwright, J. (ed.), The Journal of Lady Knightley of Fawsley (1915).
Clarke, T.E. Guide to Merthyr Tydfil (1848).
Cliffe, C.F., The Book of South Wales, the Bristol Channel, Monmouthshire and the Wye (1847).
Disraeli, B., Lothair (Bradenham edn, vol. XI, 1927).
Evans, J., Letters Written During a Tour Through South Wales in the Year 1803 and at Other Times (1804).
Hare, J.C.A., The Story of my Life (6 vols., 1896–1900).
Lewis, W.S. (ed.), The Yale Edition of the Letters of Horace Walpole (New Haven, 1937–).
Malkin, B.H., The Scenery, Antiquities and Biography of South Wales from Materials Collected During Two Excursions in the Year 1803 (2 vols., 1807).
Matthews, J.H. (ed.), Cardiff Records: Material for a History of the County Borough (6 vols, 1898–1911).
Pearson, A., Some Account of a System of Garden Labour (1831).
Phillips, S., The History of the Borough of Llantrisant (1866).
Rammell, T.W., Report on a Preliminary Inquiry into the . . . Sanitary Condition of the Inhabitants of the Town of Cardiff (1850).
Rees, T., Description of South Wales (1815).
Ryskamp, C., and Pottle, F.A. (eds.), Boswell: the Ominous Years, 1774–76 (1963).
Santayana, G., Persons and Places: the Background of my Life (1944).
Smyth, W.H., Nautical Observations on the Port and Maritime Vicinity of Cardiff (1840).
Stuart Wortley, Mrs, A Prime Minister to his Son (1925).
Trounce, W.J., Cardiff in the Fifties (1918).
Turner, W., The Port of Cardiff (1882).
Wilson, J., Tourists' Guide to Rothsay and the Isle of Bute (1862).

I have omitted a comprehensive list of dissertations and modern printed sources, as the references are themselves a running bibliography. A full bibliography of the Bute estate in Glamorgan is available in J. Davies, Cardiff and the Marquesses of Bute (1981), 301–16.

NOTES

1 A Sketch of the Life of John, Second Marquess of Bute, reprinted principally from the Cardiff and Merthyr Guardian (1848), 24; J.H. Matthews (ed.), Cardiff Records, Materials for a History of the County Borough (6 vols., 1896–1911), IV, 459; Daily Chronicle, 10 October 1900.

2 M.J. Daunton, *Coal Metropolis: Cardiff, 1870–1914* (1977), 229.

3 J. Davies, 'Glamorgan and the Bute estate, 1776–1947' Ph.D. thesis, University of Wales, 1969); *idem, Cardiff and the Marquesses of Bute* (1981).

4 Not all these estates were retained by the senior line of the family. The Mackenzie and Wortley lands went to the third earl's second son, James; the wealth inherited from Thomas Coutts went to the first marquess's children by his second marriage and the Guilford lands reverted to the North family following the death of Maria, marchioness of Bute, childless, in 1841.

5 F. Brady and F.A. Pottle (eds.), *Boswell in Search of a Wife.* (1957), 50.

6 *The letters of Horace Walpole* (Yale edition), X, 237.

7 Davies, *Cardiff*, ch. 2.

8 *Ibid.*; T. Lever, *The Herberts of Wilton* (1967); J. Davies, 'The Dowlais lease, 1748–1900', *Morgannwg*, XII (1968), 37–66.

9 Valuation, 1774 (National Library of Wales, Bute collection (hereafter cited as NLW, Bute), box 104).

10 Survey and valuation, 1825 (*ibid.*); Rentals (*ibid.*, boxes 73–5).

11 F. Brady and F.A. Pottle (eds.), *Boswell on the Grand Tour, Italy, Corsica and France* (1955), 9; C. Ryskamp and F.A. Pottle (eds.), *Boswell, the Ominous Years, 1774–76* (1963), 130.

12 Cardiff Central Library, Bute collection (hereafter cited as CCL, Bute) IX, 18 and 19.

13 G. Williams (ed.), *Glamorgan County History*, IV, 396, 407, 414; L.B. John, 'The parliamentary representation of Glamorgan, 1536–1832' (M.A. thesis, University of Wales, 1934), 17–35.

14 Letter to Lord Mountstuart, 1789, quoted in L.B. John, *op. cit.*, 115–18.

15 G. Williams, *op. cit.*, 160, 188–91; D.G. Walker, 'Cardiff' in R.A. Griffiths (ed.), *Boroughs of Medieval Wales* (1978), 103–30; W. Rees, *Cardiff, a History of the City* (1962).

16 L. Owen, 'The population of Wales in the sixteenth and seventeenth centuries', *Trans. Hon. Soc. Cymmrodorion* (1959), 99; B.H. Malkin, *The Scenery, Antiquities and Biography of South Wales* (1807), 136–7.

17 G. Williams, *op. cit.*, 354–61; M.I. Williams, 'Cardiff – its trade and its people', *Morgannwg*, VII (1963), 83–6; *idem*, 'Some aspects of the economic and social life of Glamorgan, 1600–1800', *ibid.*, III (1959), 33–4.

18 J. Bird, *The Directory of Cardiff* (1794); A.H. John, *The Industrial Development of South Wales, 1750–1850* (1950); G. Williams and A.H. John (eds.), *Glamorgan County History*, V, 430–8; C. Hadfield, *Canals of South Wales and the Border* (1960), 89–97; W.H. Smyth, *Nautical Observations on the Port and Maritime Vicinity of Cardiff* (1840), 9.

19 J.P. Grant, *Cardiff Castle, its History and Architecture* (1923); Malkin, *op.cit.* 142; J. Wilson, *Tourist's Guide to Rothesay and the Isle of Bute* (3rd edn, 1862), 8.

20 *Cambrian*, 19 June 1818; Vouchers (Glamorgan RO, Bute Estate Papers (hereafter cited as GRO, Bute) D/DA 56–117).

21 R. Richardson, *Coutts and Co., Bankers, Edinburgh and London* (1901), 45; L.B. John, *op. cit.*, 115–18.

22 Matthews, *op. cit.*, II, 28, 113; III, 408–9, 477; IV, 330–73, 419; V, 360–61, 527; Rees. *op. cit.*, 43; S. and B. Webb, *The Borough and the Manor* (1908), I, 254–6; PP, XXIII (1835), 186–94.

23 W. R. Williams, *The Parliamentary History of Wales* (1895), 104–10; R.D. Rees, 'The parliamentary representation of South Wales, 1790–1830' (Ph.D. thesis, University of Reading, 1962), I, 9–12, 198–248.

24 *Ibid.*, I, 88; G. Williams, *op. cit.*, IV, 415–29; Matthews, *op. cit.*, IV, 342–4; CCL, MS 2.716, Diary of John Bird, 19 June 1790.

25 *Cambrian*, 13 June 1818; *ibid.*, 29 May 1818.

26 Opinion of Mr Warren, 1818 (NLW, box 31).

27 See D. Spring, *The English Landed Estate in the Nineteenth Century: Its Administration* (1963), 53, and W. A. Maguire, *The Downshire Estates in Ireland, 1801–1845* (1972), 7.
28 Stewart to Richards, 25 February 1822 (GRO, Bute, D/DA 9).
29 *A Sketch of the Life*, 24.
30 NLW, Bute, box 60; CCL, Bute, X, 1 and 2.
31 CCL, Miscellaneous Bute Papers, 4. 850, Survey of Bute Mineral Property, 1823.
32 PP, XII (1919), 654; CCL, Bute, VII, 13, 4; Coal House, Llanishen, Claim Files, R.O. 8.
33 Bute to Smyth, 9 January 1841 (NLW, Bute, box 70, letterbook 7).
34 CCL, Bute, VII, VIII and XVI; J. H. Morris and L. J. Williams, *The South Wales Coal Industry, 1841–1875* (1958), 112–13; E.D. Lewis, *The Rhondda Valleys* (1959), 69–70, 118.
35 CCL, Bute, VII, 44, 5.
36 *Ibid.*, IX, 19; *ibid.*, MS 4. 850; NLW, Bute, box 70, letterbook to Messrs Coutts; bond relating to Rhymney (*ibid.*, box 140).
37 Davies, 'The Dowlais lease'; Lady Bute to Bruce, 1 May 1848 (Register House, Edinburgh, Hamilton Bruce Papers (hereafter cited as Bruce Papers) 196).
38 Bute to Smyth, 25 January 1840 (NLW, Bute, box 70, letterbook 6).
39 *Archaelogia Aeliana*, 3rd ser., x (1913), 183.
40 PP, XII (1919), 230, 653–8; NLW, Bute, box 106; CCL, Bute, X, 2 and 6.
41 *Ibid.*, XI, 20; *ibid.*, Cardiff Supplementary Rental, 1927–30; *Estates Gazette*, 21 May and 9 July 1938.
42 Davies, *Cardiff*, ch. 5; NLW, Bute, box 143.
43 *Ibid.*; boxes 60, 65, 72 and 73; T.W. Rammell, *Report on . . . the Sanitary Condition . . . of the Town of Cardiff* (1850).
44 Stewart to Richards, 8 September 1824 (GRO, Bute, D/DA 11).
45 Bute to Richards, 1 December 1837 (NLW, Bute, box, 70, letterbook 6); *ibid.*, Jevons Papers, IV, 122.
46 *Ibid.*, E.L. Chappell, *Cardiff's housing problem* (1913), 5, 12.
47 J.B. Hilling, *Cardiff and the valleys* (1973), 88–9; Daunton, *op. cit.*, 73–88; PP XIII, (1887), 797; Rees to Richards, 1 June 1853 (CCL, Bute, IX, 27, 21).
48 L. Wilkes and C. Dodd, *Tyneside Classical, the Newcastle of Grainger, Dobson and Clayton* (1964); N. Pevsner, *The buildings of England, Northumberland* (1957), 222–3.
49 J.M. Crook, 'Patron extraordinary, John, third marquess of Bute, 1847–1900' in *Victorian South Wales: the Seventh Conference Report of the Victorian Society* (1970), 6–10; M. Girouard, *The Victorian country house* (1971), 125–30; Hilling, *op. cit.*, 61–70, 145–60; A. Pettigrew, *The Public Parks and Recreation Grounds of Cardiff* (1926).
50 Hadfield, *op. cit.*, 100–10; Smyth, *op. cit.*
51 CCL, Bute, XI, 3 and 4; Bute to Roy, 14 February 1832 (NLW, Bute, box 70, letterbook to Messrs Coutts); 1 William IV *cap.* CXXXIII.
52 4 William IV *cap.* XIX; Smyth, *op. cit.*, 21; CCL, Bute, XI, 56.
53 Davies, *Cardiff*, 277–85.
54 Bute to Smyth, 13 and 14 November 1839 (NLW, Bute, box 70, letterbook 7).
55 De Grave to Bruce, 22 December 1842 (Bruce Papers, 196).
56 CCL, Bute, XI, 56; W. Turner, *The Port of Cardiff* (1882); *South Wales Coal Annual* (1913); C. J. Howells, *Transport Facilities in the Mining and Industrial Districts of South Wales and Monmouthshire* (1911); I.B. Thomas, *Top Sawyer, a Biography of David Davies of Llandinam* (1938), 270–311; British Transport Historical RO, BDC 1.
57 57–58 Victoria *cap.* CLIV; *South Wales Daily News*, 14 and 15 July 1907.
58 Minutes of the Bute Docks Company, 1 November 1894 (British Transport Historical RO, BDC 1).
59 CCL, Bute, X, 1–6, XI, 56, XII, 20, 31 and 32.
60 Davies, *Cardiff*, 263–70, 276–7; Daunton, *op. cit.*, 26–7; W.E. Simnett, *Railway*

Amalgamation in Great Britain (1923), 5, 50–1, 230, 262; British Transport Historical RO, BDC 1 and RAC 1/55.

61 Crawshay to Bute, 19 December 1833 (NLW, Cyfarthfa Papers, III).

62 *South Wales Daily News*, 29 September 1906.

63 J.H. Morris and L.J. Williams, *op. cit.*, 26, 100–2; W.H. Jones, *History of the Port of Swansea* (1922).

64 Davies, *Cardiff*, 282–7, 298–9; H. Carter, *The Towns of Wales* (1965), 110–17; Daunton, *op cit.*, 53–4.

65 Matthews, *op. cit.*, II, 113.

66 *Ibid.*, IV, 270–71, 361–7; W.R. Williams, *op. cit.*, 109–10.

67 Walker to Richards, 18 October 1820 (GRO, Bute, D/DA 8); king against Wood (NLW, Bute, box 31); L. Hargest, 'Cardiff's "spasm of rebellion" in 1818', *Morgannwg*, XXI (1977), 69–88.

68 Richards to Walker, 5 and 14 July 1817 (GRO, Bute, D/DA 5).

69 *Ibid.*, D/DA 6; N.L.W., Calendar of the diary of L.W. Dillwyn, May and June 1818; R.D. Rees, *op. cit.*, I, 208–15; J. Ballinger, 'Elections in Cardiff and Glamorgan, 1818–32', *Cymru Fu*, I (1889), 348–59; CCL, box labelled 'Posters etc.', Papers relating to the political affairs of Cardiff, 1815–19.

70 CCL, Bute, IX, 19.

71 Letters in GRO, Bute, D/DA 11 and 12; CCL, letterbooks of E.P. Richards, MS 4. 713 and Bruce Papers, 196.

72 NLW, Bute, boxes 60, 72 and 73; Richards to Bute, 8 September 1828 (CCL, MS 4. 713).

73 Bute to Richards, 27 January 1825, 25 December 1846 (GRO, Bute, D/DA 12 and 30).

74 Bute to Richards, 18 June 1836 (NLW, Bute, box 70, letterbook 6). See also *ibid.*, letterbooks 7, 13 and 1842–4 and PRO, HO 40/40 and 52/25.

75 Letters in NLW, Bute, box 70, letterbook 1845–46.

76 Bute to Richards, 31 January 1838 (*ibid.*, letterbook 6).

77 *Ibid.*, 24 August 1836 (*ibid.*); *Parliamentary Debates*, 3rd ser., 25, 274.

78 *Ibid.*, 2nd ser., 16, 1269.

79 Mrs Rickards to Richards, 3 June 1848 (Bruce Papers, 196).

80 Richards to Bute, 9 March 1846 (NLW, Bute, box 70, letterbook 1844–6); other letters in *ibid.* and letterbook 1847–8; *ibid.*, box 31.

81 Bute to Richards, 21 December 1846 (GRO, Bute, D/DA 30); NLW, Bute, boxes 60, 72 and 73.

82 J. Howells, 'Reminiscences of Cardiff', *Red Dragon*, v (1884), 221.

83 *Merthyr Guardian*, 21 June 1869.

84 *South Wales Daily News*, 25 March 1910.

85 CCL, Bute, IX, 19; GRO, Bute, D/DB E1 and 2, Atlas and Terrier of the Bute Estate, 1824.

86 Richards to Bute, 11 January 1843 (NLW, Bute, box 70, letterbook 1842–4).

87 Walker to Richards, 21 October 1817 (GRO, Bute, D/DA 5); Richards to Bute, 16 October 1824 (CCL, MS/4. 713).

88 Richards to Bute, 16 October 1824 (*ibid.*); Tyndall to Bute, 25 November 1825 (Bruce Papers, 196).

89 Richards to Bute, 15 December 1832 (CCL, MS letterbooks of E.P. Richards, 4. 713); L.V. Evans, 'The Royal Glamorgan Militia', *Glam. Historian* VIII (n.d.), 146–66.

90 NLW, Calendar of the diary of L.W. Dillwyn, 9 June 1818.

91 Bute to Richards, 17 January 1825 (GRO, Bute, D/DA 12).

92 Wheeler to Richards, 29 January 1820 (*ibid.*, 8).

93 Bute to Melbourne, 28 April 1832 (PRO, HO 52/21); NLW, Bute, box 60.

94 Bruce to Bute, 2 December 1825 (Bruce Papers, 196); letters of Richards, December 1832 and January 1833 (CCL, MS letterbooks of E.P. Richards, 4. 713).

95 Richards to Bute, 29 January and 26 February 1825 (*ibid.*); Bute to Richards, 3

February 1825 (GRO, Bute, D/DA 12).
96 Richards to Bute, 25 January 1840 (CCL, Miscellaneous Bute Papers, MS 4. 860).
97 Bute to Thomas, 21 December 1838; to Lady Hall, 6 January 1840; to Bickens, 21 October 1840 (NLW, Bute, box 70, letterbook 13); to Campbell, 10 January and 10 March 1845 (*ibid.*, letterbook 1845–46).
98 Williams to Richards, 12 January 1829 (GRO, Bute, D/DA 5); Richards to Bute, 18 November 1831 (CCL, MS, letterbooks of E.P. Richards, 4. 713); Bute to Richards, 11 February 1835 (NLW, Bute, box 70, letterbook 6); A. Pearson, *Some Account of Garden Labour* (1831), iii.
99 Rickards to Richards, 10 September 1825 (GRO, Bute, D/DA 12).
100 Bute to Richards, 4 February 1836 (NLW, Bute, box 70, letterbook 6).
101 Richards to Bute, 9 December 1837 (CCL Miscellaneous Bute Papers, MS 4. 860).
102 Bute to Richards, 22 December 1825 (GRO, Bute, D/DA 12); Richards to Tyndall, 15 May 1826 (Bruce Papers, 196).
103 Richards to Bute, 8 October 1832 (CCL, MS letterbooks of E.P. Richards, 4. 713); Bute to Smyth, 9 August 1839 (NLW, Bute, box 70, letterbook 6).
104 Bute to Richards, 29 September 1845 (*ibid.*, letterbook 7); Richards to Bute, 10 October 1845 (*ibid.*, letterbook 1845–6).
105 Letters in GRO, Bute, D/DA 11–17 and in Bruce Papers, 196.
106 Letters in *ibid.* and CCL, MS, letterbook of E.P. Richards, 4. 713; G.A. Williams, *The Merthyr Rising of 1831* (1978).
107 Richards to Stuart, 26 September 1832 (CCL, MS, letterbooks of E.P. Richards, 4. 713).
108 *The Times*, 22 October 1832; Richards to Bute, 10 October 1832 (CCL, MS, letterbooks of E.P. Richards, 4. 713).
109 *Merthyr Guardian*, 1 December 1832; Richards to Bute, 12 February 1828, 5 January 1831 (CCL, MS, letterbooks of E.P. Richards, 4. 713).
110 Bute to Richards, 19 February 1824 (GRO, Bute, D/DA 11); Richards to Bute, 8 September 1832 (CCL, MS, letterbooks of E.P. Richards, 4. 713).
111 Richards to Bute, 31 August 1832 (*ibid.*).
112 Richards to Bute, 11 January 1833 (*ibid.*); Pryce to Bute, 23 November 1839 (CCL, Bute, XX, 81).
113 Bute to Richards, 18 April 1835 (GRO, Bute, D/DA 20).
114 Richards to Bute, 24 October 1842 (NLW, Bute, box 70, letterbook 1842–4).
115 *The Times*, 28 January 1846.
116 *Parliamentary Debates*, third ser., 87, 469–70.
117 *Ibid.*, 29, 1422; *PP* XXIII (1835), 186–94, 221–4, 313–14; Richards to Bute, 28 September and 2 October 1833 (CCL, MS, letterbooks of E.P. Richards, 4. 713); Bute to Richards, 23 July, 19 and 21 August 1835 (GRO, Bute, D/DA 20).
118 Matthews, *op. cit.*, V, 413.
119 Bute to Richards, 19 and 20 August and 25 November 1835 (NLW, Bute, box 70, letterbook 6).
120 Bute to Richards, 21 January 1836 (*ibid.*); Matthews, *op. cit.*, IV, 418.
121 Richards to Bute, 22 February 1842 (NLW, Bute, box 70, letterbook 1842–4).
122 Lord Bessborough (ed.), *Lady Charlotte Guest, Extracts from her Journal, 1833–52* (1950), 53; Bute to Smyth, 13 August 1839 (NLW, Bute, box 70, letterbook 6).
123 Bute to Richards, 17 April 1839 (*ibid*).
124 Richards to Bute, 5 November 1838, 11 November 1839 (*ibid.*); *ibid.*, 11 November 1836, 13 August 1839 (CCL, MS, letterbooks of E.P. Richards, 4. 860).
125 *Ibid.*, 21 and 27 July 1840 (*ibid.*).
126 Matthews, *op. cit.*, IV, 434.
127 Bessborough, *op. cit.*, 206.
128 Lady Bute to Richards, 7 March 1849 (GRO, Bute, D/DA 33).
129 Abstract of a deed of management (NLW, Bute, box 140); Minutebook of the trustees

of the marquess of Bute (*ibid.*, box 70); will of the marquess of Bute (*ibid.*, box 137); 11/12 Victoria *cap.* 20; 16/17 Victoria *cap.* 22.

130 McNabb to Bruce, 10 May 1848 (Bruce Papers, 196).
131 Davies, *Cardiff*, 70–5.
132 CCL, Miscellaneous Bute Papers, MS 4. 937, and CCL, Bute, X, 1–6; Bute to Roy, 26 December 1844 (NLW, Bute, box 70, letterbook to Messrs Coutts).
133 S. Philips, *The History of the Borough of Llantrisant* (1866), 37–8.
134 Richards to Bute, 14 February 1835 (CCL, MS, letterbooks of E.P. Richards, 4. 713); Matthews, *op. cit.*, V, 119.
135 G. Santayana, *Persons and Places, the Background of my Life* (1944), 137–8.
136 Letters in GRO, Bute, D/DA 32–36 and Bruce Papers, 198.
137 McNabb to Bruce, 22 May 1848 (*ibid.*).
138 Stuart to Richards, 20 and 22 November 1863 (GRO, Bute, D/DA 43); CCL, Bute, X, 1–6; NLW, Bute, boxes 60 and 65.
139 G.M. Young and W.D. Handcock (eds.), *English Historical Documents, 1833–1874* (1956), 78.
140 Rammell, *op. cit.*; letters, 1849–56 in GRO, Bute, D/DA 33–7, CCL, Bute, XI, 43 and Bruce Papers, 197–8; Matthews, *op. cit.*, IV, 540–4.
141 *Ibid.*, IV, 438; *Merthyr Guardian*, 23 May 1857; *Merthyr Express*, 21 January 1888.
142 *Cardiff Times*, 14 October 1864.
143 W.J. Trounce, *Cardiff in the Fifties* (1918), 47.
144 Bruce to Richards, 27 February and 24 March 1849 (GRO, Bute, D/DA 33).
145 Lady Bute to Bruce, 8 August 1853 (Bruce Papers, 198); *Cambrian*, 18 June and 10 July 1852; Trounce, *op. cit.*, 23; I. Humphries, 'Cardiff politics, 1850–1874', *Glam. Historian*, VIII (n.d.), 108.
146 C. Williams, *A Welsh Family* (1893), 185.
147 *Merthyr Guardian*, September 1868; *Illustrated London News*, 19 and 26 September 1868; CCL, box labelled 'Posters etc.'; CCL Bute, IX, 27, 20; J.H. Matthews, *op. cit.*, IV, 458–60.
148 D.H. Blair, *John Patrick, Third Marquess of Bute, K.T., 1847–1900, a Memoir* (1901), 1–77; N. Macpherson, *The Appelate Jurisdiction of the House of Lords in Scotch Cases, Illustrated by the Litigation Relating to the Custody of the Marquess of Bute* (1861).
149 J.C.A. Hare, *The Story of my Life* (6 vols., 1900), V, 169–71.
150 Crook, *op. cit.*, 5; Blair, *op. cit.*, *passim*.
151 M.E.G. Duff, *Notes from a Diary, 1851–72* (1897) II, 201.
152 Blair, *op. cit.*, *126*.
153 *Western Mail*, 10 October 1900; B. Disraeli, *Lothair* (1927 edn), 25, 91.
154 CCL, Miscellaneous Bute Papers, MS 4. 937 and CCL, Bute, IX, 29–33, X, 1–6; indenture, 1902 (NLW, Bute, box 137); British Transport Historical RO, BDC 1, 1–3.
155 Blair, *op. cit.*, *passim*; *Western Mail*, 10 October 1900; *Cardiff Tide Tables and Almanack* (1893), 133; DNB, *sub.* marquess of Bute.
156 *Ibid.*; Matthews, *op. cit.*, V, 119, 136, 143–44; CCL, Bute, IX, 29.
157 *Ibid.*, IX, 31; *Parliamentary Debates*, 4th ser., XXV, 273; Blair, *op. cit.*, 79; *The Buteman*, 6 February 1869.
158 *Cardiff Times*, December 1868; *Merthyr Guardian*, December 1868; I. Humphries, *op. cit.*, 109–17.
159 Lord Riddell, *The Story of the Western Mail* (1927); CCL, Miscellaneous Bute Papers, MS 4. 459; CCL, Bute, X, 6; Blair, *op. cit.*, 80.
160 *Western Mail*, 27 January, 11 and 14 February 1874.
161 See GRO, Bute, D/DA 50–51.
162 J.M. Davies, 'A study of the effect of the Reform Act of 1884 and the Redistribution Act of 1885 upon the political structure of Glamorgan' (MA. thesis, University of Wales, 1979), *passim*.
163 *Cardiff Times*, 31 January 1874.

164 *Western Mail*, 11 February 1874; Daunton, *op. cit.*, 167–68; Humphries, *op. cit.*, 111–13.
165 *South Wales Daily News*, 24 October 1872.
166 Matthews, *op. cit.*, IV, 489.
167 CCL, Bute, XI, 5; *Weekly Mail*, 18 February 1882.
168 *Cardiff Times*, 1 July 1882; *South Wales Daily News*, 26 February, 5 March, 26 June, 16 August 1884; Daunton, *op. cit.*, 155–59.
169 PP, XII (1919), 654.
170 Blair, *op. cit.*, 174.
171 NLW, Jevons Papers, IV, 122.
172 *Western Mail*, 2 July 1886. The *South Wales Daily News*, however, attacked the estate officials rather than the marquess himself. 'Happily', it wrote (10 July 1882), 'Lord Bute is as popular as ever. The common sense of the community can always distinguish between the nobleman and his lackey.'
173 E.g., *ibid.*, 24 October 1892, 20 and 28 June 1894, 11 May 1895, 23 June 1907, 25 March 1910, 20 June 1914.
174 PP, XII (1919), 653–8.
175 *The Times*, 26 and 29 April 1947; J.A. Jones, 'Dysgu Cymraeg i'r ardalydd Bute', *Y Gwrandawr (Barn)*, August 1965, v–vi; *Western Mail*, 26 April 1947.
176 *Ibid.*, 27 July and 4 August 1928.
177 *Western Mail*, December 1910; *South Wales Daily News*, December 1910; NLW, Jevons Papers, IV, 122.
178 *Western Mail*, 28 November, 4 and 7 December 1918; *South Wales Daily News*, November and December 1918.
179 Will of the marquess of Bute (NLW, Bute, box 137).
180 *South Wales Daily News*, 27 and 29 September 1906; *Western Mail*, 13 November 1906; CCL, Bute, XI, 56.
181 Simnett, *op. cit.*, 5, 50–1, 230, 262; D.S. Barrie, *The Taff Vale Railway* (1939), 39. The total trade of the Bute docks fell from 13,054,419 tons in 1914 to 6,863,563 tons in 1938, coal exports falling from 10,278,963 tons to 4,980,479 tons.
182 NLW, Sale catalogue collection, 52, 213, 214, 219; *Estates Gazette*, 6 December 1919, 3 January 1920; J. Davies, 'The end of the great estates and the rise of freehold farming in Wales', *Welsh History Rev.* (1974), 193.
183 *Colliery Guardian*, 19 January 1915, 18 July 1919; *Western Mail*, 30 July and 1 August 1924.
184 *Ibid.*, 9 October 1926; *Estates Gazette*, 21 May and 9 July 1938; *Economist*, 31 December 1938; files relating to the Mountjoy Company (Companies House, Cardiff).
185 Claim Files, RO 8 (Coal House, Llanishen); *The Times*, 17 December 1938; Central Valuation Board, *Valuation Regions*, PP (1938)) (Cmd. 5904).
186 *The Times* and *Western Mail*, 7 August and 11 September 1947.

Peers on an industrial frontier: the earls of Dartmouth and of Dudley in the Black Country, c. 1810 to 1914

RICHARD TRAINOR

Peers on an industrial frontier: the earls of Dartmouth and of Dudley in the Black Country, c. 1810 to 1914

RICHARD TRAINOR

1 Introduction

> As an hour and a half will take the traveller from the heart of the Black Country to a typical agricultural neighbourhood so, in the higher social influences dominating town and country, is there a near relationship. The fact that the great country landlord is also, in many cases, the great proprietor of mines and factories, is at once a guarantee and a sign of the fusion between the different elements of English life, and the diverse sources of our national power. The new is ever being incorporated with the old, and the result of the process is a growing identity of interests and of feeling.[1]

Thus in 1885 T.H.S. Escott suggested the importance for the Black Country, as for other British urban areas, of the wealth and influence of the landed interest. This study of two aristocratic families with extensive landholdings in the region, explores their changing social and political rôle there during the nineteenth and early twentieth centuries. As such, it forms part of a broader investigation[2] into middle-class as well as aristocratic leaders. That larger project extends the emerging discussion of the identity, aims, methods and influence of Victorian élites[3] through a comprehensive examination of social leadership in a Midlands area which, as a major producer of coal, iron and basic metal manufactures, had an economy distinct from, although complementary to, that of neighbouring Birmingham (see fig. 6).[4]

The Black Country is an appropriate subject for an élite study for two reasons. First, although the overwhelming majority of its nineteenth-century inhabitants were working class, the region had a numerous resident middle class (broadly defined) which formed nearly 10 per cent of the local population at mid-century.[5] Moreover, despite an unusually large share of small entrepreneurs, the Black Country economy also included several big firms and many businesses employing dozens of men.[6] Thus local masters, in combination with professional and commercial men, formed a substantial, though relatively small and modest, middle class. Second, the economic and social context in which these groups operated also justifies attention. During the nineteenth century the Black Country experienced rapid expansion and subsequent relative decline. Reacting to social disorders in the early 1840s, the upper and middle classes in these grimy 'frontier' towns at first had to build up public and voluntary institutions from a primitive level. Then from the mid-1870s the protracted slump in the region's basic industries produced heavy demands on philanthropy and the Poor Law. Consequently the Black Country case is especially useful for understanding the rôle of élites in the maintenance of social stability in nineteenth-century urban Britain.

The Black Country as a whole was too large for detailed examination: in 1901 its population of nearly 675,000 was spread across 100 square miles and 19 towns (see fig. 6 and table 3). Moreover, many aspects of the area's class relations can best be observed at the level of its individual localities – which acquired many institutions and firmer local identities during the nineteenth century. Accordingly three towns – chosen for their industrial, demographic and political variety – received comparative study: West Bromwich (in greatest detail), Dudley and Bilston. West Bromwich, still mostly rural at the start of the century, soon experienced rapid expansion of industry and population. Its diverse trades then cushioned the town against the worst effects of the region's slump in the late nineteenth century. Containing a major market as well as industries, Dudley was at first a more substantial town, with more elaborate local government. However, with a less diversified economy, it was the greater victim of the region's later economic troubles. Bilston, the most thoroughly industrialized of the three, and the town most heavily committed to the Black Country's traditional trades, suffered an absolute fall in population after 1861.

Table 3   The growth of the Black Country, 1801–1911

	West Bromwich	Dudley	Bilston	Black Country*
1801	5,700	10,100	6,900	97,200
1811	7,500	13,900	9,600	129,000
1821	9,500	18,200	12,000	159,900
1831	15,300	23,000	14,500	205,900
1841	26,100	31,200	20,200	284,900
1851	34,600	38,000	23,500	362,000
1861	41,800	45,000	24,400	457,300
1871	47,900	43,800	24,200	498,500
1881	56,300	46,300	22,700	546,600
1891	59,500	45,700	23,500	591,700
1901	65,100	48,700	24,000	671,000
1911	68,300	51,100	25,700	729,000

* the Registration Districts of Dudley, Stourbridge, Walsall, West Bromwich and Wolverhampton (slightly modified).
Source: Published census; G.J. Barnsby, 'Social conditions in the Black Country in the nineteenth century' (Ph.D. thesis, University of Birmingham, 1969), 2.

Investigation of the élites of these towns first involved scrutiny of the number, and the social, political and religious backgrounds, of the individuals who held leading positions in principal local institutions. It was then appropriate to consider the methods – and, more speculatively, the success – of the involvement of these élites in industrial relations, partisan and religious activities, philanthropy and the Poor Law, and local government. This analysis revealed the growth – mainly during the second half of the century – of larger, more diverse and more coherent élites, whose increasingly elaborate social interventions played a major rôle in promoting and preserving the relatively great degree of social harmony which characterized the Black Country from the 1850s.

Since local patricians made significant contributions to these élites, the Black Country is also an attractive place in which to study the urban activities of the nineteenth- and early twentieth-century peerage. Many aristocrats resided in parts of Staffordshire and Worcestershire not far from the smoke and bustle of the Black Country.[7] Moreover, several grandees – notably the dukes of Sutherland and Cleveland, and lords Bradford, Dartmouth, Dudley and Hatherton – owned Black Country land of considerable mineral or residential value, and several participated in the social and political life of the region.[8] Accordingly, the Black Country provides an excellent locale for analysis of problems related to the aristocracy which have concerned historians of nineteenth- and early twentieth-century Britain.[9] Here, in particular, one may find indications of the means by which peers preserved so much of their influence in an increasingly urban and industrialized nation.

This essay explores these themes by investigating the activities of the Legges, earls of Dartmouth, in West Bromwich, with comparative reference to the participation of the even wealthier Wards, earls of Dudley, in the affairs of Dudley. This comparative exercise breaks new ground by analysing aristocratic influence from the perspective of differing but basically similar industrial towns as well as from the viewpoints of the peers themselves. These aristocrats are particularly suitable subjects for this purpose, since they combined major Black Country economic interests with significant social and political activities in the area. Because the essay focuses on particular patricians and towns, it cannot exhaust the subject of aristocratic influence in the Black Country. However, reference is made, where appropriate, to the broadly similar, though often less intense, interventions of grandees such as Bradford, Hatherton and Lichfield.

This contribution is an expansion of those parts of the thesis which deal with the aristocracy and, by frequent reference to other aspects of that work (especially to the activities of leading middle-class industrialists), it places aristocratic leadership in the context of local élites generally. The scope of this study differs from that of the thesis in two additional respects. First, it focuses on two towns rather than three, omitting Bilston which lacked active aristocratic social and political influence for most of the period. Second, it begins earlier and ends later: by starting with the 1810s rather than the 1830s, it covers a period of local aristocratic strength which was ebbing two decades later; and by ending in 1914 rather than in the 1890s, it is able to deal more fully with two additional holders of the titles. Inevitably, though, the conclusions reached are more firmly based for the years c. 1840–c. 1890 than for the preceding and succeeding decades.

After a survey of the lucrative economic activities of the Dartmouths and Dudleys, attention will fall first on the period, ending in the mid-1830s, when the earls extracted from their estates largely unquestioned social and political influence. The essay will then consider the following 25 years, which brought challenges

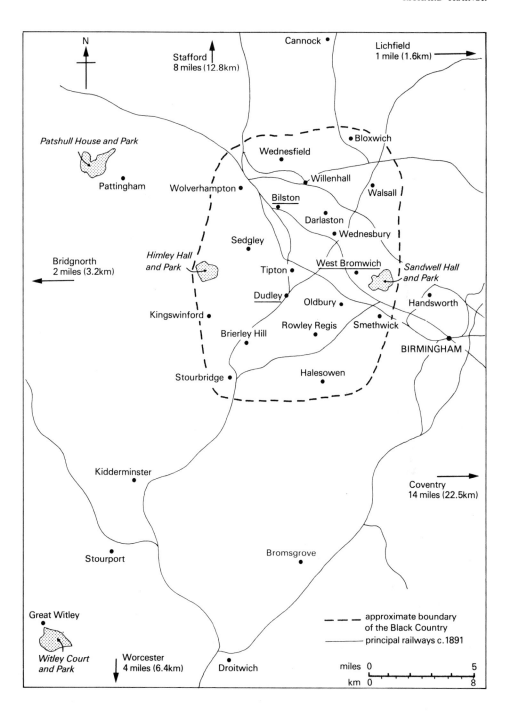

Figure 6. The Black Country and its vicinity in the later nineteenth century.

to the peers' authority from the local middle class. However, the section dealing with the period from approximately 1860 will demonstrate that the earls developed a more modest but more effective local social rôle, as they wisely abandoned attempts to dominate society and politics in these localities, and instead adjusted to rôles as celebrities with significant but limited influence. In this fashion they supported increasingly active voluntary societies and local authorities which were now led principally by members of the local middle class. Although economic, partisan and sectarian tensions persisted, by the end of the century the middle class leaders of both towns had generally satisfactory relations with their respective peers. By cooperating to promote 'civic unity', the earls gained goodwill towards their estates, while the local middle class secured contributions and prestige for their own projects. Thus both formed part of an urban élite whose coherence and effective authority, like its size and activities, increased substantially during the second half of the century.[10] An epilogue will suggest that only after 1914 did class-based politics and the earls' economic and social withdrawal virtually destroy their local influence.

2 The families, their seats and their estates

The Legges, earls and barons of Dartmouth, and viscounts Lewisham (the heir's courtesy title), had acquired their barony in 1682 and their two remaining titles in 1711. By the time the third earl died in 1810, conspicuous public service, royal largesse and marriages to well-selected heiresses had made the Dartmouths a family of talent and fortune. Four of the heirs to this legacy are relevant to this essay (see Appendix 1). William, the fourth earl, succeeded his father at the age of 26 and fathered 15 children. The eldest, William Walter, the fifth earl assumed the title in 1853. The sixth earl, William Heneage succeeded his father in 1891. Twelve years earlier he had married a daughter of the earl of Leicester; she gave birth in 1881 to William, the future seventh earl.[11]

The Wards – variously barons Ward, viscounts Dudley and Ward, and earls of Dudley – traced their association with the titles and the region back to the 1640s. By the early nineteenth century they had established themselves as one of the wealthiest landowning families in the West Midlands. The family provides six characters for this story (see Appendix 2). William, third viscount Dudley and Ward, and eighth baron Ward, had inherited the title and estates from his brother in 1788. His son John William succeeded as fourth viscount in 1823 and was named earl of Dudley and viscount Ednam four years later. (He is referred to as the fourth viscount throughout this essay in order to avoid confusion with the earls of the second creation.) When he died unmarried in 1833 the earldom and viscountcy became extinct, but the barony of Ward passed to a second cousin, the Rev. William Humble Ward. On the latter's death in 1835 his son William Humble succeeded as eleventh baron Ward. The younger Ward had already inherited the estate, which was held in trust for him until 1845. He became earl of Dudley and viscount Ednam (the heir's courtesy title) of the second creation in 1860, and is referred to as Ward until 1860 and as Dudley thereafter. William Humble succeeded his father as second earl in 1885, and was followed in 1932 by his son William Humble Eric (1894–1969).[12]

The Dartmouths had owned the estate of Sandwell, in the parish of West

Bromwich, since 1701. By the later eighteenth century Sandwell Hall had become the family's chief residence. But by 1840 it was 'much injured by smoke'. Desiring an unpolluted and more prestigious seat, the fourth earl purchased in 1848 for £297,000 a large estate and house at Patshull, a village on the western edge of Staffordshire about eight miles west of Wolverhampton and fourteen miles from West Bromwich (see fig. 6). The fourth earl moved to Patshull shortly before his death, and his son, who had preceded him there, never again lived at Sandwell.[13]

The Wards, having abandoned Dudley Castle as a residence in the seventeenth century, had settled at Himley, four miles west of Dudley (see fig. 6). However, by the late 1830s nearby industry had made Himley, like Sandwell, unsuitable as the 'Residence of a Nobleman of considerable income'. Therefore, in 1839 Ward – backed by the trustees – agreed to pay the huge sum of £668,000 for Witley Court, a house and estate in the rural Worcestershire parish of Great Witley, about 20 miles southwest of Dudley. From 1846 Witley Court was Ward's chief residence and Himley Hall became a dower house.[14]

Both families had substantial incomes – rising for much of the nineteenth century – and landholdings with which to support these acquisitions and the lifestyle they entailed. In the early 1880s Dartmouth owned 19,518 acres. According to Bateman's figures of gross annual income – which underestimated the family's urban revenues – this land yielded the considerable sum of £58,657. Dudley's 25,554 acres provided the yet higher total of £123,176.[15] Moreover, unlike many landowners, neither family suffered drastic diminutions in income in the late nineteenth century. Agricultural problems and stagnation in Black Country trades only gradually cut Dudley's receipts from the peaks of the 1880s. Similarly, the Dartmouths' mining and building revenues evidently more than compensated for rural woes.[16] In addition, buoyant incomes meant that neither family was crippled by debt. The Dudley estate paid off the Witley Court purchase by 1854 and apparently borrowed little thereafter, until the second earl's personal spending soared in the early twentieth century.[17] With more limited means the Dartmouths took longer to repay mortgages incurred for buying Patshull: lingering debt, and the burden of supporting relatives, distressed the sixth earl when he inherited in 1891. Yet by the end of the decade he was able to take on a lavish London town house.[18] Thus, though the Dudleys were significantly better off, the Dartmouths too were well-heeled and perhaps reduced the gap between the families towards the end of the period.

In income and wealth these noblemen surpassed all but a few peers and upper middle-class businessmen in the region. Of those aristocrats with significant holdings in Staffordshire, only Anglesey (£110,598), Cleveland (£97,398), Shrewsbury (£62,382), and Sutherland (£141,667) had gross incomes in the early 1880s greater than Dartmouth. Only Sutherland – and five other peers in the entire nation – surpassed Dudley.[19] Comparisons with businessmen lacking broad acres are more difficult. Probate values give rough estimates of wealth but understate the peers' means because of the omission of all real estate until 1898, and of settled realty until 1925. Because of this anomaly the first earl of Dudley's probate value of £1,026,000 (1885) trailed that of the atypically well-landed and especially well-to-do ironmaster W.O. Foster (£2,588,000 in 1899). But the earl's total approximately equalled that of another major ironmaster, Sir Alfred Hickman (who died in 1910), and it far exceeded the values of such leading Black Country businessmen as Sir Benjamin Hingley (£158,697 in 1905), J.H. Chance (£253,013 in 1900) and Timothy

Kenrick (£156,479 in 1885). These smaller sums, substantial enough in themselves, were more comparable to that of the fifth earl of Dartmouth (£119,811 in 1891). But if the latter's gross annual landed income is converted to the approximate sale value of his land,[20] an estimate of £1,936,00 emerges, far behind Dudley's £4,065,000, but well ahead of the probate values of most upper middle-class rivals. Whatever the exact comparison, at least one of the Black Country's top iron-masters thought Dartmouth much his superior in wealth.[21]

Both families held much of their land in the West Midlands, and drew a substantial portion of their income from property there. This pattern was especially marked in the case of the Dudleys (see table 4):

Table 4   The earls of Dudley and of Dartmouth: acreage and income, c. 1883

	county	acres	%	gross annual value in £	%
Earls of Dudley	Worcestershire	14,698	57·5	48,545	39·4
	Staffordshire	4,730	18·5	68,460	55·6
	Merioneth	4,472	17·5	3,114	2·5
	Roxburgh	1,086	4·2	2,825	2·3
	Shropshire	568	2·2	232	0·2
	total	25,554	99·9	123,176	100·0
Earls of Dartmouth	Yorkshire, West Riding	8,024	41·1	20,520	35·0
	Staffordshire	7,316	37·5	16,356	27·9
	Buckinghamshire	2,195	11·2	4,700	8·0
	Shropshire	1,096	5·6	2,711	4·6
	Sussex	454	2·3	550	0·9
	Kent	391	2·0	10,470	17·8
	Middlesex	42	0·2	3,350	5·7
	total	19,518	99·9	58,657	99·9

Source: J. Bateman, *The Great Landowners of Great Britain and Ireland* (1883 edn), 119, 140. Note: The metropolis is *not* included in these figures.

In the 1880s over three-quarters of their land, and 95 per cent of their income, came from Staffordshire and Worcestershire, and roughly three-fifths of their acres in these counties lay in the Black Country. Despite fluctuations in revenue, the family estates there were more valuable than their nearby rural properties.[22]

The estates from which the Dartmouths drew significant income were more numerous, more widely scattered, and more heterogeneous. Most of their hold-ings, including those in and around the Black Country, had substantial agricultural components. Yet the family's Kent property, situated around Lewisham, was already valuable as building land in the 1880s, and evidently became more lucrative in succeeding decades.[23] The Dartmouths had also developed an estate in St Pancras, and their West Riding properties, yielding more than one-third of gross income, included mines and property let for building and industrial purposes, as well as farms.[24] Altogether, Staffordshire contained almost 40 per cent of Dartmouth's acres, and of these about two-fifths lay in the Black Country. They were of disproportionately great value, and their yield was increasing; but since the revenue from the Dartmouths' urban estates elsewhere was also bouyant, it seems unlikely that Black Country receipts – though substantial and perhaps increasingly important – ever became dominant in the earls' income.[25]

Despite this contrast between the two families, within the Black Country both earls were major landowners. Dudley, indeed, was the greatest of the district's proprietors. In the 1880s the earl possessed over one-third of the total acreage of Dudley and eight nearby parishes. He held just over half of the town of Dudley itself, and was also lord of the manor. Dartmouth, too, ranked as one of the 'great landed proprietors' of south Staffordshire. Within the Black Country most of his property lay in West Bromwich where he owned almost two-fifths of the land subject to tithe at mid-century.[26] Nevertheless, other aristocratic families, notably the Bradfords and Hathertons in Walsall, also held valuable Black Country property, and even within their home parishes Sir Horace St Paul in Dudley, and the ironmaking Williams family in West Bromwich, owned large parcels. Moreover, there were many small freeholders and copyholders in the Black Country towns.[27] So, while the Dudleys and Dartmouths were by far the largest landowners in these localities, and substantial proprietors in the region as a whole, they by no means monopolized local landed property.

Both earls enhanced their economic importance by developing their Black Country estates. For Dartmouth the Sandwell property continued to yield substantial agricultural revenues throughout the period. But mining and building receipts became predominant by the 1880s. Following a helpful early nineteenth-century enclosure act, the fourth earl had drawn significant profits from West Bromwich pits as early as the 1820s. And from mid-century the family's costly removal from Sandwell both allowed and necessitated more intensive non-agricultural exploitation of the estate. Mining revenue increased, especially after the unusually large Sandwell Park Colliery began yielding substantial royalties in the 1880s – a time of general distress in Black Country coal. Meanwhile, the earl had also begun a middle-class residential scheme on the estate. These developments made Sandwell more profitable, and Dartmouth, whose relative economic importance had declined as the town and its industry expanded rapidly in the second quarter of the century, thereby became a more substantial figure in the local and regional economy.[28]

The Dudley estate's diversification accelerated during the late eighteenth and nineteenth centuries. In that period it undertook 'a wide range of economic activities including agriculture, extensive mining and quarrying operations, the manufacture of bricks, pig-iron and finished iron goods, and . . . its own canal and railway systems.' The Wards secured especially favourable enclosure acts which guaranteed them access to minerals without liability for surface damage. Improved management of coal, combined with expansion into high-quality iron manufacture, further enhanced the economic position of the properties in the decades surrounding mid-century. The estate reached its industrial peak during the period 1860–85 when the region as a whole had mixed fortunes. Although some contraction and reorganization occurred after 1880, the Dudleys began steel production and – like the Dartmouths – sank a large new colliery. Urban cottage rents and sales supplemented the earls' income. However, in contrast to the Dartmouths, the Dudleys did not engage in systematic building development. From the early nineteenth century, industrial sources, especially coal, provided most estate revenue.[29]

Because of such non-agricultural activities, the peers' importance in the local economy paralleled their shares in the area's landownership. Each was a major economic force in his home parish, though both – especially Dartmouth – had upper middle-class rivals. Dartmouth was formidable enough for his coal explorations to alarm the managers of the Dudley estate.[30] Yet even in West Bromwich few enterprises depended on Dartmouth for land or for raw materials. Dudley was a much larger employer as well as a significantly greater and more diversified producer. He was by far the greater economic force.

In fact, the earl of Dudley – as the landlord of many firms and a key supplier of raw materials to others – exercised more control over the Black Country economy than any other single proprietor. Only one other ironmaster enjoyed independence in raw materials, and the quantity and quality of the earl's iron output gave him additional leverage. Especially from the 1840s the estate enjoyed leading influence over regional prices for coal and iron. These were agreed by associations of ironmasters and coalmasters which the agents often headed.[31] Of course, the size and complexity of the region's economy – and its increasing vulnerability to outside economic trends – prevented dictation by the estate. For example, smaller producers often defied the decisions of the price-setting bodies. More substantial firms could also be difficult: in the 1840s a coalition of businessmen, led by significant opposition within Dudley itself, successfully defied the estate's railway plans in the 'battle of the gauges'. Nevertheless, even the victorious scheme had to make special concessions to Lord Ward's interests. In price determination, too, the threat of estate action frequently won cooperation from the recalcitrant.[32]

The estate's formidable economic power had mixed effects on its popularity. Dudley and his agents gained goodwill as well as acquiescence from the fact that the estate was 'the most extensive iron making and coal producing establishment in South Staffordshire, and one which has done as much as any other to keep up the reputation of the district'. In addition, its coordination of prices, like its extension of credit to other firms in the slump of the early 1840s, often served the interests of the trade as a whole. But smaller producers, in particular, were frequently unenthusiastic about the estate's influence.[33] At some cost to the estate's standing within the local middle class, then, the economic might of the earl's enterprises allowed him and his agents considerable leverage over the region's economic policies. In this respect Dartmouth counted for much less.

How far were the peers themselves involved in the economic activities of their Black Country estates? Like most nineteenth-century titled industrialists the Dartmouths were usually lessors rather than entrepreneurs. The fourth earl had engaged in detailed, often acrimonious negotiations with the lessees of his mines.[34] But with the accession of his son the implementation – and, to a large degree, the making – of policy devolved on the family's agents, Messrs Thynne of London. The Thynnes – operating through correspondence, periodic visits and resident subordinates – executed the absentee earls' policy of securing enhanced returns from the Sandwell estate.[35]

The earls of Dudley were exceptional among great landowners in their continued direct entrepreneurship. In the later nineteenth century this policy covered the estate's iron works and its more profitable pits. However, the peers had much help in the oversight of their industrial interests. After reorganization during the trusteeship period the estate included a well-developed bureaucracy headed by a mineral agent who resided in an imposing house in Dudley. For 19 years from 1845, Richard Smith took much responsibility for estate affairs, becoming a figure of economic and social importance in his own right. His son Frederick played a similar if less intense rôle between 1864 and 1870, as did his grandson Edward Fisher Smith (1870–86) and C. Tylden Wright (1886–91).[36] The Dudleys, therefore, had perhaps even less occasion to intervene in estate business than did the Dartmouths. Although the second viscount had been a skilful economic strategist, his two successors had little interest in trade. The young Lord Ward kept an eye on his interests before obtaining full control of his property, and he discussed business affairs with his agents afterward. But he was not active in day-to-day management. The second earl 'was never too taken with the world of business'.[37] Increased responsibility thus fell on Gilbert Claughton. As the earl's cousin as well as his agent (1891–1912) Claughton further developed the rôle of surrogate peer which the Smiths had pioneered.

On neither estate, however, did the agents reduce the earls to impotence. True, the subordinates (especially on the Dudley estate) handled routine matters without reference to the aristocrats, and even on basic decisions the agents' recommendations carried great weight. Yet the peers' consent remained crucial for major initiatives, and they received regular briefings on estate business generally. So they could intervene in business affairs if they wished, but kept their days free from humdrum estate operations.[38] Lords Dartmouth and Dudley had leisure, therefore, for aristocratic socializing: they also had time and attention to spare for social and political interventions connected with these valuable estates.

3 Dominance and deference, c. 1810–35

For most of this period the landownership, early industrial activities and prestige of the Legge and Ward families gave them predominant influence in these localities. For while the local middle class was expanding rapidly, its institutions were, as yet, poorly developed: insofar as they existed, they were mainly Tory, Anglican and sympathetic to the nobility.

Throughout the eighteenth century, and into the fourth decade of the nineteenth, the earls of Dartmouth were the single most important religious, philanthropic and political force in West Bromwich. In many respects they dominated the town's affairs, and they were active in the county, and in other West Midland localities as well. The fourth earl served as Vice Lord Lieutenant of Staffordshire on various occasions; in Birmingham he continued a family tradition by supporting several of the town's major philanthropic institutions with contributions and visits; and he also spread his largesse to his estates elsewhere, notably in Yorkshire.[39]

In particular, the Dartmouths gradually accelerated their involvement in the increasingly substantial town of West Bromwich. The second and third earls spent much time at Sandwell. They were more interested in national than in parish affairs, but their wives helped to compensate for this preoccupation. The third countess, for example, promoted a local school in the early nineteenth century.[40]

Moreover, the fourth earl made a direct personal impact on West Bromwich, largely because his personality and career differed so much from those of his father and grandfather. Like them, the fourth earl had a strong sense of religion and duty. As a fellow of the Royal Society he also showed some intellectual distinction. But in contrast to his predecessors the fourth earl, a 'shy silent peer', played little part in national politics. This was not surprising. One observer had never seen a man 'so little calculated for publick meeting'. Yet Dartmouth took a great interest in West Bromwich, where he resided for much of the year. There the characteristics which disqualified him from national fame were – at least until the 1830s – more assets than liabilities. Lack of personal ostentation and kindness to the local poor earned him the affectionate nickname of 'Billy-my-Lord'.[41]

The Dartmouths were particularly dominant in local religious affairs. The second earl's intense interest in the evangelical revival prompted him to use his religious patronage, in West Bromwich and elsewhere, to reward clergymen of his persuasion. He also provided a new house for the incumbent. His grandson, though considerably less evangelical, was 'before all things, a faithful son of the Church'. The fourth earl improved the fabric and enlarged the endowment of the parish church. Various middle-class businessmen joined him in founding the first three district churches in the town. But Dartmouth obtained two of the livings, laid the foundation stone of one church, subscribed more than half the initial sum for the second and involved himself personally in its promotion.[42]

Although by no means the only philanthropist in West Bromwich, the fourth earl was the town's largest single benefactor in secular as well as religious causes. His giving was diverse and substantial. He made annual donations of bedding and clothes to the local poor, increasing this relief in years of special distress. In 1817, for instance, it was reported that 'The sums he has expended in charity must be immense . . . his draper's bill, for bed-clothes alone, amounts to £500. A hundred quarts of soup are also daily distributed by his cooks'.[43] Dartmouth supported local Anglican schools, built the town's first public baths, and made part of his estate available for recreational alternatives to bullbaiting and dogfighting. He played an active part in many of these causes, and also indulged in eccentric, locally-famous projects, such as giving donkeys to the poor. Such conspicuous generosity, combined with a reputation for discreet aid to individuals in difficulty, created considerable goodwill for the earl in West Bromwich and elsewhere. As a Birmingham paper remarked, 'Few persons have generously given away so much money, and rendered such substantial benefit to the cause of religion and philanthropy, yet with so little noise and ostentation.'[44]

The Dartmouths were also predominant in West Bromwich local government until the 1830s. The fourth earl, an active J.P., was the leading local magistrate. In 1835, for example, the vestry requested the churchwardens to approach Dartmouth concerning the suppression of Sunday drinking.[45] Manorial authority at first proved more troublesome. In the eighteenth century the first earl lost a legal battle with a 'little litigious citizen', a London merchant who was lord of the manor of West Bromwich. However, Dartmouth did not recognize the victor's authority, and his descendant acquired the manor in 1823. Its court leet and baron played no important rôle in local government. Still, until the 1830s the earls experienced little difficulty in their dealings with the more important vestry. In addition, Dartmouth became the first chairman of the West Bromwich Board of Guardians.[46]

The first three earls of Dartmouth had found West Bromwich a deferential retreat from national politics. As one eighteenth-century bard put it, around Sandwell 'the peaceful hamlet' was 'spread content', rendering 'submission due'. The fourth earl, too, was 'one of the institutions of the place in the days when West Bromwich was still a village.'[47] Assuredly, during the early nineteenth century the town's industry, population and middle class were expanding rapidly, and the existence of considerable support in West Bromwich for parliamentary reform – which Dartmouth opposed – suggested future diminution of influence. But the earl had expanded his economic and social activities as the town grew: in the early 1830s the family remained prominent, and it enjoyed considerable local esteem, especially (but not exclusively) among Tories and Anglicans.

The influence of the Ward family in Dudley in the early nineteenth century was in some respects even more firmly based. Because of the Wards' massive local wealth and many involvements, Dudley seemed, as late as 1868, 'The *apanage* of one noble family, whose name overshadows or drowns in its illumination all the lesser stars.'[48] The latter were already of some economic and social importance by the 1810s; but well into the century most followed the lead of the Wards.

Neither the third nor the fourth viscount matched the fourth earl of Dartmouth's enthusiasm for parish affairs. Yet the Wards interested themselves in the Black Country from time to time. The third viscount 'preferred port wine and fiddling to the pursuit of either politics or literature'. Still, he could stay in touch with local affairs from nearby Himley, where he spent most of the year.[49] His son, a bookish eccentric who became Canning's foreign secretary, cared much more for national politics and travel than for parish life or domesticity. However, after inheriting the estates the fourth viscount frequently stayed at Himley and manifested concern for local problems – until insanity overtook him shortly before his death.[50] And, whatever their preoccupations, the Wards already had agents to watch over the family's local interests.

The family's philanthropy gained it a local reputation for benevolence. The third viscount was known as 'the rich man's model and the poor man's friend'. He repaired the castle, landscaped its grounds and opened them to the public. In addition, he headed the list of contributors to soup kitchens and to the rebuilding of the parish church.[51] His son continued this tradition. As well as subscribing to charities in other Black Country localities – and in Birmingham, Stafford and Worcester – the fourth viscount gave regularly to Dudley's Anglican schools and churches and to its fledgling voluntary societies. The amounts were substantial but not huge. The local middle class, which developed earlier than in West Bromwich, bore a greater share of Dudley's philanthropy than did its equivalent in Dartmouth's parish. But the Wards' donations were often crucial.[52]

In local government the Wards did not, like Dartmouth, dominate the Bench personally. However, they could rely on local J.P.s who, for instance, called in troops during the strikes of 1842. In addition, the family enjoyed the cooperation of an active court leet and, from 1791, of town commissioners. Besides transacting some estate business the court leet enjoyed a measure of control over roads and markets. On one occasion they ordered Lord Dudley and Ward to mend a street. In general, though, this body protected the estate's interests while exercising limited supervision over local health and safety.[53] These were the more direct responsibility of the commissioners, 'a self-perpetuating body . . . Tory in composition and generally considered to be under the influence of the Castle.' The town's market tolls caused friction between the commissioners and the estate. But eventually the fourth viscount made a generous settlement, and the two parties cooperated in planning new streets. By the 1830s the businessmen brothers Isaac and Thomas Badger – commissioners and magistrates – coordinated 'a small Tory clique which . . . ran the town in cooperation with the Castle.'[54]

Such lieutenants and superior local wealth enabled the Wards to maintain, into the 1830s, a predominance in Dudley at least equal to that which greater personal exertion and less well-developed institutions secured for the Dartmouths in West Bromwich. Moreover, unlike the Legges, the Wards enjoyed much influence in several other Black Country localities as well. Nevertheless, the Wards experienced some local difficulties before the fourth viscount's death in 1833. In industrial relations, rival coalmasters had combined with estate subcontractors and colliers to force the abandonment of an attempt by the estate to employ its miners directly, and the miners' riots menaced Himley and the family's pits. These crises were infrequent, but such episodes revealed a vulnerability that lurked beneath the estate's economic might. In town affairs early stirrings of civic self-confidence had surfaced in the first of many disputes concerning access to the castle grounds. In the 1820s protests forced the estate to drop plans to build its agent's house there.[55]

Parliamentary politics, too, had begun to pose problems. The family's acreage and wealth created the potential for significant influence in the politics of the area. All four viscounts had held seats in the West Midlands, but neither the third nor, especially, the fourth holder of the title seriously attempted to achieve more. At the end of the latter's life, however, his opposition to reform, contempt for the numerous Dudley reformers and indirect kinship to the aspiring Tory candidate aroused his interest in the forthcoming election to the new parliamentary borough of Dudley. The fourth viscount's reference to a 'hornet's nest . . . of Jacobins and Dissenters of the most noxious breed' indicates that local radicals had already created difficulties for the estate and its allies. The Ward interest apparently played little part in the election: the viscount had gone insane beforehand. But the victory of the Whig Sir John Campbell did not augur well for estate influence in the town.[56] Storm clouds were looming, then. But during the period preceding the 1830s the Wards had enjoyed a great deal of influence both in Dudley and in the Black Country generally.

4 The challenge to aristocratic authority, c. 1835–60

During this period the Legges and Wards suffered a diminution, though by no means the destruction, of their local influence, as the growing size and self-confidence of the local middle class, the rise of radicalism and of militant dissent, and the peers' own misjudgments, combined to erode their earlier predominance.

By the 1830s – a decade when the population of West Bromwich increased by a staggering 71 per cent – the town contained many potential rivals to the Dartmouths for social and political leadership. These ranged from large-scale manufacturers and ironmasters to smaller tradesmen and petty landlords who often spoke for a host of small ratepayers, many of whom were workingmen. Some of these businessmen, mainly Tory Anglicans, provided allies for Lord Dartmouth in his philanthropic and political efforts. However, many others, usually Liberal nonconformists, acted independently or in direct opposition to the earl. The Kenricks, for example, had occasionally cooperated with the Dartmouths in philanthropic projects. But these Unitarian manufacturers placed more emphasis on their own schools, and later supported self-improvement institutes for which Dartmouth had little enthusiasm.[57] Less polite competition for the Legges emanated from the lower ranks of the middle class. Through such vehicles as the local political union, men like the barber George Wilkes battled for radical, nonconformist and pinchpenny 'ratepayers' causes inimical to the Dartmouths.[58] Of course the parish had long contained nonconformists: the Kenricks had moved their factory to West Bromwich as early as the 1790s. But it was only from the 1830s, in a highly-charged national and regional political atmosphere, with local institutions starting to expand, that these groups began to assert themselves independently of the Legges and the Tory Anglican élite which they headed.

Whatever the religious and partisan alignments had been, the general increase in middle-class numbers and wealth must necessarily have undermined the family's influence. Eventually, the earls would alter their approach to the locality in order to preserve what remained of their position; but in the interim, with a large number of militant nonconformist radicals confronting a resident peer unused to rivals and reluctant to compromise, the Dartmouths' position in West Bromwich experienced turbulence and decline.

In local public affairs the fourth earl first encountered difficulty over church rates, as his fervent Anglicanism confronted a local nonconformist majority. Church Rates soon became a sore point for dissenters, radicals and other rate-payers. In order to prevent a direct clash some West Bromwich Anglicans urged reliance on voluntary contributions. Dartmouth played a key rôle in preventing such a compromise, yet was unable to avoid a clear defeat for the church rate party in an 1837 poll. He then pursued a vendetta against the leading local abolitionist for an allegedly libellous pamphlet. The controversial nature of Dartmouth's position on this issue further revealed itself in the anonymous payment of the £20 fine which he secured against his antagonist. No further attempt was made to levy a church rate in West Bromwich. Dartmouth's role in the dispute revealed important limits to his influence and left much bitterness in its wake.[59]

The earl's activities during the strikes of 1842 give further indications of the weaknesses, and lingering strengths, of his local position. On the positive side, Dartmouth played a leading rôle – as commander of the militia, acting Lord Lieutenant, and chief local magistrate – in restoring order in the county generally and in West Bromwich in particular. Until late August he helped to keep the peace without seriously alienating either the employers or the men. However, his situation became more difficult when miners' representatives asked the magistrates to arrange a meeting with the coalmasters. Though favouring conciliation he stressed the limitations of his official position:

> Lord Dartmouth – I do not see that you can do better than appoint men to meet the masters . . . and state your grievances.
> Shelton [a collier] – Will your Lordship call the masters to meet us?
> Lord Dartmouth – I have no power as a magistrate to call together either masters or men.
> Shelton – Your Lordship has great influence.
> Lord Dartmouth – In my individual capacity I will do all I can for you.[60]

After further calls for a meeting Dartmouth commissioned one of his lessees to use his name in summoning such a conference. But the meeting proved a fiasco. Although the proceedings were amiable and produced promises of reform by both sides, very few masters attended. The strike was already failing, the employers thought, and there was resentment that the gathering had been called by 'a comparatively young and small master'.[61] Yet the businessmen's absence also indicated Dartmouth's limited leverage over Black Country bosses.

This episode revealed and worsened Dartmouth's awkward position between workingmen and employers. As he told the meeting, he was neither a friend of the workers nor a coalmaster. Subsequently both parties would realize that Dartmouth lacked 'enough influence to have got . . . men and masters together'. The working men might wonder whether a property owner who drew industrial income, however indirectly, could be a reliable ally in such disputes. To the masters Dartmouth evidently seemed an outsider prone to excessive sympathy with working men. He was sufficiently involved in trade to clash with businessmen but not adequately engaged to bully them. In a town and region undergoing rapid expansion and experiencing tense relations between masters and men, an 'amphibious' figure like Dartmouth was increasingly isolated. The events of 1842 indicated that he remained a figure of importance in the region as well as the single most prominent person in West Bromwich; yet the strike had also demonstrated the limitations of his position.[62]

Dartmouth's interventions in local government during the 1830s and 1840s provide further evidence that his earlier predominance had given way to diminished and disputed influence. By 1839 the estate was locked in battle with the 'Radical Overseers of the Bye Roads' concerning damage caused by Dartmouth's pits. In 1844 he condemned the rate-conscious guardians he had once headed for their opposition to a Union workhouse. On the same occasion he successfully opposed, at Quarter Sessions, a West Bromwich petition calling for the replacement of the county police by less expensive local constables. Over 2,000 ratepayers, ranging across the social spectrum and representing more than three-quarters of the total assessment of the town, had called for the removal of a force Dartmouth had been instrumental in introducing into the parish.[63]

The terms in which the earl fought this challenge to his authority demonstrated his isolation from poor and rich alike. On the one hand, Dartmouth provided evidence of his unpopularity with the volatile smaller ratepayers of West Bromwich by citing local protests against his allegedly light rate assessment. But he also launched an attack on the town's industrialists, arguing that 'during a period in . . . which the population of West Bromwich had increased more than threefold, and the wealth more than sevenfold, the annual subscriptions to the national schools (exclusive of those of my own family) fell off about one-half'. A year earlier, he went on, the town had failed to take advantage of a national relief fund: 'not one of the recipients of the large income of West Bromwich . . . not one of those opulent individuals who have signed the memorial, stood forth to second the motion'.[64] Thus did Dartmouth's reply bristle with rage at the impudence as well as the meanness of the petitioners.

It may well be that the charity of the middle class had not increased as fast as its wealth, at least among businessmen of medium and small means. But Dartmouth ignored contributions to local nonconformist schools as well as substantial middle-class donations to the town's district churches. In any case, the fact that so many citizens, wealthy and struggling, Conservative and Liberal, Anglican and noncon-formist, called for the removal of a force so long supported by Dartmouth underscored the considerable decline in his local influence. And his ill-tempered response probably further weakened his position.

Like their other interventions, the Dartmouths' involvement in parliamentary elections during this period brought the family an embattled, precarious promi-nence. Between the 1830s and the 1850s, aristocratic influence in Black Country politics faced a sharp challenge.[65] The First Reform Act created largely urban constituencies – Wolverhampton, Walsall,[66] Dudley and south Staffordshire – fraught with difficulty for management by landed, often Tory interests. Yet, here as elsewhere, the aristocracy retained much economic power and social prestige, and local businessmen were slow in turning to Liberalism. As a result, landed influence over Black Country elections, especially for county seats, only gradually declined. For example, Liberal and Tory representatives of the landed interest divided the two south Staffordshire seats until 1854. Still, by the 1850s, in the Black Country as in other urban areas, peers exercised such leverage only where they adjusted to the increasing importance of the middle class.[67]

Various factors hindered the Dartmouths' successful exploitation of this awk-ward rôle. First, the fourth earl staunchly defended causes which were dead or dying in the Black Country. One of only 22 peers who resisted the Reform Bill to the end, Dartmouth also served as president of the Wolverhampton District Agricultural Protection Society. Second, unlike his grandfather, and in contrast to his contemporary Hatherton, Dartmouth did not play an important part in representing the views of local businessmen in the House of Lords.[68] Third, even in their days of national political prominence the Dartmouths had not wielded much influence over elections, either in Staffordshire or elsewhere. Nevertheless, the family also had advantages, especially once the future fifth earl came of age in 1844. Since the Dartmouths were now proprietors of 'a large landed property and also . . . a mining property', they were especially suitable for a constituency such as south Staffordshire with significant rural as well as urban elements. In addition, the fourth earl's energetic support of Tory organization efforts, in other parts of the region as well as in West Bromwich, made him one of the area's leading Conservatives.[69]

When the 'Tory' seat for south Staffordshire fell vacant in 1849 the family's standing propelled Lord Lewisham into an unopposed return. Yet he had to submit to interrogation by the leaders of the Black Country iron trade, and they accepted Lewisham only when no ironmaster stood for election. Moreover, re-election in 1852 depended on the heir's disguising his continued support for Protection. Worse still, the 1854 by-election which followed Lewisham's elevation to the Lords produced a sharp defeat for his cousin at the hands of a free-trading Liberal eldest son backed by the ironmasters who soon produced their own M.P.[70] Thus the young earl found himself an advocate of a style of politics and a political cause which were in decline in the Black Country in the 1850s. Strong support in West Bromwich in 1854 (as in 1835) for the Liberal candidate, with sharp criticism of the deceased fourth earl, underscored the bleakness of his son's position.[71]

During the 1830s, 1840s and early 1850s, the fourth earl had found himself in opposition to the consensus in West Bromwich regarding Church Rates, strikes, local government and parliamentary elections. Most members of the local middle class preferred Liberal nonconformity and inexpensive social provision to the earl's more lavish Tory paternalism. The many smaller ratepayers, meanwhile, were too well-off to benefit much from the earl's philanthropy, but lacked the resources to enable them to support expensive parish projects with equanimity. In addition, many members of both groups apparently resented the earl's frequent, forceful interventions in local affairs. Of course, Dartmouth retained many allies as well as much leverage in philanthropy, in Tory politics and on the Bench. And many opponents conceded that 'Though he differed from many . . . in politics, not a man could say that his politics ever interfered with his charity.'[72] Nevertheless, despite lingering influence and popularity, the earl experienced increasing difficulty in transforming his preferences into the collective will of the parish. The rift between the earl and many local inhabitants may have contributed to his decision to move the family seat from Sandwell to rural Patshull. In any case, that move, and the advent of a new earl in 1853, would bring many changes to the family's relationship with West Bromwich.

Like its West Bromwich counterpart the Dudley estate, under the direction of the Trust and then of Lord Ward, experienced increasing challenges to its local influence during these years. Undoubtedly, the Wards had greater success than did the Dartmouths in keeping pace with local economic expansion; but the estate had to cope with a well-developed local radical movement and with stirrings of independence even among its increasingly wealthy and respectable Tory allies.[73] Moreover, Lord Ward's personality provoked at least as much opposition as did Dartmouth's. Ward was much more stable than his quarrelsome father, who had died in 1835, although as a young man his strong will and his debts had caused conflicts with the trustees. Once in full control of his estates, however, the intelligent Ward left his youthful excesses behind. He became an amiable ornament of aristocratic society, a great art patron and collector, and a formidable orator. Nevertheless, he remained eccentric and extravagant, impulsive and moralistic and – above all – fond of getting his own way. Yet he was not aloof from the region: during this period he spent part of his year either at Himley or, from the 1840s, at Witley Court.[74]

Ward had chequered relations with local government in Dudley during these decades. He cooperated with the commissioners concerning market tolls and the elimination of dilapidated buildings, and the advent of the more powerful board of health in 1853 owed something to his advocacy and that of his agents. However, the estate clashed with the 'Tory clique' during the early years of the board. Ward's well-off candidates, led by agent Richard Smith, backed stern, expensive action and at first triumphed over 'ratepayers' agitation led by the Badger brothers. But the latter successfully counter-attacked in subsequent elections. Under their control the board made few improvements and occasionally bickered with the estate.[75] As in West Bromwich, resistance from men who paid larger shares of their incomes in rates than did the peers undermined aristocratic paternalism.

Ward's problems, like Dartmouth's, also stemmed from the increasing sensitivity of an expanding town to slights by a grandee on its rights and dignity. Even at a Dudley dinner celebrating Ward's marriage in 1851, speakers objected to the estate's proposal to lease the Castle grounds to a railway company. If the firm controlled access the citizens would have 'bartered their independence'; townsmen should keep 'the rights and privileges they possessed'.[76] Ward attempted to mollify the town but implied, as in his public health intervention, that he knew best. Thus his proposed assault on a cherished local amenity demonstrated his hauteur as well as the town's prickliness.

A similar clash surfaced in parliamentary elections. Ward's early political career was idiosyncratic: he began as a Tory, voted for Repeal, remained a restless Peelite and then moved cautiously towards Palmerstonianism. Less conventionally, he chartered a vessel which distributed supplies to English and Turkish soldiers in the Crimea. But his overriding political interest lay in securing the revival of the family earldom.[77] As a Black Country employer and lessor of increasing means, he could aspire to political influence surpassing that of his predecessors – especially in Dudley itself, but also in the neighbouring county divisions and in seats near his new rural estates. By the late 1830s Ward and his trustees were eager to exercise such political leverage to safeguard estate interests and to indulge his political convictions.[78]

In this effort Ward's agents could supplement deference with economic coercion and the threat of mob action against the property of recalcitrants. Yet in such a turbulent era even this formidable power base would have encountered serious difficulty long before it did if the local political climate had not favoured Ward's influence.[79] In Dudley he could initially depend on the Conservatives who, with the estate's encouragement, had long dominated local government. Moreover, that group and the local clergy, rather than the nobleman or his agents, drew most of the fire of Dudley radicals during the 1830s and 1840s. The middle-class Tories led the protracted and acrimonious local defence of church rates, for example. These allies lacked Ward's glamour and isolation, yet were no less involved than the estate in the contentious labour disputes of the period. Nevertheless, the family's local political influence had its potential weaknesses. The town contained many middle-class Liberals and nonconformists, albeit fewer proportionately than in West Bromwich. And especially from 1847 local radicals strenuously opposed the estate's interventions.[80] In addition, those members of the 'Tory clique' not directly dependent on the earl could afford to protect their own political interests if necessary.

Ward's involvement in Dudley elections developed gradually. Preoccupied with its own affairs, the estate took little part in the contests of 1834 and 1835. On those occasions the limited electorate – angered by the Whig member's attack on local magistrates – ended its brief flirtation with reform. Yet the Tory victor, the popular local manufacturer Thomas Hawkes, received some estate support in his subsequent successes in 1837 and 1841. When financial woes rendered Hawkes inactive, estate pressure forced him to resign, and his replacement, the London lawyer John Benbow, Ward's solicitor and trustee, was 'well-known to be the nominee of the young Lord Ward and his trustees'.[81]

Benbow's career in Dudley displays both the strength of Ward's influence and the growing challenge to it. Benbow, who rarely visited Dudley, had no claim to the town's seat other than his connection with the estate. In 1844 estate support was an unmixed blessing for him. But three years later resentment of Castle influence occasioned an unsuccessful attempt to persuade one of the Badger brothers to stand. By 1852 even Benbow felt it advisable to attempt to deny that he was Ward's nominee. Still, references to the M.P.'s 'personal influence . . . in their neighbourhood' indicated the cause of the local electorate's continued, but increasingly reluctant, tolerance of this imposed octagenarian. Ward's last successful electoral intervention in Dudley came in the mid-1850s.[82] In 1855 he nominated his latest political favourite, Sir Stafford Northcote, as successor to the deceased Benbow. As Ward's choice, a 'Liberal-Conservative' and an administrative reformer of distinction, Northcote proved acceptable to the Dudley electorate, despite his lack of previous contact with the town. Soon local opinion regarded him as a considerable improvement on his predecessor.[83]

But the general election of 1857 brought a crisis in Ward's influence over the Dudley seat. Northcote, moving towards the Tories, had ignored Ward's advice to support Palmerston on the China question. Ward, now an enthusiastic admirer of the Prime Minister's policies, also hoped that the removal of this 'Derbyite' from Dudley would advance his campaign for the earldom. So he effectively dismissed Northcote. Intending to defer to the constituency's Tory past, Ward nominated as a replacement a former Conservative M.P. who, like himself, 'tho avowing himself a Peelite shall promise Lord Palmerston his support.'[84]

This flagrant ejection of a popular and accomplished representative ignited the long-smouldering local resentment of Ward's political influence. The Whigs and radicals had never had close ties to him; now the Tories, the bedrock of Ward's support, found a Derbyite evicted in favour of an unknown Palmerstonian. In the absence of a local candidate, a Liberal London barrister, H.B. Sheridan, became the candidate both of the Tories and of the more radical wing of the local Liberals. Sheridan adapted himself to the anti-Ward mood, claiming that he 'did not depend upon aristocrats for support, but "vox populi".' Resentment against an interfering peer had become the dominant sentiment. As a local newspaper argued, 'politics have formed a very trifling element in the . . . struggle. Whatever may have been the real motives of the originators of the opposition, the people believed it to be a struggle for independence, and nobly have they fought the battle.' With Ward's consent his candidate withdrew without a contest, and Ward conceded that his 'political preponderance', already weakened, had vanished.[85]

In 1859, however, Ward's Palmerstonian candidate trailed Sheridan by only 71 votes, suggesting a partial restoration of Ward's position – the result of natural recovery, coercion, and Tory disaffection with Sheridan. But the M.P's renewed condemnation of aristocratic domination, combined with Dudley's participation in the rising strength of Liberalism in the region as a whole, allowed him to withstand the reassertion of Ward's influence.[86]

After these two elections, then, the political strength of the estate in Dudley was at a low ebb. As an emerging Liberal, Ward had severed his ties to the previously loyal Tories. Yet he had not forged strong links to the radicals in the borough. His Palmerstonianism fell between the two major blocs of opinion in Dudley, and his style of intervention alienated many. Ward's greater economic power and the support of a strong local Tory élite had made his initial political influence much superior to Dartmouth's leverage. But his dominance could not survive blatant manipulation in an era of increased constituency independence.

Serious as these parliamentary and other setbacks were, the influence of the ever-wealthier Ward had by no means disappeared. His philanthropy, for example, generated much respect even if his politics no longer did so. Even Sheridan conceded to Ward 'all due praise for his public liberality and manly generosity'; the Liberal had found 'one universal feeling of respect to his lordship.' Such benevolence, a local newspaper opined, merited influence even if electoral dictation were unacceptable.[87] And from a political point of view Ward's policies eventually had some success. In 1860 Palmerston rewarded his now formal political conversion with the long-coveted earldom.

By the 1850s, therefore, the confident, ambitious paternalism of the Legges and Wards had been swamped by rising middle-class confidence, working-class assertion and adverse political and sectarian trends. With the local middle-class élites and their institutions becoming even more entrenched, the peers' continued exercise of their reduced influence would require new approaches.

5 From frustrated autocrats to civic celebrities, c. 1860–1914

The personal, family and local contexts

In dealing with the years from the later 1850s to the First World War, it is appropriate to examine the families themselves, their many commitments, and the growth of the towns' élites, before discussing the earls' involvements in various aspects of local society.

During this period changing personalities made both families better suited to social and political activities. Like his father, the fifth earl of Dartmouth was modest and endowed with a deep sense of duty. But he proved more socially adept. Although not a skilled orator, he could be 'humorous' and 'jocular' as well as earnest on public platforms in the Black Country. From 1891 his son brought a still lighter touch to the Dartmouth tradition of conscientious public service and rural domesticity. More a sportsman than a scholar, the sixth earl's combination of 'courtesy . . . tact . . . humour and general *savoir faire*' made him a natural public performer.[88] The Dudleys, too, mellowed. During the quarter of a century preceding the first earl's death in 1885, his earldom and happy second marriage provided a more serene existence than heretofore. The second earl lacked his father's intellectual and artistic inclinations. Yet he surpassed him in his 'genial disposition' and 'complete absence of assumption'.[89] Rescued from the turf by his wife, the young earl turned to the public career his father had foregone. By 1914, though, his 'profligate habits and expenditure' had disrupted his marriage and had begun to strain the revenues of the estate.[90]

With greater wealth and a more pronounced taste for conspicuous consumption, the Dudleys pursued a more extravagant lifestyle than did the Dartmouths. Both families, however, enjoyed grand and peripatetic existences during this period. Each had the use of several fine residences: their principal seats near the Black Country, a shooting lodge or two elsewhere and a series of splendid town houses. The Wards and the Legges regularly savoured their 'bit of London'.[91] Each family travelled extensively, often abroad or to aristocratic seats such as Holkham and Wilton. Yet each also passed part of the year – except when the second earl of Dudley held office abroad – at Witley Court or Patshull. Both peers gave large, elaborate house parties at their West Midland seats. In 1903, for instance, the Dartmouths hosted nine such occasions at Patshull. The Dudleys entertained guests such as the future Edward VII on an even grander scale at Witley Court, which the first earl had made 'a palace, regal in size and grandeur'.[92]

Such socializing mainly involved other aristocrats, often from far afield. Yet both families also had close ties with the 'quality' of the West Midlands, on both sides of politics. In addition, the peers' sponsorship of local sport increasingly brought contact with the gentrified members of the Black Country's upper middle class.[93]

Moreover, the earls' local celebrations of family and national festivals involved lavish hospitality for rich and poor alike, with much favourable publicity, and well-reported entertaining of the upper crust reminded nearby urban communities of the prestige and grandeur of these titled industrialists. The visit of the Duke and Duchess of York to Patshull in 1900, for example, involved elaborate commuting between the house and Wolverhampton, where the royal couple and the Dartmouths participated in civic functions.[94] Thus the social lives of these grandees were not divorced from their activities and standing in the surrounding area.

In any case, during this period the Dartmouths and Dudleys, like most landed families, remained active in local public affairs as well as in domesticity, sport, hospitality and business. Their incomes were large, and regional interventions, especially of a ceremonial kind, did not take much time – a few hours spent now and then in a provincial locality might make a large impact. Also, many factors combined to keep them interested in local, social and political events: a sense of *noblesse oblige*; attachment to localities long connected with their families; enthusiasm for particular causes; eagerness to prove themselves or their sons capable leaders; anxiety regarding the security of rank and property generally; and concern for the image and practical interests of their estates. Nevertheless, the diversion of their social and political energies to the county level, and to their other estates, formed a potential limit to their influence in the Black Country, and their involvement in other localities in the West Midlands might reduce their impact in West Bromwich and Dudley.

The Dartmouths continued their social involvement in their other estates, especially in Kentish London and the West Riding. The former supplied a living for the fifth earl's clerical brother and, eventually, a seat in the Commons for his eldest son. The family made occasional non-political appearances in the area – which attracted slightly less than a sixth of the earl's donations to specific localities in the early 1880s. The Yorkshire estates received some personal attention and even more largesse – almost half the earl's gifts, in fact. The family's lavish generosity there stemmed from their fondness for the region, the paucity of rival philanthropists, and the large income they drew from the district.[95]

Nevertheless, Staffordshire, the Dartmouths' home, attracted most of their social and political activities and much of their generosity. A good deal of this involvement focused on county affairs rather than on the Black Country itself. The fifth earl was 'devoted to Staffordshire'. Indeed, but for his Toryism he might have been Lord Lieutenant as early as 1863, for he was 'popular both as a landlord and as a liberal supporter of every good object.' Dartmouth continued to take an active supporting role in county business until appointment to the lieutenancy in 1887 intensified his involvement. The sixth earl secured the post on his father's death and became one of the leading Staffordshire figures of his generation. He wielded 'powerful influence' on the new county council which he served as alderman for 44 years. The council had limited business concerning West Bromwich, a county borough. Yet Dartmouth's connection with 'almost every county movement' involved his urban as well as his rural estates.[96]

Some of the family's local cash and attention went to the rural parishes of Patshull and Pattingham which surrounded the new Dartmouth residence, where they soon established themselves as the pre-eminent figures. In these localities family gifts were essential for much-appreciated improvements such as schools and

Figure 7. Witley Court, c. 1900 (by courtesy of the Hereford and Worcester Record Office).

Figure 8. Arrival of the duke and duchess of York at Patshull, 1900 (by courtesy of Mr and Mrs J.K. Winter).

village halls. Yet the Dartmouths did not become detached from the life of the Black Country – a natural focus for 'improving' efforts only a few miles away – merely because they lived at Patshull and were county enthusiasts. Such charities as the district's educational prize scheme attracted their support, and the grounds at Patshull proved an ideal location for fêtes involving Black Country tenants and Conservative loyalists.[97]

The move from West Bromwich to Patshull entailed alterations in the pattern of the family's activities in the Black Country. The Dartmouths increased their involvement in the political, philanthropic and civic life of Wolverhampton, the nearest industrial town, while the greater distance to West Bromwich prompted the ageing fifth earl to attempt to reduce his activities there. Yet the Dartmouths retained a keen interest in West Bromwich. Their long-standing connection with the town promoted a sentimental attachment which especially aroused the family's sense of duty. Also, during this period the Dartmouths wished to protect the interests of the rapidly-developing Sandwell estate. Local aristocratic activity would serve both types of goal by insuring that 'the old connections between the family of Sandwell Hall and their neighbours of various classes were still maintained'. West Bromwich attracted almost all the Dartmouths' contributions to particular Black Country towns in the early 1880s, and the earls and their families frequently visited the town.[98] From the 1860s the fifth earl gave personal as well as pecuniary support to the institutions of West Bromwich. His successor, who had never resided in West Bromwich, perhaps felt less identified with the town; but he, too, often appeared publicly there, although less frequently than his father had done.

The Dudleys, meanwhile, had no other major estates to distract them from their properties in the West Midlands. However, within the region they were much involved in county activities and in the affairs of localities outside the Black Country. For example, the first earl served for many years as an active chairman of Worcestershire Quarter Sessions. The second earl's absorption in national affairs prevented him from equalling his father's importance in the county's public life. However, his agent Gilbert Claughton was an influential councillor and later alderman in Staffordshire, the county which provided the bulk of the Dudleys' income. In addition to these county activities, the Wards had philanthropic and ceremonial ties to Great Witley, Kidderminster and Worcester (see fig. 6). Projects dealing with the Black Country as a whole – the district hospital, for example – also gained their attention.[99]

Nevertheless, much of the earls' social and political activity remained focused on the southwestern side of the Black Country where their urban estates lay. Even their county involvements had much relevance to this area. The first earl, for example, was instrumental in persuading Worcestershire Quarter Sessions to improve county facilities in Dudley. And although the peers and their agents contributed cash and personal service to various localities in the vicinity, none benefitted more than Dudley – the focal town both of the area and of estate activities – which attracted more than a third of the estate's Black Country subscriptions in 1857, before its institutions were fully developed.[100] In Dudley both the family's sense of obligation and its instinct for self-preservation were particularly strong. The second earl confessed to a Dudley audience the 'large debt of gratitude we owe to the people of this district'. Yet he told the same crowd that 'it is decidedly important that I, largely connected . . . with the industries of this country, should ever preserve as far as I can the relations that have existed so friendly between my family and the inhabitants of this district'.[101]

Both types of consideration encouraged Dudley to lend maximum support to the town's activities at a time of increasing municipal powers, rising workingmen's demands and estate reorganization. Such stimuli also meant that the town received much personal attention from the estate. The first earl had made few appearances there in his youth; in the final years of his life illness kept him away. But in the interim he visited frequently, especially on grand ceremonial occasions. The second earl followed this pattern until public business took him abroad from the turn of the century. Afterward – and throughout the period – the earls' agents or relatives were often on hand when the peers themselves were not. Thus the Wards, like the Legges, retained their strongest local social involvements in their principal Black Country base.

During this period the towns themselves produced powerful élites – large and diverse yet united and respectable – with which the peers could cooperate. As late as the 1830s these localities contained few reputable organizations and élite positions. Places of worship (especially churches) were relatively few, and political party organizations had little substance between elections. Philanthropy was sparse and ephemeral. Local government consisted only of the county Bench, old-style town commissioners and humble parochial institutions such as vestries and highway boards. During the rest of the century, however, prestigious institutions and the leadership posts within them, expanded dramatically. Churches and chapels, with their auxiliary organizations, increased quickly; the political parties established active, permanent local associations with affiliated clubs. In philanthropy, likewise, mechanics and technical institutes, temperance societies, hospitals, workingmen's clubs, Y.M.C.A.s and football clubs developed. In local government West Bromwich and Dudley acquired guardians of the poor, health commissioners, school boards, incorporation and borough J.P.s. The number, prestige and achievements of these bodies accelerated after mid-century as population growth slowed, the towns became more coherent, and the earliest of the new organizations had time to settle down.

In the 1830s, most local institutions either had homogeneous memberships or were divided into battling factions. But by the 1890s, all the religious, political and social groups within the upper and middle classes were represented in reasonable harmony in the expanded élites, especially in West Bromwich.[102] In the key areas of philanthropy and local government, the major partisan and sectarian groups secured at least a third of the seats in each town. In terms of social standing, few members of the élites were workingmen; but all parts of the middle classes gained significant shares of the posts. Most of the positions, particularly in West Bromwich, went to the more substantial parts of the middle class – a pattern which reflected their greater enthusiasm for such service, and their easier fulfilment of the formal and implicit requirements of élite posts. Moreover, the upper middle class remained active and retained considerable influence, while aristocrats also participated, with potential importance disproportionate to their small numbers.[103] Yet these leading businessmen and peers were outnumbered by more modest but still well-off citizens: lesser manufacturers, more prosperous retailers, and professionals.

The number of individuals holding one or more of these posts during the period 1836–1900 was substantial – roughly 1 per cent of the 1871 population (and thus a much larger proportion of the middle class) of each town. Yet there was enough overlap between and within philanthropy and local government to permit coordination – for example in giving technical institutes both voluntary and municipal support.[104] Those leaders with multiple posts tended to be significantly more socially eminent, and more often Tory and Anglican, than the élite as a whole. Still, the more modest social levels of the middle class and Liberal nonconformists had substantial shares even of these key positions. Thus each town developed a broad and varied élite, internally linked by a significant overlap of its more socially eminent members, which provided the potential for a wide but united group with a prominent and respected leadership that included the aristocracy.

Concerning the social context in which these élites operated, the Black Country was not so harmonious in the later nineteenth century as the traditional interpretation of the social pattern of the West Midlands suggests.[105] Yet the dramatic industrial and political disturbances of the early 1840s were never repeated; the later challenges from below were more restrained – and, in general, unsuccessful. In politics, for example, the institutionalized radicalism of the Second Reform Act era began to give way, by the 1880s, to demands by local workingmen for special representatives and policy concessions. However, the independent labour movement did not establish itself effectively in the region before 1914.[106] Therefore, while local trends in social class relations resembled developments in urban Britain as a whole – becoming more tranquil from mid-century but more disturbed from about 1880 – the Black Country, which had been especially agitated at the start of the period, was relatively calm at its end.[107]

As examination of various aspects of local society will show, increasingly effective social intervention by progressively more unified élites played an important part in promoting this social stability. But could the aristocrats cooperate enough with the local middle class to have a significant rôle in this process? Both sides sometimes showed the strains involved in such a partnership. The fifth earl of Dartmouth, for example, condemned in 1857 'a vestryocracy – a small, noisy, fidgetty busybody of the middle class'. Likewise, the latter sometimes vented its resentment of aristocratic pretensions.[108] However, various forces encouraged cooperation during these decades. Both groups had stakes in the prosperity and stability of the region, and the increasingly well-off local middle class combined its resentment of hauteur with a growing regard for the grandeur of the local aristocracy – especially appealing because of the 'blackness' of the region. For example, local industrialists imitated the aristocratic lifestyle by acquiring large homes in the surrounding countryside, participating in rural sports and sending their sons to public schools and Oxbridge.[109] Informal social contact between the two groups remained limited. But, the peers banished their snobbishness from the public platform and apparently enjoyed the adulation they received there. The potential for friction remained, though, particularly at the height of sectarian and party tension in the 1870s. However, other trends facilitated collaboration: the waning of partisan animosity, the growth of respectable civic institutions, the increasing threat to local prosperity and an enhanced awareness of shared separation from an organized working class.

In examining the interaction between these grandees, local middle-class élites and the other residents of West Bromwich and Dudley, it is appropriate to look first at areas especially fraught with difficulty – industrial relations, partisan politics and religious activities. Afterwards attention shifts to the peers' rôle in the more promising spheres of philanthropy and local government. It will then be possible to assess the aristocrats' overall position during the period c. 1860–1914.

Potential irritants: industrial relations, party politics and religion
Black Country industrial relations underwent many changes during these decades. Confused confrontations between temporary workers' combinations and frightened masters had given way, by the 1860s, to more disciplined battles between more stable trade unions and better-organized employers. The conciliation boards which soon developed involved tacit recognition of trade unions. Yet they also legitimized the bargaining advantage which the depressed condition of local industry conferred on employers. Some local unions became more coherent in the 1890s. But the division of the local workforce into many trades and levels of skill kept local unions in a weak position compared to their counterparts elsewhere – at least until a wave of strikes just before the First World War.[110]

The Dartmouths and Dudleys had sharply diverging involvements in this difficult social sphere. The Dartmouths delegated much responsibility even for their agricultural employees. As lessors, their relations with the workers in their collieries were even more indirect and less substantial. The fifth earl recognized that 'my interest in the trading district is very small, and I am not directly concerned in the management of it.' This position encouraged him to attempt to calm clashes between employers and trade unions. Thus Dartmouth occasionally joined other local peers such as Lord Lichfield in trying to mediate in industrial conflicts. In West Bromwich in 1873, for example, he helped to seek a solution to the troublesome problem of a permanent colliery relief fund.[111] Yet his detachment both from direct industrial employment and, for most of the period, from the Lord Lieutenancy, limited the frequency and importance of his interventions. Moreover, local conciliation efforts increasingly involved standing wage tribunals, with 'sliding scales' and presidents such as Joseph Chamberlain, rather than *ad hoc* interventions by titled grandees.

For the Dudleys, however, industrial relations were inevitably of great importance. The peers, and more directly their agents, had to deal with several thousand estate employees. In addition, the Dudleys' position as the region's largest direct employers, and the estate's general economic might, conferred on it a leading rôle in the efforts of Black Country masters to cope with trade unions and wage boards.

Like other landed industrialists, the Dudleys had a mixed record as employers. They continued to employ subcontractors, including the notorious coal 'butties'; yet the estate had attempted to eliminate this system, and its bureaucracy's comparatively tight control of these subordinates perhaps reduced casualties in the earl's mines. And, in contrast to many middle-class masters in the area, the Dudleys prevented their subcontractors from forcing colliers to accept payment in kind. But there is no clear evidence that the estate's disdain for such practices had much effect on other local employers. Nor were the Dudleys entirely enlightened concerning pay practices: one of their managers admitted that the estate's timing of cash payments to ironworkers provided 'a lien upon them which prevents them from occasionally moving away without giving notice.'[112]

Concerning benefits, the Dudleys were comparatively generous in providing treats and contributions to workmen's sickness funds. However, the latter often proved troublesome. The second earl personally led the national fight to allow workers and employers to 'contract out' of employers' liability legislation. The implicit compulsion on the workingmen inherent in this arrangement eventually made it controversial in the district. Also, to the extent that the estate was relatively generous in such matters, its work discipline – often reinforced by prosecution – was especially strict, at least in the ironworks.[113] So, although the Dudleys' working conditions and benefits were superior to contemporary local standards, their practices made many concessions to Black Country customs and often ran foul of workers' preferences.

This moderately enlightened record probably boosted the estate's standing with the local middle class – already much impressed with the earl's contribution to the region's prosperity. But the workmen's overall reaction is more elusive. At the famous Round Oak ironworks favourable working conditions and paternalistic rhetoric apparently produced much approval for the earls and their agents. And, at least one local labour leader thought Lord Dudley a good person to rule the trade because in slumps he kept prices up and his works open.[114] Yet neither in the ironworks nor in the less deferential pits could paternalism protect the estate from labour disputes. Wage levels remained controversial, and the agents' leading rôles in local employers' organizations projected them into conflicts involving workingmen other than those who profited from the estate's practices. As a result, the Dudley interest frequently found itself in the thick of industrial battles. In 1882, for example, 3,000 colliers struck because of a wage reduction coordinated by the agent E.F. Smith.[115] In some instances the estate's comparatively good record as an employer apparently eased its own labour difficulties. But, in most major Black Country strikes the estate was fully, contentiously, and in the end often victoriously, involved.[116]

What effect did such disputes have on the estate's local standing? Often, as in 1858, great resentment resulted. The agents attracted most of the criticism, though they could deflect some unpopularity onto subcontractors and lessees. The peers themselves usually escaped most of this opprobrium. During the 1884 coal strike, for instance, tradesmen, employers and miners directed a petition to the earl and countess against the wage reduction in which their agents were involved.[117] On the other hand, since the appeal brought no result, presumably the earl shared, to some degree, in the backlash. Such unpleasantness – however distributed among the estate's principals – probably diminished slightly during the period as grudging acceptance of trade unions made direct confrontations less frequent and less fraught with social tension.

Thus for the Dudleys, far more than for the insulated Dartmouths, industrial relations constituted a controversial, involuntary sphere of social involvement. The estate gained some credit for its record as an employer, but it remained unpopular, especially with local workers, for its rôle in labour disputes. These difficulties complicated as well as stimulated the other social interventions of the Dudleys.

These decades also brought changes that made the political position of the Dartmouths and the Dudleys more difficult. The Second Reform Act introduced large numbers of working-class electors into the expanded number of Black Country seats. Partly as a result, the period to 1885 was one of Liberal dominance in the region – a handicap, in the event, for both families. In addition, local M.P.s increasingly came from trade and the professions rather than from the local landed interest. Yet the Legges and Wards – in contrast to the Hathertons but like many landed families elsewhere – maintained their interest in local elections. In a political climate featuring a broad electorate, middle-class representatives, and sophisticated party organizations, the aristocrats' influence could not equal even the level of the 1840s and 1850s, but the peers' wealth, prestige, experience and varied local involvements ensured that they did not become political ciphers in their urban bases. Moreover, the local revival of Toryism from the mid-1880s – until the partial and temporary Liberal recovery of 1906 – both eased and profited from their participation.[118]

During the first half of this period the fifth earl of Dartmouth and the first earl of Dudley made some adjustments to these changed circumstances. Yet each retained some of the combativeness and overconfidence of the years, ending in the 1850s, when the aristocracy could realistically aspire to control Black Country politics.

The fifth earl of Dartmouth was an enthusiastic Tory. He adjusted to unwelcome political change more easily than his father had done, and he was more active in national politics. But his abilities and application were not adequate to bring him either office or the Garter that he sought. National mediocrity, however, did not prevent local importance. As Dartmouth said, 'what he lost in doing good to the public in London he would . . . make up in the country'.[119] Having kept the Sandwell estate in part for political purposes, he retained great interest and considerable influence in Tory politics in the Black Country, especially in West Bromwich, which was part of the Wednesbury constituency 1867–85, thereafter a separate seat. Only to a slight degree did Dartmouth pursue political advantage through his estate's economic power.[120] In any event, even within West Bromwich, his tenants and direct employees formed a small proportion of the population. Insofar as the estate itself gave Dartmouth political influence, the process was more subtle, as his local property and investment gave him legitimacy as an actor in the area's political affairs.

The fifth earl's encouragement of Conservative organizational efforts and campaigns in the Black Country constituted the most important aspect of his local political rôle. Dartmouth filled honorary posts in the constituency associations which sprang up after 1867. He subscribed to their funds and frequently delivered vigorous partisan speeches at their public meetings, especially in Wednesbury and West Bromwich. In addition, as Lord Lieutenant he served the interests of local Conservatives. For example, he put many Tories on the Bench after four decades of nominations by Liberals – and incurred much criticism for doing so.[121]

Like his father, the fifth earl found a seat for his eldest son. Although mentioned as a possible candidate for Wednesbury, the future sixth earl sat for East Kent between 1878 and 1885 and then for Lewisham until he succeeded to the title. This successful intervention in the neighbourhood of the family's Kent estates – where one contest reportedly cost £11,000 – might suggest lessening interest by the Dartmouths in Black Country politics. However, political prudence rather than indifference dictated the choice. Lewisham came of age politically at a time when the Liberals dominated south Staffordshire elections; Kent, in contrast, was a safe Tory haven. By the time that the Black Country swung towards the Conservatives in the mid-1880s, Lewisham was firmly established in the southeast. In his son's absence, the fifth earl's support for Tory candidates in south Staffordshire helped both to preserve family influence and to promote the Conservative cause.[122]

The first earl of Dudley became disaffected with Liberalism, except on foreign policy issues, soon after his formal adherence to the party. He never formally renounced the Liberals, but his ambivalence ended whatever chance he may have had of national office. In addition, this partisan wavering prevented any substantial personal activity by the earl in the developing party associations of the Black Country. The widening of the parliamentary borough of Dudley in 1867 to encompass outlying industrial districts – where radicals as well as estate industry were strong – further complicated local political interventions by Lord Dudley. So too did the Ballot Act. Nevertheless, the great economic importance of the estate promised continued influence, and the earl's agents could provide organizational support and potential candidates.[123] In addition, he evidently retained some of his old zest for area politics.

Although bruised by the defeats of the 1850s and constrained by divided party allegiance, Lord Dudley and his agents occasionally attempted to decide contests during this period. The earl continued to support Liberals in county elections, especially in 1880 when the Eastern Question engaged his interest. But in Dudley itself the earl and his subordinates backed what was, in effect, the Tory side. Lord Dudley never reconciled himself to his old antagonist Sheridan, who compounded past bitterness by supporting causes such as workmen's compensation which were anathema to the estate. In 1874 Dudley's former agent Frederick Smith (now Smith-Shenstone) stood as a 'Liberal-Conservative', with estate backing, against Sheridan. Yet the incumbent won by almost one thousand votes. When the attendant widespread rioting necessitated another contest Shenstone, discouraged and feuding with local Tories, gave way to a local ironmaster, Noah Hingley who, despite connections with the estate, personal popularity and the ostentatious support of his own employees, only cut Sheridan's majority by three hundred votes.[124]

The results of 1874 demonstrated the limitations of the 'Castle interest' in this area. True, the estate's support, more tactful than the interventions of 15 years before, had some positive effect. The earl's power and goodwill helped Smith-Shenstone and Hingley to fare as well as any Tory aspirants in Dudley before 1886. Although Sheridan's sympathy for labour hampered them, this factor would have handicapped any employer–candidate.[125] Nevertheless, the estate could not prevail, in a mass electorate balloting in secret, against 'advanced Liberalism' in flood tide.

In the adverse political climate of the early part of this period, then, neither Dartmouth nor Dudley withdrew from local politics, though both attempted less than in earlier years. Dartmouth's focus on aid to constituency associations proved reasonably successful – although his fierce local partisanship sometimes caused a reaction. Dudley and his agents were moving towards a similar rôle, but in the interim the estate's efforts to win elections, and to do so more through direct intervention than through aid to party organizations, were largely frustrated.

Under the new earls the families usually swam with, rather than against, the partisan currents of the Black Country. Their more equable dispositions also diminished the acerbity and high-handedness of aristocratic political interventions. At first both families simply aided the new local Tory M.P.s whose prominence gave a further indication of the reduced political importance of the region's landed interest. Then, early in the new century, family members attempted to win both seats. But these interventions, undertaken through local party organizations, illustrated the diminished though less troubled influence that the families now enjoyed.

The sixth earl of Dartmouth surpassed his father in political aptitude. He proved an effective junior whip and agricultural spokesman while serving as Vice-Chamberlain of the Household 1885–6 and 1886–91. Yet his national political career effectively ended when he inherited in 1891.[126] Henceforth, despite a partial revival of his interest in affairs at Westminster from the late 1890s, the focus of the sixth earl's political life, like that of his father, was primarily local. In the West Midlands he proved less zealous and marginally less active than the fifth earl but still a partisan of importance. As Lord Lieutenant he was less fiercely partisan than his father yet did the Tory cause no harm. He reduced some of his father's political contributions, but he remained personally active, both in individual Conservative associations – notably at West Bromwich – and in regional efforts such as an attempt to fuse Tory and Liberal Unionist organizations.[127]

The second earl of Dudley – unlike his father a Conservative from the outset – became active in national politics from the early 1890s. He served as a parliamentary secretary at the Board of Trade (1895–1902) and dealt capably in the Lords with a host of labour and commercial issues. His posts as Lord Lieutenant of Ireland (1902–5) and Governor General of Australia (1908–11) brought added glamour, if also some controversy. His national political prominence gained him considerable popularity in the Midlands during this period, among both Liberals and Conservatives.[128] But it left little time and attention to spare for Black Country partisanship. He served as officer of local Tory organizations but once launched into affairs at Westminster he made few personal appearances. Nevertheless, the estate's agents, especially Claughton, compensated for this inactivity at the top.

Dudley and Dartmouth assisted the middle-class Conservatives, J.E. Spencer and Brooke Robinson, who sat for West Bromwich and Dudley respectively between 1886 and 1906. The combined impact of Home Rule, Fair Trade, the M.P.s' local connections and their support for some workingmen's causes, proved more significant than aristocratic backing. Still, Spencer and Robinson gratefully reciprocated the latter – through public praise of the peers and by specific services such as the Dudley M.P.'s mediation in a compensation dispute involving the estate.[129] When both incumbents declined to stand in 1906, the replacement candidates were the future seventh earl of Dartmouth in West Bromwich, and family member Claughton in Dudley. These ventures reflected personal ambition and stopgap service for the local parties more than the reassertion of the 'landed interest' or the defence of specific estate policies. Yet the candidates' aristocratic ties attracted much attention.

Both lost, Lewisham by 1216 votes, Claughton by 754. In each case a poor electoral legacy was responsible. Spencer had recently been inactive, and Robinson's majority had been falling. The local Tory organizations were weak while their Liberal counterparts were thriving. Lewisham, moreover, lacked experience, was adopted late and had to cope with an internally divided local party. Most importantly, the 'aristocrats' faced an adverse national 'swing' while fighting distinguished local Nonconformists.[130] Nevertheless, aristocratic connections probably brought both Unionists more good than harm. Contemporaries thought that Lewisham bore 'a name to conjure with in West Bromwich' which would exert 'considerable influence in his favour'. His opponent attacked the Dartmouths' royalties and argued that their 'great interest' in the town was 'what they can get out of it'. But Lewisham's supporters could point to the family's benefactions. In Dudley, Claughton's position as the representative of an often controversial local employer hindered his attempt to compete for the rôle of defender of the workingman. Yet he also profited from being a personally popular agent for an estate which generated large numbers of jobs. He did well in the normally Liberal outlying districts where many estate works were located.[131] In both towns the 'aristocratic' candidate, combining prestige and local connections, very likely polled more than any alternative Unionist would have done.

In the more favourable electoral climate of 1910 the earls' candidates fared better. Both Lewisham and Claughton had gained esteem from the gentlemanly style of their campaigns in 1906.[132] Claughton declined to stand again but persuaded Sir Arthur Griffith-Boscawen to contest Dudley. Estate assistance helped this outsider to come within 187 votes of victory in January and to achieve a December triumph by a margin of 360. Lewisham, with London County Council experience now behind him, won by 735 votes in January and by 2 in December (after an inquiry which found irregularities by party workers on both sides). The Lords issue apparently made less impact in 1910 in West Bromwich than did organization. The Tories were very active in January, and the stunned Liberals counter-attacked 11 months later. Lewisham's aristocratic lineage – which he proudly displayed – attracted less criticism than it had four years earlier.[133] Also, his enhanced personal stature made the family tie more useful than in 1906: Lewisham had now earned the right to favour as a Dartmouth. In both towns family influence was only one helpful factor among many; but in such a finely balanced election year it may have been decisive. In any case, both families had more success in 1910 than they had had locally in the early decades of the period.

Because these aristocrats lowered their political ambitions and adapted to cooperation with local political élites their activity and resources sustained real, if reduced, influence in Black Country politics. And if noble assistance was only one of several forces aiding local Unionism, the peers' cash and glamour made them especially useful to the middling businessmen and professionals who undertook most of the organizing work of the party in these towns. The aristocrats faced competition – as Black Country donors, candidates, and celebrities – from top local industrialists such as the Chamberlains and Hickmans, but the peers' contribution was of comparable importance within their particular towns. The Dartmouths had less economic weight and less national political distinction during this period than did the Dudleys, but their industrial rôle was less controversial and their contribution to local politics was more consistently personal. Thus both families made a significant, though by no means an overwhelming, impact on local partisan affairs.

What was the effect of the peers' political activities on their local position generally? Aristocratic support usually delighted fellow partisans. Yet firm advocacy of controversial positions antagonized other local residents. By plunging eagerly into contentious issues the fifth earl of Dartmouth, in particular, seemed to have 'a most unfortunate knack of introducing debatable topics at inapropos seasons'. The earls' opponents could be at least as vitriolic. For instance, the Liberal M.P. for West Bromwich proposed to the Commons in 1906 – no doubt with Dartmouth in mind – that a tax be imposed on holders of hereditary titles. Even the peers' philanthropy could be thrown back at them in the heat of political battle.[134]

Thus the Dartmouths and Dudleys, like their titled counterparts in other towns, experienced difficulty in the dual rôle which placed them simultaneously 'above politics, as the embodiment of the established order, while often at the same time being involved in politics as partisan participants.'[135] Yet the local trend towards Unionism eased this dichotomy. Moreover, much of this antipathy only emerged during, or soon after, elections; it had much less impact, especially later in the period, at other times. In any event, the peers and their agents involved the estates in a host of less controversial interventions which brought them more success than did their political adventures. Particularly for the later earls, whose local partisan activities were less intense, these other involvements overshadowed their political escapades.

The peers' interventions in religious affairs, like their party-political exertions, were often controversial. In these towns at mid-century, dissenting majorities confronted top industrialists and landowners who were predominantly Anglican.[136] Conflict was inevitable as rising nonconformist businessmen sought to establish themselves in local society and politics. Partly as a result, for much of this period religious issues such as disestablishment occupied considerable public attention in the Black Country. To the extent that the aristocrats served as Anglican leaders in such struggles, they risked perpetuating the alienation from Dissenters which the Dartmouths, in particular, had experienced before 1850. Disputes *within* local Anglicanism might also make the peers' religious leadership unpopular. On the other hand, religious convictions and institutions underpinned the paternalistic social action that appealed to nonconformist businessman and Anglican peer alike. Thus much religious activity might bind the peers to their middle-class counterparts – many of whom were Anglicans anyway – rather than divide the two groups.

The religious commitments of the elder aristocrats were strong. The fifth earl of Dartmouth participated in a variety of Anglican organizations and often gave sermon-like speeches. The first earl of Dudley also took his religion very seriously. Their sons were loyal but less intense members of the Church of England.[137]

Particularly during the elder peers' lifetimes these families, especially the Dartmouths, found their Anglicanism contentious. Yet both increasingly distanced themselves from local sectarian battles. The fifth earl of Dartmouth was an 'eager and intrepid' Anglican controversialist, who led the regional church defence institute's campaign against disestablishment. Still, even this enthusiastic Churchman kept his distance from many local religious difficulties. In an acrimonious dispute in West Bromwich concerning ritualism, for instance, the earl – a moderate High Churchman – quietly opposed the more extreme practices while attempting to calm the situation.[138] His son became a strong adherent of Anglican positions on issues such as voluntary schools, but evidently played a less prominent rôle in such struggles than his father had done. The first earl of Dudley translated his High Church sympathies into firm opposition to such causes as the 'deceased wife's sister' campaign. This must have displeased nonconformists in Dudley, though the earl apparently did not participate in local controversies on the matter. As late as 1904 the second earl and, more directly, Claughton found themselves on the losing side of a battle within Dudley Anglicanism concerning the proposed transfer of the town to the diocese of Lichfield.[139] Yet generally the peers' and agents' positions as leading local Anglicans caused them little difficulty.

The Dartmouths and Dudleys had even less troubled careers as religious philanthropists. Both families were eager for this rôle. Religious conviction combined with the view that additional church accommodation formed an essential part of the 'improvement' of the working classes.[140] Thus each family devoted much of its giving to church construction and subsequent support. The Dudleys and their agents aided churches both in Dudley and in neighbouring towns. For example, St Edmund's Dudley gained the site for a new parsonage and £100 towards the building itself from the local peer. In 1857 roughly seven-tenths (c. £1900) of the estate's philanthropy went to religious purposes.

The Dartmouths, too, 'generously supported church extension'.[141] In West Bromwich much of this aid preceded mid-century. Only one-fifth of the family's local giving in 1884 went to religious causes, compared to three-fifths on the Dartmouth estates generally. Yet the fifth earl supported the rebuilding of West Bromwich parish church in the 1870s and in the following decade provided local churches with regular contributions for repairs, affiliated organizations and clerical stipends. Local middle-class Anglicans also gave much to the Church. The peers, however, were the greatest single benefactors of Anglicanism in their localities. They proved especially important in providing sites and in launching fund-raising drives. Local vicars depended on such help. In 1901, for example, a Dudley clergyman seeking to enlarge his church wanted the earl 'to defray the entire cost himself, or to give such a generous subscription to start with as would justify me in . . . carrying it through.'[142]

Such giving was not trouble-free. The earls felt the need to scrutinize the clergymen involved and to assure themselves that other men of means were subscribing too. Also, business considerations sometimes intruded. The Dudley estate protected its mineral rights when giving sites. Later the earl's mines caused subsidence which made estate contributions for repairs virtually mandatory. As one parish spokesman wrote to Claughton, 'I am met at every request with the question "What has the Earl given?"'[143] In addition, the earls' patronage, prestige and generosity allowed them to block or shape major church projects. When they occasionally exercised such powers, resentment almost certainly followed.[144]

Nevertheless, the earls' relations with local parishes were mainly smooth. They did not interfere in the week-by-week running of the churches by the clergy and the middle- and upper middle-class laity, and most gifts were voluntary and uncontroversial. Moreover, the peers reinforced local gratitude by attending ceremonial occasions in the parishes they supported. In 1868 and 1869, for example, Lord Dudley turned up at special services in Dudley churches inaugurating improvements he had backed. In addition, the presence of the aristocracy enhanced the profits of fund-raising events. Thus the predominant impression left, at least on local Anglicans, was one of the peers' religious generosity. As an obituarist said of the first earl of Dudley, 'His purse and influence were always ready to promote any useful scheme of church work'.[145]

These patricians, then, remained active in religious philanthropy even as they reduced their participation in sectarian agitation. The peers thereby followed local trends. By the late 1870s many sectarian questions, such as church rates, had been settled, and issues such as the local slump and the advances of workers' organizations had become more pressing than the vestiges of disputes concerning such matters as religious education. As a result, well-off leaders from different denominations increasingly cooperated in efforts to win over local workingmen to organized religion. This rapprochement paralleled a decline in partisanship in local government elections and defections to Liberal Unionism in parliamentary elections. These shifts reflected and furthered accommodation between Tory Anglicans and Liberal nonconformists within the upper and middles classes of the region.

As loyal Anglicans and active partisans the Dartmouths and Dudleys were not in the vanguard of these movements. Nor did sectarianism and party rivalry entirely disappear. Nevertheless, except in 1906, such battles became less vitriolic, both for the peers and for the local better-off generally. Partly in consequence, the aristocrats and the rest of the local élites were increasingly involved in philanthropic and local government projects which bridged denominational and partisan barriers. Such participation strengthened the peers' ties to local nonconformists and Liberals. Moreover, by joining other leaders in these campaigns for civic betterment, the Dartmouths and Dudleys helped local élites to avoid, for a time, effective challenge from below.

Instruments of cooperation: philanthropy and the 'municipal gospel'
The Dartmouths and Dudleys devoted much of their local giving to secular philanthropy. In doing so they provided important financial and personal assistance to local charity – which improved considerably in amount, organizational sophistication and popular appeal during these decades. The consequences of the peers' involvement were especially positive, for them and for the towns, because the earls adjusted to collaboration with the middle-class citizens who bore most of the leadership and monetary burdens of local philanthropy.[146]

The earls' extensive participation in voluntary societies stemmed from the towns' activities as well as from the peers' preoccupations. Despite further efforts to bring religion to the masses, secular charities were the principal growth area of private social activity in the later nineteenth century. This sphere thus demanded aristocratic attention for reasons both of duty and of self-interest. For example, the first earl of Dudley felt that since Providence had given him a fortune he should provide for 'the well-being of the community at large'. Yet he and the other peers also gave evidence, in their philanthropy, of concern for social stability, reputation and specific estate advantages. The fifth earl of Dartmouth – opening an amenity that served his own residential development as well as West Bromwich generally – typified the various considerations involved in his wish 'to deserve to be spoken well of by the inhabitants of this neighbourhood'.[147]

The Dartmouths and Dudleys supported a broad range of charitable activities in West Bromwich and Dudley. In education, apart from providing sites and subscriptions to many primary schools, the earls served as officers and benefactors of various institutes, including the comparatively successful technical ventures of the late nineteenth century. The Dudleys also gave their town's adult educational organizations the substantial proceeds of the annual castle fêtes. In addition, the peers provided much leadership and cash to the hospitals launched in each town in the later 1860s, and they supported local military and sporting activities.[148]

They also engaged in substantial 'civic philanthropy': the provision of facilities for free access by all the inhabitants of the towns. In 1877 Dartmouth gave West Bromwich a long-term lease on a 56-acre park which he enlarged ten years later. The Dudleys continued to allow access to the Castle grounds as a *de facto* public park, and in 1866 Lord Dudley gave the town a huge fountain for the market square. In addition, he assisted the construction of the free library and technical institute, and his son gave sites for branch libraries and a grammar school.[149] Through these benefactions the earls' philanthropy, instead of being eclipsed by their towns' expanding municipal efforts, became an important part of them.

In supporting these various projects the peers made a substantial financial effort. Dartmouth's giving (in all regions) was at the higher end, and Dudley's probably toward the lower limit, of the typical range of 4 to 7 per cent of gross income donated by mid-Victorian aristocrats.[150] Despite worries the younger peers

103

apparently did not much alter the level of local subscriptions: the tapering off of new charitable projects by the turn of the century probably eased any perceived strain on their purses. In any event, during the peak period of local philanthropic expansion the high level of the families' incomes and their extensive land ownership had allowed the earls to provide sites and large initial contributions for new projects in addition to continued support for existing charities. For example, in the 1860s Lord Dudley, while keeping up his subscriptions to other institutions in Dudley, supplied £3,000 for his fountain and sites for a new dispensary building and the new hospital.[151]

Middle-class donations were also of great importance, especially since individual businessmen had fewer localities among which to spread their largesse. By the 1860s leading families such as the Bagnalls, Chances and Kenricks provided significant aid to town-wide charities as well as support for schools, institutes and chapels associated with their works. Moreover, upper middle-class families occasionally gave very large sums such as the £20,000 which manufacturer Joseph Guest, 'the local Peabody', provided for the Dudley hospital later named after him. Although the aristocrats often topped the donation and subscription lists, both earls' share of the total usually fell well below half: a wide range of middle-class men, supplemented by workingmen in some cases, joined the best-off industrialists in contributing most of the money. In addition, like the peers, middle-class worthies made substantial gifts to the municipalities, especially in West Bromwich. For example, that town gained a museum and a five-acre park from businessman Reuben Farley, and Dudley obtained the collections and endowments of Brooke Robinson M.P.[152]

Nevertheless, the aristocratic families were philanthropists of special importance. In almost no project was the peers' giving negligible. Overall, the Dudleys were the single greatest philanthropists in their town, and the Dartmouths may have edged out the Kenricks for that honour in West Bromwich.[153] Moreover, in both towns only the earls owned land of sufficient quantity and quality to provide large public parks as well as sites for many local institutions. The earls' acreage, prestige and reputed riches made their support especially important for initiating projects. They also served as reliable sources of cash in crises. For instance, when West Bromwich needed a fountain in 1882 the mayor, believing that too many appeals were under way, persuaded Dartmouth to finance the project himself.[154] In these ways, the resources of both peers proved significant in the expansion of local philanthropic effort during the period; the infusion of noble as well as middle-class wealth was crucial, especially in Dudley, for the degree of progress achieved.

The aristocrats' participation in the organizations themselves was largely ornamental. Both families made personal appearances at openings of buildings and similar grand occasions. Dudley, for example, spoke at the meeting inaugurating the new mechanics institute in 1863.[155] Yet the earls, who filled the largely honorary presidencies, played little part in detailed management. Active leadership fell to less eminent though highly respectable citizens – middling manufacturers, clergymen, doctors, solicitors and, to a lesser extent, larger retailers. Top industrialists such as J.H. Chance sometimes served as managers but, like the earls, they usually filled honorary positions only.

Local voluntary societies usually cherished aristocratic officers, however slight their contribution to the deliberations of the leadership. In 1883, thinking that a local head would be better than an 'ornamental one residing at a distance',

Dartmouth attempted to resign the presidency of the West Bromwich Floral and Horticultural Society. But the active leaders of the society persuaded the earl to remain: he need not 'take any part in the work' but it would help if he would 'allow his name to continue as president'. Leading industrialists such as the Kenricks and local M.P.s also served as valued celebrities.[156] Yet the eagerness of the organizations to secure appearances by the peers, and their delight when the earls came, suggest that the prestige and glamour of the aristocrats still surpassed those of the upper middle class.

Difficulties remained in the relationship between the earls and local recipients of largesse, which resulted from the determination of the peers and their agents to protect estate interests, to limit their giving to a reasonable level, to avoid serving as the towns' only major philanthropists and to support only 'deserving' causes. So they often rejected appeals, gave token sums or cut existing subscriptions. Even when they provided large amounts, the estates demanded assurances that the local middle class was also contributing. Also, the earls occasionally tried to alter the plans of schools and voluntary societies.[157] Such behaviour sometimes met resistance. For example, Lord Dudley had difficulty persuading the local mechanics institute to share the proceeds of the castle fêtes with the school of art. Likewise, Dartmouth's initial park offer received a rebuff from commissioners upset by the proposed terms and by the earl's unprompted intervention. Dartmouth also met defeat in his effort to have the West Bromwich hospital adopt a particular admissions policy.[158] Even when the aristocrats' prestige and financial importance won compliance, the recipients probably resented such treatment.

But these were only minor disturbances in a generally satisfactory relationship. To begin with, the earls and their agents learned how to preserve their own dignity without affronting the pride of middle-class philanthropists. When Dartmouth made his second, successful park offer he waited to be approached by the town's leading citizen, Farley – and improved his earlier terms.[159] Moreover, both families mixed politeness with aristocratic glamour to ease the occasions when middle-class worthies approached them for gifts. The first earl of Dudley, for example, invited representatives from the mechanics institute to lunch. The fifth earl of Dartmouth, meanwhile, was 'the most affable, frank, and approachable of men and above all a cheerful giver'. In addition, appeals from these towns, as centres of the peers' interests in the Black Country, were usually successful enough to defuse most of the resentment generated by the screening. As a local obituarist said of Dartmouth, 'It is doubtful whether he was ever approached in vain when aid was sought for any deserving movement . . . in West Bromwich.'[160] Finally, the earls, their subordinates and other middle-class allies often turned to methods more subtle than direct demands to influence policy within the institutions. The Dudleys' agents, themselves donors, and the Dartmouths' closet ally, Farley, were members of supervisory committees, especially in medical organizations. Thus in Guest Hospital, Dudley's agents eschewed special privileges for the earl and avoided direct challenges from insurgents. Yet they remained key figures in the charity.[161]

Adjusted in these ways, the earls' rôle in the launching and running of the mainly middle-class organizations was compatible with their positions as inactive but decorative officers. Both sides gained: the peers provided the organizations and their active leaders with status and money, and the charities supplied the aristocrats with humanitarian satisfaction and with conspicuous local service which tended to justify their wealth and status. This generally satisfactory aristocratic participation eased the peers' relations both with the local middle class and with local workingmen. Philanthropic activities, by including all levels of the upper and middle classes in uncontroversial activities aimed principally at the working class, helped to neutralize the internal divisions of the better-off. Social breadth was compatible with overlapping leadership by the well-to-do and with special honour for the aristocracy and top industrialists.

Religious and political differences proved more troublesome. Sectarianism caused some difficulties at the opening of Dartmouth Park, for example, and in a subsequent dispute concerning Sunday operation. However, the park, like similar benefactions by the aristocrats and their middle-class associates, generally helped to ease religious and political tensions. Both titled and other leaders of these projects emphasized their determination to exclude politics and religion. Also, especially in West Bromwich, voluntary enterprises – particularly the later, more successful initiatives – included significant numbers from both major political and religious blocs. These institutions produced cooperation among men who were often antagonists in other contexts, including Dartmouth and William Kenrick.[162] Likewise in Dudley, though it remained more troubled by partisanship and sectarianism, all denominations and parties praised the earl's benefactions. The peers' participation in philanthropy, therefore, assisted the unity of the well-to-do generally, while bringing the aristocrats into closer and warmer contact with the middle class, including its Liberals and nonconformists.[163]

As far as ties with the working class were concerned, the rapid advance of local voluntary societies in these relatively small and deprived towns may have had significant social impact. Certainly, the nature of the earls' philanthropic rôle tended to enhance their popularity among workers. Neither family had much to do with disputes concerning the rôle of workingmen in local charities and, like most members of the upper middle class, they had only limited contact with the related (but much more difficult) sphere of Poor Law administration, where problems were often severe, discretion limited, and the boards riddled by squabbling. The peers wisely left such chores to the middle- and lower-middle class, and instead supported voluntary or municipal relief efforts in times of distress.[164]

Moreover, the earls received much favourable attention at festivities connected with their benefactions – such as at the opening of Dudley's fountain in 1867 (see fig. 9) and at the inauguration of Dartmouth Park 11 years later[165] – which emphasized social unity and the generosity of the towns' chief citizens to large numbers of enthusiastic spectators. The depth of the mass reaction to such gifts and fanfare is hard to judge, but its direction was certainly positive. In West Bromwich the schools provided by the Dartmouths and by wealthy middle-class families 'enjoyed excellent reputations, and parents had much pride when their boys attended'. Similarly, when in 1861 Dudley and his mother opened schools at Pensnett he had supported, they found a cheering crowd and a banner proclaiming 'Long live the Earl of Dudley and Lady Ward'.[166] Likewise, the many working-class visitors to Dartmouth Park and Dudley Castle grounds presumably thought better of the earls because of these facilities. In all these circumstances Dartmouth and Dudley appeared as grandees dispensing largesse, rather than as landlords and industrialists enjoying handsome returns from local property.

Overall, both families considerably enhanced their local standing through their secular philanthropy. Local opinion greatly esteemed the elder peers – and eventually, if slightly less enthusiastically, their sons – as benefactors. The *Dudley*

Herald noted that 'In Dudley . . . the Earl's benefactions have always been on a scale commensurate with the large property in his hands. Our chief public institutions owe their continuance in their present efficiency, if not their existence, to Lord Dudley's influence and help.' Dartmouth also drew lavish praise, less for indispensability than for his repeated 'munificent' donations, the spread of his generosity beyond his own party and religion, and his personal efforts.[167] For both families philanthropy helped to neutralize the resentment aroused by aristocratic activity in the more contentious areas of trade, industrial relations, party politics and sectarian agitation. In charity more than in those other spheres, the peers' combination of wealth, established social position, and glamour was of significant value both to the middle class élite and to the local population as a whole.

In local government, as in philanthropy, there was much expansion and

Figure 9. Opening of the Dudley fountain by the earl and countess of Dudley, 1867 (by courtesy of the Cambridge University Library).

achievement during this period. All the subdivisions of the better-off obtained shares of the posts. Yet, as in voluntary societies, the substantial middle class predominated. The local authorities produced marked but incomplete improvements in basic services such as sanitation and elementary education. They had more success in providing 'optional' facilities, notably town halls, public parks and municipal utilities. Such projects occasioned civic festivals which emphasized the community service of the élites and social harmony. Through such activities the diverse but interconnected leaderships became more skilled at overcoming their own social, religious and partisan divisions. These élites had to cope with the demands of ratepayers' advocates and, later, of workingmen's representatives. But in these previously poorly-served towns, advances in the style and substance of local government helped to preserve ties between the well-to-do and the working class.[168]

The Dartmouths and Dudleys played important rôles in this process. The earls did not regain the paramount influence in local government which they had lost in the turbulent period ending in the 1850s. But relations and reciprocal advantage advanced from the low point of those decades. Lord Dudley's dealings with the board of health in its later years remained unsatisfactory. Similarly, in West Bromwich the commissioners rejected the earl's offer of land for a cemetery extension as well as for a park.[169] However, as each town incorporated (Dudley in 1865, West Bromwich in 1882) and stepped up its pace of achievement, the relationship between local government élite and aristocrat improved significantly. The diminution of ratepayers' agitation and, eventually, of sharp partisanship aided this process, and the peers found the new authorities, with their enhanced prestige, easier to work with and more progressive.

Unlike some other aristocrats, both Dudley and Dartmouth supported incorporation. Lord Dudley presented the council with the mace of his defunct manorial court and treated the new authority with respect.[170] In West Bromwich, Dartmouth saw the 'Staffordshire knot' in the borough's arms representing 'the triple link that would bind the lord of the manor, the Mayor and Aldermen, and the councilmen in one strong bond of union for . . . [the town's] general welfare'. The councils reciprocated such backing. The seal of the Dudley corporation bore the crest of the Wards, and the West Bromwich council presented the countess of Dartmouth with a portrait of her husband and hung a copy in its chamber (fig. 10).[171]

In both Dudley and West Bromwich, too, aristocratic donations of land and money materially assisted the councils' popular 'optional' projects. Such aid proved particularly important for municipalities with limited resources which came of age at a time of local economic uncertainty. Yet since other benefactors and the ratepayers also contributed to these efforts, no abject dependence resulted.[172] Both peers and councils profited from the success of the projects themselves and from the mutual felicitations at the opening ceremonies.

Shared advantage also arose from the earls' service as chief celebrities of the new municipalities. The aristocrats attended the most important municipal ceremonial occasions; their appearance as featured speakers and performers increased the size and enthusiasm of the crowds. At these jamborees there was much reciprocal congratulation. When the sixth earl of Dartmouth opened a museum in West Bromwich in 1898 the local M.P. praised the earl's generosity to the town; Dartmouth in turn lauded the councillors as 'public-spirited men, whose object in life was to identify themselves with some movement for the advancement of the

Figure 10. The fifth earl of Dartmouth (by courtesy of Sandwell council).

people'.[173] These ceremonies also permitted councils and peers to renew their vows of deference and benevolence. For instance, in Dudley – where the Wards were even more regular and more fêted performers than were the Dartmouths in West Bromwich – thousands watched the widowed countess and young earl unveil the statue of the late Lord Dudley in 1888. The town fathers voiced their esteem for the generous and distinguished first earl, and the countess pledged that her son would follow his father's example in aiding the town.[174]

Such festivities also allowed the peers to place their partisan and sectarian affiliations in the context of united civic effort. For instance, Dartmouth quipped at the opening of West Bromwich town hall in 1875 that he was proud of the locality's progress despite his supposedly antiquated public opinions. Councillors of all parties and religious factions complimented the earls on these occasions.[175] The peers' presence thus reinforced the developing unity of the local government élites as well as the aristocrats' own places in them. These themes also emerged in coming-of-age and marriage celebrations. Complete with addresses, presentations and treats for the poor, these festivals broadened during the period, with municipal encouragement, to include the towns as a whole.[176]

The philanthropic and ceremonial relationships between the peers and the local authorities conferred glamour on the young councils – whose 'municipal gospels' otherwise would have lacked the splendour that larger, richer towns such as Birmingham could produce more easily. The earls, meanwhile, apparently saw their rôle as a way to 'give some proof of . . . continued good will'.[177] By bolstering the councils in these ways the aristocrats fostered their families' popularity while assisting civic improvements which the peers also valued in themselves.

In Dudley this largesse and display drew reinforcement from the estate's provision of three mayors: agent Frederick Smith (1865–6), G.H. Claughton (1891–5) and the second earl himself (1895–7). Smith and Claughton gained this recognition mainly because of their key positions in the estate and their close association with Lord Dudley.[178] But why should the council honour the estate and the earl? In large measure their choice reflected a recognition of economic power: the peer held 'Dudley, and the great ring round it, in the hollow of his hand'. Civic deference might help to tame this behemoth for the benefit of local improvements. In addition, the aristocrat and his retainers provided superior versions of the high social status desired in a chief magistrate. Claughton and the second earl had resources more than adequate for mayoral dignity and hospitality – at a time when this requirement put mayors in short supply in Dudley and elsewhere. Finally, although the estate had a marked class and partisan identity, the magnitude of its status and wealth placed the selection of these men above the rivalries of social and party factions on the council.[179]

Why did these luminaries serve? Apparently *noblesse oblige* was an important spur. Also, Claughton and the earl evidently realized that their service facilitated supervision of the estate's manifold interests in municipal affairs. Indeed, as mayor, Claughton dealt with inquiries from councillors concerning estate policy. Nevertheless, this motive was probably subsidiary: the estate and the council monitored and influenced each other's activities whoever the mayor might be. More important, it seems, was a desire to further the general popularity of the estate by gratifying the strong desires of the council.[180] Elsewhere aristocratic mayors seldom attended council meetings or took much interest in their affairs. Yet in Dudley, Claughton, and to a lesser extent the earl, played more than merely decorative rôles. The former conducted negotiations for the municipality and received much credit for various council achievements. Lord Dudley, also serving at the Board of Trade and on the London County Council, stipulated in advance that he could not regularly attend the council. But he turned up at some monthly meetings as well as at the annual ceremonial gathering, and supplied useful advice on questions such as tramways and electricity supply.[181]

Whether the council placed more value on the status or on the practical accomplishments of agent and peer, their tenures of office were triumphs of public relations. For example, reciprocal goodwill emerged when the council gave Lord Dudley a silver cradle commemorating the birth of a child to the countess during his mayorality. When the earl received the freedom of the borough with great fanfare in 1899 the townsmen stressed his services as mayor. Thus in Dudley, perhaps even more than elsewhere, aristocratic mayors fostered cooperation between a still-powerful estate, local government leaders and – through civic ritual – the population as a whole.[182]

In West Bromwich the lesser economic and philanthropic importance of the Dartmouths, and the absence of a responsible resident agent, prevented an aristocratic mayoralty. Yet Reuben Farley, who became a great civic celebrity during his five terms as mayor, often extolled the virtues of the Dartmouths, producing an impression that Farley and the earl were the town's two most 'useful' men. And, even without serving as mayors, the earls rendered significant practical as well as ceremonial service to West Bromwich. The fifth earl's parliamentary assistance was of special importance before the town acquired its own M.P. Moreover, in his capacity as landlord, Dartmouth sold the borough, on favourable terms, a site that West Bromwich needed for a major sewage project. Gratitude for such help persisted. A councillor told the sixth earl in 1921 that Dartmouth 'had it in his power to help or hinder municipal progress . . . He had always been ready to help.'[183] The Dudley estate's mayoral service probably gave that family's relations with their municipality a greater boost. Still, the Dartmouths gained much from their rôle, and the Dudleys – with greater local interests and more serious recent clashes with townsmen – had more need of such help.

Of course, there were also significant tensions in the relationships between the earls and local government leaders. For while estates and municipalities were generally well-disposed to each other, occasional disputes arose in the regular negotiations between the improving authorities and these large landowners. During the early years of Dudley's incorporation, serious problems occurred concerning the amount of compensation the earl should receive for his market tolls and for his rôle in a sewage project. The latter clash, though exaggerated by local Liberals. revealed considerable resentment in Dudley against an extremely wealthy estate apparently trying to extort money from a struggling town. The earl's agents were most involved, but even the peer's standing in the town suffered from the protracted struggle.[184] Nevertheless, the estate managed to smooth its relations with the council even before the era of aristocratic mayors arrived. For example, the earl's offer to aid the town with its baths and free library coincided with the sewage dispute. Later, in the wake of the agent's and the earl's mayoralties an alderman saw even the market tolls episode in a favourable light.[185] Under the emollient Claughton such battles became less common anyway.

As a less substantial landowner Dartmouth had easier business relations with West Bromwich corporation. However, especially from the 1880s, the earl faced, both within and outside local government, fundamental criticism of his property rights. Resentment surfaced against his immunity from rates on the coal that produced his royalties, and his position as tithe owner, and as proprietor of enclosed land, became controversial.[186] The Dudleys had to deal with similar discontent. Their situation was exacerbated by ownership of undeveloped building land and by legal immunity from the property damage that estate mining caused. By the 1880s, with early mine workings collapsing, the mining compensation issue had become a major problem. From 1885, in line with legal misgivings and a more general effort to please, the estate acknowledged some liability for damages. Yet, unpleasantness persisted.[187]

Such episodes, though taken less seriously by Unionists than by Liberals, complicated the peers' relations with the local government élite and with the local population generally. Still, supporters of the earls recited their gifts to the towns when such attacks on estate privileges and policy arose. Moreover, the councillors, at least, recognized their need to cooperate with the aristocrats. As the Dudley council told the earl, 'Your lordship is the largest landowner . . . without your cooperation improvements and progress could not be carried on without great difficulty'.[188]

Another source of tension lay in the collision of the self-assurance of the peers and their agents, on the one hand, with the easily-affronted dignity of the young boroughs on the other. Deference often mixed with vexation. At an 1883 mayoral banquet in Dudley, for example, a glowing account of the town's relationship with the noble family competed for attention with evidence of irritation at the cancellation of a local engagement by the countess. Yet, as in philanthropy, the earls profited from their mistakes in this regard. For instance, Dartmouth waited until he was certain that the town would accept before offering to give West Bromwich its mayoral insignia.[189] Likewise Claughton and the second earl of Dudley were more tactful in their suggestions to the municipality than the blunt first earl had been. And, by the end of the century, in an atmosphere of partisan rapprochement and demonstrated civic achievement, local government leaders were less easily offended by aristocratic behaviour.

By the 1890s the previous chaotic mixture of condescension, deference, and hostility had evolved into a sense of reciprocal advantage laced with mutual compliments. Both sides acknowledged the double-edged nature of the benefits inherent in the association between peer and council. As the *Dudley Herald* argued, 'The honour which has been conferred upon the borough is no small one, whilst his lordship acknowledges that he too is sensible of the honour the invitation to become Mayor of Dudley necessarily confers upon him.' It had become clear that the aristocrats were as anxious, as Dartmouth said earlier, to show 'my deep interest in the progress and welfare of my native parish', as the councils were to receive this attention. Both sides gained. As a Dudley newspaper wrote in 1895, 'the noble House has recognised that wealth and position have their responsibilities, whilst the populace have shown appreciation of that recognition'.[190]

Thus, while significant tensions lingered, by the 1890s both local government élites had generally satisfactory relations with their noble families. The Dudley estate continued to have more difficulties with the council than did the Dartmouths, but the Dudleys also had more influence in local government and obtained greater glorification from local council activities. The later incorporation of these towns, the individual peers' progressive instincts and the towns' greater need for the dignity and practical help the earls could provide – these factors diminished, and shortened, the phase of aristocrat-council conflict also found in other towns.[191] In neither town was peer or council completely dependent on the other. Yet in each locality aristocrat and municipality had a significant stake in amicable interaction.

The aristocratic rôle in local government must not be overstated. In this sphere, as in philanthropy, the middle class carried greater burdens of leadership and finance than did the nobility, and leading local businessmen as well as peers provided manpower, prestige, cash and political help to these local government élites. In diminished but still significant numbers the upper middle class – especially its newer members – continued to participate in week-by-week council affairs at the end of the century. Even the longest-established dynasties such as the Kenricks remained active in municipal ceremonies and civic philanthropy, playing a rôle in local government, especially in West Bromwich, which resembled that of the earls.

Nevertheless, in municipal affairs, as in voluntary activities, the peers retained special advantages of wealth, landownership and glamour. As men of the highest prestige, the aristocrats were in the best position to help compensate for the gradually declining social level of town councillors. Moreover, the grandees' rank gave them special license to discourage council partisanship and workingmen's demands for municipal activism.[192] The earls, therefore, made a distinctive as well as significant contribution to the acceptability, style, substance, and unity of local government in these towns. This aid proved especially useful in Dudley where municipal resources were more limited, partisanship was stronger, and the social standing of councillors was lower than in West Bromwich. But the Dartmouths had significant impact as well. Local government was a more trouble-filled sphere of activity than philanthropy. Yet in municipal as in charitable affairs, the earls' performance made a substantial contribution to their positions in the towns. In local government, as in voluntary activities, adjustment to prominent and generous ceremonial rôles, in cooperation with mainly middle-class élites, brought the peers much better results than had earlier attempts to dominate.

Conclusion

Like other patricians with urban links, both the Dartmouths and the Dudleys enjoyed great popularity in their localities in the late nineteenth and early twentieth centuries. The Dartmouth name was 'a household word' in West Bromwich, and the first earl of Dudley's death created a 'profound impression' on Dudley and its environs. Even the Dudleys' agents, whose custody of that estate's difficult problems helped to protect the earls from criticism, received marks of local respect.[193] Such esteem was strongest among the earls' co-religionists and partisans, and in the upper middle class. Nevertheless, the huge crowds which watched the aristocrats' ceremonial appearances, and the unanimity of praise for them from local councils, suggest that this popularity stretched across barriers of opinion and status.

Service, glamour and personality were the most important ingredients of this respect. Especially towards the end of the period, a popular aristocrat had to prove his usefulness to the community. Yet while these towns thought they had 'a claim upon, and a right to' the services of the peers, the fulfilment of these assumptions produced gratitude. The Bishop of Saint Albans echoed these attitudes in praising his brother-in-law, the first earl of Dudley: '[Lord Dudley] had ever felt an interest in the welfare of this town and its inhabitants – (cheers). It was only to be expected that he should do so . . . But men did not always do that which might reasonably be expected of them – (hear, hear). The Earl . . . had fulfilled their best hopes and expectations – (cheers).'[194] Since the aristocrats went beyond their duties as businessmen and employers the townspeople gave them more than ordinary esteem in return.

The glamour of aristocracy also proved a great asset in cultivating popularity – which was probably disproportionate to the grandees' actual services. The earls supplied the display and excitement that these grimy industrial towns otherwise lacked. Some contemporaries intensely disliked the pomp and privileges of the aristocracy, yet repeated local invocations of 'the noble earls' suggest that this was not a majority view in Dudley and West Bromwich – at least with respect to *their* peers. General approval of the aristocrats' personalities and manners proved important as well. Ideally a grandee connected with such towns should combine domestic virtue, a proper show of lordly grandeur and courtesy toward local residents.[195] The fifth earl of Dartmouth, for example, drew praise as 'a kindly, genial, whole-souled, English country gentleman'. The second earl of Dudley's youthful gambling habits brought censure, but he won compliments because, in his early years in the title, he 'well maintained the princely traditions of his picturesque father'. Also, the Dartmouths and Dudleys increasingly earned applause for their politeness in dealing with local citizens.[196]

How far did the Dartmouths and Dudleys supplement this popularity with real power? The earls had had to abandon attempts to maintain their early dominance. Yet a 'celebrity' rôle was compatible not only with economic leverage but also with considerable, if diminished, social and political impact. The peers' popularity itself helped to discourage concerted attacks on their estates: a negative but important form of influence in a time of rapid change. Moreover, having learned how to compromise, the aristocrats had some effect on the result of parliamentary elections and on the nature and timing of philanthropic and municipal projects. The earls and their agents could not dictate policy without producing rebellions. However, the peers affected civic decisions in more subtle ways – by deciding which projects to support generously, through suggestions made by their allies, or by behind-the-scenes negotiations between town and estate leaders. Since almost every major local initiative – especially in Dudley – involved the estates, such leverage could have considerable cumulative impact. The earls helped to steer the towns toward significant 'improvements' but also away from 'fads and theories and fantastic projects', which might menace respectable leadership generally and their estates in particular.[197] Activity, flexibility and generosity combined with underlying social and economic strength to yield persisting influence. With this level of success the peers could easily do without their lost dominance.

The Dudleys had greater sway over philanthropy and local government, if not over politics, than did the Dartmouths, and this superior leverage mainly stemmed from the Dudleys' greater importance in promoting and sustaining the local economy. Also, in philanthropy and municipal affairs less prosperous Dudley was more dependent on its titular earl than was West Bromwich on Dartmouth. The latter, with his lesser wealth and more scattered involvements, drew praise for assisting all civic projects, but the town fathers of Dudley acknowledged a debt to Lord Dudley for an even more substantial role in their corresponding institutions. Despite this important contrast, at the turn of the century both cases fell between the extremes of aristocratic dominance and noble futility.[198] Each peer enjoyed considerable popularity and exercised influence on major decisions in local institutions. Yet neither could prevail in the committee rooms without significant concessions to other citizens.

This 'middling' degree of influence stemmed from a number of factors. Both families had considerable shares of the town's resources, yet neither dominated the local economy. The relatively small size of the towns enhanced the earls' influence, but by the later nineteenth century each locality was sufficiently large to develop independence. The comparatively tiny middle class encouraged aristocratic leadership, yet the middle strata, by the end of the period, proved large and prestigious enough to carry the bulk of local civic responsibility. Similarly, although the undersupply of local institutions had encouraged aristocratic dominance early in the century, their subsequent rapid growth restricted aristocratic sway. Still, local civic accomplishment was not sufficiently well-endowed, innovative or glamourous to render noble participation redundant. The peers themselves were sufficiently popular and active to sustain significant influence, yet none was so devoted to these particular towns as to produce either dominance or reaction. Finally, both families dabbled enough in contentious activities to make impossible an unspotted local record, yet each engaged in sufficient uncontroversial improvement to generate respect.

What were the consequences of the earls' social and political activities for the towns' social development? Led by top industrialists, the resident middle class – which provided most of the manpower, money and prestige of the local élites – contributed more to the success of social leadership than did the peers. Moreover, the influence of the élites as a whole must not be overstated. Basic economic and social forces – such as waning prosperity, social mobility, working class subdivisions, and the small size of the towns – also contributed to local social stability. Also, the votes and organizations of workingmen increasingly prompted concessions from these Black Country élites even before 1914.

Nevertheless, in the later nineteenth and early twentieth centuries – in contrast to the 1840s – the local well-to-do were in a strong position compared to their counterparts in other industrial areas. Furthermore, local élites had played a substantial part in achieving this relative stability. Despite the daunting problems of an urban 'frontier', they had created an approximation of the institutions, social services and ceremonies enjoyed by larger cities and by industrial areas whose social framework had developed earlier. The social substance and interconnections of these élites facilitated such gains; élite size and diversity maximized contact with, and acceptability to, the local population. The increasing harmony of the élites – partly a response to economic challenge and to advances in working class organization – promoted their practical achievements and enhanced a sense of unity across class lines.

The earls did much to produce these accomplishments. Admittedly they did not move local society in a direction it would otherwise have failed to take, but the peers *did* make distinctive contributions – in cash, land, prestige and glamour – which speeded and eased the formation of effective local élites. As generous figureheads of decreasing sectarian and political notoriety, the Dartmouths and Dudleys promoted both the practical achievements of local institutions and the growing unity of Black Country leaders on which these efforts in part depended. With special attraction both for the middle and the working classes, the aristocrats played significant parts in the promotion of 'civic unity'.

115

6 Epilogue: economic and social withdrawal since 1914

Since the First World War the Dartmouths and Dudleys have significantly reduced their personal and economic ties to the Black Country, and they have also cut back their social and political involvements in West Bromwich and Dudley. Changes in both families have diminished their contact with the region. The sixth and seventh earls of Dartmouth resided at Patshull until their deaths in 1936 and 1958 respectively. However, the latter's successors – his brother and nephew – have lived in the southeast. Thus, although descendants of the seventh earl still have homes at Patshull, the link between the title and the region has been broken. The second earl of Dudley spent little time in England between his marriage in 1924 to the former actress Gertie Millar and his death in 1932. After the family sold Witley Court in 1920, Lord Ednam (the future third earl) and his wife reopened Himley Hall, but Lord Dudley sold the house in 1947, thus ending the residential tie between peer and district.[199]

During these decades the aristocrats have also effectively severed their economic connections with the Black Country. In the 1920s and 1930s the Dartmouths continued as royalty owners at Sandwell Park and as agricultural landlords in West Bromwich and Patshull. However, after the Second World War nationalization ended their links with the colliery, and municipal acquisition for greenbelt absorbed the rest of the Sandwell estate. In addition, after the death of the seventh earl, most of his Patshull property passed to the Crown.[200] The Dudley estate underwent considerable change before as well as after 1945. In the early 1920s depression in local trades, the second earl's debts, managerial disarray and the need for modernization made drastic action essential. Ednam, a keen businessman, recruited outside capital and ended the family's direct entrepreneurial rôle. In addition, the formation of an investment company facilitated a gradual shift – accelerated after 1945 by nationalization of coal and steel – away from dependence on Black Country income. This transformation also included the sale of most of the family's land in the district. From 1926 Ednam began to break up the estate; a massive sale in 1947 in effect removed the family from landownership in the district, although they retained interests in a few local firms until the 1960s and 1970s.[201] So for both families economic as well as residential links with the Black Country, having lingered through the Second World War, virtually ceased thereafter.

In the 1920s and 1930s the Dartmouths and Dudleys still played significant parts in the social and political life of West Bromwich and Dudley. However, aristocratic activity and influence had fallen from their early twentieth century level – foreshadowing further decline in these rôles after the Second World War.

Participation by the Dartmouths in the affairs of interwar West Bromwich began badly with Lewisham's defeat by Labour candidate F.O. Roberts in the 1918 general election. The political situation in the town was much more adverse for a Conservative than it had been in 1910. The franchise had been extended; the trade unions had made gains and were firmly backing Roberts; Labour was well-organized and on the upsurge in local government; and the former Liberal M.P. supported the challenger. In addition, Lewisham, just back from wartime service abroad, was unable to fight the election in person because of influenza.[202] Even in these dire straits the Dartmouths exerted themselves to some effect. The earl appeared and spoke eloquently for his son, stressing Lewisham's war record and his support for progressive reconstruction, and little rancour against the Dartmouths surfaced. Yet Lewisham gained only 46 per cent of the vote in the two-man contest.

Although the Legges were still popular their remaining political influence was small in a town whose political complexion had altered permanently. Accordingly, they soon withdrew from active participation in Conservatism in West Bromwich.[203]

Despite this setback the sixth earl continued to serve as civic philanthropist and celebrity. Approached by representatives of the council, Dartmouth and Lewisham agreed in 1919 to give the town the freehold of Dartmouth Park. As a result the council two years later conferred the freedom of the borough on the earl. In 1923 the transfer of the title deeds occasioned a final Dartmouth-led civic jamboree, featuring large crowds and the Prince of Wales.[204] Nevertheless, this fanfare represented the culmination of a previous philanthropic initiative, and of an older ceremonial rôle, rather than the launching of a massive 'new presence'. After Sandwell Hall was demolished in 1928 Dartmouth allowed the corporation to have the site. And as the sixth earl aged and the town began a burst of municipal activity, the Dartmouth connection became more remote.[205] The seventh earl's involvements in West Bromwich were largely confined to sport (he was an active president of West Bromwich Albion for many years), and his public life lay more at Westminster (where he was Lord Great Chamberlain 1928–36) and on the county council (where he was a rural representative in the 1940s).[206]

As the Dartmouths remained active and generous in West Bromwich life even after 1945, affection for them persisted.[207] However, as participation fell away and the economic tie vanished, this pleasant relationship began to have less importance for peers and townsmen alike. This change is reflected in the diminishing press coverage in West Bromwich of the deaths of the fifth, sixth and seventh earls. West Bromwich Albion mourned the latter, but in the town as a whole the Dartmouth connection was a rather distant memory by the late 1950s.[208]

Although starting from a position of greater strength, the Dudley's local rôle has undergone a similar shrinkage. In his later years the second earl's public appearances in the Black Country were infrequent, although his son, Ednam, played an active part in the region's social and political affairs in the interwar period. He was an important benefactor of Guest Hospital; he assisted campaigns to alleviate unemployment and poor housing; in the propitious year of 1931 he ousted a Labour incumbent from Wednesbury and aided the successful Unionist candidate in Dudley; and at Westminster he helped to organize a federation of M.P.s from the district. In addition, having accompanied the Prince of Wales abroad on official visits, he addressed meetings of local businessmen concerning foreign competition.[209]

Nevertheless, this activism brought problems as well as successes. Ednam's 'tactless' manner and zealous defence of estate interests annoyed local worthies. Moreover, his partisan interventions naturally produced controversy in a region in which, except in 1931, Labour was making significant advances.[210] These difficulties punctuated the estate's relations with Dudley corporation in the 1920s and 1930s. The second earl pleased the town by selling land which the council then covered with houses.[211] Yet an attempt to renew the estate's rôle as civic philanthropist backfired. The second earl and his son gave the municipality a 99-year lease on Dudley Castle and its grounds. But the agreement's conditions – designed to protect the estate and to preserve free public access – ran foul of the dignity, financial woes and growing political diversity of the council. Matters came to a head after Ednam successfully prosecuted the corporation for allowing a celebration at the castle of Labour's temporary capture of the Dudley seat in the 1929 general election. One Labour councillor argued that 'The Dudley family as regards the civic life of this town are as dead as mutton . . . [They] have treated the town like a schoolboy does an orange – sucks the best out of it and throws the peel into the gutter.' Other civic fathers disagreed; but the council returned the castle to the estate shortly before the death of the second earl.[212] Two years later the new peer's enhanced status and his resolution to moderate his political interventions facilitated a public reconciliation: in laying the foundation stone of new municipal buildings Lord Dudley earned praise even from a Labour alderman.[213] However, the third earl's civic contacts never equalled those of his father's early career in frequency and warmth. The castle dispute was symptomatic of the pitfalls inherent in perpetuating the 'celebrity' rôle into an era of sharpened political conflict and diminished economic involvement.

In these circumstances, the Wards experienced a gradual but significant decline in their local standing. The second earl's long absence had undercut his popularity, although a large throng, including representatives from the council and other major local institutions, attended his funeral at Himley. The third earl's activities in the region, contentious though some were, temporarily sustained keen interest in the family.[214] However, following Lord Dudley's service as regional commissioner for the Midlands during the Second World War, his activities in the region fell off drastically. Partly as a result, his death in 1969 attracted much less local attention than had that of his father 37 years earlier.[215] The current earl's philanthropic and civic ties have survived the reduction of his local business interests, but such connections no longer form major preoccupations either of the family or of the town.[216]

In the years immediately preceding 1914 rising social tension and the infrequency of the earls' local appearances may already have begun the twentieth-century decline of the influence of these estates. In any case, the First World War weakened such ties by straining aristocratic finances and by boosting class-based politics. In both towns the lingering economic involvement of the estates and the continued activity of the families sustained a lessened social and political rôle into the interwar period. With the local economy often ailing and social conditions still problematical, aristocratic glamour and gifts remained useful. But these towns were now well-established: their active councils, in which Labour played an increasing rôle, required such help less than had their predecessors. Aristocrats with diminishing local property, similarly, had less cause to foster civic goodwill.

Since the Second World War the breaking of most economic ties and the advent of another shift in political and social atmosphere have further reduced the significance of the connection between peers and towns. The magnitude of the aristocrats' original strength, the lingering impact of their successful adjustment to earlier challenges, and persisting feelings of affection on both sides – these factors account for the survival after 1945 of a vestigial local aristocratic rôle. However, in an era of general prosperity and expanding government activity such localities have had relatively little need for noble prestige and cash. Likewise the peers have had neither the practical incentive to provide these benefits nor the local resources with which to do so. The postwar sale of Himley Hall to the National Coal Board and the motorway's incursion into the former Sandwell estate thus serve as apt symbols of the great but protracted decline of the aristocratic dominance that these towns had experienced in the early nineteenth century. The presence of the Sandwell gatehouse arch above the motorway roundabout, and of Dudley Castle atop its town, constitute – with remnants of the philanthropy of these families – the only reminders of once overwhelming patrician influence and involvement.

APPENDIX 1

Genealogical table of the Dartmouth family (simplified).

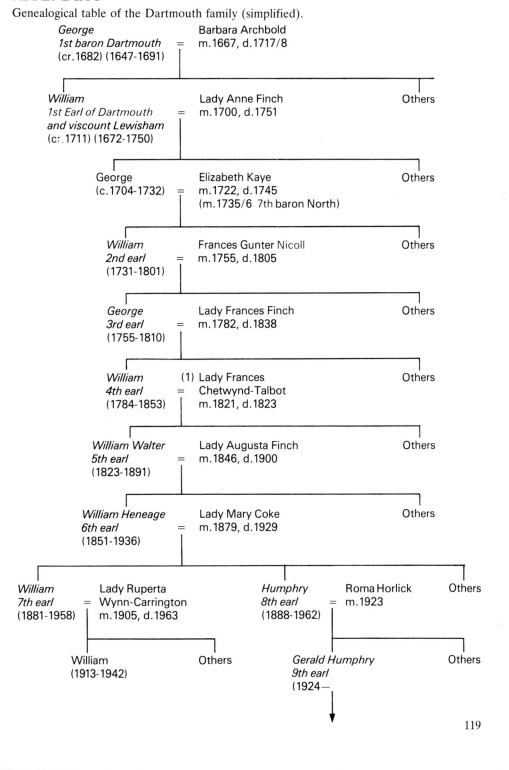

APPENDIX 2

Genealogical table of the Dudley family (simplified).

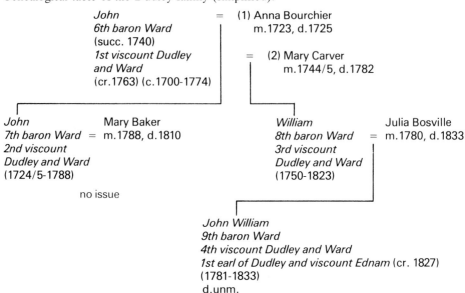

John
6th baron Ward
(succ. 1740)
*1st viscount Dudley
and Ward*
(cr.1763) (c.1700-1774)
= (1) Anna Bourchier
m.1723, d.1725

= (2) Mary Carver
m.1744/5, d.1782

John
7th baron Ward
2nd viscount
Dudley and Ward
(1724/5-1788)
= Mary Baker
m.1788, d.1810

no issue

William
8th baron Ward
3rd viscount
Dudley and Ward
(1750-1823)
= Julia Bosville
m.1780, d.1833

John William
9th baron Ward
4th viscount Dudley and Ward
1st earl of Dudley and viscount Ednam (cr. 1827)
(1781-1833)
d.unm.

succeeded by his second cousin:

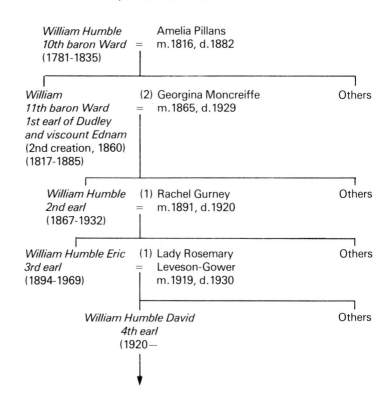

William Humble
10th baron Ward
(1781-1835)
= Amelia Pillans
m.1816, d.1882

William
11th baron Ward
1st earl of Dudley
and viscount Ednam
(2nd creation, 1860)
(1817-1885)
= (2) Georgina Moncreiffe
m.1865, d.1929
   Others

William Humble
2nd earl
(1867-1932)
= (1) Rachel Gurney
m.1891, d.1920
   Others

William Humble Eric
3rd earl
(1894-1969)
= (1) Lady Rosemary
Leveson-Gower
m.1919, d.1930
   Others

William Humble David
4th earl
(1920—
   Others

BIBLIOGRAPHY

1 Primary sources

Dudley Library:
  Dudley Estate Collection
  Dudley Dispensary Records
  Dudley Government School of Design and Technical Institution Records
  Dudley Guest Hospital Records
  St Edmund's Church Vestry Minute Book
  St Thomas Church Vestry Minute Books
  Dudley Town Commissioners, Board of Health, Town Council and County Borough
    Minute Books
Greater London Record Office:
  Legge (Dartmouth) Papers
Hatfield House, Hertfordshire:
  Political Papers of third marquess of Salisbury
Hereford and Worcester Record Office:
  Palfrey Collection: Volumes of cuttings on Dudley
Kent Archives Office:
  Political Papers of first Viscount Chilson
Miss Dorothy Meynell:
  Diary of Lady Dorothy Legge (1904)
  Materials relating to Patshull House
Staffordshire Record Office:
  Dartmouth Estate and Political Papers
  Hatherton Collection: Dudley Trust Papers
  Lichfield Estate and Political Papers
  Sandwell Park Colliery, Ltd., Records
  South Staffordshire Ironmasters Association Minute Book.
West Bromwich Library:
  All Saints Church Vestry Minute Books
  Christ Church Vestry and National Free School Minute Books
  West Bromwich Improvement Commissioners, Town Council and County Borough
    Minute Books
  West Bromwich Institution for the Advancement of Knowledge Minute Book
Mr and Mrs J.K. Winter:
  Diary of Lady Dorothy Legge (1904)
  Diary of Lady Joan Legge (1902–11)
  Diary of Mary, countess of Dartmouth (1881–1915)

2 Newspapers

Aris's Birmingham Gazette
Birmingham Daily Mail
Birmingham Post
Dudley Herald
Dudley Weekly Times
Free Press (West Bromwich)
Midland Counties Express (Wolverhampton)
The Times
Staffordshire Advertiser
Wednesbury and West Bromwich Advertiser (later *Midland Advertiser*)

Weekly News (Oldbury) (later *West Bromwich Weekly News*)
West Bromwich and Oldbury Chronicle (later *The Chronicle for West Bromwich*, etc.)
Wolverhampton Chronicle

3 Parliamentary Papers

1843, vol. XIII, *Midland Mining Commission*
1867–8, vol. XXXIX, *R.C. on Trades Unions*, fifth report
1871, vol. XXXVI, *R.C. on Truck System*
1873, vol. X, *S.C. on Coal Industry*

4 Published contemporary sources (local)

Blocksidge's Dudley Almanacks (1881–1914)
Burritt, E., *Walks in the Black Country and Its Green Border-Land* (1868).
Clark, C.F.G., *Curiosities of Dudley and the Black Country, from 1800 to 1860* (1881).
Coplestone, E. (ed.), *Letters of the Earl of Dudley to the Bishop of Llandaff* (1841)
Hackwood, F.W., *A History of West Bromwich* (1895).
Jewell's Annual and Year Book: Borough of West Bromwich (1894).
Jones, W.H., *Story of the Municipal Life of Wolverhampton* (1903).
Perkins, M., *Dudley Tradesmen's Tokens* (1905).
Prince, H.H., *Old West Bromwich* (1924).
Reeves, J., *The History and Topography of West Bromwich and its Vicinity* (1836).
Rickword, G., and Gaskell, W., *Staffordshire Leaders, Social and Political* (1907).
Romilly, S.H. (eds) *Letters to 'Ivy' from the First Earl of Dudley* (1905).
Turberville, T.C., *Worcestershire in the Nineteenth Century* (1852).
White, W., *History, Gazetteer and Directory of Staffordshire* (1851).

I have omitted a comprehensive list of dissertations and modern printed sources, as the notes are themselves a running bibliography.

NOTES

1 T.H.S. Escott, *England: Its People, Polity and Pursuits* (1885), 75.
2 R.H. Trainor, 'Authority and social structure in an industrialized area: a study of three Black Country towns, 1840–1890' (D. Phil. thesis, University of Oxford, 1981).
3 Among others: M.J. Daunton, *Coal Metropolis: Cardiff 1870–1914* (1977); J.Foster, *Class Struggle and the Industrial Revolution: Early Industrial Capitalism in three English towns* (1974); D. Fraser, *Power and Authority in the Victorian City* (1979); E.P. Hennock, *Fit and Proper Persons: Ideal and Reality in Nineteenth Century Urban Government* (1973); P. Joyce, *Work, Society and Politics: The Culture of the Factory in later Victorian England* (1980); H.E. Meller, *Leisure and the Changing City, 1870–1914* (1976); H. Perkin, 'The recruitment of élites in British society since 1800', *J. Social History*, XII (1978); W.D. Rubinstein, 'Wealth, élites and the class structure of modern Britain', *Past and Present*, LXXVI (1977). Also sections of studies focusing on the working class: G. Crossick, *An Artisan Elite in Victorian Society: Kentish London 1840–1880* (1978), ch. 5; R.Q. Gray, *The Labour Aristocracy in Victorian Edinburgh* (1976), chs. 4–5, 7. See also note 9.

4 Black Country élites have hitherto attracted little attention from social historians. For a survey of the literature, see R.H. Trainor, 'George Barnsby and the social and political history of the nineteenth-century Black Country', *The Blackcountryman*, XII (1979), 53–8.

5 For details see Trainor, 'Authority and social structure', ch. 2.; G.J. Barnsby, 'The standard of living in the Black Country during the nineteenth century', *Economic History Rev.*, 2nd ser. XXIV (1971), 232, has a lower estimate. The definition used here includes: industrial and retail-drink-craft employers (in effect excluded by Barnsby); professional and commercial men; and white collar employees. This approach is appropriate for a heavily working class area where claims to nonmanual and employer status had scarcity value.

6 G.C. Allen, *The Industrial Development of Birmingham and the Black Country 1860–1927* (1929), 112, 132–4, 142, 146.

7 The Black Country, which contemporaries often referred to as 'South Staffordshire', contained parts of both counties. West Bromwich was in Staffordshire, Dudley in Worcestershire.

8 E. Richards, 'The industrial face of a great estate: Trentham and Lilleshall, 1780–1860', *Economic History Rev.*, 2nd ser., XXVII (1974), 416 & n. 6; D. Spring, 'English landowners and nineteenth-century industrialism', in *Land and Industry: The Landed Estate and the Industrial Revolution*, ed. J.T. Ward and R.G. Wilson (1971), 30, 32, 42; R.W. Sturgess, 'Landownership, mining and urban development in nineteenth-century Staffordshire', in Ward and Wilson, *op. cit.*, 174–6, 186–7; Ward, 'Landowners and mining', in Ward and Wilson, *op. cit.*, 75–6, 99–100.

9 Among others: W.L. Arnstein, 'The survival of the Victorian aristocracy', in *The Rich, the Well Born and the Powerful: Elites and Upper Classes in History*, ed. F.C. Jaher (1973); D. Cannadine, *Lords and Landlords: the Aristocracy and the Towns 1774–1967* (1980); D.C. Moore, 'Social structure, political structure, and public opinion in mid-Victorian England', in *Ideas and Institutions of Victorian Britain*, ed. R. Robson (1967); H. Perkin, *The Origins of Modern English Society 1780–1880* (1969); D. Spring, 'The role of the aristocracy in the late nineteenth century', *Victorian Studies*, IV (1960); F.M.L. Thompson, *English Landed Society in the Nineteenth Century* (1963); *idem*, 'Britain', in *European Landed Elites in the Nineteenth Century*, ed. D. Spring (1977).

10 By 'civic unity' is meant social solidarity based on the towns' communal institutions (cf. 'cultural unity' in Meller, *op. cit.*, 14–15 and *passim*). 'Authority' is taken to be legitimized power, exercised through voluntary as well as government institutions.

11 F.W. Hackwood, *A History of West Bromwich* (1895), 57–60.

12 T.J. Raybould, *The Economic Emergence of the Black Country: A Study of the Dudley Estate* (1973), 27 n. 4; *idem*, 'The Dudley estate: its rise and decline between 1774 and 1947' (Ph.D. thesis, University of Kent, 1970), 570.

13 Staffs. RO, Dartmouth MS (hereafter cited as SRO, Dartmouth), D761/3/4, Bailey to Dartmouth, 24 September 1840; M.W. Greenslade (ed.), *VCH Staffs.*, XVII (1976), 19–20; R.W. Sturgess, 'The response of agriculture in Staffordshire to the price changes of the nineteenth century' (Ph.D. thesis, University of Manchester, 1965), 69, 79; Hackwood, *op. cit.*, 60, 62.

14 Staffs. RO, Hatherton MS (hereafter cited as SRO, Hatherton), D260/M/F/5/19/4, legal document, 6 June 1838, 2; Raybould, *Economic Emergence*, 76, 115, 118; *idem*, 'The Dudley estate', 388; D.M. Palliser, *The Staffordshire Landscape* (1976), 182–3; E. Burritt, *Walks in the Black Country and Its Green Border-Land* (1868), 313.

15 Sturgess, 'Response of agriculture', 115; J. Bateman, *The Great Landowners of Great Britain and Ireland* (1883 edn), 119, 140.

16 Raybould, 'The Dudley estate', 452–3, 552, 566; Sturgess, 'Response of agriculture', 103–6; *idem*, 'Landownership, mining and urban development', 180–2, 186. It should be noted, however, that the incomplete nature of the Dartmouth estate papers prevents certainty concerning overall income trends.

17 Raybould, 'The Dudley estate', 341–2; D. Cannadine, 'Aristocratic indebtedness in the nineteenth century: the case re-opened', *Economic History Rev.*, 2nd ser., xxx (1977), 628–9.

18 *Wolverhampton Chronicle* (herafter cited as *WC*) 16 September 1891; Kent Archives Office, Chilston MS, C161/3, Dartmouth to Akers-Douglas, 15 October 1891; 'Dartmouth House' (pamphlet in possession of Miss D. Meynell).

19 Bateman, *op. cit.*, 10, 94, 406, 431 and *passim*; Raybould, *Economic Emergence*, 15, 113.

20 Rubinstein, 'Wealth, elites and the class structure', 100–2; *idem*, 'British millionaires, 1809–1949', *Bull. Inst. Historical Research*, xlvii (1974), 204 n. 2. For probate values, *ibid.*, 211, 213 and Probate Calendars.

21 P. Williams, *WC*, 23 December 1857.

22 Raybould, *Economic Emergence*, 96, 130; *idem*, 'The Dudley estate', 390; cf. Ward, 'Landowners and mining', 76.

23 R.W. Pepper, 'Urban development of Lewisham – a geographical interpretation' (M.A. thesis, University of London, 1965), 54–6, 108, 113–14, 193, 204–5, 216–24; H. Evans (ed.) *Our Old Nobility* (1907 edn), 173; Hon. V. Gibbs (ed.), *The Complete Peerage*, IV (1916), 92.

24 Sir George Gater and W.H. Godfrey (eds.), *The Survey of London*, XIX: *Old St Pancras and Kentish Town* (1938), 36–8; Ward, 'Landowners and mining', 75, 99; C.A. Hulbert, *Annals of the Church and Parish of Almondbury, Yorkshire* (1882), 176, 212.

25 Sturgess, 'Response of agriculture', 87, 115.

26 Raybould, 'The Dudley estate', 462; R.W. Jeffery (ed.), *Dyott's Diary 1781–1845*, I (1907), 258; William Salt Library, S.MS.430, West Bromwich Instrument of Apportionment of Tithe, 1849. The family also owned much of the other land in the parish (*VCH Staffs.*, XVII, 22).

27 Sturgess, 'Landownership, mining and urban development', 185, 192, 194; West Bromwich Instrument of Apportionment; W.H.B. Court, *The Rise of the Midland Industries 1600–1838* (1938), 154 n.1.

28 Hackwood, *op. cit.*, 60; Sturgess, 'Response of agriculture', 80, 87–103, 107–8, 111–12, 114–20; *idem*, 'Landownership, mining and urban development', 174–6, 180–2, 184–6, 189.

29 Raybould, *Economic Emergence*, 10–11, 15, 40, 44–6, 51, 112, 182; *idem*, 'The Dudley estate', 553, 564–5; *VCH Staffs.*, II (1968), 96.

30 S.D. Chapman, 'Black Country industrial history', *The Blackcountryman*, ii (1969), 40; Raybould, 'The development and organization of Lord Dudley's mineral estates, 1774–1845', *Economic History Rev.*, 2nd ser., xxi (1968), 542.

31 Raybould, *Economic Emergence*, 10, 152; *idem*, 'The Dudley estate', 382, 387, 471; *idem*, 'Development and organization', 543; D. Philips, *Crime and Authority in Victorian England: the Black Country 1835–1860* (1977), 194 and n.37; E.F. Smith, *S.C. Coal*, PP, 1873, X, 125.

32 *WC,* 24 June and 1 July 1868; Raybould, *Economic Emergence*, 77–86; *idem*, 'The Dudley estate', 381–2; *Midland Counties Express*, 20 June 1874.

33 *WC*, 5 January 1870; Raybould, 'The Dudley estate', 423, 449–50; *Free Press* (hereafter cited as *FP*), 1 December 1883.

34 Thompson, *English Landed Society*, 171–5, 264–5; Spring, 'Landowners and industrialism', 51; SRO, Dartmouth, D761 and D853, *passim*; cf. Ward, 'Landowners and mining', 63, 71–2, 75.

35 SRO, Dartmouth, D564, *passim*; Sturgess, 'Response of agriculture', 81, 84, 87.

36 Raybould, 'The Dudley estate', 451, 489–90, 570; *idem*, 'Development and organization', 543; *idem, Economic Emergence*, 182, 206, 208, 225–34, 243. Ward, 'Landowners and mining', 77; R.P. Fereday, 'The career of Richard Smith (1783–1868), manager of Lord Dudley's mines and ironworks' (M.A. thesis, University of Keele, 1966).

37 *Ibid.*, 86; A. Birch, *The Economic History of the British Iron and Steel Industry 1784–1879* (1967), 289; Raybould, 'The Kingswinford estate of Lord Dudley: its development and organisation between 1774 and 1833', (M.A. thesis, University of Birmingham, 1966), 227–30; *idem*, 'The Dudley estate', 391, 451, 548; C. Knox, *Steel at Brierley Hill: The Story of Round Oak Steel Works 1857–1957* (1957), 23.

38 Dudley Library, Dudley Estate Archive (hereafter cited as DL, DEA), *passim*; SRO Dartmouth, D564, *passim*; Sturgess, 'Response of agriculture', 78–87.

39 *Dyott's Diary*, II, 98; 'The late Earl of Dartmouth' (1854; copy in the William Salt Library), 7–8; Cannadine, *Lords and Landlords*, 129; *WC*, 4 December 1844.

40 B.D. Bargar, *Lord Dartmouth and the American Revolution* (Columbia, South Carolina, 1965), 2; D. Dilworth, *The Tame Mills of Staffordshire* (1976), 38; SRO, Dartmouth, D(W) 1778/V/963, Lady Dartmouth to Lewisham, 3 September [1809].

41 *Dyott's Diary*, I, 329, II, 185; *WC*, 30 November 1853; Hackwood, *op. cit.*, 60; R.D. Woodall, *West Bromwich Yesterdays* (1958), 19; S. Lees, 'Billy-my-Lord', *West Bromwich and Oldbury Chronicle*, 14 May 1901; H.H. Prince, *Old West Bromwich* (1924), 122–3.

42 L.E. Elliott-Binns, *The Early Evangelicals: A Religious and Social Study* (1953), 139–40, 293–4; *VCH Staffs.*, III (1970), 65; *ibid.*, XVII, 50, 52, 54–6; Hackwood, *op. cit.*, 60; Vestry Minute Book, St James, West Bromwich, 15 November 1844; W. White, *History, Gazetteer and Directory of Staffordshire* (1851), 683.

43 William Salt Library, newspaper cuttings, new vol., 167.

44 *VCH Staffs.*, XVII, 75–6; White, *op. cit.*, 682, 684; *WC*, 12 November 1845; Minute Book of National Free School, 1811–38, *passim* (Christ Church, West Bromwich); Woodall, *op. cit.*, 17; *FP*, 8 November 1907; 'The late earl of Dartmouth', 7, from *Birmingham Mercury*.

45 E. Lissimore (ed.), C.H. B[ayley], 'List of occurrences in West Bromwich', 8 August 1835 (West Bromwich Library).

46 SRO, Dartmouth, D742/VIII/1/4, September 1723 (I owe this reference to Mr M.W. Greenslade); Staffs. RO, West Bromwich Manor Court MS, D(W) 515, *passim*; *VCH Staffs.*, XVII, 16 and n.97, 43–4; Hackwood, *op. cit.*, 101.

47 'Edge hills', quoted by J. Reeves, *The History and Topography of West Bromwich and its Vicinity* (1836), 38; *FP*, 8 November 1907.

48 Burritt, *op. cit.*, 157.

49 *Quarterly Rev.* LXVII, 84, quoted by S.H. Romilly (ed.), *Letters to 'Ivy' from the First Earl of Dudley* (1905), 6; SRO, Hatherton, D260/M/F/5/27/29 no. 5, J.W. Ward to Coplestone, 25 May 1812 (copy).

50 *DNB*, LIX, 324–6; Raybould, *Economic Emergence*, 235; Romilly, *op. cit.*, 39, 217, 348, 351, 372, 380–1.

51 M. Perkins, *Dudley Tradesmen's Tokens . . .* (1905), 4; G. Chandler and I.C. Hannah, *Dudley as it was and as it is to-day* (1949), 47; V.L. Davies and H. Hyde, *Dudley and the Black Country 1760 to 1860* (1970), 28–9; Palliser, *op. cit.*, 200.

52 SRO Hatherton, D260/M/F/5/19/4, 'List of annual subscriptions paid by the late earl of Dudley'. In 1799 the third viscount subscribed £63 of £1804 given to a soup kitchen (Davies and Hyde, *op. cit.*, 28); W. Page and J.W. Willis-Bund (eds), *VCH Worcs.*, III (1913), 103.

53 G.J. Barnsby, *The Dudley Working-Class Movement 1832 to 1860* (1967), 34; DL, DEA, D/DE/27–8, Court Minute Books 1794–1866; Raybould, 'The Kingswinford estate', 242–4; Chandler and Hannah, *op. cit.*, 46, 146–7; J.S. Roper, *Dudley: The Town in the Eighteenth Century* (1968), 21–2.

54 Barnsby, *The Dudley Working-Class Movement 1750–1832* (1966), 6; *idem, The Working Class Movement in the Black Country 1750 to 1867* (1977), 151; Chandler and Hannah, *op. cit.*, 149, 158; Bourne and Owen, 'Dudley market tolls' (c. 1866; Dudley Library), 3–4.

55 Raybould, *Economic Emergence*, 188–93; C.F.G. Clark, *Curiosities of Dudley and the Black Country, From 1800 to 1860* (1881), 7–8; *Birmingham J.*, 26 April 1851.

56 Romilly, *op. cit.*, 19–20, 315; E. Coplestone (ed.), *Letters of the Earl of Dudley to the Bishop of Llandaff* (1841), 54–5, 245; SRO, Hatherton, D260/M/F/5/27/29 no. 5, J.W. Ward to Coplestone, 25 May 1812 (copy); M/F/5/27/7 no. 97, Dudley to E.J. Littleton, 16 December (?) 1831.

57 G.W. Hannah, *All Saints' Parish Church West Bromwich* (1975), 27–8; R.A. Church, *Kenricks in Hardware: A Family Business 1791–1966* (1969), 42, 283; *VCH Staffs.*, XVII, 77; West Bromwich Library, Minute Book of the West Bromwich Institution for the Advancement of Knowledge, *passim*.

58 Barnsby, *Working Class Movement in the Black Country*, 24.

59 West Bromwich Library, All Saints Churchwardens' Book 1832–1964, 16 June 1837; Jephcott, 'Old West Bromwich', *Midland Chronicle and Free Press*, 17 September 1943; PP, 1856, XLVIII, 148; *WC*, 17 April 1844 and 25 January 1854.

60 'The late earl of Dartmouth', 14–16; *Aris's Birmingham Gaz.*, 25 July, 1 August and 29 August 1842; F.C. Mather, *Public Order in the Age of the Chartists* (1959), 51–2; PP, 1843, XIII, *Midland Mining Commission*, appendix, 11.

61 *Ibid.*, 12–14. The district's masters had already rejected a mediation attempt by the Lord Lieutenant, Talbot. (D. Philips, 'The Black Country Magistracy 1835–60: a changing elite and the exercise of its power', *Midland History*, III (1976), 178).

62 *Aris's Birmingham Gaz.*, 5 September 1842; Rev. Barnard Slater (another mediator), *Midland Mining Commission*, Appendix, 16; SRO, Dartmouth, D761/3/4, Dartmouth to Bailey, 28 June 1847.

63 *Ibid.*, Bailey to Dartmouth, 17 July 1839; *WC*, 17 April 1844 for Dartmouth's letter of opposition; a year earlier he had appeared in person to fight a similar petition (*Staffordshire Advertiser*, 21 October 1843); Staffs RO, Quarter Sessions Records, Q/SB E.1844; and Q/ACp 3, *passim*; D. Philips, 'Crime and authority in the Black Country 1835–60: a study of prosecuted offences and law enforcement in an industrialising area' (D.Phil. thesis, University of Oxford, 1973), 60–5.

64 *WC*, 17 April 1844.

65 The once-great Gower interest had declined as early as 1820: E. Richards, 'The social and electoral influence of the Trentham interest, 1800–1860', *Midland History*, III (1975).

66 The Hathertons and Bradfords battled each other there: G.B. Kent, 'Party politics in the county of Staffordshire during the years 1830 to 1847 (M.A. thesis, University of Birmingham, 1959, chs. 6, 8).

67 V. Tunsiri, 'The party-politics of the Black Country and neighbourhood (1832–1867)', (M.A. thesis, University of Birmingham, 1964), 78, 376–7 and *passim*; Thompson, *English Landed Society*, 274–6.

68 *Complete Peerage*, IV, 90 note c; *WC*, 19 February 1845; M.W. McCahill *Order and Equipoise: The Peerage and the House of Lords, 1783–1806* (1978), 69, 194–8, 205–7; SRO, Hatherton, D260/M/F/5/17/10.

69 Bargar, *op. cit.*, 55, 196; Sir L. Namier and J. Brooke, *The House of Commons 1754–1790*, III (1964), 29–30; SRO, Dartmouth, D564/12/14/9, Lewisham to Dartmouth, 7 September 1780; *WC*, 14 July 1852; Kent, *op. cit.*, ch. 4; *Dyott's Diary*, II, 196, 252, 258; Cannadine, *Lords and Landlords*, 149–51.

70 *WC*, 24 January, 7 February and 21 February 1849, and 23 June 1852; Tunsiri, *op. cit.*, 76–9, 105, 114–15.

71 William Salt Library, 1835 South Staffordshire Poll Book; *WC*, 25 January and 15 February 1854.

72 J. Williams, *WC*, 25 January 1854.

73 Barnsby, *Dudley Working Class Movement 1832 to 1860, passim*.

74 Fereday, *op. cit.*, 64; Raybould, 'The Dudley estate', 358–65, 390, 422; *Dudley Herald* (hereafter cited as *DH*), 28 April 1888; Countess of Cardigan and Lancastre, *My*

Recollections (1909), 44–8; modified by SRO Hatherton, D260/M/F/5/27/23 no. 21, Ward to Hatherton 21(?) November 1851; and by *Complete Peerage*, IV, 490–1 and notes a, b; *WC*. 30 April 1851.

75 Bourne and Owen, *op. cit.*, 6; Davies and Hyde, *op. cit.*, 29; *DH*, 9 May 1885; Dudley Library, Minute Books of Board of Health and of Committee on Small Tenements, *passim*; *WC*, 18 June, 25 June, 9 July and 15 October 1856, and 15 October 1858; Clark, *op. cit.*, 166–72, 194–6.

76 P. Williams, *WC*, 30 April 1851.

77 Fereday, *op cit.*, 149–50; Raybould, 'The Dudley estate', 457; Tunsiri, *op. cit.*, 78, 114–15; SRO, Hatherton, D260/M/F/5/27/30 no. 28, Ward to Hatherton, 21 March 1857.

78 For surveys of Dudley elections during this period: Barnsby, *Working Class Movement in the Black Country*, 207–11; Chandler and Hannah, *op. cit.*, 111–29; Raybould, 'The Dudley estate', 378, 384–6; and Tunsiri, *op. cit.*, 169–74, 243–6, 282–3, 304–5.

79 Fereday, *op. cit.*, 124–5; Clark, *op. cit.*, 134. An 1837 intervention in Wolverhampton, where estate interests were comparatively weak and Liberalism especially strong, proved a fiasco (Raybould, 'The Dudley estate', 383, 409–12).

80 T.C.Turberville, *Worcestershire in the Nineteenth Century* (1852), 53–4; *Dudley Weekly Times*, 28 March 1857. Compare Raybould, 'The Dudley estate', 384–5, 423.

81 *Ibid.*, 384–5, 558; Turberville, *op. cit.*, 53. Ward's half-mad father had had some ties with local radicals (Clark, *op cit.*, 60–1; *Hansard*, 3rd ser. XXVII, 1835, 832); Clark, *op. cit.*, 191. On Hawkes, J.A. Smith, in Chandler and Hannah, *op. cit.*, 129.

82 *WC*, 14 July 1852; Clark, *op. cit.*, 101, 103–4, 110, 154–60, 173–6; Chandler and Hannah, *op. cit.*, 111. The estate backed the successful Liberal candidate for South Staffordshire in 1854.

83 *Midland Counties Express*, 21 January 1903.

84 SRO, Hatherton, D260/M/F/5/27/30 Nos. 23 and 28, Ward to Hatherton, 4, 21 March 1857; A. Lang (ed.), *Life, Letters, and Diaries of Sir Stafford Northcote, First Earl of Iddesleigh* (1891 edn), 87, 92–3; *DH*, 9 May 1885.

85 *Dudley Weekly Times*, 28 March 1857; SRO, Hatherton, D260/M/F/5/27/30 no. 1, Ward to Hatherton, n.d. (1857).

86 Clark, *op. cit.*, 275–87; *WC*, 2 February and 30 April 1859.

87 *Dudley Weekly Times*, 28 March 1857.

88 *FP*, 7 November 1885; *Staffordshire Advertiser*, 8 April 1905; *The Times*, 12 March 1936.

89 *The Times*, 30 June 1932; Hereford and Worcester RO, Palfrey Collection (hereafter cited as HWRO, Palfrey), BA 3762/51 Dudleiana xi, 2 July 1932.

90 J.L. Garvin and J. Amery, *Life of Joseph Chamberlain*, VI (1969), 671; HWRO, Palfrey, BA 3762/48 Dudleiana iii, 3 July 1920; Raybould, 'The Dudley estate', 522.

91 F.H.W. Sheppard (ed.), *The Survey of London*, XXXIX: *The Parish of St James, Westminster*, Pt I, *South of Picadilly* (1960), 81; HWRO, Palfrey, BA 3762/46 Dudleiana i (c. 1908); Diary of Mary, Countess of Dartmouth, I, 12 August 1891; II, 1896.

92 Diary of Lady Joan Legge, I, 1903, *passim*; N. Pevsner, *The Buildings of England: Worcestershire* (1968), 171; J.S. Leatherbarrow, *Worcestershire* (1974), 72–5; Raybould, 'The Dudley estate', 390–1, 457.

93 Diary of Countess of Dartmouth, II, 1902; Diary of Lady Joan Legge, I, November 1906.

94 Diary of Countess of Dartmouth, II, 21 July 1900. Characteristically, the Dartmouths' royal ties were mainly with this couple and Victoria; the Dudleys were closer to Edward VII and Edward VIII.

95 *FP*, 5 November 1881; H. McLeod, *Class and Religion in the Late Victorian City* (1974), 171, 173, 185, 189 n.4; calculations based on SRO, Dartmouth, D564/5/12/1 for the period 4 October 1883–15 October 1884; Hulbert, *op. cit.*, 8, 179–80, 212 and *passim*; cf. Joyce, *op. cit.*, 298.

96 *Staffordshire Advertiser*, 8 August 1891; Staffs, RO, Lichfield MS, D615/P(L)/1/7, Lichfield to Palmerston, n.d. [late 1862 or early 1863]; *Midland Chronicle and Free Press*, 13 March 1936.

97 'Twelfth Annual Report, South Staffordshire Prize Scheme Association' (1865), Staffs RO, Lichfield MS, D615/P(L)/6/18; Diary of Countess of Dartmouth, II, 1902; *FP*, 19 June 1886.

98 W.H. Jones, *Story of the Municipal Life of Wolverhampton* (1903), 230, 300 and *passim*. In contrast, Birmingham attracted little of the cash or activities of the fifth and sixth earls (SRO, Dartmouth, D564/5/12/1); *FP*, 7 November 1885. Sandwell Hall became the home of various Anglican charities backed by the family (*VCH Staffs*, XVII, 20).

99 *DH*, 9 May 1885; Staffs. County Council, *Year Books*, 1889–1920; Raybould, 'The Dudley Estate', *passim*; HWRO, Palfrey, BA 3762, *passim*; DL, DEA, D/DE/IV/10, Accounts of George Taylor for 1857.

100 *DH*, 9 May 1885; DL, DEA, D/DE/IV/10, Accounts of George Taylor for 1857.

101 *DH*, 21 November 1891.

102 For details on élites see Trainor, 'Authority and social structure', ch. 3.

103 Cf. Hennock, *op. cit.*, 308; and Fraser, *Urban Politics in Victorian England: The Structure of Politics in Victorian Cities* (1976), 18. By 'more substantial' is meant the upper- and middle-middle classes: employers with at least ten workers (in industry) or five workers (in retailing), with other criteria also used; and professional and commercial men. The relative proportions of generally high-status industrialists and usually lower-status retailers are also taken into account.

104 Approximately one-quarter of the members of each élite held posts in both philanthropy and local government.

105 For the standard view see A. Briggs, *History of Birmingham*, II (1952), 1; for a sharp contrast, Barnsby, *Working Class Movement in the Black Country, passim*.

106 For further details see Trainor, 'Authority and social structure', ch. 7; D. Philips, 'Riots and public order in the Black Country, 1835–1860', in *Popular Protest and Public Order*, ed. R. Quinault and J. Stevenson (1974); and E. Taylor, 'The working class movement in the Black Country 1863–1914', (Ph.D. thesis, University of Keele, 1974).

107 G. Best, *Mid-Victorian Britain 1851–75* (1973 edn), 279; W. L. Burn, *The Age of Equipoise: A Study of the Mid-Victorian generation* (1965 edn), 15–16; H. Pelling, *A Short History of the Labour Party* (1976 edn), 2.

108 *WC*, 23 December 1857; W.H. Jones, *op. cit.*, 88–9.

109 'The Thorneycroft's Patents and Inventions . . .' (1891; Wolverhampton Library), *passim*; F[rederic] W[illett], *Osney Foss: A Story of the Black Country* (1908), 9–10, 15; *VCH Staffs.*, II, 361.

110 For further details: Trainor, 'Authority and social structure', ch. 4; Taylor, *op. cit.*' chs. 2–9; A. Fox, 'Industrial relations in Birmingham and the Black Country, 1860–1914' (B. Litt. thesis, University of Oxford, 1952).

111 SRO, Dartmouth, D564/7/1/21, E.L. Thynne to J. Jarvis, 10 and 11 August 1874; Staffs. RO, Sandwell Park Colliery MS, D1117/SP1, SP5, Minutes of Directors and Annual General Meetings, *passim*; *WC*, 23 December 1857, 24 September 1873; *FP*, 8 June 1878.

112 PRO POWE 6/75, 'Charter Master System in Lord Dudley's Collieries' (1906–7); Raybould, *Economic Emergence*, 191–3; Smith Casson, *R. C. Truck System*, PP, 1871, XXXVI, Q.37911.

113 *Hansard*, 4th ser. XIX, 1893–4, 64–7; Staffs. RO, D888 South Staffordshire Ironmasters Association Minute Book, 116–19; Taylor, *op. cit.*, 122–3, 213–21; 'Rules . . . of the Round Oak Ironworks' (1858), in Knox, *op. cit.*; Philips, *Crime and Authority*, 193–5.

114 *DH*, 9 May 1885; *WC*, 6 August 1862; *Weekly News*, 17 April 1880.

115 *FP*, 8 April 1882.

116 In the 1865 iron lockout, for example: F. Smith, *R. C. Trade Unions, Fifth Report*, PP, 1867–8, XXXIX, QQ.10840ff. Compare Fereday, *op. cit.*, 136 and Raybould, *Economic Emergence*, 213–14.

117 *WC*, 13 August 1858; SRO, Hatherton, D260/M/F/5/6/2, Hogg to Hatherton, 3 October 1858; Philips, *Crime and Authority*, 216–17; Fox, *op. cit.*, 82.

118 Sturgess, 'Landownership, mining and urban development', 199; J. Cornford, 'The parliamentary foundations of the Hotel Cecil', in Robson (ed.), *op. cit.*; Taylor, *op. cit.*, chs. 10–12, including accounts of the elections discussed in this section; Trainor, 'Authority and social structure', ch. 5, pt B.

119 Hatfield House, Salisbury Papers, Dartmouth to third marquess of Salisbury, 18 July 1890 and *passim*; *Midland Advertiser*, 23 June 1875.

120 H. Pelling, *Social Geography, of British Elections 1885–1910* (1967), 186; Sturgess, 'Response of agriculture', 80, 85, 560–1; *Midland Counties Express*, 31 January 1874.

121 *FP*, 7 August 1891; *Staffordshire Advertiser*, 8 August 1891; *DH*, 4 August 1888.

122 *Midland Advertiser*, 11 December 1875; *FP*, 19 April 1902; Sturgess, 'Response of agriculture', 562–3; Hatfield House, Salisbury Papers, Dartmouth to Salisbury, 2 August 1886.

123 *The Times*, 8 May 1885; *Complete Peerage*, IV, 490 n. b; Raybould, 'The Dudley estate', 451; *WC*, 29 July 1868, 30 October 1878 and 6 July 1892; Pelling, *Social Geography*, 185–6.

124 *DH*, 9 May 1885; *Midland Counties Express*, 31 January and 2 May 1874; HWRO, Palfrey, BA 3762/46 Dudleiana i, 20 January 1906.

125 *Midland Counties Express*, 13 June 1874; compare Taylor, *op. cit.*, 377–9.

126 Viscount Chilston, *Chief Whip: The Political Life and Times of Aretas Akers-Douglas 1st Viscount Chilston* (1961), 218; G. Rickword and W. Gaskell, *Staffordshire Leaders Social and Political* (1907), 3; Kent Archives Office, Chilston MS, C161/3, Dartmouth to Akers-Douglas, 15 October 1891; Hatfield House, Salisbury Papers, Dartmouth to Salisbury, 10 July 1895.

127 *Hansard*, 4th ser., CLVIII, 1906, 1081–3; SRO, Dartmouth, D564/7/1/43, E.L. Thynne to W.P. Dix, 25 March 1892; *Jewell's Annual and Year Book: Borough of West Bromwich* (1894), 89; Briggs, *Birmingham*, II, 190.

128 HWRO, Palfrey, BA 3762/46, Dudleiana i, 19 August 1911; *ibid.*, Dudleiana xi, 30 June and 2 July 1932; Raybould, *Economic Emergence*, 16; *DH*, 28 July 1894.

129 HWRO, Palfrey, BA 3762/46, Dudleiana i, n.d.

130 Dr A.E.W. Hazel, a barrister, Oxford don and native of West Bromwich; and A.G. Hooper, a prominent local solicitor.

131 *Birmingham Daily Mail*, 1 January 1906; *The Chronicle for West Bromwich*, 6 January 1906; *DH*, 16 December 1905 and 13, 20 January 1906.

132 *The Chronicle for West Bromwich*, 19 January 1906; HWRO, Palfrey, BA 3762/46, Dudleiana I, 20 January 1906.

133 *DH*, 2 July 1921; Taylor, *op. cit.*, 458; A. Griffith-Boscawen, *Memories* (1925), 128; *Birmingham Post*, 29 September and 16 December 1909; West Bromwich Library, Scrapbook 27, *passim*.

134 *FP*, 6 March, 16 October and 11 December 1886; *Hansard*, 4th ser., CLXVII 1906, 131; *The Chronicle for West Bromwich*, 19 January 1906.

135 Cannadine, *Lords and Landlords*, 60.

136 *WC*, 26 January 1859; PP, 1859, XX, 129–35, 229–37. In distribution of total attendances in 1851, 'Other Protestants' led Anglicans by margins of 60.1 per cent to 34.7 per cent in West Bromwich and 68.1 per cent to 25.1 per cent in Dudley (calculations based on PRO H.O. 129). Cf. Trainor, 'Authority and social structure', ch. 5, pt B.

137 *Staffordshire Advertiser*, 8 August 1891; *WC*, 24 June 1868; *WC*, 24 December 1856; SRO, Hatherton, D260/M/F/5/27/23 nos. 21 and 72, Ward to Hatherton, 21(?) and 22 November 1851; information from Mrs J.K. Winter.

138 *Staffordshire Advertiser*, 8 August 1891; *WC*, 8 November 1876; *Wednesbury and West Bromwich Advertiser*, 9 September 1871; *Midland Advertiser* 1 March 1873, 23 June 1875 and 11 November 1882; *VCH Staffs.*, XVII, 53.

139 Hatfield House, Salisbury Papers, Dartmouth to Salisbury, 23 December 1895;

Hansard, 3rd ser., CCXIV, 1873, 1898; DL, DEA, D/DE/V/5, Mines Dept, Ecclesiastical Matters 1840–1905, Bishop of Worcester to Claughton, 15 August 1904 and Claughton to Bishop, 17 December 1904.

140 *WC*, 30 October 1851; *Midland Counties Express*, 28 November 1874.

141 Calculations based on DL, DEA, D/DE/IV/10, accounts of George Taylor, 1857, excluding Anglican schools which are considered with secular philanthropy; Dudley Library, Vestry Minute Book of St Edmund's 1845–1968, entry for 1852; Raybould, 'The Dudley estate', 380; *VCH Staffs.*, XVII, 50.

142 D564/5/12/1; *VCH Staffs.*, XVII, 54; DL, DEA, D/DE/V/5, Mines Dept, Ecclesiastical Matters 1840–1905, Packet 527, St Thomas Church, Dudley, Rev. A.G. Maitland to Claughton, 6 March 1901.

143 SRO, Dartmouth, D564/7/4/6, Dartmouth to F. Thynne, 21 March 1859; B. Lovering, 'The earl of Dartmouth's Sandwell Estate' (Wolverhampton Teachers College, 1975), 25; Raybould, 'The Dudley estate', 331–2; DL, DEA, D/DE/V/5, Mines Dept, Church Schools etc., W.E. Thompson to Claughton, 16 August 1920 (copy).

144 *WC*, 15 November 1865; Dudley Library, St Thomas Vestry Minute Book 1856–1936, 7 April 1885.

145 *WC*, 2 December 1868 and 7 July 1869; *DH*, 28 April 1888, 9 May 1885.

146 For further details see Trainor, 'Authority and social structure', ch. 7, pt B. In 1883–4 roughly four-fifths of the Dartmouths' giving in West Bromwich went to 'secular' objects (including schools); the Dudley proportion in 1857 was only three-tenths, but it had almost certainly risen in the interim as local secular philanthropy expanded (SRO, Dartmouth, D564/5/12/1; DL, DEA, D/DE/IV/10).

147 *WC*, 27 February 1856; *FP*, 8 June 1878.

148 *DH*, 9 May 1885; *FP*, 7 August 1891; local press accounts; various records listed in Bibliography.

149 *VCH Staffs.*, XVII, 5, 9–10, 92–3; *VCH Worcs.*, IV (1924), 523; *DH*, 9 May 1885 and 28 July 1894; *WC*, 23 October 1866. Cf. Meller, *op. cit.*, 74–5, 112–13.

150 Sources as in n. 146; estimates allow for rising Dudley contributions since 1857 but exclude land values for both families; cf. Thompson, *English Landed Society*, 210.

151 *WC*, 23 October 1866; L. Jones, 'The Guest Hospital, Dudley: 1871–1948' (Wolverhampton Teachers College, 1972), 15, 18.

152 *WC*, 27 November 1867; *DH*, 2 August 1884; *FP*, 7 August 1891; *VCH Staffs.*, XVII, 7, 9–10, 25, 81–3; HWRO, Palfrey, BA 3762/46, Dudleiana i (n.d.).

153 On the Kenricks: Church, *op. cit.*, 42, 80, 227, 279, 282–3; T.C.T. [D. Plant], *Life's Realities* (1922), 232–3.

154 *FP*, 10 June 1882.

155 *WC*, 30 December 1863.

156 *FP*, 3 February 1883, 6 August 1897.

157 SRO, Dartmouth, D564/7/4/58, Lady Dartmouth to E.L. Thynne, 2 July 1891 (copy); *DH*, 9 May 1885; Lovering, *op. cit.*, 64, 69–70.

158 *WC*, 1 November 1865; West Bromwich Commissioners Minute Book (West Bromwich Library) and *WC*, June-November 1862, *passim*; *Wednesbury and West Bromwich Advertiser*, 4 February 1871.

159 *Midland Advertiser*, 5 August 1876.

160 *FP*, 7 August 1891; *WC*, 1 November 1865.

161 DL, DEA, D/DE/V/5, Mines Dept, Correspondence, Schools, Churches, Roads 1869–1900, draft 'Scheme for the Government of Guest Hospital' (1870), and Claughton to W.F Taylor, 15 November 1920.

162 *FP*, 9 April 1881, 21 January 1882, 4 March 1882, 9 December 1882 and 4 April 1885; *Weekly News*, 20 September 1879.

163 For this trend generally see J.M. Lee, *Social Leaders and Public Persons: A Study of County Government in Cheshire since 1888* (1963), 52.

164 For elaboration of the local Poor Law see Trainor, 'Authority and social structure' ch.

7, pt A. Only E.F. Smith, among the Dudleys' chief mineral agents, was a Guardian, and his service ceased before his appointment to the post.

165 *Illustrated London News*, 26 October 1867; *FP*, 8 June 1878.

166 Plant, *op. cit.*, 236; *WC*, 5 June 1861.

167 *DH*, 9 May 1885; *FP*, 7 August 1891.

168 For details see Trainor, 'Authority and social structure', ch. 6.

169 *WC*, 13 January 1864; West Bromwich Commissioners Minute Book (West Bromwich Library), 21 March 1859.

170 J.E. Williams, 'Paternalism in local government in the nineteenth century', *Public Administration*, XXIII (1955); *WC*, 1 November 1865 and 29 May 1867; *DH*, 28 April 1888.

171 *WC*, 25 October 1865; *FP*, 8 April 1882, 9 December 1882, and 24 December 1887.

172 For example, ratepayers in West Bromwich paid to develop the park Dartmouth had given (*FP*, 8 June 1878).

173 *DH*, 2 August 1884; *Weekly News*, 30 July 1898.

174 *DH*, 28 April 1888.

175 *Midland Advertiser*, 14 August 1875; *FP*, 24 December 1887; *DH*, 28 July 1894.

176 For example, *DH*, 21 November 1891; cf. Cannadine, *Lords and Landlords*, 48.

177 *Ibid.*, 50; West Bromwich Commissioners Minute Book (West Bromwich Library), 1 March 1882.

178 Mayors from outside the council were unusual in the Black Country: G.W. Jones, *Borough Politics: A Study of the Wolverhampton Town Council, 1888–1964* (1969), 259.

179 Dudley Library, Local Government Scrapbook, 1965; *DH*, 14 and 21 November 1891, and 16 November 1895; Cannadine, *Lords and Landlords*, 50–3.

180 *DH*, 12 November 1892, 9 November 1895.

181 Cannadine, *Lords and Landlords*, 55–6; *DH*, 16 November 1895, 18 April, 11 July and 12 September 1896, 14 January 1899; HWRO Palfrey, BA 3762/51 Dudleiana xi, 2 July 1932.

182 *DH*, 13 November 1897, 14 January 1899; Cannadine, *Lords and Landlords*, 53–5.

183 *FP*, 6 October 1877, 10 August 1878 and 5 March 1887; *Weekly News*, 6 September 1879; *Midland Chronicle*, 4 November 1921.

184 *WC*, 1 May 1867; Dudley Council Minute Book 1877–82 (Dudley Library), 133–4, 155, 350–1; *DH*, 16 April 1881; *Dudley and District News*, 5 February 1881.

185 Ald. Bagott, *DH*, 14 January 1899.

186 SRO, Dartmouth, D 564/7/1/20, E.L. Thynne to E. Pincher, 24 January 1874, and *passim*; *FP*, 1 January 1887; West Bromwich Library Scrapbook 28, 80–85 *re*: 1908; *The Chronicle for West Bromwich*, 19 November 1909.

187 *WC*, 12 November 1892; DL, DEA D/DE/V/5, Property and Land, E.M. Warmington to E.F. Smith, 31 December 1880 and copy of reply, 1 January 1881; Raybould, 'The Dudley estate', 495; *idem, Economic Emergence*, 49–50.

188 *DH*, 18 June 1892, 14 January 1899.

189 *DH*, 27 October 1883; West Bromwich Council Proceedings 1882–3 (West Bromwich Town Hall), 17; *FP*, 6 January 1883.

190 *DH*, 5 October 1895, 9 November 1895; *Midland Advertiser*, 14 August 1875

191 Cannadine, *Lords and Landlords*, 49–50.

192 *Ibid.*, 53; *DH*, 14 January 1899.

193 *FP*, 11 November 1882; *The Times*, 8 May 1885; *WC*, 17 August 1864 and 29 July 1868. Cf. Raybould, 'The Dudley estate', 429–30; and Fereday, *op. cit.*, 137.

194 Cannadine, *Lords and Landlords*, 351; *Weekly News*, 30 July 1898; *DH*, 2 August 1884.

195 Arnstein, 'Survival', 249; M. Girouard, *Life in the English Country House: A Social and Architectural History* (1978), 270–1; Cannadine, *Lords and Landlords*, 37.

196 *FP*, 7 August, 30 October, 1891; HWRO, Palfrey, BA 3762/51, Dudleiana xi, 2 July 1932; *WC*, 12 August 1891.

197 *DH*, 14 January 1899.
198 *DH*, 9 May 1885, 1 September 1888; Cannadine, *Lords and Landlords*, 40–1, 45, 223–4, 387–8.
199 Information from Lady Barbara Kwiatkowska; HWRO, Palfrey, BA 3762/51, Dudleiana xi, *Birmingham Gaz.*, 30 June 1932; Raybould, *Economic Emergence*, 124, 127.
200 *VCH Staffs.*, XVII, 6; West Bromwich Library, Scrapbook 10, 27 (12 July 1946).
201 Raybould, 'The Dudley estate', 457–8, 486–7, 525, 531, 566; *idem*, *Economic Emergence*, 16, 106–7, 124–8, 242–3; Dudley Library, Cuttings 34: 89 (*Express and Star* [Wolverhampton], 23 December 1969); information from the earl of Dudley. The family is still involved in a local brick company.
202 *FP*, 29 November, 31 December 1918, 3 January 1919.
203 *FP*, 6, 13 December 1918; *Midland Chronicle*, 4 November 1921. Excepting 1931, Labour has won every subsequent election.
204 *Midland Chronicle*, 4 July 1919; *Midland Chronicle*, 4 November 1921; *FP*, 22 June 1923.
205 Jephcott, 'Old West Bromwich', *Midland Chronicle and Free Press*, 25 June 1943; *VCH Staffs.*, XVII, 47.
206 *Midland Chronicle and Free Press*, 18 October 1946 and 7 March 1958; *The Times*, 12 March 1936; Staffs. County Council, *Year Books*.
207 *Midland Chronicle and Free Press*, 18 October 1946; *VCH Staffs.*, XVII, 80.
208 *FP*, 7 October 1891; *Midland Chronicle and Free Press*, 13 March 1936 and 7 March 1958.
209 L. Jones, *op. cit.*, 99, 101; DL, DEA, D/DE/VII, Box 3, folder on meeting 15 April 1935; HWRO, Palfrey, BA 3762/51, Dudleiana xi, 2 July 1932; 'GRB', 'Round Oak steel works 1925–1958', *The Acorn*, II (1957; Dudley Library), 3, 6.
210 DL, DEA, D/DE/IV/13, cutting from *DH*, 11 July 1931. Labour had only once won a Black Country parliamentary seat before 1914; during the interwar period it secured 28 results, though its inroads remained in peril until 1945.
211 Raybould, 'The Dudley estate', 326.
212 DL, DEA, D/DE/IV/13, cuttings from *DH*, 27 June and 11 July 1931, 18 January and 5 March 1932, and from *Express and Star*, 5 May 1932. Ednam also experienced problems at Guest Hospital (L. Jones, *op cit.*, 109).
213 Dudley Library, Cuttings 4:145–7 (*DH*, 30 June 1934).
214 HWRO, Palfrey, BA 3762/51, Dudleiana xi, 2 July 1932.
215 A revival in his local activities in the early 1960s was partial and brief. (See Dudley Library, Cuttings: 6:62 [*DH*, 11 June 1949]; 19:52 [*DH*, 24 September 1960]; 21:112–13 [*DH*, 23 November 1962 and unidentified]. *DH*, 2 January 1970.
216 Dudley Library, Cuttings: 39:3 (*Express and Star*, 27 October 1970); 58:79 (unidentified, 11 October 1974); and 63:28 (*Express and Star*, 30 May 1975).

Estate management and land reform politics: the Hesketh and Scarisbrick families and the making of Southport, 1842 to 1914

JOHN LIDDLE

Estate management and land reform politics: the Hesketh and Scarisbrick families and the making of Southport, 1842 to 1914

JOHN LIDDLE

1 Introduction

The relationship between the size of land holdings and the quality of ninteenth-century urban development has rightly received much recent attention from social, economic and urban historians alike.[1] A general conclusion has been reached that, with a few odd exceptions, the towns under the leasehold control of one or two large landowners had higher standards of planning and development than those towns that fell into the hand of multifarious commercial developers. There has been agreement that this resulted from the large estates having neither the need nor the desire to maximize profits. The aristocratic families, from the great dukes of Portland and Westminster in London to the moderate Calthorpes in Edgbaston, were socially secure and sufficiently affluent to enable them to plan the long-term development of their estates, and to combine their own self-interest with that of their lessees and the community at large, without the prime counteracting motivation of profit and immediate financial return that preoccupied smaller men making their way in the world.[2]

Nowhere was this contrast more in evidence than in the seaside resorts. Although by their very function, in providing a setting for leisure and escapism, they nearly all afforded standards of spaciousness, amenities and recreational facilities rarely found in their industrial and commercial counterparts, it was in the resorts such as Eastbourne, under the dominant control of the dukes of Devonshire, or Bournemouth, much of which was owned by the Tapps-Gervis family, that the highest class of development was to be found.

The north-west of England provides the most graphic contrast. The ill-planned terraced lodging houses which characterize the area's working-class holiday image were the product of the fragmented patterns of land distribution found at Morecambe, New Brighton and, most importantly, at Blackpool, where only 24 freeholders had holdings of over 25 acres.[3] They contrast sharply with the broad, tree-lined avenues of red brick middle-class villas which characterize Lytham-St

Annes and Southport, developed under the exclusive control of the Clifton family and the Hesketh and Scarisbrick estates respectively.

At Southport the two land-owning families controlled 97 per cent of the land in the resort.[4] During the second half of the nineteenth-century the town grew at a rate which few could equal. The resort was transformed from a sprawling and undistinguished village of less than 8,000 people in 1841, to a relatively sophisticated better-class residential resort, with a population of over 51,000, in 1911. This growth was achieved by small-scale speculative enterprise working under the strict leasehold control of the two estates. On the face of it, Southport provided the classic example of the single landowner town, where controlled development under the short leasehold system had directly beneficial effects on the rate and quality of urban growth. My original research was undertaken to prove or disprove this point, and themes and areas of study were developed from this basic framework.[5]

In the first place, the physical development of the town and its changing social composition was examined and outlined. The rôle of the estates was then placed in the context of other factors which helped to determine the growth and the social and economic characteristics of the town. Areas of concern included the rôle of communications (Southport was quick to obtain excellent railway services, and by the turn of the century had more suburban railway stations than any other town in England); the rôle of the local building industry and the provision of building capital; the fashionable spread of popular sea-bathing holidays, and its relationship with residential development; and socio-economic considerations such as the prevalence of unhealthy living conditions in the towns and cities of industrial Lancashire, and the desire by their rapidly expanding middle classes for social segregation.

An exhaustive examination then took place into the nature of the two estates, their economic links with the area, and their rôle in the development of the town. It was found that their estate management methods, especially their administration of the leasehold system, although basically complementary to the rapid and largely distinguished growth of the town, were particularly commercial and insensitive, and reflected the untraditional background of the two estates. In all, it was concluded that the Southport landowners had been particularly fortunate in having had their virtues extolled by historians seeking merely to explain economic, edificial and social divergences between Southport and its immediate neighbouring contemporary, Blackpool.[6]

This essay is concerned with the social and political consequences of the landowners' estate management methods and involvement in the town. Section 2 will briefly examine the historical background of the two estates and how their economic links with Southport developed. More importantly, the circumstances, motivation and purpose behind the 1842–3 purchases by Charles Hesketh and Charles Scarisbrick will be examined as having an important bearing on future social and political interactions between town and estates. Sections 3 to 5 will explore the changing relationship between landowners, local government and lessee-residents. They will explain how a period of mutual harmony and shared aims, involvement and expectations developed into one of bitter conflict, culminating in the Foreshore dispute of 1883. Questions such as who had the natural right to control local government, and in whose interests was the town best served, placed this conflict at the heart of the land agitation of the 1880s. The importance of this reform agitation is examined in relation to the management of the estates. The final phase deals with the manner in which the landowners traded their exclusive social and political power for continued financial success. The inherent weaknesses of the local land reform movement, symptomatic of those at national level, as contributing to the gradual, yet permanent, reconciliation between town and estates is also considered. Finally, section 6 explains how the estates' links with the town have been gradually severed during the twentieth century.

2 Economic links and estate development

The Heskeths and Scarisbricks were among those old Roman Catholic families who managed to rise out of the mild impoverishment which characterized minor gentry families in pre-industrial Lancashire to positions of some social, political and territorial importance as a result of careful marriage consolidation during the eighteenth century.[7]

The Scarisbricks consolidated their holdings with those of two other minor gentry Catholic families (see Appendix 1). In 1742, Basil Scarisbrick, a younger son who had branched out to become a Liverpool and Cádiz merchant, married into the Dicconsons of Wrightington and Parbold, an industrious yeoman family who had worked their way up during the seventeenth century to become lords of the manor. At the same time he also succeeded to the Eccleston family estate as a result of a slightly earlier alliance. From this consolidated foundation, Basil's son, Thomas Eccleston, was able to add to this inheritance with the purchase of additional surrounding estates. He was also a keen agricultural improver, effecting extensive drainage works to reclaim 3,600 acres of marshland at Martin Mere. Although their continued Catholicism excluded them from some positions of social and political prestige, careful management and estate consolidation within strict social and political lines ensured that by the time of Thomas Eccleston's death in 1809, the Sacrisbricks had attained an overwhelming territorial dominance over the coastal plain of south-west Lancashire, and were firmly entrenched in the upper ranks of Lancashire gentry.[8]

The Heskeths had held part of the joint moiety to North Meols, an ancient parish situated on the Lancashire coast midway between Preston and Liverpool, and adjacent to the Scarisbrick's inland estates, since the thirteenth century, but prior to the marriage of Roger Hesketh to Margaret Fleetwood, heiress to the Fleetwood and Rossall estates, in 1733, had been little more than minor squiredom (see Appendix 2). This alliance, however, made the Heskeths very considerable landowners. The Fleetwood estate ran a long way south from Rossall Point at the mouth of the Wyre, and included the land on which Blackpool now stands. The North Meols estate consisted of the area of Southport's future development, stretching from the northern boundary of the West Derby Hundred down to the Birkdale boundary. Their earlier Catholicism and lack of territorial influence had denied them participation in the kind of social and political activity expected of a landed family, yet within a generation they had risen to one of the foremost county families in their own right. Indeed, Peter Hesketh Fleetwood, who inherited the estate in 1824, came to embrace all the trappings associated with being the head of a landed family. He held the office of High Sheriff in 1830, sat in parliament as a member for Preston from 1832 to 1847, was created a baronet in 1838, and when 'in town' resided at a fashionable Piccadilly address.[9]

It was not until the 1840s when the land at North Meols was purchased by Charles Scarisbrick and Peter Hesketh Fleetwood's brother, Charles Hesketh, that either estate began to forge serious economic links with the infant resort. The Heskeths paid their isolated, sparsely populated and unproductive Meols estate little attention during the eighteenth century. They resided at Tulketh Hall near Preston and at Rossall, and rarely visited North Meols. It was left to the Bold family, the other holders of the joint moiety at North Meols, to take an initial interest in the village. Though resident at Bold Hall near Warrington, by the turn of the century they had become frequent visitors 'for the sake of the sea bathing' and Bold House in Churchtown was rebuilt to accommodate them in 1802. North Meols had long been a popular bathing place with local farm workers and their families, but in the pattern of so many English seaside towns, it was the Bold's unassuming patronage which drew the attention of neighbouring gentry and established the small village as a 'locally fashionable' resort.[10]

During the next four decades the development of Southport was steady rather than dramatic, as table 5 indicates:

Table 5   The growth of Southport, 1801–1841

	population	no. of houses
1801	2,096	327
1811	2,496	479
1821	2,763	539
1831	5,132	875
1841	7,774	1,273

Source: LRO, Census return summaries, 1801–41.

The first hotel was built in 1798 by William Sutton, a small-time innkeeper and entrepreneur, on a five-acre plot adjacent to the shore. Other settlers followed in his wake, and marine villas and cottages became clustered in the sandhills surrounding the original Southport Hotel. They were mainly for the accommodation of paying summer guests. The land was taken on life leases at very small annual rentals. A second hotel, The Union, was built in 1805, and in 1818, Wellington Terrace, a row of rather fine Regency company houses was built alongside it by a consortium of Wigan businessmen. By the 1820s the long valley through the sandhills along which visitors had to pass to reach the new shoreside settlement, was straddled with cottages as the famous Lord Street was brought into being.[11]

Such growth did not pass unnoticed by the Bolds or the Heskeths, yet it did little to affect the overall picture of their estates. The land at Southport was still technically 'wasteland'.[12] Apart from the infant streets, the estate consisted almost entirely of barren ranges of sandhills interspersed with watery slacks and marshland. Edwin Beattie remembered that during his childhood (the 1850s) it was 'a place which consisted more of sandhills than houses . . . from the Royal Hotel to the Claremont on the Promenade was sandhills . . . so also they were in evidence in Lord Street . . . opposite to Chapel Street Station (which was just built) was a sandy waste . . . There was hardly a street that was free from all the pervading sand.'[13]

When the Bold estate presented leaseholders in Lord Street with extra land in order to make the frontages in the main thoroughfare more uniform, 'A very large number of the owners complained very much of having to add lumps of dirty swampy ground to their gardens . . . [and] when Sir Henry was pushed for want of the needful he sent a printed paper round to all the leaseholders in the town offering to make their leases into freeholds for the sum of forty pounds.'[14] Fewer than 20 people took up the offer, such was the value attached to land in Southport at that time. Certainly, the landowers derived very little income from it. As late as 1841, Peter Hesketh Fleetwood's rental from the 14 acres of new building development was worth only £215 *per annum*; indeed, his entire North Meols estate realized only £4,600 *per annum*.[15]

Both families were willing to grant short and life leases on very easy terms as and when they were asked, and obtained an Act of Parliament in 1825 physically to partition the jointly held land in order to facilitate the easier granting of building leases. They gave land freely and readily for public purposes and donated moderately to local subscriptions and charities; but by and large their interests lay elsewhere.

Peter Hesketh Fleetwood's main preoccupation was the development of Fleetwood on his Rossall estate. From the early 1830s he borrowed heavily to finance personally the costs of street works, public buildings, hotels, terraces and sea defences in an over-ambitious and financially disastrous attempt to create a thriving sea port and resort on his isolated estate. By the early part of 1840 he had debts of £184,000 and had to meet forthcoming expenses of a further £100,000. The need to raise money by the sale of his Southport property was obvious. In order to clear heavy debts owed to other members of the Hesketh family, he went back on an earlier agreement of sale with Charles Scarisbrick, and in 1842 sold his Meols estate for £148,000 to his younger brother, the Reverend Charles Hesketh, who had been resident at North Meols as rector since 1835.[16]

Later the same year Charles Scarisbrick showed his determination to get a stake in the growing resort, when he paid Sir Henry Bold-Hoghton, who was also heavily in debt, £132,000 for his 2,700 acres of land at North Meols, together with some small holdings in Wigan. By March 1843, Charles Hesketh was finding the burden of mortgages very heavy on his newly-acquired estate, and Scarisbrick paid £91,000 to extend and consolidate the boundaries of his new estate. In this way the Scarisbrick estate became possessed of the whole of the town centre of Southport from Seabank Road and Union Street to the Birkdale border and all the land co-extensive to the east, together with more agricultural land at Crossens, Banks and Martin Mere. Charles Hesketh retained an estate to the north extending from the site of Hesketh Park to Crossens, and also a detached central strip, together with manorial rights.[17]

This chain of events and change of ownership was crucial to the nature of estate management in Southport and the social and political interaction between landowner, local authority and lessee-resident which resulted from it. Firstly, the financial ruin which the Fleetwood enterprise brought on his brother had a critical and longlasting effect on Charles Hesketh and his administration of the Hesketh estate in Southport. He found the break up of the family estate a bitter and painful experience. Besides the Meols sale, the Blackpool property was sold to Thomas

Clifton of Lytham in 1841. Tulketh Hall, the old Hesketh family home near Preston, followed in 1842.[18] In 1843–4 the Fleetwood home at Rossall was lost. On being informed of the sale, Charles wrote to his brother, 'Thank you for your kind invitation to come and visit Rossall once more before it is sold. I have thought again and again on the subject, but I really feel it would be so painful to see the dear old place under such trying circumstances that I cannot encounter such a distressing visit.'[19] Matters did not end there. More land at Norbreck and Bispham fell into the hand of his mortgagor in 1850, and when all that remained was the heavily encumbered Fleetwood property, the inevitable sale of family and personal effects began. After his death the need for sales continued. In 1869 land was sold to the Lancashire and Yorkshire railway company, and finally in 1875 the Fleetwood Estate Company acquired the rest of his property together with the manorial rights.[20]

Throughout the rest of his life Charles was plagued by the aftermath of the Fleetwood disaster. His fraternal correspondence acted as a painful and constant reminder of the consequences of overspeculation. By the late 1850s, Sir Peter's position had become quite dire. He wrote asking for food parcels, 'I hope I do not ask what you feel you feel you cannot send me, when I ask for some game – remember hares pay their expenses of carriage by saving in butcher's meat.'[21] At another point, needing to sell his house at Windsor, but without the means to make the place look warm and comfortable for prospective buyers, he explained how 'at one each day Mrs Hornsby gets dressed to show the place and so we sit till five – like rabbits hopping into holes when people come with an order to view.' But, above all, there was the self-doubt, reflection and recrimination – 'Sometimes my heart sinks within me as I look forward, and backward too.'[22]

He died penniless in 1866, unable to bear the cost of his own funeral. Even after his death the wreckage of Rossall continued to be washed up before Charles and his successors. Charles was continually harassed by long standing creditors demanding money or security, and after his death in 1876, his widow, Mrs Anna Maria Hesketh, had to live with the remaining family debris. Sir Peter's son, Louis, born illegitimately to his low-born mistress who later became his second wife and took the name of Lady Fleetwood, joined the Church and sponged on relatives before trying his luck abroad. Mrs Hesketh was informed by a 'well wisher' that he had died in abject poverty in Monte Carlo in 1880. In 1870 Lady Fleetwood married Henry Willis, a schoolmaster, but the marriage broke up when she went to live with John Orrell Lever, a bankrupt ex-Irish M.P. Willis subsequently made constant demands on Charles's widow for financial assistance. She reluctantly sent him postal orders for 10s. in an attempt to keep him quiet.[23]

This was the trauma through which the Hesketh family lived as their economic links with Southport developed. Charles Hesketh felt a great and personal lesson had been learned on the dangers of overspeculation. He saw his brother's position as the complete vindication of his own opposed views. He had repeatedly warned his brother about unnecessary speculation, as Mrs Hesketh later revealed in a letter refusing to subscribe to Fleetwood church: 'The ground on which Fleetwood now stands was then a rabbit warren – and if his advice had been taken would have remained such and not caused the ruin of his brother . . . who owing to speculations was afterwards obliged to sell his estate . . . calling up to my mind many sad recollections of bygone days.'[24]

Charles made certain that the same mistakes were not repeated in Southport.

Indeed, all features of urban estate management employed at Fleetwood were excluded. He felt that to lay out capital on new streets and amenities to create a demand for new building land was both reckless and unnecessary. The local press reported a speech where he prided himself on the fact that 'Southport had grown gradually, had not been forced by undue speculation, but had crept up by degrees'.[25] Equally, he felt his duty as an urban developer lay not with any ideological position – Sir Peter, as a Liberal social reformer had once planned a second New Lanark at Rossall and had tried to plan Fleetwood in a manner consistent with his ideal view of society – but rather with his family and their continued financial prosperity.[26]

Because of this, Southport could not expect, nor did it get, the same material and altrustic help afforded to other contemporary leasehold resorts. The extraordinary circumstances in which Charles Hesketh came to manage his estate ensured that he had neither the means nor the inclination. As will be seen, the Heskeths were willing to donate land for churches or public parks as and when it suited their own religious, moral, political or financial ends; but there was never the entrepreneurial drive in the shape of plans, capital or ideas which characterized the urban process in other single or joint landowner-controlled towns.[27] They were simply willing to take the returns that natural demand and the application of straightforward business methods had to offer, and although it was mainly as a result of their lack of initiative, those returns were never great. Apart from the Hesketh Park and High Park areas, the greater part of the Hesketh land remained undeveloped until the inter-war years, by which time it had passed out of their hands. On taking over the estate, Hesketh's income in 1842–3 was a mere £3,905 *per annum*, of which £2,620 went in mortgage repayments. Although in the intervening years their income was often boosted by the sale of urban land, such as that for the Promenade extension in 1878–9 which brought in £8,000, by 1896–7 the gross income stood at only £10,000, with urban ground rents accounting for slightly less than half. By 1914 it had risen to £16,500, and immediately prior to the estate sale in 1927, to £21,000.[28]

Secondly, and of even more far reaching significance to estate management at Southport, was the fact that the resort came under the dominant control of, initially, a man as singular, indeed possibly unique, as Charles Scarisbrick, and later, men as business-like and purposeful as the Scarisbrick trustees. Charles Scarisbrick was born in 1801, the youngest of Thomas Eccleston's three sons. A life in the clergy or as a minor landowner seemed to be ready mapped out for him, yet by the time of his death in 1860 it was felt that 'he was probably the wealthiest commoner in Lancashire.'[29] Although his father's will had bequeathed him the least valuable Eccleston estate, which yielded a mere £5,000 *per annum*, he worked from the very beginning with a ruthless and singleminded resolve to revoke and improve his natural inheritance. In so doing he cared little for those who got in his way, and his early years were marked by a long and difficult, though finally successful legal battle to disinherit other members of his own family. By February 1838, following the deaths of his two elder brothers and a four-year litigation against his sisters which culminated in a House of Lords hearing, he had managed to secure the title to all of his father's estates, the combined gross income being about £40,000 *per annum*.[30]

Not unnaturally, for a man of his burning ambition, Scarisbrick did not rely on the outcome of this legal battle for his future fortune. Besides involving himself in coal mining, brick making, stone quarrying and various speculations and fanciful inventions, he undertook a venture, which for a rather obscure Lancashire landowner, was nothing short of remarkable. Following his death there were rumours that he had kept a gambling house in Paris, but in fact he had become heavily involved in land speculation there. By February 1833 he owned 'more than 100 large acres under the walls of Paris', and later the same year described himself as 'the largest proprietor in the environs of Paris.' His object was quite clear: 'Though it has been a present outlay I shall be a heavy gainer in a short time as the Government cannot stir in any one direction in their works without buying me.'[31] This land speculation was carried out under the strictest veil of secrecy. All correspondence with his agent was sent first to London, then posted on with a London postmark to keep his whereabouts unknown. In later years he informed the Inland Revenue that he did not own property, nor had he ever received income, from property abroad.[32]

As a result the estate papers do not make it clear if Scarisbrick indeed became a 'heavy gainer'. But in view of the fact that he was able to finance the purchase of Southport and other property totalling £314,000, following years of expensive litigation and modest income, was able to spend something in the region of £85,000 employing Augustus Welby Pugin in the rebuilding of Scarisbrick Hall, was able to fill it with valuable pictures and works of art which realized £45,000 on his death,

Figure 11.
Charles Scarisbrick.

and that at the time of his death in 1860 had £161,000 deposited with his Wigan bankers and an outstanding mortgage of only £25,000, it seems not unreasonable to suppose that he did rather well out of the venture, and certainly, even before the Southport purchase, he enjoyed a reputation among his peers as a noted man of business.[33]

His main purpose in purchasing the land at Southport was to provide an inheritance and assured future income for the three illegitimate children born between 1837 and 1841 to Mary Ann Braithwaite, a former family servant with whom he lived from the early 1830s until his death. All the purchased property was left in trust to these children, namely, Charles, later Sir Charles (1838–1923), William (1837–1904) and Mary Ann (1841–1902). His settled estates had to pass to his sisters and were gradually broken up, the ancient Scarisbrick property being sold in various lots in the 1920s for over one million pounds.[34]

He did not view his territorial aggrandizement in terms of social prestige and political power. He led the life of a somewhat eccentric recluse, never involved himself in county society, and steadfastly refused to take part in local or national politics. Similarly, he did not view the estate's rôle in the development of Southport as encompassing any duty other than the maximizing of profit. Although in terms of territorial holdings and personal wealth he could rub shoulders with all but the greatest, he did not do so as a result of normal aristocratic inheritance. He was a landowner who had won his fortune *in spite* of his birthright – through the law courts, through the full exploitation of coal and mineral resources on his estates, through ambitious investment, through land and art speculation, through fact, the full nineteenth-century entrepreneurial spectrum. Unlike some of his contemporaries he cared little for the creation of a model town or society on his land, in which he and his successors could bask in reflected glory. Rather, his outlook and character can best be summarized by pointing out that he never wrote or answered a letter unless it was on a matter of business. The accumulation of wealth was his abiding obsession, and estate management at Southport was governed accordingly.

The Trustees who followed him were men of the same mould. Thomas Part (1799–1885), an able and assiduous Wigan solicitor whom Scarisbrick had known since his schooldays at Wigan Grammar School, and William Hawkshead Talbot (1813–75), an experienced and conscientious Chorley land agent and surveyor, who had acted as Scarisbrick's agent since the early 1830s, were his only 'worthy friends' and close advisers.[35] They knew the background to his personal motivation, understood his aims and far sighted plans and concurred with and embraced his estate management methods. Land, for Scarisbrick and his Trustees, was a source of wealth and power, but carried with it few traditional responsibilities. The fact that the Scarisbrick estate initiated a system of development marked in the main by a standard of town planning control remarkably good by the normal rules of the time, is no evidence to the contrary. Far from seeing their development policies as being formulated for the public good, Scarisbrick and his Trustees offered large plots, generous terms and well planned development precisely because they came to realize that in a town such as Southport, 'space has its profits no less than its density', and acted accordingly.[36]

During Scarisbrick's own lifetime the income from the new development at Southport remained small. As late as 1856, building leases at Southport contributed a mere £910 to his total annual income of £56,000, his vast agricultural estates and

Wigan coal mines making the Southport yield appear paltry. However, during the time of the Trust his far-sightedness began to pay dividends. The will had directed that the Trust Estate should provide the beneficiaries with an annual income of £3,000 each, in addition to a division of any surplus capital which might remain after the payment of expenses and other annuities. From the 1870s they never drew less than £10,000 each. In addition, from 1884 there was a series of three-way partitions of surplus residuary capital. Between 1884 and 1908 £261,809 was divided up amongst the beneficiaries. It was the contribution made by the new building development to the Trust's income which made this possible. Between 1860 and 1904 the Trust Estate realized £253,000 from the sales of land in Southport.[37] As table 6 shows, despite these sales, the income from new building leases continued to grow in relation to gross estate income.

Table 6   Scarisbrick Trust Estate annual income, 1861–1901

year	total gross income	income from agricultural rack rents at North Meols		income from new building leases at Southport		income from agricultural rack rents at Scarisbrick and Wrightington and miscellaneous income		income from 3% consols and other investments	
	£	£	%	£	%	£	%	£	%
1861	18,132	7,698	42.5	1,052	5.8	3,571	19.7	5,811	32.0
1866	23,468	8,008	34.1	3,682	15.7	5,289	22.5	6,489	27.7
1871	25,215	8,520	33.8	4,165	16.5	5,611	22.2	6,919	27.5
1876	31,209	8,218	26.3	8,967	28.7	6,998	22.4	7,026	22.6
1881	39,477	11,203	28.4	13,160	33.3	6,503	16.5	8,611	21.8
1886	31,605	11,335	35.8	10,764	34.1	5,547	17.5	3,959	12.6
1891	33,437	12,018	35.9	14,449	43.2	3,293	9.8	3,677	11.1
1896	41,230	13,571	32.9	18,092	43.9	6,929	16.8	2,638	6.4
1901	49,270	not known		22,270	45.2	not known		583	1.2

Source: LRO, Scarisbrick MSS, DDSc, 89/1, Trustees Ledger, 1860–97.

Such, in outline, were the economic links between the Hesketh and Scarisbrick families and town of Southport during the second half of the nineteenth century. The remainder of this essay seeks to explore the social and political consequences of this economic relationship.

3 The politics of deference and morality, 1842–63

Charles Scarisbrick did not delay in bringing change. The possibilities of developing a seaside estate to cater for working-class holidays-with-pay were as yet unforeseen, and Scarisbrick, acting on Southport's early start as a locally-fashionable watering place and convenient railway links with Liverpool and Manchester, decided to develop his estate as a select middle-class residential town. Closely-managed leasehold development soon replaced the rather haphazard, inefficient, and certainly unprofitable management which had governed Southport's development prior to the 1842–3 purchase. Hawkshead Talbot was quick to inform his employer that, 'There have been many applications for building land in Southport – several of the applicants not being able to obtain an answer have gone to other watering places. The delay of not having rules laid down being an injury to your property.'[38] Within a month a set of printed rules and terms for building land had been distributed to all potential applicants, and estate aid for Southport's development was put on a strict financial footing. The customary policy of the landowner paving streets prior to letting was discontinued on the understanding that it would only be done 'when there is sufficient contract for the land made to justify my outlay.' The unprofitable bargains which Hesketh Fleetwood had made to stimulate development, such as the letting of large 2,000 square-yard plots on the Promenade at 1s. *per annum*, were either immediately sold off or bought back by the estate.[39]

All direct financial aid to local improvements practically ceased. For example, by 1854 the portion of the Promenade owned by Scarisbrick was being described as 'an eyesore, a nuisance and a reproach' and was said to be having a serious effect on the local holiday trade. Appeals by the Improvement Commissioners fell on deaf ears for nearly three years, until all the adjacent building plots had been taken. Then the lessees were instructed by the estate to put the Promenade in order at their own expense under the repairing clauses in their leases.[40] This contrasted sharply with the generous estate help given to contemporary resorts by such as the Devonshires at Eastbourne or the Cliftons at neighbouring Lytham.

More important was the Scarisbrick estate's refusal to accept some responsibility for local sanitary improvements. Anxious in the first instance to increase revenue and encourage builders, the estate allowed building to go on quite indiscriminately, before the streets had been properly laid out or sanitary facilities provided. They later accepted no financial responsibility for the levelling, paving or sewering of the streets. The wealthier classes were encouraged because in the beginning they were generally willing to undertake such improvements at their own expense. It was considered a small price to pay for the haven of exclusive middle-class respectability which the estate's social policies were intended to guarantee. The estates were indeed fortunate that demand from the wealthier classes was such that, with the aid of the strict restrictive convenants, large plots and minimum values which the estates imposed, they were found in sufficiently large numbers to be able to isolate themselves in neatly-defined villa communities, and earn the town a reputation as a select middle-class retreat without either estate having to contribute materially towards that reputation.

In truth, in the lodging-house, artisan and older areas of the town, the estate's attitudes led to a real, though largely unpublicized, decline in public ammenities and sanitary conditions during this period. Within the limited boundaries of the 1846 Improvement Act the burden fell on the Improvement Commissioners and public money to provide the necessary improvements. In the rapidly expanding districts on the periphery of the town, nothing was done. In 1862, Ecclesfield, a district on the very edge of the town centre, was described in the following way: 'It is a misappropriation to speak of its sanitary condition – it has none. No drainage exists, and everything, even the laying out of the streets and the levels of the houses is unsatisfactory in the extreme . . . there is no gas, no pavement, no footpath.'[41] Local builders told the Incorporation Enquiry of 1864 that the estates allowed new streets to block ancient water-ways, which led to extensive flooding. Temporary surface drainage was put in, 'to get off the water from the surface until the Lord of the Manor can sell the land. It is not put there for the convenience of the houses that are built, but for him to sell the land that is not built upon.'[42]

What were the social and political consequences of such a uncompromising attitude? By the 1880s it was to lead to open conflict between the estates and the town, yet this period was marked by relative harmony and shared aims and involvement. Why was this? In the first instance the reasons why the landowner's critics met with little success need to be outlined.

A small opposition group of Liberal nonconformists was formed in the early 1850s, led by two Improvement Commissioners, Henry Forshaw, a prominent local solicitor, and Samuel Boothroyd, the town's Congregational leader and owner of a large drapery business.[43] They agreed that the insanitary condition of the town could only be remedied by increased local powers – more especially, by the adoption of the Public Health Act and the acquisition of private land and concerns, such as the Southport Waterworks Company. Because the 1846 Improvement Act, which the Public Health Act would have abolished, was an Act designed to protect the interests of the landowners, and the lucrative Waterworks Company was promoted and largely financed by Charles Scarisbrick, these measures were rightly seen as a direct challenge to the power of the estates.

Indeed, their main object, as they made quite clear, was to curb the landowners' powers by making them more accountable to the town's elected representatives. Henry Forshaw, reacting to an order from Scarisbrick relayed to the Board by his agent and Commissioner, Richard Wright, was reported as saying,

> He was certainly astonished at the few observations which had fallen from Mr. Wright who spoke about 'his instructions from Mr Scarisbrick' and said that 'Mr Scarisbrick orders this' and 'Mr Scarisbrick orders that.' He had been accustomed to hear the authoritative 'we' spoken of at the Board . . . and how Mr Wright was justified in saying that he had orders from Mr Scarisbrick to interfere with public property, which it was their duty to take care of for the benefit of the ratepayers, was to him something . . . marvellous and monstrous. He had no desire to dictate to Mr Scarisbrick in the same way in which that gentlemen seemed to him to dictate to that Board.[44]

Boothroyd was similarly explicit when demanding the right to access and consultation over the estates' development plans: 'as a Commissioner of Southport, he thought he ought to be consulted. The interests of the ratepayer had been committed to their trust and they ought not to allow those interests to be tampered with.'[45]

Unfortunately for Boothroyd and Forshaw, the Board had neither sufficient numbers of radical members nor adequate finance effectively to challenge the landowners. The resort at this time was still little more than a large village, dominated by a Conservative, long-established oligarchy of elderly residents, unaffected by the landowers' attitudes, sympathetic to their cause, and opposed to most forms of rateable public interference. It was a situation perpetuated by the élitist and conservative nature of the property qualifications in the 1846 Improvement Act, as reflected in the social and political composition of the Board of Commissioners, and also the slow rate of urban growth at this time, particularly in the professional middle class sector.[46] It was ironic that the landowners' very success in attracting this latter class of resident during the 1870s was also the means to the success of the Radical Liberal challenge in the later period.

'Retrenchment' and 'Economy' were the watchwords throughout the pre-Incorporation era. All public spending was stringently monitored by a public critical of even the most modest expenditure. As a result, the rates were kept artificially low, rendering the Board's finances inadequate to meet the demands of essential local improvements. For instance, between 1846–55 the Highway Account income of £6,178 failed to meet actual expenditure of £9,708, despite the fact that only the most modest improvements were undertaken, leaving most of the town without parapets and Lord Street with an open ditch sewer. By 1856 mortgages on the Board's several estates stood at nearly £16,000, and all surplus from the profitable estates, such as the market and slaughterhouse, went towards meeting the necessary repayments.[47]

All attempts to undermine the position of the landed estates were compromised by this lack of finance. For example, the acquisition of the Waterworks Company and adoption of a proper civic sewerage scheme would not only have necessitated rates of four to five shillings in the pound – figures totally unacceptable to the town's ratepayers – but would also have meant the expense and later consequences of opposing Charles Scarisbrick. Proponents of the scheme were warned by Thomas Hunt, one of the main dependants within the Scarisbrick faction, that Scarisbrick, 'has given his support to this company . . . he has given his word and he is not a man to be trifled with. You may as well offer to go through the Scarisbrick delf without tools, as to attempt it without his sanction. His word is his bond, and I can assure you that if you go against him, he will oppose you all he possibly can and make you pay dear for your whistle when you buy it.' The warning was fully heeded and in the end all hope of the scheme had to be abandoned.[48]

The Radical opposition could not escape the fact that the need for local improvements could only be met by cooperation with the landed estates because of the town's financial and organizational shortcomings. The town's inability to provide the financial aid, social stature and land essential to the success of any civic, social and religious improvement, meant that the landowners' involvement in public life and limited dispensation of patronage earned them an undue amount of deference and respect, and created an ephemeral atmosphere of mutual harmony in which their parsimonious estate management methods could thrive.

Nobody was more important in this regard than Charles Hesketh. Although as unwilling, and less able, to provide direct financial support for civic improvements as the Scarisbrick estate, he immersed himself in the activities of the growing town. He was particularly active in the resort's many temperance and sabbatarian societies, was instrumental in reinstating the North Meols Local Dispensary, a patron of the Marine Fund, President of the Lifeboat committee, and President and founder of the local Savings Bank. His obituary notice stated that 'There is scarcely any charity in the town with which his name has not been associated.' He sat as one of the original members of the Board of Commissioners and held the position until poor health forced him to retire in 1863: 'He rendered most efficient service, his clear headedness, business aptitude and great administrative powers making him one of the most prominent amongst those who managed the affairs of the town.'[49]

As a staunch Conservative and evangelical he felt that conflict between the landed élite and the middle and lower classes could and ought to be avoided by the paternal hierarchy assuming responsibilities commensurate with their privileged place in society. Apart from some grudging donations of land, the Scarisbrick estate never assumed these responsibilities; but such was Hesketh's involvement in public life that he more than compensated for their inactivity during these years. The backbone and purpose of his public work and his expense of patronage was to maintain the 'classless society' of localized hierarchical structures in which each individual was linked by a vertical relationship based on patronage and dependency to a patron above and a client below. It was a society in which Hesketh's own position of relative wealth and power was assured, and in which the town's later class-based conflicts could never have taken place.

Conflict was also avoided during this period because of the need on both sides for a common social policy towards the town's holiday industry. Before 1860 Southport was almost exclusively a holiday town. Besides the lodging house keepers, traders and shop keepers who clearly profited by the seasonal trade, there were the scores of genteel spinsters and widows, hidden behind the social acceptability of more

Figure 12.
Charles Hesketh
(by courtesy of
Colonel R.F. Hesketh).

147

ambiguous terms in the Census Enumerators Books, who 'also render accommodation to visitors'.[50] Nathaniel Hawthorne, one of Southport's earliest rail commuters, wrote as late as 1856, 'It is a large village . . . which seems to be entirely made up of lodging houses, and at any rate has been created by the influx of summer visitors.'[51]

Despite later claims for exclusivity, these visitors were rarely of the wealthy, leisured upper class. Hawthorne was rather disappointed and did not think 'that the visitors of Southport are generally of a very opulent class,' and indeed it is only very rarely that one comes across a titled entry in the visitor's list of the *Southport Visitor*.[52] The dukes, earls and marquesses preferred to monopolize the more fashionable resorts of the south coast and the more exclusive inland spas where the social tone was fixed by strict rules of exclusivity. The rules for the Cheltenham Assembly Rooms stated, for instance that 'No clerk hired or otherwise in this town or neighbourhood; no person concerned with the retail trade; no theatrical or performers by profession, be admitted.' Despite Southport's attempt to ape such pretentions by the construction of her own Assembly Rooms in 1830, no such restrictions were evident – indeed, those concerned in retail trade were considered the life-blood of the town's holiday traffic.[53]

By the mid 1850s the social tone sank further as the railways brought new industrial, working-class trippers in their thousands, especially at Bank Holidays. The editor of the *Southport Visitor* reflecting on the summer of 1855, wrote:

There are few who are at all acquainted with this town, but must have observed and felt the vast difference in Southport of the summer just ended and that of any other which has ever preceded it . . . Where we have been want in former years to count by scores those who come amongst us . . . it has been our gratification to see many thousands . . . The new links of railway have made this town accessible at rates of fare hitherto unheard of to thousands in the thickly populated districts.[54]

Local fishermen became boating proprietors and farmers rushed their donkeys to the shore to join the itinerant amusement stalls and sideshows that arrived to cater for the trippers, 'who flowed in the streets in one vast living stream, and swarmed on the wide expanse of shore like a newly disturbed anthill.'[55]

The landed estates and the town's middle class élite were drawn together in a united attempt to counter this development. The social tone of the town's earlier holiday trade was barely compatible with the projected rôle of a select residential retreat: the popular working-class tone was intolerable. The commuting and retired middle classes had not escaped to their havens by the sea to be followed by hordes of the very class they had sought to segregate themselves from. Whilst for the estates, the tripper offered the same threat to their agreed policy of select development as that posed by peripheral lower class urbanization to the middle-class suburban 'transit camps' of the main cities.[56] Political hatchets were buried as the landowners and the town's leaders presented a united front in the face of this common threat. The Scarisbrick estate was stirred from its position of abdicated responsibility to throw its considerable weight behind the efforts to promote a higher social tone. At the Licensing Sessions which followed the 1855 season, Thomas Part appeared on behalf of Scarisbrick to oppose applications for beer licenses. He said that 'the prosperity of Southport depended rather upon quiet and respectability than upon the increase of public houses.' The estate was anxious 'to have established only hotels of good character and suitable for such company as resorted to hotels of that description.' The applications were duly refused.[57]

Charles Hesketh was again important. He held positions of influence in the estate office, the local board and the pulpit. As effective guardian of the town's morality, he faced popular ridicule in promoting a strict puritanical moral tone. The holiday faction labelled Hesketh as 'a gentleman notoriously addicted to water drinking' who threw cold water on all popular projects because 'it might have interferred with the sale of the sacraments . . . or the monopoly of the pulpit performances.' Nevertheless he won the support of the town's leaders in discouraging and legislating against all forms of popular amusement calculated to attract cheap trippers. He was responsible for prohibiting race meetings shortly after his arrival in the town. He was the founder of the Southport Total Abstinence Society in 1836, and the main mover in the formation of the Lord's Day Society in 1855. He saw Sunday trading as a 'glaring evil', and successful attacks were made on Sunday trains, the Sunday opening of the Victoria Baths, on Sunday sea-bathing and all forms of popular Sunday entertainment.[58]

Among the town's leaders, even those most politically opposed to the land-owner's cause lent their unqualified support to these social policies. Henry Forshaw urged the adoption of the Lord's Day Act to legislate against Sunday trading. Samuel Boothroyd was the most forceful of the Improvement Commissioners in denouncing the cheap tripper and his effect on the respectable morality of the town. He led the Association to Promote the Improvement and Prosperity of Southport, in which he urged that the town be advertised 'both as a place of permanent residence and also as a place of resort for invalid visitors.' He felt that Southport prospered because of 'the wise provision made for the accommodation of the religious public, by the erection of churches and chapels.'[59]

This attitude reflected the strong links between respectable morality, religious nonconformity and political radicalism which characterized the town throughout the latter half of the nineteenth century. In a period when the ideals of respectable morality encompassed within religious nonconformity were threatened, political radicalism was clearly compromised since the threat came from a class which was not as yet the natural political enemy of the aspiring middle classes, but was indeed averted by the landed estates, who pursued the very social policies considered necessary to maintain an orderly, moral and tranquil society.

4 The tide goes out, 1863–88

As the town's population expanded, its dependence on the landowners to fill the financial and status vacuum declined. New town leaders emerged who wanted to free themselves from the shackles and restrictions of the earlier period. In 1863, Thomas Evans resigned his seat on the Board because he was neither a ratepayer nor resident in the town. He explained that, 'seven years ago they were rather short of gentlemen in Southport to fill the office of Commissioner, now, however, the difficulty was . . . how to find places for all who were qualified to fill them.'[60] Many of the newcomers brought essential experience gained in the political cauldron of the expanding industrial towns. For example, by the early 1860s Dr Robert Craven had emerged as Southport's main Incorporationist. He was a former Leeds Town

Councillor and a leading sanitary reformer. His main ally, William Halliwell, had been prominent in the Anti-Corn Law League and was one of Cobden's closest supporters. It was both ironic and ominous for the landowners that the families who came to occupy the red brick mansions which rapidly spread over their estates were headed by former Anti-Corn Law Leaguers, Free Traders and men who represented the very essence of Radical Liberalism.

These men were quick to take on civic responsibilities. They felt Southport needed its own corporate identity and civic standing, and they provided the necessary self-conscious and experienced leadership to achieve it. It was felt that Incorporation, 'would give the town a different standing and cause people to have more confidence in its authorities . . . Then, too, they might get the County Court here, and gain something like a position in the country.'[61] These were the sentiments of Walter Smith, the town's main building contractor and a staunch Liberal, who typified the new spirit. He involved himself in virtually every enterprise which took place in the town during his lifetime. At one time he was chairman of the Winter Gardens Company, the Botanic Gardens Company and the Southport Tramways Company. He had large financial interests in many local companies, ranging from the Southport and West Lancashire Bank, the Baths Company and the Birkdale Land Company, to the Cheshire Lines Extension Railway, which he promoted and constructed. He was made an alderman of the Borough in 1870 and between 1871 and 1876 he served as mayor four times. Such involvement made the landowners' limited paternalism largely redundant.[62]

At the same time the retired cotton princes provided philanthropic aid to local improvements on such a scale as to make the landowners' efforts inconsequential. William Atkinson, a former Manchester and Preston cotton manufacturer, built the Atkinson Library and Art Gallery at a cost of £13,500. John Fernley, a Stockport spinner, purchased the land for the Infirmary (1870), built the Observatory in Hesketh Park (1871) and bore the entire cost of Trinity Wesleyan Church (1864). By comparison, the Scarisbrick estate, even at the height of its financial success, never contributed more than a few hundred pounds a year to local charities and voluntary organizations.[63]

The new leadership was anxious to divorce the town's interests from those of the landed estates. In 1863 Walter Smith led a coalition to prevent Scarisbrick's agent, Richard Wright, from becoming chairman of the Commissioners. He said that 'he did not think a man could serve two masters.' This attitude, together with the continued insanitary condition of the town, made the movement towards Incorporation irresistible. The Charter was granted in 1867 after a fierce struggle with the estates.[64]

The 1870s witnessed an unprecedented increase in Southport's resident population and a rapid rise in the rateable value of the town. This, together with the various Improvement Acts which the new Corporation was able to enact, placed the local authority on a reasonably sound, if narrow, financial foundation, from which they assumed a more radical and independent stance. At the same time the landowners themselves began to assume a new rôle – one of privilege and financial security based on Southport's development, but lacking in the responsibilities of public office and involvement which they had previously undertaken. Charles Hesketh was forced to retire from public life in 1863 because of poor health. His son Edward 'seemed to have a keen dislike to touching anything which had been prominently associated with his father.' Indeed his father ensured that most of his property passed to his wife, and left only the sandhills, wastes and foreshore in the hands of Edward.[65]

His years as part-ground landowner and Lord of the Manor were in stark contrast to those of his father. The development and affairs of the estate were left almost entirely in the hands of his Preston agent and solicitors, and he took little or no interest in the affairs of the town. His years were notable for the frequency for which he held extravagent banquets, of which his mother, reflecting the economical attitudes of her husband, distinctly disapproved. He also made a vain attempt to introduce horse racing to the town. His mother urged him, 'to forego its pecuniary advantage . . . Let me earnestly beg you to have nothing to do with what in plain language would be the *gains of ungodliness* – do not bring upon what was so lately your father's property an institution he would have so grieved over.'[66] Even his Preston agent, Edward Gregson, felt the need to write and restrain him: 'It should be borne in mind the *lessees* as much as the lessors have great interests in Southport – these interests, I am sure you as a lessor and Lord of the Manor would not wish to overlook, or look lightly upon in any event.'[67]

During this period, then, the Hesketh estate was led by a man who did not readily assume public responsibilities, but rather had to be constantly reminded of them. After his sudden death in 1886 the whole of the estate passed to his mother, Mrs Anna Maria Hesketh (1809–98), who, because of old age, was not able to resume her husband's rôle.

The inactivity of the Scarisbrick estate in this capacity had always been marked, of course, governed as it was by Trustees for the pecuniary advantage of three illegitimate beneficiaries who had never set foot in the town. William Scarisbrick, one of the beneficiaries resident in Hannau, felt that their annual income should take clear precedence over all other considerations. Writing to Talbot in 1863, he stated:

It is not my brother's or my intention to ever live in England, except should we receive very different incomes. As regards Southport (the will says) the executors are to encourage the sale of building land as much as possible – and by that means diminish the praiseworthy remarks sometimes let fall from the mouths of the Southport gentlemen upon landowners . . . It is perfectly reasonable that Southport should be properly represented and cared for, but not at our expense.[68]

An estate run on these uncompromising financial lines made conflict with the 'Southport Gentlemen' inevitable. William Talbot, one of the Scarisbrick trustees, resigned his seat as Alderman in 1870 as the balance of power began to shift towards the radical élite. In his resignation speech he stated that 'he thought he was hardly in the right place, as he had an interest to serve besides that of the council.' The Scarisbrick estate's abdication of responsibility and the total separation of interests could not have been more complete.[69]

The policy of residential development which the landed estates pursued ensured they travelled down two roads simultaneously during this period; one to further financial success, the other to conflict and diminished power and independence. Residential development provided the Corporation with the means to effect local improvements without the landowners' cooperation. It was only by virtue of their ownership of land that the estates possessed a commodity which the Corporation could not provide for themselves. It was inevitable, therefore, that the landowner's abdication of responsibility and the rising challenge of the town's middle-class leaders should result in conflict – at the heart of which was the problem of land.

If the harmony of the earlier period was mainly a product of the alliance between the estates and the town's leaders to combat the threat of a popular holiday trade, the conflict over the land problem during the 1880s was the result of a breakdown in this alliance. This came about because the type of holiday trade which the alliance fostered was not able to meet the challenge which came its way in the late 1870s. Throughout that decade all forms of popular entertainment came under moralistic fire. Punch and Judy shows were threatened with fines or imprisonment, and amusement booths were driven off the shores. W.H. Stephenson neatly captured the spirit of the times: 'The Southport fathers, casting a contemptuous glance across the estuary to Blackpool, said they would never sully the fair expanse of Southport sands with such vulgar aids to amusement . . . They ordained that the sacred area of the Southport Sahara should be preserved at any sacrifice. They literally made the foreshore a desert and called it peace.'[70]

The more enlightened warned that 'pleasure seekers do not visit watering places in order to ascertain their particular standard of ultra-respectability, but for amusement and recreation.' Such warnings, though, went unheeded as unnecessary ripples on a sea of calm, assured, morally-based complacency – for the years that immediately followed were brilliant ones for the town's holiday trade, years which seemed economically to justify the moral tone promoted by the alliance. Because of this the early 1870s witnessed an unprecedented scale of investment by the town's middle-class élite in the holiday industry. But the forms of entertainment which this investment created – the Cambridge Hall (1874), the Winter Gardens and Aquarium (1874), the Botanical Gardens (1875), and a little later the lavish Prince of Wales Hotel, which was built to accommodate the flood of well-to-do visitors which Southport's investors were confident would pour into the town – were all projected with the social object in mind of attracting the wealthier, cultured class: 'The tripper was regarded with high disdain; the town's leaders flew at higher game . . . who were supposed to be ammenable to the influence of the ozone laden climate, while refined entertainments represented by the original orchestra of the Winter Gardens, its Aquarium and well-filled conservatory were thought to be quite sufficient to satisfy any reasonable appetite.'[71]

Their aim was not merely to tolerate the holiday trade, but to mould it to a form of their own liking. Unfortunately this form was too narrowly based to withstand the effects of the depression of 1878–9, as it hit most fiercely at the very class of visitor which Southport had come to rely upon: 'Visitors who came to inhale the ozone laden breezes were not numerous enough to bring prosperity, and the seekers after refined intellectual pleasures did not discover the charms of Southport in sufficient numbers to do it any good.'

The years 1876 to 1881 were disastrous for the town. News, fed by Blackpool-sponsored publicity, of a smallpox epidemic, kept visitors away during 1876. This clearly had a bad effect on a town which had sold itself as a recuperative health resort. The following year was just as bad – 'We are now in the most glorious part of the summer . . . still but for our residents the town would be empty.' 1878 saw the town's fortunes sink to their lowest ebb, and although the following years did witness a slight recovery, all longed for a return to the successes of the pre-1876 years.[72]

As the middle-class investment in the holiday trade suffered, the landowners' investment in residential development continued to prosper. The early 1870s witnessed an unprecedented rush to take up building leases, and although the influx of new residents after 1876 never matched the numbers of new houses on the market, the scramble to take up leases was unabated. The builders continued on the assumption that economic recovery would be well underway by the time their houses were completed, and were certainly insensitive to sudden changes in market conditions. Many got into dire financial difficulties. 'Only liquidating accountants seemed to be really busy,' recalled William Ashton.[73]

The landowners remained immune to all this. Their financial success depended purely on the demand for building leases. During the period 1870 to 1879, 1,042 building leases were granted by the Scarisbrick estate, compared with only 468 during the previous decade. The picture was the same in the rapidly emerging select residential suburb of Birkdale, where the Weld-Blundell estate granted 700 building leases between 1870 and 1879, compared with only 228 for the period 1860–9.[74]

Leasehold development gave the landed estates a steady source of income divorced from the world of risk and speculation which beset the builders and those engaged in the holiday trade, and which led to the bankruptcy of not a few. Walter Smith was the most notable victim of these years. He was declared bankrupt in 1883, and local dignitaries had to rally round to prevent the sale of his silver presentation sets given him by the Corporation in 1877. This economic divergence between the estates and the town's civic leaders led to open conflict. The latter had to be seen to be acting, had to find a scapegoat for their failure of policy. They found it in the town's foreshore.

By the 1880s the sea was retreating from Southport's shores with a rapidity which was at the same time both worrying and reassuring. It was leaving the foreshore, the very focal point of the resort, unwashed by the tide and an embarrassing eyesore. The Corporation assured themselves that they could not contend with the anomaly of purporting to be a seaside town when practically being an inland one. They approached the Duchy of Lancaster to purchase the rights of the foreshore. It offered them the chance at an important strategic point to redevelop and make the town more attractive to visitors. It also presented them with the opportunity to become larger landowners in their own right, and to be seen to be acting independently of the landed estates who were no longer seen as allies in the creation of a model middle-class society, but as parasites who were content to take rich financial rewards without contributing to the material well-being of that model.

The Scarisbrick Trustees immediately denied the right of the Duchy to treat with the Corporation, and claimed that the landed estates were the lawful owners of the foreshore. Thomas Part then moved smartly and offered to drop all pending litigation against the Duchy and pay them £14,000 for any rights which they 'might' have to the foreshore. A party of Southport Councillors in London to oppose the Ribble Navigation Bill agreed to stand as personal guarantors to match the landowner's offer. The following day it was announced that the Duchy had resigned all rights to the Southport landowners.

This simple announcement resulted in a complete breakdown in relations between the Corporation and the landed estates.[75] The Corporation refused to recognize the landowners as the rightful owners. They argued that the rights and claims of a public body should have received preference over those of private individuals. This point was seized on by other local authorities, as the Foreshore Dispute became for a while a minor *cause célèbre*, and an issue of national discussion and importance. Within a few weeks 25 town councils and 65 local boards had all publicly pledged their support and petitioned Prime Minister Gladstone and their parliamentary members.[76]

Radicals within the Council claimed that the landowners were 'landgrabbers' who were content to sacrifice the best interests of the town for their own financial gain. Feelings ran high. Alderman Griffiths declared that, 'They would burn the effigies of some of these men before long unless they gave them equity'.[77] In return the landowners were indignant at the Council's challenge to their celebrated position. Mrs Hesketh wrote to her son in 1883: 'I have been reading the Southport papers and all that has been said. I am thoroughly disgusted! . . . I should show no generosity whatever. What generosity could they expect from a land-grabber?'

Alderman Griffiths felt that Southport was 'in the van of the fight' for land reform, and he and other radicals clearly saw the dispute as part of a much wider programme of land reform agitation.[78] In the November local elections, Liberal candidates favouring municipal acquisition of the foreshore all presented a platform offering support for widescale land and leasehold reform. The dispute was part and parcel of a much deeper tension and conflict in society. It was not simply a matter of legal rights to a foreshore, but a question of who had the legitimate moral right within the new urban and industrial society to determine a town's future development. In essence it challenged the right of land to confer natural wealth and power.

The landowners naturally claimed that their ownership of the land on which the town stood entitled them to legitimate exercise of power and influence. Their solicitors wrote advising the Duchy that their clients were the owners of 95 per cent of the land in Southport, 'and have therefore, a far greater interest in the prosperity of the town than members of the Corporation have.'[79] In short, the Trustees asserted that the rights and privileges of a private estate were greater than those of a public authority, and that the interests of the inhabitants of Southport were better served and safeguarded by the Scarisbrick estate than by the Southport Corporation.

This assertion was vehemently denied. The Town Clerk, John Henry Ellis, argued that the Scarisbrick estate was merely interested in obtaining the highest possible income for the beneficiaries, whose interest, he told the Select Committee on Town Holdings, was best displayed by the fact that they were not resident in the town. He felt that the foreshore should be left to the Corporation 'as the representative of the inhabitants to deal with in such a manner as they think fit,' for, he insisted, 'to say that the landowners have a greater interest in the prosperity of the town than the members of the Corporation is to say that they are more interested in the town than the inhabitants themselves.'[80] Ellis rightly felt that the Trustees' moves were part of a general attempt to undermine the middle-class challenge to the privileged position of landowners in society. It was a challenge which the landowners saw as a real threat to their survival as a class, for it was a challenge which not only denied the right of land to confer natural wealth and power, but by so doing also denied their moral and economic justification as a class. The challenge of the land reform movement was based on 'the denial of the economic necessity of the landowning class. Brought up upon a gospel of work and horror of waste common to the Evangelical and Benthamite, they could not separate unearned income from the idea of sin.'[81]

It was the way in which Southport's landowners were able to live a life of luxury based on the town's residential development, without actually *doing* anything, that so offended her middle classes. The landowners did not lay out the streets, nor did they build the houses. They did not provide capital, nor did they directly provide amenities. They simply leased land. A *Southport Guardian* editorial complained that, 'The ground landowners of Southport have had princely fortunes built up for them from the bare sand . . . without paying for as much as a brick.' Land provided them with an income and a place in society wholly incommensurate with their actual rôle.[82]

Of course the estates argued that the leasehold system, and their particular administration of it, had accounted for the rapid, beautifully-planned development of the town. They wanted their imposition of stringent covenants and conditions and their donations of land for public and recreational purposes to be seen by all as part of a general town planning scheme designed for the public good. The Hesketh estate solicitors insisted that, 'The natural advantages of Southport are few, yet it has grown at a rate which no other watering place can compare.' They claimed that this had been done by leasing land cheaply, which 'has enabled them to secure large open spaces by attaching to each house a large area of land, and also to impose restrictions as are conducive to the prosperity of the town . . . they are insisted upon for the benefit of the town generally, and not for their own pecuniary profit.' The Town Clerk, Ellis, rejected this argument. He asserted that, 'Southport has grown in spite and not in consequence of the actions of these parties.'[83] The conflict between the estates and the town's middle-class leaders arose very much out of this rejection of the claims made for the leasehold system, and the landowners' rôle in the development of the town.

The restrictive convenants and conditions which the landowners inserted into their leases formed the basis of their claims for the system. They were, of course, a form of social and planning control, and were extensively evident in all the Southport leases. Building plans were carefully vetted by the estate offices to ensure that they conformed with the minimum building standards and values demanded. Restrictive convenants were wide ranging, prohibiting sub-letting and various trades and nuisances. In principle such measures were fully supported by Southport's lessee-residents to maintain the respectable internal social standards of the town. Their objection was to the way in which they were used by the landowners, and the Scarisbrick estate in particular, as a lever for enforcing payments of money. Covenants were often allowed to be broken in exchange for an increased ground rent or payment of a substantial fine. It was argued that if a covenant was based on a genuine desire to protect the values and residential standards of a district, it should not be allowed to be breached in return for monetary compensation. Ellis complained to the Select Committee on Town Holdings, 'The rule on the Scarisbrick estate seems to me to be to seize on every breach of covenant for the purpose of obtaining a higher ground rent.'[84] The restrictive covenant thus came to be seen as little more than a form of legalized extortion – another means of profiting from the development of the town without actually contributing anything.

Further, it was felt that the landowners, by virtue of their ownership of land and the covenants they could impose to restrict its use, were in a position to exploit the local authority, and ratepayers' money, whilst claiming to act in a purely philanthropic and altruistic manner. Radicals pointed back to Charles Hesketh's donation of Hesketh Park in 1865. The Board of Commissioners was initially prepared to pay for the outright purchases of the 30 acres of sandhills, but Hesketh insisted that he should *donate* it to the town. Not only did this buy time for the landowners in their fight against Incorporation, it also placed Hesketh in a better position to impose conditions and restrictions favourable to the development of the surrounding area than if he had sold it at a full economic rate. He insisted that the Commissioners lay a wide crescent-shaped road around the perimeter of the park and that they provide proper sewerage facilities. The Improvement Commissioners also funded the planting and landscaping of the park.[85] As a result the adjacent land was instantly eligible for building, and Hesketh's barren range of sandhills was dramatically transformed into one of the town's most lucrative development areas. This was done at no cost to the owner, who emerged in the eyes of most as a benevolent and kindly benefactor.

The foreshore offered a similar opportunity to manipulate the local authority. Having acquired the rights from the Duchy, the landowners' intention was to win public favour by selling the land at a nominal sum – but with conditions which would ensure that the value of their adjacent property would be be enhanced, not at their own, but at the ratepayers' expense. In the climate of the 1880s their strategy was only too transparent. The editor of the *Southport Guardian* was quick to complain that the estates,

> would spend no money in reclaiming the foreshore if they could induce other people to do the work, their policy being to remain ground landowners while public bodies enrich it . . . if the scheme satisfied the landowners, that is to say, if it would enhance the value of their adjacent property, it would be approved . . . In short, what the Corporation would have to consider would be not what would serve the interests of the town, but what would pay the landowners.[86]

Against this, the estates argued that Councillors' interests in the town were fleeting and their policies potentially detrimental to the long-term prosperity of the town. In contrast they claimed that their landed interest was the more long-term, that they were above immediate financial gain, and any measures calculated to increase the value of their residential estates were automatically in the best interests of the town.

It was a common enough argument. Yet in a town of Southport's middle-class residential character, the Corporation, as much as the landed estates, was concerned and anxious to preserve standards of town planning compatible with their high notions of respectability and morality. Moreover, the Corporation was responsible for many of the town's fine planning features, such as the tree-lined avenues, Lord Street's boulevards and the splendid landscaping which character-ized civic improvements, such as the Marine Gardens and the various Promenade extensions. And there is no doubt that the landowners' development strategy, and the argument they deployed to justify it, was motivated by the desire deliberately to cover both the keen distrust and resentment they felt towards the Corporation, and the uncompromising, financially selfish attitude they displayed towards the town's urban development.

The argument, often accepted and defended, that the leasehold system secured minimum standards and large plots of land for each house purely for reasons of sound town planning in the interests of the residential public, was clearly spurious. Southport set the standards for fine planning simply because the Scarisbrick estate was aware that careful planning and financial profit went hand in hand in the development of Victorian residential resorts. High-class development also ensured a more valuable reversionary interest, a factor which was never far from the lessor's mind. Large plots were also given for reasons of direct profitability. Hesketh's agent explained to his employer: 'It is not desirable to let land only 25 yards in depth . . . you have a street to give for much *less depth* of land leased – therefore less profitable to you.'[87]

In a system where sound town planning was only found in partnership with sound financial return, Southport's leasehold development led to several pernicious features of urban growth, of which the local authority became only too well aware as it extended its areas of concern. Consequences of the landowners' reversionary interest, such as poor housing conditions at the fag end of leases, a general reluctance to make improvements, and an acute shortage of working-class housing due to the landowner's reluctance to allow land to be leased for such purposes because of its poor reversionary value, all began to make their mark during the 1880s. The cheap housing problem continued well into the twentieth century. In his annual report of 1911 the Medical Officer of Health, John Weaver, pointed out that although the general standard of housing was good, it was too uniformly expensive in relation to the average income levels of the town's working classes, with the result that overcrowding and poverty was rife.[88] It was only after the local authority attained compulsory powers that the problem was effectively tackled, with the construction of sponsored cheap housing in the 1920s.

The leasehold system, then, was the source of many real grievances. The town's rejection of the claims made for it, and the general denial of the landowner's moral and economic justification, formed the basis of the conflict between town and estate during this period. There is no doubt that Southport's landowners received an income from and achieved a celebrated position within the town, based on a system of development which did not morally entitle them to it. The legitimacy of the Radicals' cause made the conflict particularly bitter and the issues embodied especially important.

5 Old enemies, new friends, 1883–1914

The Land Reform movement enjoyed an Indian Summer in Southport. After the Settled Lands Act of 1882, which gave added powers and benefits to tenants-for-life, the years which followed witnessed a real plethora of national organized agitation. The Land Nationalisation Society, the Georgist Movement, Hyndman's Social Democratic Federation, the Leasehold Enfranchisement Association and the Free Land League were all products of these years and Southport was quick to adopt local branches.[89] In the wake of the foreshore dispute and extreme Radical fervour, the local elections of 1883 swept the entire landed interest out of office, including the Scarisbrick estate agent, John Betham.

Land Reform remained the recurring political cause in the town throughout the remainder of the century, and formed the main platform of all the town's Liberal candidates in the general elections between 1886 and 1900. Indeed the movement almost enjoyed a final eccentric success in the election of 1910. In this particularly bitter fight, the Unionists argued that land was being valued at inflated figures preparatory to the taxation of land values. At the prompting of the Hesketh estate solicitor and Tory Council leader, J.J. Cockshott, they challenged the Liberal candidate, Baron de Forest, to buy the undeveloped land of Southport at the official figure of £585,000. To their complete astonishment, de Forest, heir and son of Baron Hirsch, the builder of the Orient Railway, agreed to the figure and deposited the money in a local bank! De Forest lost the election by 400 votes, but won a moral victory as no land owner accepted his offer.[90]

During these years the land owners' political bullying of tenants, their open prejudice against Radical builders, their refusal to allow nonconformist day schools to be built on their land and their increasingly excessive reversionary demands, all fuelled the fires of a movement which lingered on into an Edwardian senility which well became both the town and the protagonists. As late as 1913, the veteran Victorian Radical, Alderman Griffiths, who had sat on the Council since 1870, opposed a draft Omnibus Bill because it would prevent the town's acquisition of the foreshore, which he stressed was, 'the most important question Southport ever had, or ever will have.' He was told to sit down and shut up.[91]

The truth was that the Land Reform movement, perhaps because of the very legitimacy and fundamentality of its equivocation, outstayed its welcome, indeed outlived most of its adherents, and certainly outlasted the contemporaneity of its appeal. In the political context of the years leading up to the First World War, Radical demands for sweeping Land Reform had become too tainted with the spectre of socialism to have any appeal to Southport's new generation of middle class leaders. The new men were concerned to preserve the establishment, in the face of threats from organized labour, rather than undermine it by legislating against its principal pillar. The red brick villas had turned Tory, and were to remain so. Following the Liberal Mayor's support for Trade Unionism, the Tories captured the keys to the Town Hall for the first time since Incorporation in November 1907. This result, though, was but the immutable political evidence of the change in the relationship between town and estate which marked this period.[92]

It was a period characterized by a gradual movement towards the permanent reconciliation of the Edwardian era and beyond. By the early years of the twentieth century the Town Clerk was no longer the landowners' most ardent and skilful opponent, but their staunchest ally and a keen defender of their residential development policies.[93] The harmony of the Edwardian era overflowed with fanciful affirmations of the new consensus. In 1902, Charles Scarisbrick's grandson, Thomas Talbot Leyland Scarisbrick, expressed sentiments about the Council very different from those uttered 20 years earlier: 'I think we may be justly proud of Southport . . . and how has Southport been developed? How has Southport been made beautiful? It has been developed in consequence of the progressive policies which have been pursued by the Southport Corporation.' And the Liberal Mayor was equally obsequious: 'The members of the Corporation have always cheerfully and freely acknowledged that their host's grandfather and his successors, and the Hesketh estate also, deserved a fair share of praise in connection with the laying out and management of this beautiful town.'[94] The battles were over. Old enemies had become new friends working in mutual harmony, with each party prepared to credit the other with responsibility for the town's development. This came about because of the ultimate failure of the town's Land Reform movement, and because of the landowners' considered resumption of traditional responsibilities.

The landed estates survived the agitation of the 1880s remarkably well. The parliamentary bill to acquire the foreshore, which was promoted by the Radicals to ensure that any victory would receive maximum publicity and legitimacy, never materialized in the face of practicality and economy. Throughout the 1880s the Scarisbrick agent John Betham repeatedly warned the beneficiaries that extreme political agitation on the estate, 'backed up by a lot of land leaguers' and 'supported by socialists and communists . . . [whose] manoeuverings are secret and adroit,' would inevitably undermine their position. He felt that the abolition of the 99-year lease and some form of leasehold reform with the compulsory purchase of reversions was certain, and a series of contingency plans were drawn up.[95] In fact such measures did not become effective until nearly a century later with the Leasehold Reform Act of 1967, ammended by the Housing Act of 1974.

Why did the movement fail so miserably? The weaknesses of the Southport campaign were symptomatic of national failings. Firstly, Southport's protagonists could never agree just how far they wanted their compaign against the landowners to go. The extremists, led by Alderman Griffiths, supported the programme of the Free Land League. They declared that all of Southport had at one time been common waste land, which was reclaimed from the sea and marshes by the erection of sea-defences built by boon-labour in the early years of the nineteenth century, and subsequently enclosed by the landowners. They thus argued that 'the land they stood upon was squatted upon by the landowners of the district. They had no more bought it than they did.' This argument was used throughout the land agitation of the 1880s and 1890s, particularly by John Taylor, the local secretary of the Land Nationalization Society. He constantly campaigned that the wealth of the estates was based on the 'land-grabbing of Squire Scarisbrick and Old Parson Hesketh.' He declared that, 'Those humble squatters in their lowly huts have more rights to their homesteads, than all the breeds of Heskeths and Scarisbricks.'[96] The majority shyed away from this argument and preferred instead to put their weight behind the less radical leasehold enfranchisement movement. Even here, though, the situation factionalized into parties who saw enfranchisement as an end in itself and others who saw it as merely part of a much wider programme of land transfer reform.

Secondly, the movement was hampered by the stand made by the legal profession. They, as much as the landowners themselves, stood to gain by the maintenance of the existing leasehold and land transfer system, with its cumbersome and costly methods of conveyancing. Licences to assign and lengthy searches of title were all claimed to be in the best interests of the purchaser to assure his good title, but in truth were devices perpetuated to assure healthy profits. The Real Property Commissioners advocated the abolition of private conveyancing and its replacement by the public registration of title as early as 1829. But because the men with the professional ability to enact this programme were the lawyers themselves, a rational system of land transfer was prevented, and has been so denied even to the present day. All forms of Land Reform agitation came up against this legal barrier of 'the monstrous regiments of the law,' against what the Duke of Marlborough termed 'the permanent conservative majority, not of the House of Lords, but of the legal profession and conveyancing interest.'[97]

The Southport campaign reflected the influence of this conservative lobby. The landowners had no trouble raising a legal army to defend their interests. Southport's considerable number of solicitors, led by the Hesketh estate solicitor John James Cockshott, were beside themselves in their rush to align with the estates. On the reformers' side members of the legal profession were notably absent, the weight of professional expertise falling on the overburdened shoulders of Town Clerk Ellis. This conservative interest was especially relevant to Southport's land agitation because of the peculiar organizational structure of the Radicals' bitterest enemy, the Scarisbrick estate, which was protected by a massive web of legal machinery. The Trustees themselves were invariably solicitors, who in turn were protected by the considerable weight of the Court of Chancery, to whom they were nominally accountable and to whom they had to apply for approval of changes in the administration of the estate. Because the Trustees were less concerned with or accountable to public opinion, and because they possessed an expert knowledge not normally found amongst the ranks of English landowners, they were in a better position to deal with the agitation which came their way, especially since they could argue that they were legally obliged to protect the interests of the beneficiaries regardless of all else. In short, any effective challenge to the Scarisbrick estate involved the undoing of a complicated legal structure. Because of the conservative interest of the legal profession, and because of financial limitations, Southport's reformers had neither the money nor the expertise to undertake such a task effectively, as their campaign ultimately demonstrated.

Thirdly, the foreshore dispute in particular provided an illustration of the way in which Gladstone's government flinched at the land problem. Despite the considerable national support which the dispute received, Gladstone refused to take up the case and preferred instead to cloud the issue with technicalities to avoid involvement. His secretary wrote that, 'Mr Gladstone cannot help thinking that there exists considerable misapprehension as to the position of the parties interested . . . it is not a question of a proposed sale . . . but of a sale actually concluded.' He deliberately ignored the wider implications and argued that the case was simply a local issue, and as such, 'It seems unnecessary for Mr Gladstone to enter into details on the points raised.'[98] The dispute thus became part of the Liberal government's steadfast refusal or inability to enact Chamberlain's radical Free Land programme of the 1870s.

Given this lack of central government support, a good deal of the onus for land reform agitation fell on the local authorities. The Southport campaign illustrated the weaknesses of these bodies. Despite the ever-increasing rateable value of the town, and the wealth of talent and expertise which residential development provided, the Southport Corporation was forced into concession as early as December 1883 as a result of the narrow financial foundation which characterized all local authorities at this date. The local rates were virtually the Corporation's sole source of income, and the financial demands made on them by the host of local improvements essential in an expanding town ensured that this acted as a definite check to the Corporation's freedom of action. Indeed, although in terms of residents Southport was one of Lancashire's wealthiest towns, its rateable values had been kept artificially low to attract prospective residents. The burden of the rates fell most heavily on the owner of a few houses since it acted as a tax on his source of income.[99] Property was a favourite form of investment among Southport's middle classes due to the easy terms which the leasehold system offered.

160

Because of this there existed a very numerous lobby of ratepayers who were especially wary of Corporation expenditure.

The professional and business élite who made up the hard core of radicals were in an economic position to assume an ideologically radical stance; but they could not act independently of the hundreds of residents with a small stake in property, whose main concern with Council expenditure, overriding the grievances they held against the landowners and the genuine sympathy they felt for the radicals' cause, was simply 'Will It Pay?' As E.P. Hennock has argued, 'This was the Nemesis built into the functioning of urban local government.'[100] Because a parliamentary bill would not have paid in financial terms, it was dropped, concessionary terms were accepted and the landowers' position consolidated.

It was only during the 1890s with the increased exchequer grant, and particularly after the Education Act of 1902, that the local authorities gained a financial foundation less exclusively dependent on the rates. But by this time the Liberal government was in even less of a position to enact their land programme, whilst in Southport at least the landowners had heeded the warnings of the 1880s and adjusted their uncompromising stance. They traded their exclusive social and political power for continued financial success, and not only tactfully resumed traditional, if merely titular, responsibilities, but also came to embrace common political stances with their old enemies.

In 1888, on the urging of local Conservatives and Anglican clergymen, Charles Scarisbrick, the youngest of the three beneficiaries of his father's estate (see Appendix 1), came to reside in Southport in a carefully-considered attempt to heal old wounds and weaken the radical campaign. He was a man particularly ill-suited to public life, and he suffered the early indignity of being an unsuccessful Conservative candidate in the municipal elections of 1889. However, he gradually overcame his natural reticence as he became more involved in local affairs due to the constant prompting of anxious Tory party organizers. He later became President of the Conservative and Unionist Association, a County Magistrate in 1890, Mayor of the Borough in 1901, Park Ward Councillor from 1903 to 1906, and was knighted in 1903. He also worked hard to gain the reputation of a benevolent philanthropist. Even a radical *Southport Guardian* columnist had to admit, 'I don't know of an object, society or institution for which his pecuniary support has not been asked – and in few cases has it been asked in vain.'[101] Most notably he gave £7,000 in cash towards the building of Southport Infirmary.

His son, Thomas Talbot Leyland Scarisbrick (1874–1933) succeeded him as mayor in 1902. His year of office was memorable for his accommodation of the British Association delegates who visited the town that year. The Scarisbricks had no ancestral home on the estate which could be used as a social centre. To overcome this immediate difficulty, and to impress all with their new found interest in the town's affairs, Thomas built Greaves Hall, resplendent in mock Tudor style with a large banquet hall especially designed to accommodate the British Association visit. Thereafter he rarely visited the Hall, which was later sold to the local authority and converted into a home for the mentally retarded.[102]

The Heskeths also acquiesced in the new alliance. Edward Hesketh had always sympathized with the radicals' cause, but he was a weak man, without the strength of character to reform in the face of the intransigent position of the Scarisbrick estate. Charles Hesketh Bibby Hesketh (1871–1947) succeeded to the estate in 1899 (see Appendix 2). He was rather less sympathetic to the land issue, but in the

Figure 13.
Sir Herbert
Scarisbrick
Naylor-Leyland,
cartoon drawing,
c. 1895
(by courtesy of
the Southport
Public Library).

162

context of his period, his willingness to serve as mayor in 1905–6, as a Conservative councillor (albeit for a term of office noted for his absenteeism at meetings), and as Deputy-Lieutenant and High-Sheriff of the County, was sufficient to cement the new ties between town and estate.

The most remarkable feature of the period, though, was the Scarisbrick estate's belated conversion to Liberalism. In February 1895, Sir Herbert Scarisbrick Naylor-Leyland, the grandson of Charles Scarisbrick, surprisingly resigned as Conservative Member of Parliament for Colchester, and changed over to the Liberal cause. He unsuccessfully contested Southport against Lord Curzon in July 1895. With an astonishing about-face he even made his main platform the cause of land reform and leasehold enfranchisement. At a public meeting held in July 1895 he was reported as saying that, 'the whole course of their land history had been designed to keep the land in as few hands as possible and to give as much power as possible to the owner of land . . . but the object of the Liberal party was distribution, not aggregation. They desired to bring about free trade in land.' In 1898 he stood again. During this campaign he even took the rather unlikely step of charging the Trustees' administration of the Scarisbrick estate with 'seriously retarding the growth and development of the town . . . and in my opinion deserves to be censured and condemned.'[103]

Although he captured the seat from Lord Skelmersdale, he died the following year at the age of 35, before he had chance to act on what many thought were hollow pledges to reform the management of the estate, pledges uttered merely to appease the town's leaseholders for the benefit of the estate and the procurement of votes. Certainly, in the 1898 campaign he was quick to take refuge behind the Scarisbrick estate's legal machinery, and detached himself from any direct future responsibility for the affairs of the estate. He pointed out that, 'In law the real owners of the estate, and the persons who are really responsible, are the Trustees, and nothing can be done except by the Trustees.' The Trustees thus conveniently bore the brunt of the responsibility for the management of the estate, whilst at the same time they made Sir Herbert 'one of the wealthiest men in the country' and provided him with the means to move in the most exclusive London society circles.[104]

In the circumstances of all that had gone before and all that they feared for the future, one would have to be extremely generous to interpret the landowners' sudden philanthropy, their surprising advocacy of land reform and their unexpected willingness to credit the Corporation with responsibility for the town's past and future progress as coincidental bursts of genuine idealism and sentiment. Rather, it was surely a conscious and deliberate attempt to consolidate and strengthen their position in the town. By joining forces with the very group which had once sought to remove them, the Southport landowners found themselves in their most comfortable position for 40 years.

6 Epilogue: economic and social withdrawal since 1914

The 1910 elections concluded the vigorous political interaction between town and estate. It was a relationship which in many ways had typified the social and political developments of nineteenth-century Lancashire. The red-brick villas, headed by the leaders of Lancashire's industry and commerce, challenging the position and authority of the landed estates, who had adapted remarkably well to the new opportunities which the period presented, characterized the metamorphosis in the region's socio-political life. This relationship rightly hinted at the vitality of the Victorian era, yet suggested a strength and permanence on both sides which finally proved illusory.

The end came quickly. By the 1920s the large Victorian villas had become anachronisms, out of place in a world where their prerequisites of a buoyant local economy and a cheap and plentiful supply of domestic servants had all but disappeared. These Liberal castles became private schools and convalescent homes, were sub-let as cheap bed-sitters, or fell into disrepair and decay in the hands of widows living off the remains of Victorian fortunes.[105] The middle class influx into Southport *did* continue. As F.W. Brown remarked in 1926, 'Good Lancashire folk, before they die, take up residence in Southport.'[106] But they were no longer the leaders of industry and commerce, men anxious to lead and direct society. Rather, they were concerned to keep up appearances in their stuccoed semis, content to be socially seclusive and politically subdued.

The landed estates mirrored this quiet retreat. The urban ground rents, which had been seen by Charles Scarisbrick as a never-ending source of income for his descendants, were soon found to be a poor defence against twentieth-century inflation and taxation, and even before the First World War sales of reversions were taking place at every opportunity. The Heskeths were the first to sever their landed connections with the town. In January 1927 it was announced that Charles Bibby Hesketh had sold the whole estate, except Meols Hall itself, for £380,000 to a syndicate of merchant bankers and businessmen, headed by the Earl of Verulam, who formed the Hesketh Estate Company. *The Times* felt that the sale was 'one of the most important of its kind ever affected,' comprising as it did of over 5,000 acres of agricultural land and the reversions to 2,500 properties held on building leases.[107]

In many ways it was a surprising decision. By careful pruning and management, mortgages on the estate had been reduced from their peak of £131,000 in 1914 to £77,000 in 1926. Clear estate profits of £8,000 *per annum* for each of the years 1925–7 had been the highest since Bibby Hesketh took control of the estate in 1899. The demand for building land was steadily increasing; 38 leases were granted in 1923–4, 44 in 1924–5 and 62 in 1925–6.[108] And unlike the Scarisbrick estate, which had virtually exhausted its land, the Heskeths still had 500 acres ripe for immediate development. Bibby Hesketh's son, Colonel Roger Fleetwood Hesketh, explained that although it was a time marked by agricultural depression and a fear of impending legislation against landowners, there was no historical reason for the sale, and that it was sold for purely personal motives. He and his brother, Peter, opposed the sale 'tooth and nail, but lost the battle.' His father thus cleared the outstanding mortgages and invested the balance in War Stock, Corporation Bonds and Railway Stock. Roger Hesketh explained that, 'The town property was the biggest loss. Peter and I had so many plans. We were only young, I was about twenty, but we had given it much thought and were very involved. I was very attached and really saw it as my duty in life to save as much of the bacon as I could. In 1929 we barred the entail and split what was left, so I got a bit of money.'[109]

With the entail money Roger repurchased the agricultural land, though not the foreshore, and most of Churchtown village, but control of the urban development in Southport was irrevocably lost. Still, Roger Hesketh used his regained portion as a base for retaining strong social and political ties with the town. He served as mayor in 1950, and as Conservative M.P. from 1952 to his retirement in 1959. Throughout his life he has campaigned to conserve the architectural integrity of the town. For instance, to compensate for his loss of influence over the speculative builders at work on the lost portion of his estate, he bought the 'Master Builder', the official organ of the Federation of House Builders, in 1930, and in 1936 he was instrumental in saving the Botanical Gardens from falling into the hands of speculative builders. Indeed, in the post-war period he lent his active support to most voluntary and charitable organizations, and Meols Hall became the town's most prominent centre for a host of social events and fund-raising efforts. In all this, Roger Hesketh has managed to earn a modern respect for the rôle of the estates which they rarely earned or deserved during the nineteenth-century. After his retirement he spent four years redesigning Meols Hall from a house devoid of any architectural distinction and character into one of imposing classical style. With the neat white-washed thatched cottages grouped near the gates to the Hall, the illusion of the traditional ancestral estate was complete.

The Scarisbrick estate's withdrawal was less reluctant and more complete. The

Figure 14. Scarisbrick Hall (by courtesy of the Cambridge University Library).

heavy sales of reversions that characterized the decade leading up to the First World War continued unabated after 1918. This was a policy more or less forced upon the Trustees by new taxation, in the form of succession, reversion and death duties, and by the beneficiaries' insistence on regular and substantial cash payments to support lavish life-styles adopted in spite, or, indeed, perhaps because of, the threat of further fiscal measures. As a result the function of the Trust was completely undermined, and in 1925, after years of prompting by Sir Thomas Talbot Scarisbrick, application was made to the Court of Chancery and the Trust terminated. The estate was physically partitioned into three undivided lots and for the first time the beneficiaries became landowners in their own right.[110] Sir Thomas Talbot, who had purchased his grandfather's ancestral home, Scarisbrick Hall, in 1923, sold his partitioned share. The remaining two-thirds was gradually whittled away by the sale of reversions at each opportune moment. The Naylor-Leyland third was finally sold off in the 1950s, and only the share descending from William Scarisbrick's grandson, Charles Ewald Scarisbrick, remained in any way intact.

This economic withdrawal was matched socially. Sir Thomas Talbot's son, Sir Everard Talbot Scarisbrick, retired to Norfolk where he died without heir in 1955. For those with a remaining stake in the town, their visits were confined to management meetings with the estate agents. The family had never taken on the traditional rôles and duties of local landowners, but after 1925 their withdrawal was total. The Naylor-Leylands lived for the most part in London and kept on the family seat at Nantclwyd Hall. In the 1970s they took up residence in the West Indies.

Finally, in 1978, David Scarisbrick severed the remnants of their 800-year-old association with the area, when the share descending from William Scarisbrick was disposed of. It was a sale not without irony. Earlier fund-raising plans to turn wasteland into an animal cemetery and to convert the Estate Office into a casino for Arab visitors had been refused planning permission by the Sefton Council. Then in April 1978, the 5,500 acres of foreshore and 850 acres of agricultural land, which realized an annual income of over £30,000 from tenant farmers, was offered for sale at £1.5 million.[111]

The estate agreed a sale with a Southport businessman and a Dutch tycoon, but the Nature Conservancy Council and the Royal Society for the Protection of Birds persuaded the Government that their plans to drain and develop the area as agricultural land would have a disastrous effect on an area ranked as the fourth most important in Europe for wintering wading birds, and a compulsory purchase order was served to purchase the area as a nature reserve for the nation.[112] The Government thus paid over £1 million for part of an area it had resigned all rights to for £14,000 less than a century earlier. It was a fitting conclusion to the Scarisbricks' involvement in Southport, underlining as it did their spectacular financial success and the final cruel consequence of the land reformers' failures in the 1880s and 1890s.

APPENDIX 1

Genealogical table of the Scarisbrick family (simplified)

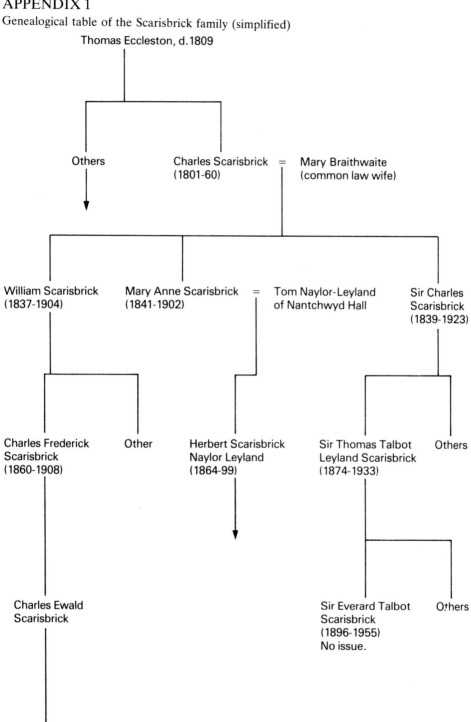

Thomas Eccleston, d.1809

Others

Charles Scarisbrick (1801-60) = Mary Braithwaite (common law wife)

William Scarisbrick (1837-1904)

Mary Anne Scarisbrick (1841-1902) = Tom Naylor-Leyland of Nantchwyd Hall

Sir Charles Scarisbrick (1839-1923)

Charles Frederick Scarisbrick (1860-1908)

Other

Herbert Scarisbrick Naylor Leyland (1864-99)

Sir Thomas Talbot Leyland Scarisbrick (1874-1933)

Others

Charles Ewald Scarisbrick

Sir Everard Talbot Scarisbrick (1896-1955) No issue.

Others

APPENDIX 2

Genealogical table of the Hesketh family (simplified)

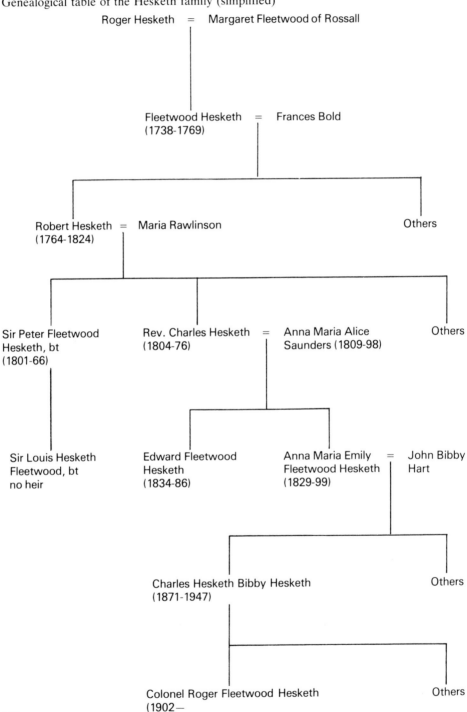

Roger Hesketh = Margaret Fleetwood of Rossall

Fleetwood Hesketh = Frances Bold
(1738-1769)

Robert Hesketh = Maria Rawlinson   Others
(1764-1824)

Sir Peter Fleetwood   Rev. Charles Hesketh = Anna Maria Alice   Others
Hesketh, bt   (1804-76)   Saunders (1809-98)
(1801-66)

Sir Louis Hesketh   Edward Fleetwood   Anna Maria Emily = John Bibby
Fleetwood, bt   Hesketh   Fleetwood Hesketh   Hart
no heir   (1834-86)   (1829-99)

Charles Hesketh Bibby Hesketh   Others
(1871-1947)

Colonel Roger Fleetwood Hesketh   Others
(1902—

BIBLIOGRAPHY

1 Primary sources

Lancashire Record Office:
  Clifton Estate Papers
  Formby Estate Papers
  Hoghton Estate Papers
  Scarisbrick Family, Estate and Trust Papers
  Weld-Blundell Estate Papers
Meols Hall, Southport:
  Hesketh Family and Estate Papers
Scarisbrick Estate Office, Southport:
  Scarisbrick Estate Papers
Southport Public Library:
  Census Enumerators Returns, 1841
  Cheetham Papers
  Council Minutes, 1867–1910
  Improvement Commissioners: Miscellaneous Committee Minutes
  Reports of Medical Officer of Health, 1903–24
Wigan Record Office:
  Scarisbrick Estate Papers

2 Newspapers

Liverpool Mercury; Manchester Guardian; Preston Chronicle; Preston Pilot; Southport Guardian; Southport Journal; Southport Visitor; The Times

3 Parliamentary papers

1883, vol. liv, Correspondence re. Southport foreshore
1866, vol. xii ⎤
1887, vol. xiii ⎥
1888, vol. xxii ⎬ *S.C. on Town Holdings*
1889, vol. xv ⎦

4. Published contemporary sources (local)

Abram, W.A., 'The Scarisbricks of Scarisbrick', *Lancashire and Cheshire Antiquarian Notes*, ii (1885–6).
Aiken, J., *A Description of the Country from Thirty to Forty Miles Around Manchester* (1792).
Alsop, W., *A Concise History of Southport* (1832).
Baines, E., *History and Directory of Lancashire* (1824).
Barron, G.B., *Southport as a Residence in Health and Disease* (1858).
Beattie, E.R., 'The Southport of sixty years ago', *Transactions of the Historic Society of Lancashire and Cheshire*, new. ser., xxx (1914).
Cheetham, F.H., 'Scarisbrick Hall, Lancashire', *Transactions of the Lancashire and Cheshire Antiquarian Society*, xxiv (1906).
Granville, A.B., *The Spas of England, and Principal Sea-Bathing Places*, vol. i, *The North* (1841).

Glazebrook, T.K., *A Guide to Southport* (1826).
Grazebrook, H., *Lights Along the Line* (1855).
Hall, E. (ed.), *Miss Weeton, Journal of a Governess* (2 vols., 1936).
Head, Sir George, *A Home Tour Through the Manufacturing Districts of England in the Summer of 1835* (1968).
Hewitson, A., *Places and Faces* (1875).
Hocking, S., *My Book of Memory* (1923).
Jacson, C., *Formby Reminiscences* (1897).
McNicholl, D.H., *Handbook for Southport* (1859).
Robinson, F., *A Descriptive History of Southport* (1838).
Sumner, J., *A Guide to Southport and the Surrounding Neighbourhood and Parish* (1849).
Whittle, P., *Marina: or, an Historical and Descriptive Account of Southport, Lytham and Blackpool* (1831).
Winter, C., *A Winter in Southport, or the Journal of an Invalid* (1871).

5 Published contemporary sources (land reform)

Banfield, F., *The Great Landlords of London* (1888).
Broadhurst, H., and Reid, R.T., *Leasehold Enfranchisement* (1885).
Brodrick, G.C., *English Land and English Landlords* (1880).
—, *The Law and Custom of Primogeniture* (1872).
Collins, E.A., *Leasehold Enfranchisement* (1913).
Fabian Society, *Land Nationalisation* (1890).
—, *Leasehold Enfranchisement* (1890).
—, *Unearned Increment* (1891).
—, *Capital and Land* (1904).
Lloyd George, D., *The Urban Land Problem* (1914).
Holdsworth, W.S., *An Historical Introduction to the Land Laws* (1879).
Pollock, F., *Land Laws* (1883).
Tarn, A.W., *The Samuel Brown Essay on the Enfranchisement of Leaseholds and the Tax of Ground Rents* (1893).

I have omitted a comprehensive list of dissertations and modern printed sources, as the references are themselves a running bibliography.

NOTES

1 The pioneer work here is H.J. Dyos, *Victorian Suburb: A Study of the Growth of Camberwell* (1973).
2 J.T. Ward and R.G. Wilson (eds.), *Land and Industry: The Landed Estate and the Industrial Revolution* (1971), 9; D.J. Olsen, *Town Planning in London in the Eighteenth and Nineteenth Centuries* (1964), 9–10; D. Cannadine, *Lords and Landlords: The Aristocracy and the Towns, 1774–1967* (1980), 219.
3 H.J. Perkin, 'The "social tone" of Victorian seaside resorts in the north west', *Northern History*, XI (1976), 180–94; C. Widdowfield, 'The local Board of Health of Poulton, Bare and Torrisholme, and the development of Morecambe, 1852–94' (M.A. thesis, University of Lancaster, 1973); M.J. Winstanley, 'Conflicting responses to New Brighton's role as a popular seaside resort, 1896–1914' (M.A. thesis, University of Lancaster, 1973); J.K. Walton, *The Blackpool Landlady* (1978), 58–79.
4 Lancs. RO, DRL I/57, North Meols Tithe Commutation Award (1840).

5 J.G. Liddle, 'Castles in the sand: the urban development of Southport, 1792–1910'
   (Ph.D. thesis, University of Lancaster, forthcoming).
6 C. and R. Bell, *City Fathers: the early History of Town Planning in Britain* (1972),
   136–7; Perkin, 'Social tone', 186.
7 For the background, see: R.O. Knapp, 'Social mobility in Lancashire society, with
   special reference to the social origins of landowers in the "Modern Domesday" returns,
   1873–6' (Ph.D. thesis, University of Lancaster, 1970), 265–7.
8 *VCH Lancs.*, III (1907), 289; W.A. Abram, 'The Scarisbricks of Scarisbrick', *Lancs.
   and Cheshire Antiq. Notes*, II (1885–6), 248.
9 Knapp, *op. cit.*, 264–5; J.H. Sutton, 'The early development of Fleetwood, 1835–47'
   (m. Litt. thesis, University of Lancaster, 1968), 9–10, 26–9; C. Rothwell, 'A history of
   Fleetwood on Wyre, 1834–1934' (Fellowship of the Library Association dissertation,
   1974), 158–69; R.F. Hesketh, *Sir Peter Hesketh Fleetwood: a Monograph* (1951);
   Southport Visitor (hereafter cited as *SV*), 28 July 1923.
10 F.A. Bailey, *A History of Southport* (1955), 46; *SV*, 27 April 1854, 22 April 1899.
11 F.A. Bailey, 'The origin and growth of Southport', *Town Planning Rev.*, XXI (1951).
12 Wigan RO, Scarisbrick MSS, D/DSc E/2, A report drawn up by Thomas Part on the
   proposed purchase of the moiety of North Meols, 4 September 1841.
13 E.R. Beattie, 'The Southport of sixty years ago', *Trans. Historic Soc. Lancs. and
   Cheshire*, n.s. xxx (1914).
14 J. Whitehead, 'Recollections of Southport fifty years ago', from a collection of articles
   published in the *Southport Guardian* (hereafter cited as *SG*), 1892–5, transcribed into
   two volumes by F.H. Cheetham, in the Southport Public Library, 60–1.
15 Meols Hall, Hesketh MSS (hereafter cited as Hesketh MSS), O.T. Alger to Peter
   Hesketh Fleetwood, 28 January 1840.
16 Sutton, *op. cit.*, 138; Hesketh MSS, T.J. Knowlys to Anna Maria Hesketh, 27 February
   1840. It was estimated that Hesketh Fleetwood owed over £125,000 to his family,
   including £75,000 to his aunt, Anna Maria Hesketh, alone.
17 Wigan RO, Scarisbrick MSS, D/DSc E/1, Abstract of Title of Rev. Chas. Hesketh to
   land in North Meols, 1842; *ibid.*, E/9, Abstract of Title of Chas. Scarisbrick to land in
   North Meols (n.d.); Instruction to settle contract and advise on title, Henry Hoghton to
   Chas. Scarisbrick, September 1842; Abstract of Title of Charles Scarisbrick to a moiety
   of the manor of North Meols purchased from Henry Hoghton, 1853; E. Bland, *Annals
   of Southport* (1903), 121.
18 Rothwell, *op. cit.*, 138.
19 Hesketh MSS, Charles Hesketh to Peter Hesketh, 9 December 1843.
20 Sutton, *op. cit.*, 239–49; Rothwell, *op. cit.*, 154, 396.
21 Hesketh MSS, Peter to Charles Hesketh, 17 December 1857.
22 *Ibid.*, Peter to Charles Hesketh, 14 January 1857, 27 March 1857.
23 *Ibid.*, correspondence between Mrs Charles Hesketh and her solicitor, William
   Dickson, 1886, *passim*; correspondence between Mrs Charles Hesketh and Henry
   Willis, September 1887 to June 1980, *passim*.
24 *Ibid.*, Mrs Hesketh to Mrs Pearson, April 1882.
25 *SV*, 27 April 1854.
26 Sutton, *op. cit.*, 26–9, 34, 45–6.
27 Compare the Devonshires at Eastbourne and the Cliftons at neighbouring Lytham, who
   both gave substantial financial assistance to urban development: Cannadine, *op. cit.*,
   esp. chs. 18–19; see G. Rogers, forthcoming Ph.D. thesis (University of Lancaster) on
   the estate management policies of the Cliftons of Lytham.
29 Hesketh MSS: Early financial papers; Agent's report, 7 December 1898; Financial
   summaries, 1905–27.
29 *Preston Chronicle*, 12 May 1860.
30 Wigan RO, Scarisbrick MSS, D/Sc L/1, case of Mary Eccleston and others v. Chas.
   Scarisbrick in House of Lords, 1835; legal papers re. case of Chas. Scarisbrick v. Mary

Eccleston and others, 1837–8; *The Times*, 10 March 1834; *Preston Chronicle*, 15 March 1834, 11 August 1838.

31 Lancs RO, Scarisbrick MSS, DDSc, Charles Scarisbrick to William Talbot, 10 February 1833, 21 June 1833, 21 June 1844. Besides his extensive coal mines around Wigan, Scarisbrick also invested in mines in Virginia.

32 *Ibid.*, Charles Scarisbrick to William Talbot, 10 February 1833, 29 June 1845.

33 *Ibid.*, 4001, Trunk 7 (A); Succession Duty Papers; Abram, *op. cit.*, 254; P. Fleetwood, *Murray's Architectural Guide to Lancashire* (1955), 104–9; F. H. Cheetham, 'Scarisbrick Hall, Lancashire', *Trans. Lancs. and Cheshire Antiq. Soc.*, xxiv (1906).

34 Lancs. RO, Scarisbrick MSS, DDSc, Will of Charles Scarisbrick, dated 28 February 1857; Abram, *op. cit.*, 251–3; F.M.L. Thompson, *English Landed Society in the Nineteenth Century* (1963), 331.

35 This was the term used by Scarisbrick in his will.

36 W. Ashworth, *The Genesis of Modern British Town Planning* (1965), 45.

37 Lancs. RO, Scarisbrick MSS, DDSc: Trunk 7, Conspectus of accounts; 89/1, Trustees ledger, 1860–97; Abstracts of capital, receipts and disbursements, 1860–1908.

38 *Ibid.*, Talbot to Scarisbrick, 16 February 1844.

39 *Ibid.*, Scarisbrick to Talbot, 7 March 1844; Scarisbrick Estate Office, Southport, General deed of covenant, 1845.

40 *SV*, 26 October 1854, 12 February 1857.

41 *Ibid.*, 11 February 1862.

42 *Ibid.*, 3 December 1864.

43 J.H. Porter, 'Samuel Boothroyd: a Southport draper', *Business Archives*, xlii (1976), 15–21.

44 *SV*, 25 January 1855.

45 *Ibid.*, 29 March 1855.

46 Clergymen and retired gentlemen made up 50 per cent of the original board. See: B. Sandham, 'The municipal politics of a mid-Victorian seaside resort: Southport, 1867–75' (M.A. thesis, University of Lancaster, 1973).

47 *SV*, 10 April 1856.

48 *Ibid.*, 2, 16, 17 March 1854.

49 *Ibid.*, 18 July 1876.

50 W. Alsop, *A Concise History of Southport* (1832), 19; J.G. Liddle, 'The Southport foreshore dispute of 1883' (M.F. Howson prize essay, University of Lancaster, 1976), 3; F. Robinson, *A Descriptive History of Southport* (1838), 17, 104.

51 N. Hawthorne, *English Notebooks*, ed. Randall Stewart (1962), 397–8. Hawthorne lived in Southport from September 1856 until July 1857, while employed as U.S. Consul in Liverpool.

52 *Ibid.*, 398.

53 G. Hart, *A History of Cheltenham* (1965), 191; L. Gregory, 'The role of sea bathing in the development of Southport' (M.A. thesis, University of Lancaster, 1973), appendix i, 56–7.

54 *SV*, 11 October 1855, 2 April 1857.

55 *Ibid.*, 7 June 1855.

56 H.J. Dyos, *Urbanity and Suburbanity* (1973), 16, 23.

57 *SV*, 13 September 1855.

58 *Ibid.*, 28 June, 6 September 1855.

59 *Ibid.*, 15 January 1857.

60 *Ibid.*, 1 September 1863.

61 *Ibid.*, 22 May 1863.

62 Bailey, *History of Southport*, 141.

63 *Ibid.*, 204; Lancs. RO, Scarisbrick MSS, DDSC, Trustees Ledger, 1860–97.

64 *SV*, 10 July 1863.

65 *Ibid.*, 19 October 1886; Hesketh MSS, Will of Charles Hesketh, 14 March 1876.

66 Hesketh MSS, Mrs Hesketh to E. Gregson, no date (c. 1880); Mrs Hesketh to E. Hesketh, 28 August 1877.
67 *Ibid.*, E. Gregson to E. Hesketh, 23 August 1877.
68 Wigan RO, Scarisbrick MSS, D/Dsc E/9, William Scarisbrick to Thomas Talbot, 13 November 1863.
69 *SV*, 12 July 1870.
70 *Ibid.*, 21 June 1870; W.H. Stephenson, *Albert Frederick Stephenson, a Lancashire Newspaper Man* (1937), 37. A. F. Stephenson came to Southport in the 1870s, and was the controlling interest in the *SV* until his death in 1934.
71 *SV*, 1 July 1870; Stephenson, *op. cit.*, 36–7.
72 *Ibid.*; F.P. Smith, *The Unexpected* (1933), 36; Gregory, *op. cit.*, ch. 3; G.B. Barron, *Southport as a Residence in Health and Disease* (1858); D.H. McNicholl. *Handbook for Southport* (1859); *SV*, 21 July 1877.
73 *Southport J.*, 16 July 1906.
74 Scarisbrick Estate Office, Southport, Schedule of real and personal estate of the Scarisbrick Estate (1899); Lancs. RO, Weld-Blundell MSS, DDIn, Draft lease book.
75 Details of the dispute and the events leading up to it can be found in: PP (1883), LIV, 677ff; Liddle, *op. cit.*, 22–6.
76 *SG*, 23 June to 14 July 1883; *The Times*, 9 May to 7 June 1883.
77 *SG*, 5 May 1883.
78 *Ibid.*, 13 October 1883; Hesketh MSS, Mrs Hesketh to E. Hesketh, 28 July 1883.
79 PP (1883), LIV, Woodcook and Partners to Duchy of Lancaster, 19 April 1883.
80 *Ibid.*, Ellis to Duchy of Lancaster, 9 May 1883; *SV*, 5 May 1883; *SG*, 28 June 1883.
81 H.J. Perkin, 'Land reform and class conflict in Victorian England', in *The Victorians and Social Protest*, ed. J. Butt and I.F. Clarke (1973), 183. The challenge was inspired by John Stuart Mill's *Principles of Political Economy* (1848), esp. 272.
82 *SG*, 14 July 1883; D.A. Reeder, 'The Politics of urban leasehold in late Victorian England', *International Rev. of Social History*, VI (1966), 415.
83 PP (1883), LIV, 753–5.
84 *Ibid.*, 360–72.
85 SPL, Minutes of Park and Town Hall Committee, XV, 1865–8, *passim*.
86 *SG*, 5 May 1883.
87 Hesketh MSS, Gregson to Hesketh, 1 January 1878.
88 *SG*, 3 October 1896; SPL: Town Council Minutes, 1895–6, 29304, 804–11; Medical Officer of Health, Annual Report (1911), 17.
89 Southport does not support D.A. Reeder's argument that leasehold reform received little support in seaside towns: cf. Reeder, *op. cit.*, 421.
90 *SG*, 1 to 22 January 1910; A.J.P. Taylor, *Beaverbrook* (1972), 44.
91 *SG*, 15, 22 February 1893, 1 January 1913. The Hesketh estate refused leases to 'radical' builders, and both estates claimed that Anglican church schools were sufficient for the town's needs. Nonconformist arguments against this stand raged in the local press throughout the 1890s and 1900s.
92 D.N. Smith, 'Southport Corporation tramwaymen: a study of working conditions and problems of organisation' (M.A. thesis, University of Lancaster, 1977), 34.
93 *SG*, 30 November 1909.
94 *SG*, 9 June 1900, 12 November 1902.
95 Lancs. RO, Scarisbrick MSS, DDSc, Letter Book 1, 29 July, 2 September, 8 August 1883; Letter Book 2, 7 May 1891.
96 *SV*, 5 May 1883, 9 July 1898.
97 F.M.L. Thompson, 'Land and politics in England in the nineteenth century', *Trans. Royal Historical Soc.*, 5th ser., xv (1965), 40–1; D. Spring, 'The English landed estate in the age of coal and iron, 1830–1880', *J. of Economic History*, XI (1951), 23.
98 Hesketh MSS, E.W. Hamilton to W. Summers, M.P., 25 June 1833.

99 E.P. Hennock, 'Finance and politics in urban local government in England, 1835–1900', *Historical J.*, VI (1963), 215–16.

100 *Ibid.*, 217.

101 *SG*, 16 April 1895; 17, 20 January 1923.

102 *Ibid.*, 8 November 1902; 20 May 1933.

103 *Ibid.*, 3 June, 13, 16, 17 July 1895; 17 August 1898.

104 *Ibid.*, 17 August 1898; 10 May 1899. The Prince of Wales, the Duke of York and the Duke of Cambridge all stood as godfathers to his children.

105 Hesketh MSS, Buck and Cockshott's Annual Reports, 1920–2.

106 *Manchester Guardian*, 1 October 1926.

107 *The Times*, 31 July 1926, 12 January 1927; *SG*, 13 November 1926, 6, 29 January 1927.

108 Hesketh MSS: Mortgage summaries, 1906–27; Financial papers, 1905–27; Building leases granted on the Hesketh Estate, 1899–1926.

109 *Ibid.*, Investments and Income, 1928–9; interview with Col. R.F. Hesketh at Meols Hall, 24 February 1977.

110 Lancs. RO, Scarisbrick MSS, DDSc 64/6, Trustees Minutes, 1920–4.

111 *SV*, 26 June 1976; 13 April 1978.

112 *Ibid.*, 8 July 1978.

Leasehold estates and municipal enterprise: landowners, local government and the development of Bournemouth, c. 1850 to 1914

RICHARD ROBERTS

Leasehold estates and municipal enterprise: landowners, local government and the development of Bournemouth, c. 1850 to 1914

RICHARD ROBERTS

1 Introduction

'From the date of its foundation, in the early years of the last century, right down to the present, Bournemouth has grown and developed under a system of land tenure almost exclusively leasehold, and probably there is no town in the kingdom where that system can be said to have worked so well as it has here', wrote Charles Mate, editor of the *Bournemouth Times*, in May 1921 on the occasion of the first large sale of freeholds by one of the Bournemouth estates. He continued, 'That is not to say that the system is at all a perfect one, still less that it is popular. It has its advantages and its disadvantages, and both alike are illustrated in our local history'.[1]

In 1838 Bournemouth did not exist. Settlement in this part of the extensive heathland which stretched from Poole in the west to Christchurch in the east and north to Dorchester was no more than some scattered cottages and a few larger houses. The commencement in 1838 of a street of detatched villas overlooking the mouth of a picturesque stream, the Bourne, was a speculative venture on the part of the principal local landowner, the Lord of the Manor of Holdenhurst, Sir George Tapps Gervis, who set out to build a watering place. He commissioned a local architect, Benjamin Ferrey of Christchurch, to draw up a plan for a resort and set to work laying out the land for building. Adjacent landowners took up the idea and also laid out areas of their estates. So, from the outset, Bournemouth was the deliberate creation of local landowners who initiated development where otherwise there might have been none.

The landholding pattern at Bournemouth arose out of the award of the Inclosure Commissioners who were appointed under the Bournemouth Inclosure Act 1802. The heathland was shared among the parties with claims to it. As a result of this distribution the bulk of the land upon which Bournemouth grew up was owned by a few individuals. Development was ultimately undertaken by about a dozen privately-owned estates and about half a dozen land companies. Only small pockets of land were developed freehold. The concentrated landholding pattern coupled with the leasehold system led to a form of estate development which gave the town a special character.

Holiday towns faced special commercial problems as local livelihoods depended almost entirely upon the continuing patronage of visitors. The seaside industry suffered both from the seasonal fluctions of demand and from a disturbing fickleness in the tastes of consumers. Resorts were always vulnerable to the vagaries of fashion, which might spell ruin for local tradesmen. Insurance against shifts in the preferences of holiday makers was necessary to ensure the continued prosperity of the local economy. Moreover, bold initiatives might even win a larger part of the market from other resorts. Measures might be taken to add to the attractions of the town by, for example, the building of a pier, a promenade, or the opening of a park, which would enhance its standing in a highly competitive market. Alternatively energy and expenditure might be devoted to advertising the resort, reminding the public of its existence and building up an image. In addition, steps might be taken to ensure that the reputation of the town did not suffer from unfavourable local events. Bournemouth's reputation for salubriousness and serenity, for instance, was a vital asset, which was safeguarded by ensuring that local sanitation and building were of a high standard, to prevent the outbreak of an epidemic in the resort, and by controlling the business practices of tradesmen and the behaviour of the public, to minimize unseemly nuisance.

There was a common recognition in resorts that it was essential to take action to promote the reputation of the town for the benefit of the whole local economy. The necessary measures were usually costly, and while they might yield a high social return they were often unattractive as business ventures. Only a large enterprise, taking a broad and long view of its interests, or a public body, could reconcile the difference between the financial yield and the social return. In some resorts, landowners and railway companies were prepared to shoulder the burden of investment in an infra-structure of attractions and the cost of promotion.[2] In most seaside towns, however, it was the local authority which assumed responsibility for both these undertakings and, in addition, exercised a degree of control over development, trading and public order on behalf of every local tradesman, shopkeeper, hotelier and builder.

Bournemouth's local economy, composed of hundreds of small-scale service industry enterprises, required coordination for the common good. Finance was needed for investment in the infra-structure of amenities and attractions, initiatives had to be taken to publicize the resort, and measures of social and economic control were necessary. The landowners, particularly the Meyrick, Dean and Tregonwell families who initiated the development of the resort, did have large leasehold estates, and commensurately large interests, in the town. But although they might have been expected to provide the necessary cash and local leadership, they confined their activities to the crucial, if unspectacular, control of the development of their estates, which determined the overall character of the resort. They did not, by and large, get involved in the promotion of the resort itself: by default, it was the local authority which increasingly took the necessary initiatives. The emergence of this energetic local authority was by no means inevitable: had the landowners taken a more active part, it might well have been but a shadow of its actual self. As it was, however, the successful development of Bournemouth in the late nineteenth and early twentieth centuries was the outcome of a fruitful – if unequal – partnership between landowners who preferred to retain a low profile in the public and economic affairs of the town, and a more assertive and energetic municipal body.

It is this partnership between landowners and local government in Bournemouth which forms the subject matter of this essay. The active part played by the local authority in the promotion of the resort and in the provision of recreational amenities are the subjects of prime interest in a larger study – of which the work on Bournemouth forms part – of the development of the economic functions of local government.[3] Bournemouth is an interesting case, since its local authority went further than most in municipal ownership of entertainments and in bye-law control of public behaviour. In the major study, the activities of the local authority, which are of necessity only presented in outline below, are examined in detail. But the contributions of the landowners and the landholding pattern to Bournemouth's development are more fully examined in this essay than in the larger study, as shortage of space there dictates that the focus is kept firmly on municipal matters.

Accordingly, this essay explores the rôle of landowners in Bournemouth's economy, society, politics and public life, with particular reference to their evolving relationship with the town's local government. Why, given their corporate territorial preponderance, did Bournemouth's landowners not play a more conspicuously active part in the town's affairs? Were the powers wielded by the landowners and the local authority compatible in the long run? And what happened when the interests of the landowners and the local community collided? Section 2 sets the general context by outlining the growth of Bournemouth, with special reference to patterns of landownership and estate development. This is followed by an account of the limited part played by the landowners in the public life of Bournemouth, and by an examination of the fluctuating relationship they had with the necessarily energetic local government body. The effect of all this on the public life of the town is then investigated, and the essay concludes with an account of the disappearance of the great leasehold estates from Bournemouth in the early 1920s.

2 Bournemouth: its growth, landowners and estate development

Resort towns grew rapidly from the mid-nineteenth century, expanding to cater for the rising demand for seaside holidays. This growth of holidaymaking resulted from the combined effects of the spread of the railway network, which gave easy access to the seaside, rising real incomes, which enabled an evergrowing part of the population to afford a vacation away from home, and an increasing amount of leisure time, including Bank Holidays and other days off.[4] Many resorts, such as Bournemouth, acquired large populations of resident rentiers in addition to local tradesmen and transient holidaymakers. The retired, the invalid, and the affluent flocked to the seaside in ever larger numbers, a movement which initially anticipated, and later complemented, the late nineteenth-century redistribution of urban population from city centres to suburban locations. The outcome was the mushroom growth of the resorts; in 1861 their population was 430,000, by 1901 it had risen to 1,200,000, and by 1911 it had reached 1,400,000.[5]

Bournemouth grew faster than most. The population recorded at each census from 1851 to 1911 is shown in table 7.

In 50 years, 1861 to 1911, Bournemouth grew from a village of under 2,000 inhabitants into an important County Borough of almost 80,000 people. Accounts

Table 7 The growth of Bournemouth, 1851–1911

year	population
1851	695
1861	1,707
1871	6,507
1881	16,859
1891	37,650
1901	59,762
1911	78,674

Source: Census of England
and Wales, 1851–1911.

of the growth of its various neighbourhoods have been written by local historians so the process of spatial expansion from 1870 to 1910 is summarized in fig. 15.[6]

The development of Bournemouth to 1914 falls into three stages. Each phase was the product of distinct social and economic circumstances and is reflected in the types of properties which were built and the uses to which buildings were put. The first period lasted from the 1840s to the early 1870s and witnessed the building of the 'marine village in a pine forest'.[7] Estates of large detached villas in generous plots were developed around the valley of the Bourne and on the East Cliff and the West Cliff. Business premises were restricted to the Commercial Road to the north of the villa estates; working-class accommodation was entirely absent; servants lived in with their employers; and other workers travelled in from Poole, Christchurch or one of the surrounding villages. During these years Bournemouth catered to an exclusive colony of upper-class visitors, particularly invalids and their families, who took refuge there to escape the rigours of the English winter.

The second period lasted from the 1870s into the 1890s. The opening of a branch line to Bournemouth in 1870 greatly reduced the journey time from centres of population, although the resort remained sufficiently inaccessible for excursion visitors (except from nearby towns) to remain exceptional. During these years a clientèle of middle-class summer visitors was added to the town's leisured and valetudinarian winter residents. Bournemouth became the 'two season resort', as the guide books liked to describe it; a winter health resort and a summer seaside town. These changes in its economic and social functions were reflected physically in new buildings of the 1870s and 1880s. Villa construction continued on the East Cliff and the West Cliff and spread westwards at Branksome and northwards at Dean Park. Boscombe, to the east of the villa estates, was developed as a summer holiday resort. Semi-detached houses of a moderately substantial sort were built at Boscombe and many of them soon became boarding houses.

The construction of terraces and small semi-detached houses to accommodate the growing number of workers in the holiday and service industries began in the late 1860s. Springbourne, Pokesdown, Malmesbury Park, Winton and Morodown began to emerge as satellite settlements to the north of the resort areas, during the 1870s and 1880s; economically they were part of Bournemouth though physically detached from it. This spatial pattern resulted from the absence of working-class housing on the Branksome, Meyrick, Dean, and Tregonwell estates. Their landlords believed that the strict social segregation of housing was essential to

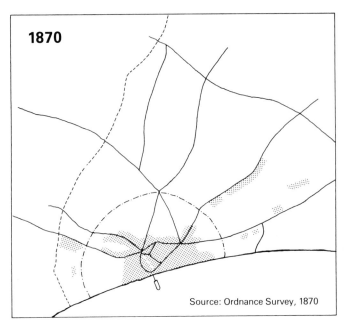

1870

Source: Ordnance Survey, 1870

built-up area

county boundary

local authority
boundary

road

railway

pier

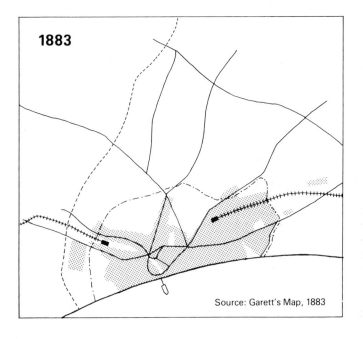

1883

Source: Garett's Map, 1883

Figure 15.
The spatial growth
of Bournemouth,
1870–1911.

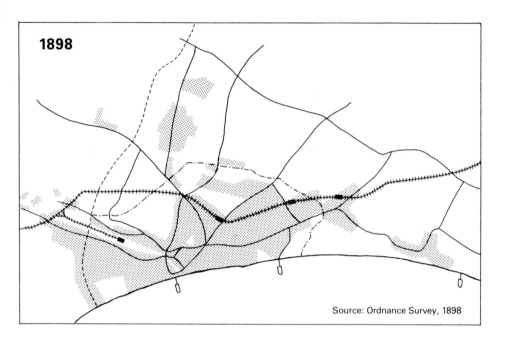

1898

Source: Ordnance Survey, 1898

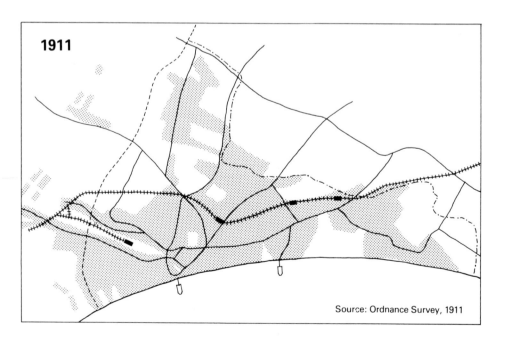

1911

Source: Ordnance Survey, 1911

safeguard the resort's reputation for respectability among the rentiers who rented their villas, and they were determined to preserve the exclusiveness of the villa estates in order to protect their substantial interests and investments.

The disappearance during the first decade of the twentieth century of the *cordon sanitaire* of undeveloped land which separated the dwelling places of Bournemouth's workers in the north of the town from the villa residences of rentiers and visitors was testimony to a further change in the pattern of the resort's patronage. Phase three of Bournemouth's development dates from the early 1890s to the outbreak of the First World War. These years saw the decline of Bournemouth's function as a winter health resort, a growing popularity as a summer holiday resort, and a large increase in its permanent population of retired pensioners. The town benefited from the lapse in continental vacationing by the British upper classes during the 1870s and 1880s as British rentiers found themselves hard hit by the low levels of dividends associated with the period of the Great Depression. They resumed their flight abroad during the 1890s, and their departure from Bournemouth was hastened by the enormous improvement in accessibility by rail from London with the opening of the 'direct line' to the town in 1888. At the same time, however, excursionists and ordinary middle-class holiday makers arrived in ever greater numbers.

These shifts in clientèle were reflected in the property market. The last of the large detached villas were built in the early twentieth century at Boscombe and Southbourne and on the few sites still empty on the West Cliff. By contrast to the burgeoning demand for modest semi-detached houses, the market for large residences was depressed and estate agents reported that letting them was increasingly difficult.[8] In the early twentieth century there was an acceleration of the rate at which the large villas in the centre of the town were converted to hotels or boarding houses. Vacant land to the north and north east of the villa estates was filled with row upon row of semi-detached houses to meet the booming demand for properties of a suitable size and price to match the means of pensioners and the aspiring keepers of small boarding houses. Outlying residential districts of working class and lower middle class housing at Winton, Moordown, Pokesdown and Southbourne grew rapidly after the opening of the municipal tramway system in 1903.

The pattern of landholding at Bournemouth was set by the 1805 award of the Inclosure Commissioners appointed under the terms of the Christchurch Inclosure Act, 1802. The site of Bournemouth at the turn of the nineteenth century was open heathland and it was the Commissioners' task to decide the allocation of 'certain Commonable lands and Waste Grounds within the Parish or Chapelry of Holdenhurst in the County of Southampton'.[9] The 5,000 acres were divided according to the Commissioners' estimation of the value of the claims of the Lord of the Manor, Sir George Tapps, the owner of tithes, the earl of Malmesbury, and 41 other persons described as 'owners, proprietors, lessees and customary tenants' who received awards 'in proportion to their several and respective lands, Common Rights and all other Rights whatsoever in, over and above'.[10] Further plots were sold to cover the costs of enclosure and 425 acres were reserved for the exercise of turbary rights (to cut turf) by local inhabitants.

The result of enclosure was a concentrated landholding pattern by which nine recipients of holdings over 100 acres owned 81 per cent of the land at Bournemouth, three of their number accounting for 59 per cent of this total. The lands received by the principal beneficiaries of the enclosure award, Sir George Tapps, the earl of Malmesbury and William Dean formed the basis of Bournemouth's three leading leasehold estates, the Meyrick Estate, the Malmesbury Estate and the Dean Estate. The areas they developed later in the nineteenth century (which are referred to as the 'enclosure estates') are shown in fig. 16. The lands awarded by the Inclosure Commissioners to these estates were substantially greater to begin with but sections were subsequently sold to other parties.

The vogue for winter residence on the south coast was set by the Prince Regent at Brighton in the late eighteenth century. The windswept heath at Bournemouth offered few attractions to those who looked for fashionable parades and fast living. It was, however, an ideal spot for those spirits of the Romantic Age who preferred to be surrounded by an untamed wilderness, and yet still wished to pursue the medically-recommended activity of sea bathing. Louis Tregonwell, the first of the 'proprietor resident' landowners, was such a man, and in 1810 he purchased 40 acres at the mouth of the Bourne stream and built a house called Exeter House.[11] Later, around the middle of the century, other men of means also purchased lands at Bournemouth for the purpose of erecting a large house set in substantial grounds. Like Queen Victoria, whose remote seaside residence at Osborne on the Isle of Wight was purchased in 1843, it was doubtless the seclusion and natural beauty of Bournemouth which drew them there. In the early 1850s Sir Percy Shelley, Charles Packe, M.P., C.A. King, George Durrant, and Miss Talbot purchased large tracts as sites for their residences as did Sir Henry Drummond Wolff and Lord Portman in the late 1860s. These estates, which are referred to as the 'proprietor resident estates,' are shown in fig. 17.

Also shown in fig. 17 are the Westbourne and the Springbourne Estates, which constitute a third class of Bournemouth land, the 'developer estates'. Robert Kerley and Peter Tuck, their respective owners and the individuals responsible for their development, were not proprietor resident landowners like the owners of the estates hitherto described, but building contractors. The land was acquired not through the inclosure award, nor for personal habitation, but for building. The motive for the purchase of the land makes the rôle of Kerley and Tuck akin to that of the builders and land companies responsible for the development of those small areas developed on a freehold basis which fall outside the estates marked on figs. 16 and 17. The difference is that the Westbourne and Springbourne estates followed the leasehold pattern of building under the careful control of an estate office.

The owners of the proprietor resident estates each built themselves a large house which they, or their family, occupied for at least part of the year. The owners of the enclosure estates, on the other hand, each had a residence near Bournemouth but not in the town. As absentee landowners, however, they suffered no conflict of interest between the gains to be reaped from development and its detrimental effects upon the features which made Bournemouth an attractive place of residence. One by one, usually following the death of the original purchaser of the grounds, the proprietor resident estates also began to lay out their land for development and the burgeoning resort slowly closed in on the big houses. By the turn of the twentieth century, with the exception of the Portman and Talbot estates, the proprietor resident estates had become as built-up as the enclosure estates. The form, the style and density of building which development took on an estate was the outcome of three interrelated factors: the location of the estate, the date it was laid out for building, and the development policy pursued. The

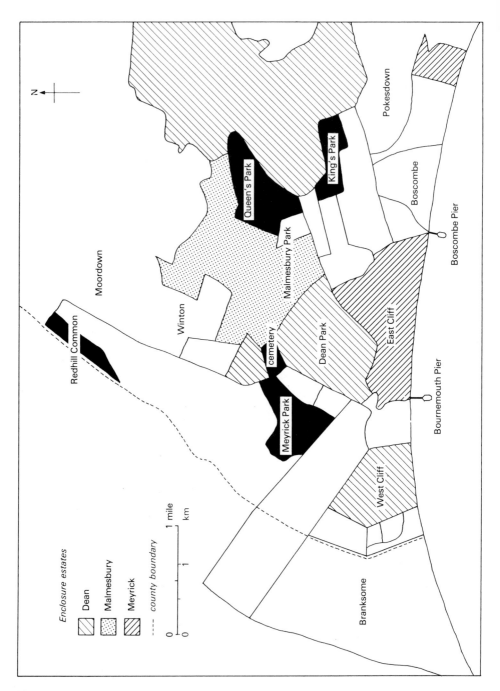

Figure 16. Estate ownership at Bournemouth during the nineteenth century: the enclosure estates.

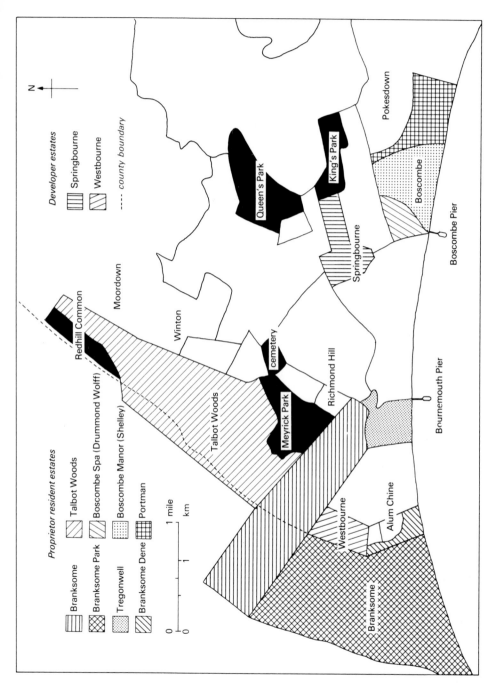

Figure 17. Estate ownership at Bournemouth during the nineteenth century: the proprietor resident and developer estates.

significance of the final factor is illustrated by fig. 15. The pattern of development shows little respect for the neat concentric movements of location theory, and the gaps between neighbourhoods are testimony to the importance of the independent decisions of landowners with regard to the development of their lands. The ownership and descent of the enclosure and proprietor resident estates shown in figs. 16 and 17 is summarized in the appendix.

Building at Bournemouth began on land located around the valley of the Bourne and along the sea front. These areas, comprising the Meyrick, Tregonwell, Branksome, and Dean estates shown in figs. 16 and 17 were developed as villa estates. Their large detached houses, on sizeable plots, accommodated affluent visitors and set the tone for the whole resort. The development of the Meyrick Estate started in 1838. The death of Sir George Tapps Gervis, the second baronet, in 1842 led to a temporary suspension of building since he was succeeded by a minor and it was necessary to secure a private act to circumvent encumbering entails on the estate.[12] During the lifetime of Sir George Tapps Gervis Meyrick, the third baronet, a Bournemouth landowner for 54 years, the development of the lands of the Meyrick Estate lying in central Bournemouth was completed.

John Tregonwell, proprietor of the Tregonwell Estate from 1846, followed the example set by the Meyrick Estate. Although the earliest lease on the Tregonwell Estate dates from 1844, development really got under way only in the 1850s and 1860s[13] By 1885, when John Tregonwell was succeeded by Hector Monro, the estate was fully developed, having become the first of the proprietor resident estates to be turned from a seaside retreat set in substantial grounds into urban real estate. Indeed, it had already ceased to merit the description proprietor resident estate, since the family's Bournemouth residence had been turned into the Exeter Hotel. Hector Monro and his son Hector Edmond Monro lived at Edmonsham Dorset, 30 miles north of the resort, and paid only occasional visits to Bournemouth.[14]

William Gordon, owner of the Branksome Estate, was quick to imitate Sir George Tapps Gervis's initiative for the development of his holding, and in 1840 he commissioned Decimus Burton to draw up a plan for the laying out of a part of the estate. Development was delayed, however, by the financial 'difficulties of a not very pleasant character' which beset Gordon and the partners whom he recruited for the project.[15] Building eventually began in the mid-1850s, and proceeded slowly in the 1850s and 1860s. But the pace quickened during the 1870s and 1880s, and the villas pushed westwards towards the county boundary and beyond in the following decade. The orderly development was the achievement of George Durrant, a Norwich businessman and associate of William Gordon, who acquired control of the estate in 1861. Durrant moved to Bournemouth and built a large residence for himself, Hume Tower, where he lived until his death in the early 1880s. The estate passed to his daughter and then to her relatives in whose hands it apparently remained until the mid-twentieth century.[16]

The development of the extensive Dean Estate did not get under way until the late 1850s, sometime after the start of building on the other centrally-located estates. Plans for development were drawn up after the inheritance of the land by William Clapcott Dean from his mother in 1854, and building proceeded at Dean Park in the 1860s and spread to the West Cliff during the 1870s.[17]

Along the coast at Boscombe lived three of Bournemouth's proprietor resident landowners, Sir Percy Shelley, Sir Henry Drummond Wolff, and Lord Portman. Sir

Percy Shelley moved to Bournemouth in 1850 upon the purchase of 195 acres from the descendents of one of the beneficiaries of the 1805 allotment and other parties. Sir Percy and Lady Shelley took up permanent residence at Boscombe Manor and even removed the remains of their illustrious ancestors, Percy Bysshe Shelley and Mary Wollstencroft, from Paddington to the cemetery of St Peter's Bournemouth. Despite Sir Percy's devotion to his Bournemouth home, financial necessity obliged him to make sales of outlying areas of the estate in 1877, 1884, and 1888. The land was sold in blocks, with attached covenants, for residential development. Lady Shelley continued to live at Boscombe Manor for a decade after the death of her husband in 1889, but she was forced to make further land sales and by the time of her death in 1899 approximately half the estate had been developed. The new owner, Robert Scarlett, later Lord Abinger, took up residence in the 1900s before he disposed of the house and remaining grounds in 1912.[18]

For 20 years the Shelleys lived without near neighbours. But the arrival of Sir Henry Drummond Wolff, who purchased the Boscombe Spa Estate from the earl of Malmesbury in 1868, heralded the beginning of building at Boscombe. Drummond Wolff put up a large residence for himself, Boscombe Towers, and soon started to organize the development of his land. The estate was laid out for an hotel and large villas which were built during the 1870s. The estate remained in Sir Henry's hands until his death in 1908, though after 1880 he was but an infrequent visitor to Bournemouth.[19]

Two of the proprietor resident estates resisted the temptation to dispose of parts of their holdings to developers prior to the sale of the whole estate. The Portman Estate remained intact from the early 1870s, when it was purchased by Lord Portman from Sir George Meyrick, until its sale in the summer of 1922. Family ties led Lord Portman to Bournemouth. Henrietta, Lord Portman's aunt, was the wife of Louis Tregonwell and mother of John Tregonwell. But neither the first nor the second baron spent much time at Bournemouth. Wentworth Lodge, the family's Bournemouth home, was occupied by the brother of the second Baron, the Hon. Henry Berkeley Portman and his wife Emma, the widow of the Earl of Portarlington, and her son, Lord Portarlington, who was a frequent visitor at the turn of the century.[20]

The Talbot Woods Estate, an extensive holding in north west Bournemouth, remained largely intact and undeveloped until it was put on the market, again in 1922. The estate was purchased in 1856 by Georgina Talbot from Sir George Meyrick and the descendents of William Driver who had received the land in 1805. The area was covered with dense woodland and during the lifetime of Miss Talbot no development took place save for the erection of model dwelling houses called Talbot Village 2½ miles from the centre of Bournemouth. Miss Talbot died in 1885 and the woods and her residence, Hinton Wood House, passed to the Hon. Ronald Leslie Melville who succeeded his half brother as eleventh earl of Leven and Melville in 1889. Lord Leven disposed of a number of freeholds at Winton for building in the 1890s but the bulk of the estate remained undeveloped during his lifetime and that of his brother who succeeded him as twelfth earl in 1906 and himself died in 1913. In 1922 the Talbot Woods were sold freehold for development by the thirteenth earl. Miss Talbot busied herself with charitable works for the local community, but otherwise took no part in Bournemouth's public life.[21] The earls of Leven rarely visited Bournemouth. They had no pressing estate office business there since their land was either sold freehold or remained as forest. Coincidentally, there was a further family connection with the resort. In 1885, the year of his Bournemouth inheritance, the eleventh earl married Emma Portman, daughter of another Bournemouth landlord, the first Lord Portman.

The Malmesbury Estate, lying one and a half miles to the north of the mouth of the Bourne, was developed later than the Meyrick, Tregonwell and Dean estates, and the houses took a more modest form. Although the first building lease was granted in 1856 it was not until the 1880s that construction proceeded on a substantial scale. The estate was developed as artisan housing, 'garden city style', a form of housing within the means of the pensioners, boarding house keepers and 'small clerks etc' who took up residence at Malmesbury Park.[22]

A similar scale and style of residential development was adopted as appropriate to the location of the developer estates, the Springbourne Estate and the Westbourne Estate, being both remote from the villa heartland of the resort at the time of building. Two local builders became landowners as they turned their hands to development. Robert Kerley, purchaser of the Westbourne Estate, was active as a builder on the Tregonwell and Meyrick Estates.[23] At Westbourne he put up shops and houses along the Poole Road during the 1850s. The rest of the estate was laid out by him during the 1860s and by his widow in the 1870s as artisans' terraces and semi-detached housing. Peter Tuck, a prominent local builder, and James Druitt, a solicitor and future Clerk to Bournemouth Council, acquired a 90-year lease on the whole of the Springbourne Estate from its owner W.J. Farr in 1874.[24] Tuck and Druitt organized the laying out of the estate and the auction of building plots. Lying inland, a mile away from the town centre, and suffering the further disadvantage of being sliced in two by a railway track, the land was developed as terraced working-class housing.

Details regarding ownership of the Branksome Dene and Branksome Park Estates are incomplete. The paucity of evidence concerning the lives of the owners of these estates reflects the very limited parts which they played in the public life of Bournemouth. It is possible, however, to sketch in some details respecting the estates. The death in 1852 of Miss Bruce, owner of a substantial landholding in west Bournemouth, led to the dismemberment of the Bruce Estate.[25] The pattern of land ownership in west Bournemouth depicted in fig. 16 was the outcome of the sales. Charles Packe established the Branksome Park Estate and Robert Kerley the Westbourne Estate while William Cooper Dean and David Tuck acquired land respectively at Alum Chine and Richmond Hill. Charles Packe, M.P. for south Leicestershire, built a cliff top mansion, Branksome Tower, between 1854 and 1858 on his Branksome Park Estate. He resided at Bournemouth in the years of his retirement just before his death in 1867. Villa building began in the 1870s under the leasehold system. In the early 1890s the estate was acquired by a 'syndicate' which speeded development though it continued the practice of dealing directly with builders and imposed covenants to ensure that new dwellings did not compromise the neighbourhood's select reputation.[26] Branksome Dene Hall was built in 1860 on land at Alum Chine, originally part of the Bruce Estate, which C.A. King acquired from William Clapcott Dean. The house and estate was later bought by Lord Wimborne, the owner of parts of Poole and substantial areas of Dorset, who lived there during the 1890s and 1900s. Large villas were erected on the estate in the 1890s.

Estate development at Bournemouth, in most cases, followed the leasehold system. The essential features of the leasehold system were the laying out of building land by the estate, the granting of a building lease to a builder, and a 99-year lease to the householder who purchased the completed dwelling which included restrictive convenants as to the use and upkeep of the building. Ownership of the freehold of the land was retained by the estate and the estate office determined the type of development which occurred, and maintained a careful watch over the standard of building and the conduct of householders. The landowner retained an economic interest in the land and the ability to exercise close control over the estate. These features of the leasehold system were important for a resort which aspired to attract an affluent and exclusive clientèle, since only through strict control over development could changes which might be to the short term commercial advantage of a particular party, but to the disadvantage of the resort's reputation and hence its livelihood, be prevented.

The development of the villa estates followed the form of the leasehold system outlined above. Building on the Meyrick, Dean, Tregonwell, Boscombe Spa, Branksome and Branksome Park estates was strictly supervised by the estate offices which dealt directly with individual builders and tenants 'by let of the land on building leases for 99 years at a yearly ground rent'.[27] Their building leases specified the minimum value of the house to be erected, the standards of construction and sanitation to be met, the architectural style, and the time within which the building was to be completed. Restrictive covenants in the leases granted to tenants imposed a wide range of duties and prohibitions. Take, for example, the lease granted to S.J. Stevens by the Dean Estate on 25 March 1876.[28] Stevens was prohibited from making additions or alterations, from touching the trees in the garden, from using the building for any commercial purpose or as a school, or a chapel, or for holding public sales or auctions. He was obliged to paint the outside every third and seventh year, to keep the house in good structural order and to make any repairs requested by the estate within three months, to insure it at an office specified by the estate and to contribute to the upkeep of parks and pleasure grounds on the estate. The estate reserved a right of entry for inspection twice a year and access to trees at all time. All fees and costs were to be born by the lessee, and the estate had a right of re-entry upon 21 days default on the payment of ground rent. Similar leases were issued by the other villa estates.

The commitment of the individual landowners of the villa estates to the creation and preservation of exclusive neighbourhoods was an important factor in the continuing prosperity of Bournemouth. The refusal of the villa estates to sell freeholds underpinned the resort's reputation. The continuing economic interest of landowners in the villa estates meant that they were managed by an estate office which enforced the restrictive convenants of the leases. A freehold market free for all, which would certainly have led to the commercialization of the front and the intrusion of such vulgarities as shops or public houses among the villas, was avoided. The Tregonwell Estate flatly refused to sell freeholds and even rejected Bournemouth Corporation's many entreaties to part with the Winter Garden. Freeholds on the Dean, Branksome and Boscombe Spa estates were 'under no circumstances' available for purchase. A minor breach of the Meyrick Estate's policy of retaining the fee simple of its developed land occurred in 1899 when money was needed to pay the estate duty due upon the death of the third baronet. The terms of the sales did not suggest any eagerness on the part of the estate for the raising of money in this manner. The tenants of commercial property along the Holdenhurst Road were allowed to purchase outstanding 63-year freehold reversions on the highly stringent terms of 80 to 110 years purchase plus all fees and costs.[29]

The development of the Malmesbury Estate was less strictly controlled than the villa estates. Instead of dealing directly with each individual builder the estate often granted block building leases for large plots to individuals or land companies which sublet the land in smaller building plots. On occasion development land was sold freehold for building and reversions were generally available at 50-years purchase, practices which greatly diminished the control of the estate over its developed lands. The casual approach of the Shelley Estate to the development of its lands also contrasts vividly with the careful control exercised by the villa estates. Blocks of land were sold to local building societies and land companies, which erected terraced cottages and modest semi-detached houses for their members. Sir Percy's sales were of leasehold blocks but in 1893 Lady Shelley began to sell freehold reversions. The effect was the redevelopment of property along the Christchurch Road as shops and a change in the character of the area. The deterioration in residential house values was resented by owners and one of them brought an action to restrain further conversion from residential to commercial use before the Court of Chancery in July 1913.[30] But the action to enforce a covenant in the original conveyance failed.

The form of development followed by the Shelley Estate resulted in the loss of control over the built-up parts of the estate which even their covenants, when put to the test, could not redress. If all Bournemeouth's landowners had pursued equally lax policies there can be little doubt that market pressures would have soon brought the town into commercialized conformity with the mass of popular resorts. It was this deliberate policy pursued by the owners of the villa estates, of building exclusive districts and of protecting them through the refusal to sell freeholds and the enforcement of covenants, which was the bedrock upon which the resort's reputation and economy was founded. In other seaside towns, landowners played a further, and complementary, part: they were active in a wide range of economic and public activities to promote the resort. But in Bournemouth they were not prominent in public life. Why did Bournemouth's landowners fail to provide the social and economic leadership which the resort required? And did the progress of Bournemouth suffer as a consequence?

3 Landed leadership and landed lethargy

Local leadership is that combination of social, economic and political activity which leads ultimately to an apt description of an individual as 'dominating the affairs of the town'. Political activity might take the form of parliamentary representation, constituency association work, or membership of the local government bodies. Economic enterprise might lead local figures to promote companies, to support schemes to improve the amenities and attractions of the resort, and often to make a personal contribution – usually by the donation of land for a park or other amenities. And the social dimension of local leadership ranged from the patronage of social events, the acceptance of the chairmanship of clubs, institutions and committees, to a ceremonial function which required the locally-eminent persons to preside, or at least be present at, important civic ceremonies.

The owners of large leasehold estates in holiday towns had good reason to take an active part in local public life. In part, this was connected with the safeguarding of their assets: as ground landlords, they had a vested interest both in promoting the success of the resort, and in the safeguarding of their property. But at the same time, local residents actually expected their landowners to exercise some degree of leadership. The two types of ratepayers found in every holiday town – the tradesmen and the other residents – agreed on the desirabilty of eminent men patronizing local events and institutions, even if they agreed on little else. Local tradesmen, mindful of their special business requirements, looked to benevolent authority figures to support trade initiatives and to mastermind the co-ordination of the local economy. And the retired rentiers, the invalids, the affluent and the idle, who resided in the resort but did not earn livings there, were often of an age, social disposition and outlook such as to revel in any attention paid to them by socially superior persons.

In the resorts where there were large privately-owned estates, the naturally qualified candidates were obvious. In the absence of such landed figures, local leadership was exercised individually by resident notables acting through the local authority. The peculiarity of Bournemouth is that, although endowed with an abundance of landed candidates, local leadership took the municipal form: with a single exception, the resident landowners refused to be drawn into the running of the resort in the rôle of active social leader. In part, this is to be explained by the complexity of the local landowning pattern. In Eastbourne, Skegness or Bexhill, for example, there was a single leading estate: the Devonshires, Scarbroughs and de la Warrs were *so* territorially pre-eminent that they had little option but to play the leadership rôles required of them.[31] But in Bournemouth there were a dozen substantial estates and half a dozen landowners, which effectively allowed a margin of choice to the suitably-qualified candidates, and in all cases but one, their overwhelming preference was to keep the affairs of the town at arm's length.

The only exception to this was a relatively small-scale landowner, Sir Henry Drummond Wolff, whose local career shows that the community welcomed patrician initiative and leadership. Moreover, his enterprise shows how large a part might be played by a landowner who was prepared to become an active local leader. He purchased a 'building property' of 50 acres from the earl of Malmesbury and Sir George Meyrick in 1868 and began the construction of a substantial residence, Boscombe Towers.[32] It was political ambition that led him to Bournemouth. Lord Malmesbury, to whom as Foreign Secretary Sir Henry Drummond Wolff had been appointed private secretary in February 1858, was Sir Henry's political patron and had secured his nomination as prospective Tory candidate for Christchurch. He contested Dorchester unsuccessfully in 1865 and Christchurch, the constituency which included Bournemouth, in 1868. He was elected in 1874 and served as a member for Christchurch until 1880 when he accepted an invitation to represent Portsmouth. His sudden 'desertion' of the seat in 1880 just before the election, a characteristically opportunist act, infuriated the Bournemouth Conservative association since it let in the Liberal Horace Davey. Bournemouth reverted to its Tory allegiance in 1885 when Henry Baring Young defeated Davey who had proved to be a 'cold fish' and an unpopular representative.[33]

Although his initial interest in Bournemouth was solely political, Drummond Wolff quickly realized the potential of the land he had acquired, and energetically set about organizing its development, with such success that the resort of Boscombe was almost entirely his creation. In 1868, it was desolate heathland dotted with a few thatched cottages, and a growing number of terraced working-class dwellings, which provided accommodation for those engaged in Bournemouth's service industries. Drummond Wolff's first moves were to erect a thatched summer house on the site of a 'supposed impregnated mineral spring' which it was said 'possessed properties similar to those of the Harrogate waters', and to adopt the name of Boscombe Spa.[34] The Boscombe Spa Estate was laid out in the early 1870s for the construction of 'Marine Villa Residences' for letting on long leases to affluent visitors. Building proceeded rapidly and by 1875 the administrative status of Boscombe had become a local issue. Despite some protests from residents, who favoured a separate Urban Sanitary District, the area was absorbed by Bournemouth in 1876.[35]

Residential development proceeded by the 99-year leasehold system general at Bournemouth, and Sir Henry gave a further spur to development by his promotion of a large hotel on the estate. The Boscombe Spa Hotel Company was formed in June 1872 with the object of building and running an 'hotel or group of hotels'. Sir Henry was the largest shareholder, putting up a quarter of the company's capital, and a member of the board, which also included the Chairman of the Bournemouth Improvement Commissioners, J. Haggard, the prominent local developers Peter Tuck and E.W. Rebbeck, and the railway contractor Charles Waring. The hotel opened in June 1874. It was not a commercial success and closed in August 1880 having incurred such trading losses that the shareholders did not recoup their investments.[36]

Drummond Wolff also lent his active support to other local commercial ventures. He took up 100 £1 shares, and became chairman of the Bournemouth Winter Garden Company, which was formed in 1873 with the object of 'affording amusements, exercise, recreation and general opportunities to the public for reading and mental and physical self cultivation.'[37] The company's early financial difficulties doubtless reflected the over-optimism of its directors, not deliberate book-keeping malpractice, although in July 1876, an accountant, acting on behalf of a disgruntled shareholder, sent an open letter to Sir Henry warning that the company 'is liable to an injuncture in Chancery to restrain them from paying such a dividend which can only be paid out of capital; and which bye-the-bye, was not unanimously voted at the meeting'. The Winter Garden eventually opened in January 1877 but failed to pay its way until it was acquired by the local authority in 1893 as a home for the newly-formed municipal orchestra.[38] Sir Henry's involvement with the scheme reflects credit upon his enthusiasm for the advancement of Bournemouth though perhaps it casts doubts upon his business judgment.

The Boscombe Pier Company was formed in 1885 by local businessmen to boost the attraction of Boscombe to holiday makers by the provision of a promenade pier, and Drummond Wolff – although now largely absentee – joined the Board and took shares in the company. A start was eventually made on the work in 1888 and the pier opened in July 1889. Again it was a financial *débâcle*, though shareholders with other economic interests in Boscombe, particularly those like Drummond Wolff who owned land and houses, may have benefited indirectly from this 'great addition to the social amenities of Boscombe'.[39] In 1903 Bournemouth Corporation purchased the pier from a near bankrupt company, in response to appeals to save this essential attraction, paying £9,000 for a structure which had cost £12,000 to erect.

Drummond Wolff's directorships of limited liability companies in Bournemouth contrast sharply with the absence of involvement by any of the other Bournemouth landowners. The lamentable commercial record of his enterprises was principally due to the nature of the projects which combined the largely irreconcilable objectives of making money and adding to the amenities of the resort. Unlike his fellow landowners he was prepared to lend his support to projects which in the opinion of leading local businessmen would promote the prosperity of the whole local economy. Unfortunately, these schemes, like the several local steamboat companies with which he was not involved, failed to be self-financing. The Winter Garden and Boscombe Pier ultimately passed into the hands of the local authority, a body which was able to reconcile the differences between their public and private returns. As a contemporary commented in 1910 with regard to the Boscombe Pier, 'it is not a profit-producing concern – but the deficits which so far have had to be met year by year are more than compensated for by other advantages conferred upon the ratepayers.'[40]

Sir Henry Drummond Wolff was also active in both the social and political rôles of a local leader. As befitted the town's parliamentary representative he took a keen interest in the work of the local Conservative Association. He was usually present at Conservative gatherings and supported the establishment of a Bournemouth Branch of the Primose League, a movement with which he was closely connected, and which, fittingly, was christened the Drummond Wolff Habitation.[41] Stepping beyond these partisan Conservative interests he was also President of the Bournemouth and Christchurch Working Men's Building Society, President of the Bournemouth Cricket, Lawn Tennis, and General Recreation Club, Vice President of the Bournemouth Amateur Dramatic Society, and a director of the Bournemouth Club, where the town's gentlemen gathered.[42] He was a steward of the Sanatorium Ball of 1872, the New Year Ball of 1875, at the annual Christmas Ball, and at the Volunteer Ball each January, an attendance record which put to shame both his fellow landowners and succeeding parliamentary representatives. He embraced the rôle of ceremonial figurehead and was usually present at important civic functions, as in 1877 for example, when he opened the Winter Garden in January, the Central Workmens' Club and Institute in May and attended the opening of the Masonic Hall in July.[43]

Drummond Wolff's close involvement with Bournemouth came to an end in 1880 when he moved to Portsmouth, and as his ever-watchful eye for the main chance noted opportunities abroad for profit, he sold Boscombe Towers in 1891 to a developer, Messrs Frederick George and Co., who erected the Burlington Hotel on the site. He kept the bulk of his estate, however, and the inhabitants of Boscombe benefited from his generosity by the lease and later sale on advantageous terms, of land at Boscombe Chine and Boscombe Pleasure Garden to the local authority for recreational uses. His obituary upon his death in 1908 was warm and respectful.[44] Sir Henry's active participation in the life of Bournemouth contrasts strikingly with the social inertia of his fellow estate owners. Of course he was also, perhaps primarily, a politician, and it is only to be expected that he should lead an active public life. Nevertheless, judged even by this criterion, his record of local participation was exceptional and outshines that of his most active successors as M.P., Baring Young, 1885–92, and Henry Croft, 1910–40.

The level of landowner involvement in the life of Bournemouth can be gauged by surveying local institutions and events and looking at the part played by the ground landlords. The catalogue is not very impressive. Predictably, the aspect of local life in which they took the most conspicuous part was constituency politics. All, save Sir Percy Shelley, were Tories. Sir George Meyrick, third baronet, was a president of the Bournemouth and Christchurch Constitutional Conservative Association, formed in 1877, as was his son the fourth baronet. The 1911 annual general meeting of the Bournemouth and Christchurch Conservative and Unionist Association saw almost a full house of Bournemouth's larger landowners.[45] In the chair was the earl of Malmesbury, chairman of the Association's council. Sir George Meyrick was re-elected president while the Earl of Leven (Talbot Estate), Lord Malmesbury, Lord Abinger (Shelley Estate), and James Cooper Dean were elected vice-presidents. Lord Malmesbury was also president of Bournemouth's second Primrose League branch, the Malmesbury Habitation, and either he or his nephew, Colonel Harris, usually attended its more important functions.

The Christchurch constituency was represented by two members of Bournemouth's landed families in the town's early days. Sir George William Tapps Gervis sat as member from 1832 to 1837 and the Hon. Edward Alfred John Harris, brother of the third earl of Malmesbury and father of the fourth earl, was member from 1844 to 1852. Thereafter, perhaps surprisingly in view of their constituency activity, none of Bournemouth's landowners, or members of their families, represented Christchurch. Charles Packe, proprietor of the Branksome Park Estate, sat in the Commons from 1836 until his death in 1867, but his constituency was south Leicestershire, and his parliamentary career had no connection with his position as a Bournemouth landowner.

Several landowners joined the town's local authority in its early days, but their enthusiasm soon waned, and after 1873 they took no part. The first Board of Improvement Commissioners included three landowners (or five if Robert Kerley and David Tuck are admitted as landowners rather than as builders) among its 11 elected members: Charles Packe, served 1856–8, John Tregonwell, 1856–67, David Tuck, 1856–60, Robert Kerley, 1856–71, and William Clapcott Dean, 1856–7. In addition, a place on the Board was reserved for the Lord of the Manor and a further place for his nominee. His representatives, agent Decimus Burton, 1856–70, and solicitor T. Arnold, 1870–90, made rare appearances at meetings, but there is no evidence that Sir George himself ever sat on the Commission. William Clapcott Dean was disqualified by non-attendance in 1857. Robert Kerley took an active part in local adminstration throughout the 1860s, but withdrew from local affairs after a disagreement in 1870 and was disqualified by non-attendance in 1871. John Tregonwell and Hector Monro, heir by marriage to the Tregonwell Estate, attended the meetings of the Commissioners on a fairly regular basis and contributed to their debates. Hector Monro, who served from 1867 to 1873, was chosen as chairman of the Board 1871–2, a position of growing importance in the locality.[46]

Bournemouth's local authority was the creation of both local landowners and local tradesmen. The initiative was taken by local residents in order to obtain an Act, 'for effecting and maintaining the necessary improvements.'[47] Uppermost in their minds were the construction of a pier and improvements to the sewerage arrangements of the locality. The formation of the Improvement Commission had the support of Sir George Meyrick and William Clapcott Dean but the opposition of Lord Malmesbury to the inclusion of 'a large portion of his lordship's cultivated acreage' led to a reduction of the areas of jurisdiction of the new local authority.[48] Landowners and tradesmen were equally represented on the first Improvement

Board of 1856. But the inactivity of the landowner commissioners soon allowed effective control to pass to local businessmen.

It is perhaps surprising, in the light of the care which had been taken to ensure that safeguards for the interests of the Lord of the Manor were written into the Bournemouth Improvement Act, and the initial participation of landowners, that they allowed the institution to pass so quickly out of their control. In fact, however, relations between landowners and local authority were harmonious throughout the existence of the Improvement Commission. Their common interests were plain. Moreover, although landowners themselves did not sit on the Board after 1873, betokening perhaps an indifference to local affairs in general, as far as their interests as landlords were concerned their opinions did not go unnoticed.

From its inception in 1856 to the opening years of the twentieth century, between a quarter and a half of the members of the Improvement Commission and, later, the Corporation, were builders or house agents, occupations which led them to work closely with the leasehold estate offices. Furthermore, several agents to large estates were themselves commissioners. T.J. Hankinson, agent to the Branksome estate, served on the local government body from 1873 to 1893 and took a prominent part in local affairs. W.E. Rebbeck, a commissioner 1868–74, and his son E.W. Rebbeck, 1878–93, leading figures in Bournemouth local government, acted as agents to the Tregonwell Estate.[49] C.T. Miles, agent to Sir Henry Drummond Wolff, sat as a councillor 1896–9, while David and Peter Tuck, contractors to the Meyrick Estate, served as commissioners from 1856–60 and 1861–77 respectively. Finally, officials to the Board also acted as agents: C.C. Creeke the surveyor to the Improvement Board 1856–1879, himself a commissioner 1883–6, was employed by the Branksome Park Estate and as 'an expert adviser' to the Dean Estate and James Druitt, Senior Clerk to the Board 1861–77, acted as agent for Sir Henry Drummond Wolff and the Malmesbury Estate.[50] At least until incorporation in 1890, Bournemouth's landowners and local authority were in close and constant contact and no serious disagreements arose.

There is a conspicuous absence of economic intitiative, of the sort which Sir Henry Drummond Wolff pursued, on the part of Bournemouth's other land-owners. Not a single one appears on the lists of subscribers or directors of local limited liability companies, even the utility companies. Their names are also absent from the circulars and lists of committee members of the *ad hoc* associations formed at various times to promote the resort such as the Towns Interest Association, active in the 1880s and 1890s, the Boscombe Interest Association, active in the 1890s, and the Centenary Fetes Committee of 1910.

Bournemouth's landowners made material contributions to the improvement of the quality of local life by the donation of land for parks, for the erection of social and charitable institutions, and for churches. In a resort where such amenities were important attractions to visitors their generosity had an economic dimension, albeit oblique. George Durrant (Branksome Estate) was regularly praised as 'a generous benefactor to Bournemouth in numerous ways,' a phrase which referred to his sale of a portion of the Upper Pleasure Gardens to the local authority for a nominal fee in 1873, to the granting of a 100-year lease on further lands, and to the gifts of the sites for the Bournemouth Sanatorium in 1852 and the Richmond Hill Chapel in 1854.[51]

The Dean Estate donated the land for the Royal Victoria Hospital in 1887, let the site of the Hahnemann Convalescent Home on a 999-year lease for a peppercorn rent in 1878, and gave generous terms to the Bournemouth Cricket Club at Dean Park in 1869. It allowed the Bournemouth Commissioners to acquire its Rush Corner Estate for a cemetery in 1878, and in 1896, after five years of negotiation, agreed to grant a lease on the 14-acre Dean Park Horse Shoe for its use as park land; but it insisted upon a commercial rate of £4,000 per acre for the two acres which the corporation wished to acquire in 1895 as a site for a town hall.[52] The Estate's insistence on what was claimed to be a punitive valuation emboldened critics of the townhall scheme and exacerbated tensions between the factions within the council. The outcome was the worst of the alternatives; the expensive land was purchased but the plans for municipal buildings were scrapped. The episode was the first of a series of disputes over open spaces which soured relations between landowners and the local authority in the 1890s and early 1900s.

By the terms of the Inclosure Commissioners' Settlement of 1805 large tracts of land at Bournemouth were set aside for the exercise of turbary rights by local residents and held in trust by the Lord of the Manor. These open spaces were made over to the local authority in the 1890s and 1900s. Meyrick Park was acquired by the corporation in 1894 and named after Sir George in gratitude for his presentation to the town of his rights as Lord of the Manor. Two further turbary commons, named Kings Park and Queens Park, were acquired by the local authority under the terms of the Bournemouth Corporation Act of 1900, and after the payment of compensation for its interest to the Meyrick Estate. In 1873 the Estate granted a lease upon the Lower Pleasure Gardens to the local authority. The hotly disputed proposals to erect a municipal pavilion in the Pleasure Gardens during the 1880s and 1890s dragged a reluctant Sir George Meyrick into local politics. Subsequent schemes to construct an undercliff and an overcliff drive led to a further deterioration of relations between the Estate and the local authority in the 1890s and early 1900s.

Bournemouth's landowners did lend their names to the letterheads of the resort's sporting clubs and charitable institutions.[53] Sir Percy Shelley was patron of the Bournemouth Amateur Dramatic Society, in which he took a keen interest, Boscombe Rowing Club and the Bournemouth Bicycle and Tricycle Club. Sir George Meyrick took over the presidencies of the rowing and bicycle clubs and the Bournemouth Golf Club in the 1890s. James Cooper Dean took on athletics, lawn tennis and cricket, in which he had a special interest, while Lord Wimborne patronized football and the Parkstone Golf Club. Henry Page Croft, who became member for Christchurch in 1910, was showered with requests for his patronage and became president of the rifle club, the Wednesday Cricket League, the hockey club and the angling society. The fifth earl Malmesbury's interests were charitable rather than sporting and led him to the presidency of the Royal Victoria Hospital, the local R.S.P.C.A., the Bournemouth and District Cage Bird Association and to the joint presidency, with the mayor, of the Gordon Boys' Messenger Corps. While it is significant that Bournemouth's landowners were prepared to serve as titular figureheads to these local bodies, suggesting the acceptance of responsibility to the community, it would be wrong to read too much into it. Their duties were minimal and their attendance, as evidenced by the almost invariable apology for absence when meetings were reported in the local press, suggests no genuine participation in the social life of the town.

A slightly more time consuming and taxing duty was the acceptance of an invitation to join the committee organizing a local ball. Sir George Meyrick and

Henry Bury (Branksome Park Estate) joined Sir Henry Drummond Wolff as stewards, on occasion, at the balls held during the 1870s. The objective of the balls was to enliven the sojourn of 'visiting gentry' so that they should not form the opinion that Bournemouth was 'a dull place'.[54] Despite the exertions of the stewards, the balls were far from glitteringly successful. The editor of the *Bournemouth Visitors' Directory* lamented in December 1876 that 'It is greatly to be regretted that the ball was not more patronized by our visiting gentry, for whose especial benefit these balls are arranged, but who upon the present, as well as upon previous occasions, have not accorded the support which after the admirable arrangements and the indefatigable zeal of the stewards, might reasonably have been expected from them.'[55]

The winter balls for visiting gentry died out around 1880. Charity balls succeeded them, both regular events such as the Volunteer Ball, and occasional efforts to assist particular causes. The landowner presence diminished with time; during the 1880s they were often among the list of patrons, during the 1890s they were occasionally present, but in the 1900s they rarely attended. The list of Lady Patronesses of the Victoria Hospital Fancy Dress Ball of April 1892, for example, included Lady Malmesbury, Countess Portarlington and Lady Wimborne, as well as Mrs E.W. Rebbeck, the Mayoress.[56] The patrons of the Royal Victoria Hospital Fancy and Full Dress Ball of 1902 listed Arthur Balfour, who became prime minister three months later, and the mayor of Bournemouth, but no landowners, although apologies were received from the earl of Malmesbury, President of the Royal Victoria Hospital. Finally, the Primrose League Ball of April 1911, exactly the milieu in which a landed Tory presence would be at a premium, was totally devoid of local landowners.[57] It did, however, boast the presence of the local member of Parliament, Henry Page Croft, the mayor, and a substantial representation of councillors. In the Edwardian era the M.P. and the mayor eclipsed both landlords and other notable local figures as the ceremonially and socially pre-eminent figures in Bournemouth.

4 Landowners and local government: conflict and compromise

The relatively limited part played by Bournemouth's landowners in the public, social and business affairs of the town, was mirrored in the growing importance of the local authority. Its economic functions were threefold: investment, regulation and promotion. Municipal investment established a physical infra-structure of amenities for visitors – the many parks and gardens, the cliff top drives and the under cliff drive. The local authority also financed municipal enterprises which extended the choice of diversions available to visitors, such as the winter garden, in which the municipal orchestra, bands and choir performed, two piers and two golf courses. Rigorous sanitary, public health and building regulations bolstered Bournemouth's reputation for good health, a crucial consideration for Victorian visitors. Further by-laws kept close control over public behaviour in the streets and on the beach, and over the commercial practices of local tradesmen for the protection of Bournemouth's respectable name. Finally, municipal advertising and the organization of special events were undertaken by the local authority to draw the visitors upon whom local prosperity depended.

By the opening of the new century Bournemouth's local authority had come to occupy a vital rôle in the resort's economy. The growth of its economic functions was a gradual process which may be divided into three phases which match the phases of Bournemouth's physical development already discussed. The first phase covers the 1850s, 1860s and 1870s. During these years the contribution of the Improvement Commission to the holiday industry was confined to running the pier, opened in 1861 and rebuilt in 1876, and to the laying out and tending of the central pleasure gardens, the 'marine village's' most important amenities.

A second phase can be identified as starting in the 1870s with the achievement of a series of by-laws to regulate public behaviour. The by-laws were the reaction of the local authority to the growing number of holiday makers and day-trippers who began to arrive as communications improved and the resort became more accessible to those with only limited time for recreation. The first bathing by-laws came into force in September 1871. Further beach by-laws of 1884 and 1890 tightened control. Powers to suppress unseemly public behaviour in parks and in the street were achieved by the adoption of clauses from the Towns Police Clauses Act, 1847, the Vagrancy Act, 1824 and the Public Health Act, 1875. A provisional order of 1887 achieved stricter control over the conduct of Hackney Cab drivers and led to a rash of prosecutions in that year.[58]

The Improvement Commissioners took action to prevent the development of slums in Bournemouth, by the adoption of model building by-laws in 1878, as the construction of terraced artisan cottage style housing began to accelerate. The local authority's exertions to safeguard the resort's unblemished reputation went beyond the enforceable scope of its legal powers. In 1876 a system of sanitary certificates was introduced by the Medical Officer of Health for houses and hotels. Certificates were issued only for buildings which met 'the highest possible standards of sanitary perfection', considerably above that prescribed by the by-laws adopted from general permissive statutes; and it soon became imperative for hoteliers and house owners to be able to produce a sanitary certificate to satisfy potential clients or tenants.[59]

The third phase of Bournemouth's civic development began on 23 July 1890. Incorporation was a victory for those citizens who wanted to see the local authority take a more active part in the promotion of the local economy and offer further positive assistance to the holiday industry.[60] The new borough council was dominated by the Progressives – an informal group of local councillors, composed of tradesmen and builders, who favoured a programme of vigorous local authority action to promote the economic well-being of Bournemouth. They advocated municipal expenditure on local amenities to make the resort more attractive to visitors. During the 1890s and 1900s they pushed the local authority to the forefront of local affairs. In 1892 a lease was taken on the Winter Garden (in use as a greenhouse at the time), and in 1893 the municipal orchestra was founded. In 1894 the first municipal golf course in the country was opened among the 118 acres of Meyrick Park, the first of the turbary commons to be acquired from the Lord of the Manor for use as a public pleasure ground. The interests of private parties in the remaining turbary commons were purchased and they were opened as parks, Queens Park in 1905, and Kings Park and Redhill Common in 1906. Cliff top drives were opened in 1902 and 1904 and two miles of under cliff drive was constructed between 1906 and 1914.

Regulation of building standards, public behaviour, business practices and public health matters was taken beyond the provisions available in the Public Health Acts by the Bournemouth Improvement Act, 1892.[61] The Act, a bold and original piece of local legislation, was drawn up by the Progressives to harness the potential of the new municipal authority to promote the prosperity of Bournemouth. It included the powers by which the Corporation was able to acquire the Winter Garden and found the municipal orchestra. The public health powers achieved were described as being, 'the most complete in England' and medical correspondents praised Bournemouth's venturesomeness. Many of the Act's provisions anticipated those of the Public Health Acts Amendment Act, 1907.

The local authority also became closely involved in efforts to publicize the resort. During the 1880s local government began to assist local associations with the organization of special sporting events, particularly the annual regatta, cricket festival and golf tournament, which passed out of the control of the respective clubs and into municipal hands during the 1890s. The growing conference trade was courted by the promise of a civic reception and offers of assistance with arrangements. From 1898 to 1900 the Corporation paid for the printing of posters which were displayed at railway stations, an expenditure which stopped abruptly in July 1900 upon a reprimand from the Local Government Board for improper use of rated revenues since municipal advertising was *ultra vires*. A further attempt to subsidize publicity for the resort in 1907 led to the celebrated surcharging of Bournemouth Council for illegal payments.[62]

The dynamic rôle which Bournemouth's local government authority played in the promotion of the local economy was of crucial importance to the continued expansion and prosperity of the resort. Credit for the creation of a thrusting local authority belongs to the men, principally local tradesmen, who made it. To some extent, however, the actions, or more accurately inactions, of landowners created the conditions which favoured the evolution of an independent and imaginative local authority. First, the absence of amenities for visitors provided either by landowners themselves or, after the example of Sir Henry Drummond Wolff, by local limited liability companies, supported by landowners and local businessmen, led to the collective provision of pier, parks, golf courses, winter garden and other attractions by the local authority. Local government emerged to fill the vacuum left by the inertia of landowners and local capitalists. Secondly, the low level of participation by landowners in local government allowed the local authority to establish an existence independent of their potentially overwhelming influence.

The nature of the relationship between land and local government changed as the functions of the local authority expanded. During the first 40 years of local government, relations between the partners were cordial and constructive. But the 1890s and early 1900s witnessed a period of discord, as the corporation attempted to extend its control over matters which the landowners considered infringed their property rights or impinged upon their sphere of influence. Predictably land lay at the root of these disputes. The corporation was eager to press ahead with improvements which would enhance the resorts attractiveness, and the refusal of the landowners to comply with the schemes of the Progressives led to acrimonious exchanges, and accusations that they were standing in the way of progress. By the time such conflicts arose, however, Bournemouth's local authority was already well established as an independent and powerful body, and it was the landowners rather than the corporation who were obliged to retreat. By the mid-1900s, reconciliation on these changed terms ushered in a final phase of harmony between landowners and town, which lasted until the demise of the great local leasehold estates in the early 1920s.

One particular point of contention in the 1890s was park land. The local authority was eager to increase the area of public gardens and drives at Bournemouth, since they were considered to be an amenity which particularly appealed to 'high-class' visitors whose patronage was eagerly sought. The transfer of the turbary commons from the Lord of the Manor to Bournemouth Corporation was effected amicably, although some councillors criticized the sums paid in compensation for rights to various parties. But a feeling that the ground landlords were asking too high a price for land which was to be put to public purposes, a use from which their property values would benefit, soured relations between land and local government during the 1890s and 1900s, as series of financial squabbles overshadowed the generous gifts of park land by landowners to the town.

The price paid to the Dean Estate for the two acres of the Horse Shoe Site in 1896 was widely regarded as exhorbitant. The high price demanded by the Tregonwell Estate for the freehold of the winter garden, during negotiations from 1897 to 1901, prevented its acquisition by the Corporation.[63] Negotiations for the purchase of all or part of the Talbot Woods proceeded between the Leven Estate and the Corporation during the 1890s and early 1900s, but were scarcely more satisfactory. The Corporation turned down Lord Leven's offer of 1894 to sell the whole of the woods for £30,000 and Lord Leven declined the local authority's final offer of £300 per acre. The development of the estate was put in hand in 1906 and some building land at Winton was sold for more than £1,000 per acre. In 1921, as a farewell gift, the Estate presented the town with 76 acres of woodland for the extension of Meyrick Park.[64]

Further conflict between landowners and local authority occurred during the 1890s and 1900s because the ground landlords seemed to stand in the way of three schemes cherished by the Progressives for the improvement of the attractions of the resort: the pavilion, and the under-cliff and over-cliff drives. The erection of a municipal pavilion, on the model of a continental casino, was first mooted in the 1880s. The proposal became a highly-charged issue in local politics and the ground landlord of the central pleasure garden, the preferred site for the pavilion, was dragged into the fray. Sir George Meyrick objected to the siting of the pavilion in the pleasure garden since it would 'block the whole of the seaward entrance to the valley and gardens', spoiling the view of his tenants and hence harming the value of their property.[65] A further complication emerged, to the dismay of councillors, during the course of negotiations with Sir George. Covenants granted to nearby occupiers safe-guarded them against any building in the vicinity so for the Council's scheme to proceed it was necessary to extinguish the rights of other parties besides the ground landlord. A scheme to build a pavilion, at one of several locations, was before the Council almost every year from 1891 to 1908 when terms were at last agreed between all the parties. Plans for the construction of the pavilion were not finalized, however, until 1914 and work had hardly got under way when it was stopped on account of the war. The Bournemouth pavilion eventually opened in 1929.

The construction of an under-cliff drive was another scheme debated for years before a start was eventually made. The project was revived by the Progressives during the 1890s who urged, 'the greater the attractions we offer the wealthy, the more they will patronise our town instead of Brighton, Hastings etc, and more especially the Riviera'.[66] The large capital cost of the works, however, frightened many ratepayers who feared large rises in rates as a result. Moreover, the spokesmen for the 'resident ratepayers', the retired and other locals with no interest in the holiday industry, protested at being obliged to pay for a costly scheme whose principal beneficiaries would be the resort's tradesmen. Their opposition to the building of the drive obliged the local authority to withdraw its proposals on several occasions during 'the negotiations which for more than twelve years have more or less continuously been carried on between the governing body of Bournemouth and the owners of the Meyrick Estates.'

But the Estate itself was keen on the under-cliff drive scheme. Its principal preoccupation was the condition of the cliffs, which were receding at an alarming rate, and the construction of a drive would afford protection to the base of the cliff while other associated works would stabilize the surface. The inertia of the negotiations with the Corporation led the fourth baronet, who had recently succeeded his father, to look favourably upon a scheme of a private developer, Archibald Beckett of Boscombe, for the construction of a drive complete with shops, hotels and houses, and they entered into a 'provisional agreement' in December 1897. Thereupon, in the words of the town's historians, 'a remarkable change of opinion soon manifested itself. Many of the most strenuous opponents saw that an under-cliff drive – for weal or woe – was bound to come, and the scheme foreshadowed by Mr Beckett included so many objectionable features that they themselves memorialised the council to re-open negotiations with Sir George.'[67]

The Town Clerk complained bitterly to Sir George that 'the Corporation cannot but feel that they have not been treated in this matter in accordance with the ordinary rules regulating business transactions'. He reminded Sir George of his responsibilities as a landowner and expressed his disbelief, 'That Sir George, who throughout the negotiation has expressed himself to be so anxious that the wishes and feelings of the inhabitants of Bournemouth should be consulted and respected would, for any pecuniary benefits to be obtained, do that which, in the opinion of the governing body and the great majority of inhabitants, will prove to be a great disaster, namely hand over the sea front to private speculators for the purposes of private gain.'[68] Sir George bowed to the strength of feeling in the town and resumed negotiations with the local authority. The Corporation moved decisively to pre-empt any revival of the private scheme and an agreement for a 999-year lease of cliffs and beach was concluded in 1902 which committed the borough to begin building within four years. The drive from Bournemouth pier to Boscombe was constructed between 1906 and 1914.

The owner of the West Cliff, James Cooper Dean, refused to allow the construction of an under-cliff drive west of Bournemouth pier since he believed that it would 'completely ruin the sands' and attract trippers to the vicinity of his residential estate. He eventually relented and the under-cliff drive to Alum Chine was opened in July 1912.[69] Despite the opposition, the Dean Estate maintained cordial relations with the local authority during the 1900s, largely because of James Cooper Dean's several gifts to the town during these years and, in particular, by his cooperation with the Council in the execution of the third of the schemes of the Progressives, the construction of an over-cliff carriage drive. In October 1902 James Cooper Dean presented 40 acres of beach, cliff and cliff-top lands to the mayor. The donation was highly praised, though the editor of the *Bournemouth*

Visitor's Directory pointed out that the scheme suited the Estate as well as the resort: 'Incidentally, it will, of course, benefit Mr Cooper Dean's West Cliff Estate, and we will not be misunderstood in saying that this gift – splendid though it is – is not philanthropy alone but business. But it is the sort of business that we would like all our ground landlords to engage in.'[70]

The Council's application to Sir George Meyrick for further land on the East Cliff for the construction of an over-cliff drive, following the protracted under-cliff drive negotiations, was not sympathetically received. Sir George eventually granted a lease on cliff top land for the drive, despite objections from his tenants, but ill-feeling remained. The mayor's remarks at the opening ceremony in 1904, festivities which Sir George Meyrick did not attend, reflected the lingering antagonism: 'The drive has been constructed, he was almost going to say under the cooperation, but certainly by the permission, of their ground landlord . . .. Although Sir George Meyrick had probably been prevented from doing what he would have liked, he thought that they would join with him in expressing gratitude to him for what he had done, and in hoping that he would do more in the future.'[71] The mayor's uncharacteristically churlish words marked the low point of relations between the local authority and the Lord of the Manor. Thereafter tensions relaxed and relations improved. By 1908 the atmosphere was transformed, and at the opening of the East Cliff Electric Lifts, a ceremony performed by Lady Meyrick, the mayor spoke in a very different tone when he extended 'a very hearty welcome and regarded it as particularly appropriate that they should thus be able to make the completion of one more advancing step in the history of Bournemouth, inasmuch as they represented a family so long identified with the place and whose interests were so closely bound up with the interests of Bournemouth (Hear, hear).'[72]

The *rapprochement* between the Meyricks and the mayor during the 1900s was mirrored in the relations between the other large estates and the local authority. A carping style of compliment for the public-spirited acts of local landowners, typical of the 1890s and turn of the century, gave way to a more wholehearted praise. At the ceremony to mark the presentation to the town of the six acres of the Boscombe Cliff Gardens in June 1900, the mayor thanked the owners of the Shelley Estate for the gift and remarked that 'he thought that the example was an excellent one for some of the other ground landlords of Bournemouth (applause) . . . They (the local authority) were always ready to receive land to benefit the town, and he trusted that there was more to follow'.[73] A thoughtful editorial, published two years later in the *Bournemouth Guardian*, the town's Liberal newspaper and no mouthpiece for the landed gentry, reflected a growing appreciation of the contribution of landowners to the amenities of the town: 'We fear that at times there is a tendency to disparage the ground landowners of Bournemouth, but the appearance of the town does not show that in considering the utilisation of land for residential purposes they have neglected the public interest . . .. (Bournemouth's many parks) are all reminders that we owe much to the gentry who sometimes get more hard words than thanks.'[74]

The underlying causes of the confrontation between landowners and local government disappeared during the 1900s. First, the Progressives eventually got their way and most of the open spaces which they coveted for the town were taken into municipal hands. Second, the local authority's assumption of policing powers through by-laws in matters relating to public health and public behaviour under the

1892 Bournemouth Improvement Act and other local legislation complemented the careful control over leasehold estates exercised through restrictive covenants. The common bond between estate offices and the local authority was strengthened by the council's actions to deal with the growing problem of maintaining decorous public order in public places, particularly the beach, which was increasingly beyond the ability of landowners while such places remained in private hands. Finally, the desertion of British resorts by the affluent during the early twentieth century made villas increasingly difficult to let to tenant residents. As the large houses were turned into boarding houses and hotels so the economic perspectives of the owners of the villa estates and tradesmen councillors converged.

A further factor was personality. The generation of landowners which had witnessed, and nurtured, the growth of Bournemouth from the days when it was no more than a village was succeeded by a new generation which was better able to come to terms with the fact that Bournemouth was a large County Borough with dynamic and determined civic institutions. A change of generations occurred around the turn of the century with the deaths of Sir George Meyrick in 1896, aged

Figure 18. Official opening of the first section of the Undercliff Drive, 6 November 1907 (by courtesy of the Cambridge University Library).

74, Lady Shelley and the Earl of Malmesbury in 1899, aged respectively 80 and 59, and Hector Monro in 1902, aged 75. The succession of new owners to the Meyrick and Malmesbury estates, in particular, brought an improvement in understanding with the local authority. Sir George Meyrick, third baronet, having witnessed the birth and childhood of Bournemouth, appeared to display the not uncommon inability of parents to recognise the maturity and independence of their offspring. He opposed the incorporation of the town during the 1880s and found himself out of sympathy with the aspirations of the new municipal body in the 1890s with the result that relations became, in the words of Alderman Hosker, 'perhaps a little strained'.[75]

The death of the fourth earl of Malmesbury brought sighs of relief from councillors. He had proved a difficult neighbour and 'the result of several years intimacy did not strengthen the relations between the rising borough and the Earl which were at times very much strained'. He was a bombastic bully of whom it was ingenuously remarked that 'his sharp and military-like speeches on local platforms will long be remembered for their blunt and forcible style'. His hostile and disdainful attitude towards the inhabitants and visitors of the nearby towns caused deep offence to the local authorities of Bournemouth and Christchurch.[76] The younger generation went some way towards the re-establishment of a landed social presence in Bournemouth during the 1900s though it is difficult to tell whether it was youthful vitality or personal inclination which, for example, induced the new Lady Malmesbury and Lady Meyrick to attend the local flower shows and charity concerts which their predecessors had shunned.[77]

The highly successful development of Bournemouth was, as already argued, the outcome of a fruitful cooperation between landowners and the local authority. The terms of the partnership altered during the course of the nineteenth and early twentieth centuries. The impulse to shift the balance of responsibility and initiative came from local government in response to the changing requirements of the local economy and the ever-increasing demands for action to promote local prosperity. The economic functions of Bournemouth's local authority were always paramount: it was a basically economic objective, the erection of a landing stage, which led inhabitants to establish the Improvement Commission in 1856, and it was economic considerations which determined the attitude of local representatives to local landowners thereafter. For most of the period after 1856 relations between land and local government were cordial, based upon a mutual appreciation of the other's contribution to the common weal. The antagonism between the parties which developed during the 1890s and early 1900s was a temporary and transitional phase, which lasted only as long as the burgeoning expectations of the reinvigorated local authority outstripped familiar conceptions of duty and interest on the part of an aged generation of landowners.

5 Local leadership and public life

The account of the changing relationships between the local landowners and the local government authority outlined in the preceding sections suggests two general conclusions. The first is that, throughout the whole period, the landowners played a much smaller part in the public, political, social and economic life of the town than did their more assertive counterparts in other resorts. But, as elsewhere, it is also true that over time, this relationship changed and fluctuated. Three periods seem to suggest themselves: the first, before incorporation in 1890, when the local board and the local landowners co-existed amicably; the second, from incorporation to the early 1900s, which was a period of conflict and confrontation; and finally from the mid-1900s to the First World War, when co-operation was re-established, albeit on a new basis, where the dominance of the local authority in the life of the town was even more emphatically re-asserted.

One significant form of civic activity which well demonstrates the validity of these conclusions is the frequency of civic ceremonial, and the changing back-ground of the celebrities who presided on these occasions. In table 8 these details are recorded for every important civic event in Bournemouth's history from 1850 to 1913 which was marked by some form of public ceremony.

Table 8 Identity of guests of honour at important civic events in Bournemouth, 1850–1913

years	landowners	outside guests	residents	local authority	total
1850–9	—	2	—	—	2
1860–9	3	1	1	—	5
1870–9	6	6	4	—	16
1880–9	2	6	1	3	12
1890–9	3	12	8	5	28
1900–09	10	7	4	26	47
1910–13	2	2	4	13	21
total	26	36	22	47	131

The occasions recorded are based upon the lists of 'Local Events' which appeared in W. Mate's annual *Bournemouth Business Directory and Year Book*, and on the summaries of the year's happenings which were published in the local press at the end of each December. They include the opening ceremonies of public halls, theatres, parks, schools, institutions and offices, and notable public celebra-tions – the milestones along the path of local history. But they exclude ecclesiastical ceremonies (of which there were an enormous number), which involved only a section of the community, political meetings, and the parochial happenings of ephemeral moment such as flower shows, balls, the annual volunteer prizegivings and the annual regattas. They are classified according to the origin of the presiding celebrity, the person who performed the opening ceremony, or in some other way was the focal point of attention according to the local press reports of the occasion. Four categories of celebrity are distinguished: local landowners, outside guests from beyond the town, residents in Bournemouth, and figures connected with the local authority, usually the chairman of the Improvement Commission before 1890, and the mayor thereafter. The scores recorded here show the number of times in each decade that a celebrity officiated at one of the 131 notable rites of passage of Bournemouth's civic development. Nominal level data of this kind has many shortcomings, but it illustrates several trends which warrant further consideration. In particular, the relatively low level of landed participation, and high degree of residents' activity stand out, as does the very limited participation of the local landowners in the 1880s and 1890s, compared with the preceding and following decades.

A closer scrutiny of the data casts further light on the limited ceremonial duties performed by Bournemouth's landowners, who officiated at 26 of the 131 recorded events, 20 per cent of the total. On 15 of the 26 occasions, the landowner was the obvious choice as celebrity since it was he who had given the land or had provided financial assistance to a project located on his estate or, in the case of the winter garden, was chairman of the company. The 11 occasions on which landowners officiated at ceremonies with which they had no material connection is half the number recorded by local residents and a third of the number recorded by visiting celebrities from outside the town.

Of course, it is possible that the figures reflect local preferences for celebrities whose distinction was founded on more exciting achievements than the inheritance of real estate, rather than a reluctance on the part of landowners to participate in local functions. If this is the case then it is necessary to look for the presence of Bournemouth landowners at civic ceremonies not just in the capacity of guest of honour. But only 27 of the 105 occasions on which non-landowners officiated witnessed landed attendance, and landowners were more inclined to turn up when the dignitary was from outside the town than when it was the mayor or a local resident. Accordingly, the visits by members of the royal family in 1890, 1892, and 1903 produced the most enthusiastic landed responses. But important local celebrations such as the elaborate reception ceremony for the municipal charter in 1890, and national festivities to mark the Jubilee in 1887, the relief of Mafeking in 1900, and the Coronation of 1911, were not graced by landed presence at all.

It is difficult to determine whether the 25 per cent landowner attendance rate at important local ceremonies was high or low since there are no comparable studies for other towns by which it may be measured. A Bournemouth yardstick, however, is the attendance rate of representatives of the local authority. The mayor or chairman of the Improvement Commissioners achieves a 40 per cent score for attendance on the occasions on which a non-municipal individual officiated, and councillors make 70 per cent. The mayor, or chairman of the Improvement Commission, in addition, was himself the celebrity on 47 occasions, on overwhelmingly greater number of times than the representatives of any individual estate. The counts for the individual estates are, Malmesbury: opened eight, attended seven; Meyrick: opened five, attended eight; Dean: opened three, attended 16; Shelley; opened three, attended seven; and Tregonwell: opened none, attended four. The most diligent of Bournemouth's landlords, the Dean family, was present on only 19 of the 131 occasions. The local authority, by contrast, was in attendance altogether on 84 occasions as personified by the mayor and 106 occasions as represented by the members of the local governing body. The presence of elected representatives at important local events is hardly surprising. The respective attendance records does, however, put the ceremonial and ornamental parts played by Bournemouth's landowners into perspective.

The empirical evidence concerning the relative contribution of Bournemouth's landowners to the ceremonial life of the town merely corroborates the conclusions already advanced concerning the general rôle of the landowners in the resort's affairs, namely that they played little part in the public or social or political life of

Figure 19. Ceremonial reading of the charter of incorporation by the town clerk at the pier entrance, 27 August 1890 (by courtesy of Bournemouth Library).

Figure 20. Opening of the enlargement of Bournemouth Pier, 5 June 1909: the lord mayor of London on *SS Majestic* (by courtesy of Bournemouth Library).

the town, and confined their economic activities to the development and administration of their estates. The fact that several of them were asked to serve as mayor,
but that none agreed so to do, is further corroborative evidence. In other resorts
with a concentrated pattern of landholding, which were likewise developed on the
leasehold system, the local landowners played a far more active part in local affairs
than has been recorded and described here in the case of Bournemouth. Why,
then, does this case seem to be the exception which proves the rule?

It is difficult to furnish an entirely satisfactory answer to any question which asks
why something did *not* happen. It is only possible to point to the circumstances of
Bournemouth's development which disinclined them from taking a more active
part. On the one hand, because there was no overwhelmingly pre-eminent estate
owner at Bournemouth, the pressures on them to take an active, assertive part in
the town's affairs were less than in, for example, Eastbourne or Bexhill. And, in
the absence of an obvious landed choice, the status vacuum thus created was
increasingly filled by representatives of a local authority which, especially in the
1890s and 1900s, came to dominate the town socially and economically, thereby
further discouraging Bournemouth's landowners from stepping forward.

Moreover, Bournemouth was not the only place of residence of its leading
landowners. The seats of the enclosure estates, the Dean, Meyrick and Malmesbury estates, were all situated outside the town. Furthermore, the incumbents of
the Meyrick and Malmesbury estates had other interests and other estates which
took them away from the neighbourhood for extended periods.[78] The owners of the
proprietor resident estates did have houses in the resort, but the motive for the
move to Bournemouth on the part of the original purchasers of these estates was
the enjoyment of a quiet seaside retreat, which meant that they were unlikely
material for active local leaders. Indeed, Miss Talbot, George Durrant and Charles
Packe were so retiring that their names hardly ever appear in contemporary
newspapers or other records and their local presence is shadowy.

In the cases of the Tregonwell, Shelley and Portman estates there was a
noticeable increase in participation in local life when a second generation succeeded the original purchasers of the estates. John Tregonwell and Hector Monro
sat upon the Bournemouth Improvement Commission in the 1860s and 1870s while
the names of Robert Scarlett and Lord Portarlington appear quite frequently in the
local press during the 1900s in contrast to the rare references to the previous owners
of the Shelley and Portman estates. But many of the owners of the proprietor
resident estates, particularly the second generation, also had distracting outside
interests. The owners of the Tregonwell Estate lived at Edmondsham in Dorset,
the earls of Leven lived in Scotland and London but not at Bournemouth, while
Lord Portman and Robert Scarlett were also only part-time residents.

Character and personal disposition must account for the inactivity on the part of
Sir Percy Shelley and the owners of the Dean Estate who lived respectively in and
adjacent to the town, since neither of them had outside property or the distraction
of public office or a job. Sir Henry Drummond Woolf described Sir Percy Shelley
as 'a gifted man, though he had never exerted himself to make any continuous
effort'. He was idle and frivolous, and 'seldom appeared in public', although he
earned praise for taking 'a lively interest in the founding of the Cottage Hospital of
which he was one of the patrons'.[79] The owners of the Dean Estate were made of
sterner stuff, but their allegiance was to country life and their energy devoted to
county affairs. William Clapcott Dean, 'a bachelor who lived a somewhat secluded

life', sat as a county magistrate from 1855 to his death in 1887, and James Cooper Dean, his heir, lived the life of 'a thorough English gentleman'.[80] His public activities were described as 'somewhat limited' with regard to Bournemouth, and were confined to the county bench, and membership of the Christchurch Board of Guardians and of the Holdenhurst Rural District Council.

County activity also distracted the attention of the owners of the Meyrick and Malmesbury estates. The Meyricks were county magistrates in Hampshire and Deputy Lieutenants in Anglesea. James Edward Harris, the fifth earl of Malmesbury, sat as a Hampshire County Councillor and served as a lieutenant in the local yeomanry, as did his predecessor. Edward James Harris, the fourth earl, exhibited most blatantly a trait which may also have disinclined other landowners from taking a more active part in the affairs of the resort: he was a snob. He had as much disdain for the tradesmen of Bournemouth as for 'the cheap destructive tripper who used to trespass on his estates near Bournemouth and wantonly destroy his beautiful flowers'.[81] Perhaps it was the nakedly commercial conduct of public affairs in the resort which led landowners to prefer to give their services to the county.

In the absence of a decisive leadership from landowners the local community in Bournemouth looked to its own. More than half the officiating dignitaries on the

Figure 21.
Sir Merton
Russell Cotes
(by courtesy of the
Cambridge University
Library).

131 occasions examined were local men, and the increased employment of the mayor as a celebrity during the 1890s and 1900s emerges clearly from table 8. In 1895, for the first time, the mayor deliberately conducted the opening ceremonies of municipally-financed amenities on behalf of the ratepayers who had paid for them, and for whom they were built.[82] The chief magistrate in that year was Merton Russell Cotes, a wealthy businessman from Wolverhampton who moved to Bournemouth in 1876 on account of his health, purchased the Royal Bath Hotel, and became the resort's leading hotelier.[83]

From the time of his arrival, he played a prominent part in the public life of Bournemouth. He was behind the invitation to the Lord Mayor of London to open the new pier in 1880, the first local celebration conducted under the auspices of the local authority, and he played a leading part in persuading the London & South Western Railway to build the direct line to Bournemouth. He acted as municipal ambassador to the Meyrick Estate during the protracted and sometimes fraught negotiations of the 1890s and 1900s, and he was invited to serve as mayor – when not already a member of the council – in recognition of his services to the resort, and in the confident expectation that he would bring to the job of chief magistrate all the gusto and glamour that his name and his efforts lent to all the civic enterprises he undertook.[84]

Nor did he disappoint, for he brought a *savoir faire* and a social self-assurance to the job which its previous incumbents, largely self-made tradesmen, had lacked. He had no difficulty in assuming the part of a celebrity on the occasions of the opening of the two local libraries in 1895, the kind of rôle which had hitherto been filled exclusively by landowners, visitors or eminent local residents.[85] Thereafter, however, the precedent was established, and the mayor became the leading figure of Bournemouth society by the opening decade of the twentieth century, as the job assumed almost presidential proportions. At one and the same time, he was the nub of the town's social and civic activity, and was also expected to play a leading rôle in municipal matters. Increasingly, as the powers of the council expanded, the job of mayor required an experience of, and commitment to, local affairs which none of the town's local landowners could provide. It was no job for an absentee or titled amateur.

The final theme to emerge from the figures in table 8 concerns the changing contours of the relationship between the landowners and the local authority. In the 1860s and 1870s, they appeared at a greater proportion of civic events than they were to do in the two succeeding decades – evidence of the relatively harmonious relations which existed between the landowners and the Improvement Commissioners. But, in the 1890s, the decade of incorporation and confrontation, landowners presided at only three out of 28 civic ceremonies. In the 1900s, however, they were the guests of honour at ten out of 47 ceremonies. The *rapprochement* between landowners and local government in Bournemouth, the rise of the mayor to civic, social and ceremonial prominence, and the efflorescence of municipal ceremonial in general, were all conspicuous developments in the first decade of the twentieth century.

In 1906, the seal was set on this new relationship between landowners and local authority. On 26 September the Countess of Malmesbury opened the new Winton Recreation Ground, an amenity laid out by the local authority on land given by Lord Malmesbury, James Cooper Dean opened the 'Rotten Row' drive, again the work of the local authority on land presented by him, and the mayor opened the new golf and athletic pavilion in Queen's Park.[86] Co-operation and mutual interest were the keynotes of the speeches at the celebration tea hosted by the mayor and mayoress in the pavilion. The new spirit of reconciliation was voiced both by the mayor, who spoke fulsome praise for landed magnanimity, and by the Earl of Malmesbury who referred to the responsibility of a landlord 'to be of use to those living at no great distance from his home'. The occasion also marked the elevation of the dignity of the leading townsman to a status equal to that of the principal ground landlords. For the first time the mayor and two landowners, one an earl, officiated at a civic ceremony as equal celebrants. The events symbolized the reality of the new relationship between land and local government in Bournemouth, in which the landowners were, as always, the subordinate partner.

6 Epilogue: economic and social withdrawal since 1914

There was a widespread feeling in Bournemouth that the leasehold estates had served the town well. The absence of a strong leasehold enfranchisement movement, in a town where freeholds were highly exceptional, is perhaps the most telling testimony to the acceptance by Bournemouth's inhabitants of the leasehold system. The Bournemouth and South of England Leasehold Enfranchisement Society held a series of meetings in 1890 and 1891 to promote its cause. But while the correspondence columns of the local press suggest some interest, there is no evidence of widespread support.[87] The issue was taken up by the local Liberal Party and featured as a platform of their electioneering during the 1890s. It seems likely that resentment of the leasehold system, and the close identification of Bournemouth's landowners with the Tory party, inclined some voters to the Liberal cause. Yet the only Liberal election victory of the period was in 1906, after a campaign in which enfranchisement was not a particularly prominent issue. The result can be satisfactorily explained without reference to leasehold enfranchisement, as the outcome of the rapid increase in the population of the lower middle-class districts of Winton, Moordown and Pokesdown, and as part of the national Liberal landslide.

By then, in any case, erosion of the leasehold system had already begun in Bournemouth, although only on the outlying estates. The Branksome Park Estate was the first villa estate to make freehold reversions generally available for purchase, as the syndicate which acquired the property in the early 1890s offered them at 25 to 30 years purchase.[88] To the West of Branksome Park lay the Canford Cliffs Estate, which was sold by Lord Wimborne to a syndicate of local builders, who laid it out for development in 1887. Building on the estate proceeded under a relaxed leasehold system, whereby purchasers were under no obligation to build, and had an open option to purchase the reversion. Moreover, from 1898, a straightforward policy of selling freeholds was adopted.[89]

Nevertheless, these minor losses aside, the leasehold system on the villa estates lasted until the 1920s. The Meyrick Estate remained intact until 1921, when the fifth baronet sold 419 lots, 'a big proportion of his Bournemouth estate', in the centre of the town. The death of James Cooper Dean in the same year brought a heavy bill for death duties, which was met by the sale of the Dean Estate freeholds in 1922 and subsequent years.[90] The leasehold system at Bournemouth suffered a further blow in 1923 when the third of the enclosure estates, belonging to the

Malmesburys, put the whole of its Bournemouth freeholds up for auction, and the Earl of Malmesbury ceased to be a Bournemouth landlord. The Earl of Leven and Lord Portman, perhaps tempted by the high prices which local land was fetching, also decided to dispose of their Bournemouth holdings, and their Talbot Woods and Portman Estates were sold for building in 1922.[91] In the early 1920s, therefore, large estates and leasehold ownership effectively disappeared as the prevailing property pattern in Bournemouth.

In 1921, Charles Mate, a local historian and editor of the *Bournemouth Times*, wrote the obituary notice of the town's leasehold system, upon the occasion of the first of the large sales of freeholds. He had no doubts that Bournemouth's landowners had served the town well in the past; but he now looked forward to the new chapter in Bournemouth's history, which opened up with the dissolution of the leasehold estates:

> In the early years, it was all to the good that the 'town planning' was in the hands of a few enlightend landowners who took long views, thought not a little of the amenities of life in a seaside health and pleasure resort, and kept within their own control the power to restrain such development as might be helpful to the individual, but harmful to the general community. To this policy, Bournemouth owes, among other things, its large open spaces, and its distinctive characterisation as 'a pleasure city of detached mansions.' But the time has come now when Bournemouth . . . needs to be freed from the swaddling clothes which are the one and only obstacle to large enterprise desirable in the interest, not of this or that individual alone, but for the general welfare of the community, the advancement of Bournemouth to a position of even greater honour and distinction than it has yet occupied.[92]

APPENDIX

Ownership and descent of estates at Bournemouth in nineteenth and early twentieth centuries

Enclosure Estates

MEYRICK ESTATE

1805	Estate created by Inclosure Award
1805–35	Tapps, Sir George Ivison. 1st Bt. (1753–1835)
1835–42	Tapps Gervis, Sir George William. 2nd Bt. (1795–1842)
1842–96	Tapps Gervis Meyrick, Sir George Eliott Meyrick. 3rd Bt. (1827–96)
1896–1928	Tapps Gervis Meyrick, Sir George Augustus Eliott. 4th Bt. (1855–1928)
1928–60	Tapps Gervis Meyrick, Sir George Llewelyn. 5th Bt. (1885–1960)

DEAN ESTATE

1805	Estate created by Inslosure Award
1805–12	Dean, William (1737–1812)
1812–33	Clapcott, William (–1833)

212

1833–54	Mrs Clapcott (–1854)
1854–87	Clapcott Dean, William (1812–1887)
1887–1921	Cooper Dean, James Edward (1840–1921)
1921–50	Cooper Dean, Joseph (1866–1950)

MALMESBURY ESTATE

1805	Estate created by Inclosure Award
1805–20	Harris, James. 1st Earl of Malmesbury (1746–1820)
1820–41	Harris, James Edward. 2nd Earl of Malmesbury (1778–1841)
1841–89	Harris, James Howard. 3rd Earl of Malmesbury (1807–89)
1889–99	Harris, Edward James. 4th Earl of Malmesbury (1842–99)
1899–1923	Harris, James Edward. 5th Earl of Malmesbury (1872–1950)
1923	Estate sold

Proprietor Estates

TREGONWELL ESTATE

1810	Estate purchased
1810–32	Tregonwell, Louis Dymoke Grosvenor (–1832)
1832–46	Tregonwell, Henrietta (–1846)
1846–59	Tregonwell, Richard (–1859)
1859–85	Tregonwell, John (1811–85)
1885–1902	Monro, Hector (1827–1902)
1902–25	Monro, Hector Edmond (1855–1925)
1925–	Monro, Hector Richard (1885–)

PORTMAN ESTATE

1873	Estate purchased
1873–88	Portman, William Henry Berkeley. 1st Baron (1799–1888)
1888–1919	Portman, Edward William Berkeley. 2nd Baron (1829–1919)
1919–22	Portman, Henry Berkeley. 3rd Baron (1860–1923)
1922	Estate sold

TALBOT ESTATE

1856	Estate purchased
1856–85	Talbot, Georgina Charlotte (–1885)
1885–1906	Leslie Melville, Ronald Ruthven. 11th Earl Leven & Melville (1835–1906)
1906–13	Leslie Melville, John David, 12th Earl Leven, & Melville (1886–1913)
1913–22	Leslie Melville, Archibald Alexander. 13th Earl Leven & Melville (1890–)
1922	Estate sold

BOSCOMBE SPA ESTATE

1868	Estate purchased
1868–1908	Drummond Wolff, Sir Henry (1830–1908)
1908–	Estate sold, date unknown

BOSCOMBE MANOR ESTATE

1849	Estate purchased
1849–89	Shelley, Sir Peter (1819–89)
1889–99	Shelley, Lady (–1899)
1899–1911	Scarlett, Robert Leopold Lawrence (–)
1911	Estate sold

BRANKSOME ESTATE

1836	Estate purchased
1836–61	Gordon, William (–)
1861–83	Durrant, George (–1883)
1883–c1913	Miss Durrant (–1913)
1913–	Durrant family

BRANKSOME DENE ESTATE

1860	Estate purchased
1860– ?	King, C.A. (–)
c1890– ?	Lord Wimborne

BRANKSOME PARK ESTATE

1852	Estate purchased
1852–67	Packe, Charles William (1792–1867)
1867–76	Bury, Henry (–1876)
1876–92	Unknown
1892	Estate acquired by development company for building

BIBLIOGRAPHY

1 Primary sources

Bournemouth Court of Quarter Sessions:
    Abstract of Cases, 1880–1914
Bournemouth Reference Library:
    Boscombe Manor Estate Papers
    Branksome Estate Papers
    'Development of Shelly Estates outlines in judgment of Mr Justice Sargant, 31 July 1915'
        (unpublished paper)
    Hawkes, C.G., 'Leaseholds in Bournemouth' (unpublished paper, 1908)
Bournemouth Town Hall:
    Commission and Council Minutes, 1890–1914
    Miscellaneous Committee Minutes, 1856–1914
    Reports of Medical Officer of Health, 1880–1914
Hampshire County Record Office:
    Tregonwell Estate Papers
House of Lords Record Office:
    Minutes of Evidence: Bournemouth Improvement and Pier Bill, 1856
        Bournemouth Improvement Bill, 1892
        Police and Sanitary Regulations Committee, 1892

Meyrick Estate Office, Hinton Admiral:
  Meyrick Estate Papers
Public Record Office:
  Series BT 31: Board of Trade Company registrations

2 Newspapers

The Architect
Bournemouth Echo
Bournemouth Graphic
Bournemouth Guardian
Bournemouth Observer
Bournemouth Times
Bournemouth Visitors Directory
The Caterer and Hotel Keepers Guide
Estates Gazette
Illustrated London News
Truth

3 Published contemporary sources

Bournemouth Corporation, *Bournemouth Year Book* (1895–1914)
  Retrospect on Sanitary Work in Bournemouth Over the Past Thirty Years (1917)
  Twenty-One Years of Municipal Music, 1893–1911 (1911)
  *The Bournemouth Improvement Act and the Public Health Acts Amendment Act, 1907, as
    they affect the county Borough of Bournemouth* (1908)
Compton, T.A., *Southbourne's Infancy* (1914)
Cotes, Sir Merton Russell, *Home and Abroad* (2 vols., 1921)
Cutler, J., *Life, Letters and Speeches* (1890)
Dobell, D.H., *Notes on Bournemouth and its Wants* (1887)
Drummond Wolff, Sir. H., *Rambling Recollections* (2 vols., 1908)
Fox & Sons, *Contacts and Contracts* (1965)
'Grandpa', *Three Weeks at Bournemouth: A Vacation Holiday, 27 August to 18 September,
  1892* (privately printed, 1893)
Hankinson, T.J., *Hankinson's Descriptive Guides to Bournemouth*
Jacob, W.H., *Hampshire at the Opening of the Twentieth Century* (1905)
Mate, C.H., & Riddle, C., *Bournemouth* (1910)
Mate, W., *Bournemouth Business Directory* (1882–1914)
'Tokio', *Revels and Reveries at Bournemouth* (Privately printed, 1909)
Tribbet and Mate, *Penny Handbook to Bournemouth* (1872)

I have omitted a comprehensive list of dissertations and modern printed sources, as the
references are themselves a running bibliography.

NOTES

1 *Bournemouth Times*, 14 May 1921.
2 For examples of this, see: J.K. Walton, 'Railways and resort development in Victorian
  England: the case of Silloth', *Northern History*, xv (1979); R.G. Armstrong, 'The rise of

Morecambe, 1820–62', *Trans. Historic Soc. Lancs. and Cheshire*, c (1948); R. Gurnham, 'The creation of Skegness as a resort town by the ninth earl of Scarbrough', *Lincs. History and Archaeology*, vii (1972); D. Cannadine, *Lords and Landlords: The Aristocracy and the Towns, 1774–1967* (1980), esp. pt III.

3 R.W. Roberts, 'The development of the economic functions of local government in England and Wales, 1880–1914, with special reference to Bournemouth' (Ph.D. thesis, University of Cambridge, 1981).

4 J. Walvin, *Leisure and Society, 1830–1950* (1978), 60–82.

5 B. Thomas, *Migration and Urban Development* (1972), 183; I. Cosgrove and R. Jackson, *Geography of Recreation and Leisure* (1972), 37–40; J.A.R. Pimlott, *The Englishman's Holiday* (1947), 172; E.W. Gilbert, 'The growth of inland and seaside health resorts', *Scottish Geographical Mag.*, iv (1939).

6 C.H. Mate and C. Riddle, *Bournemouth* (1910); D.S. Young, *The Story of Bournemouth* (1957); J. Soane, 'The significance of the development of Bournemouth, 1840–1940' (Ph.D. thesis, University of Surrey, 1977).

7 Mate and Riddle, *op. cit.*, 66.

8 *Estates Gaz.*, 9 January 1908, 25 December 1909.

9 Christchurch Inclosure Act (1802), preamble.

10 Young, *op. cit.*, 34.

11 Mate and Riddle, *op. cit.*, 57.

12 *Ibid.*, 68.

13 Hampshire County RO, Tregonwell Estate Papers, 9 M67/115.

14 *Bournemouth Guardian* (herafter cited as *BG*), 22 November 1902.

15 Soane, *op. cit.*, 101; Mate and Riddel, *op. cit.*, 90; *Bournemouth Visitors Directory* (hereafter cited as *BVD*), 18 July 1891.

16 Bournemouth Reference Library (hereafter cited as BRL), Branksome Estate Papers, Misc. Deeds Box 2, Abstract of title of George Durrant to Branksome Estate, 12 June 1861.

17 *Ex inf.* A.T. Goadsby, agent to the Dean Estate.

18 BRL, unpublished paper, 'Development of Shelly Estates outlined in judgment of Mr Justice Sargant', 31 July 1915.

19 Sir Henry Drummond Wolff, *Rambling Recollections* (2 vols., 1908), II, 102–5; *BG*, 17 October 1908.

20 *Bournemouth Times*, 19 May 1923; *BVD*, 21 November 1888; Sir Merton Russell Cotes, *Home and Abroad* (2 vols., 1921), I, 63, 197.

21 *BG*, 25 August 1906, 3 November 1906, 14 June 1913, 22 April 1922.

22 Mate and Riddle, *op. cit.*, 156.

23 *BVD*, 15 March 1872.

24 BRL, unpublished paper by C.G. Hawkes, 'Leaseholds in Bournemouth' (1908).

25 *Penny Handbook to Bournemouth* (1872), 58–9.

26 *Bournemouth Echo*, 13 September 1949; *BG*, 22 October 1892.

27 BRL, Hawkes, *op. cit.*

28 BRL, Misc. Deeds Box 3, building lease, W. Clapcott Dean to S.J. Stevens, 29 June 1876.

29 BRL, Hawkes, *op. cit.*

30 BRL, 'Development of Shelly Estates'.

31 Cannadine, *op. cit.*, chs. 20, 22.

32 Wolff, *op. cit.*, ii, 102.

33 *BG*, 17 October 1908.

34 Mate and Riddle, *op. cit.*, 150.

35 BRL, Development plan for Boscombe Spa (no date); *BVD*, 22 April 1876.

36 PRO, BT 31 1729/6352, Boscombe Spa Hotel Company: Memorandum of association, 12 June 1872; letter to Registrar of Companies, 29 March 1884; *The Architect*, 5 July 1873; *BVD*, 5 September 1874.

37 PRO, BT 31 1910/7789, Bournemouth Winter Garden Company, Memorandum of Association, 6 November 1873.
38 *BVD*, 8 July 1876; *Illustrated London News*, 9 December 1876.
39 Mate and Riddle, *op. cit.*, 154.
40 *Ibid.*, 155.
41 *BG*, 17 October 1908.
42 PRO, BT 31 1601/5370, Bournemouth Club, Ltd., Articles of Association, 11 April 1871.
43 *BVD*, 20 January 1877, 26 May 1877, 28 July 1877.
44 *The Caterer and Hotel Keepers Gaz.*, 15 August 1893; Young, *op. cit.*, 91; Mate and Riddle, *op. cit.*, 219; *BG*, 17 October 1908.
45 *BVD*, 3 May 1911.
46 *Ibid.*, 15 March 1872; Bournemouth Town Hall (hereafter cited as BTH), Records and minutes of the Bournemouth Improvement Commissioners, 1856–90, *passim*.
47 BTH, Minutes of a Committee established to obtain an Act of Parliament 1856, report of public meeting, 29 August 1854.
48 House of Lords RO, Minutes of Evidence of Commons Select Committee on Bournemouth Improvement and Pier Bill, 10 June 1856.
49 W.H. Jacob, *Hampshire at the Opening of the Twentieth Century* (1905), 265; *Bournemouth Graphic*, 21 December 1905; *BVD*, 6 December 1879; *BG*, 17 March 1913.
50 Jacob, *op. cit.*, 242; *BT*, 2 May 1930; *BG*, 18 March 1904; *BVD*, 26 May 1886; Russell Cotes, *op. cit.*, i, 54–6.
51 Mate and Riddle, *op. cit.*, 218, 226, 239; W. Mate, *Bournemouth Business Directory*, (1891), 3.
52 BTH, Minutes of General Purposes Committee, 1891–5, 30 December 1895 and *passim*.
53 The material in this paragraph is derived from the annual editions of W. Mate, *Bournemouth Business Directory*, and from the local press.
54 *BVD*, 23 December 1876.
55 *Ibid.*, 30 December 1876.
56 *Ibid.*, 23 April 1892.
57 *Ibid.*, 22 April 1911; *BG*, 12 April 1902.
58 Bournemouth Magistrates Court, Abstract of Cases, *passim*.
59 BTH, Report of Medical Officer of Health, 1893, 13.
60 *BG*, 30 August 1890.
61 Bournemouth Improvement Act, 1892, clauses 55–6.
62 BTH, Report of Auditor, 15 December 1900; *BG*, 20 July 1907.
63 BTH, Winter Garden and Band Committee Minutes, 1897–1901, *passim*.
64 Russell Cotes, *op. cit.*, i, 100; Young, *op. cit.*, 137; *BG*, 22 April 1922.
65 BTH, Report of the Town Clerk on the Acquisition of the Belle Vue and Tachbrook properties, 19 April 1911, 5.
66 *BVD*, 14 September 1901.
67 Mate and Riddle, *op. cit.*, 160.
68 BTH, Miscellaneous Reports, 1879–1901, 168.
69 BTH, General Purposes Committee Minutes, 25 July 1892; BG, 13 July 1912.
70 *BG*, 18 October 1902, 13 July 1912; *BVD*, 23 February 1901.
71 *BG*, 30 July 1904.
72 *Ibid.*, 18 April 1908.
73 *Ibid.*, 9 June 1900.
74 *Ibid.* 18 October 1902.
75 *BVD*, 14 March 1896.
76 *BG*, 27 May 1899; *Truth*, 22 September 1898.
77 *BVD*, 11 March 1896.
78 In 1876 Sir George Eliott Meyrick Tapps-Gervis inherited the 17,000-acre estate of Bodorgan in Angelsea from his great grandfather, and thereafter divided his time between his lands in Hampshire, Sussex and Wales. He added the second Meyrick to his name in the same year.

79 Wolff, *op. cit.*, ii, 102; *BVD*, 7 December 1889.
80 *Bournemouth Observer*, 7 December 1887; *Bournemouth Graphic*, 19 August 1921.
81 *BG*, 27 May 1899, quoting from the *Daily Telegraph*.
82 The laying of the foundation stone of the Victoria Hospital by the mayor in 1887 was a compromise after the failure to persuade a member of the royal family to perform the ceremony, and a row over which local dignitary should officiate.
83 *Bournemouth Times*, 1 February 1927.
84 *Ibid.*, 28 January 1927; Russell Cotes, *op. cit.*, i. 184, 261–4.
85 *BG*, 5 January 1895.
86 *Ibid.*, 29 September 1906.
87 The principal complaint of local tradesmen against Bournemouth's landlords was not, in fact, the leasehold system, but that 'not one of the ground landlords keeps an establishment within the town to benefit tradesmen': *Bournemouth Observer*, 3 December 1890.
88 *BG*, 22 October 1892.
89 *Bournemouth Observer*, 16 February 1887.
90 *Bournemouth Times*, 20 January 1923, 27 January 1923, 2 June 1923, 14 July 1923, 15 September 1923, 18 May 1928.
91 *Ibid.*, 19 May 1923, 26 May 1923; *BG*, 22 April 1922.
92 *Bournemouth Times*, 14 May 1921.

INDEX